NEW FARMERS' MOVEMENTS IN INDIA

NEW FARMERS' MOVEMENTS IN INDIA

Edited by

TOM BRASS

Preface by T.J. Byres

FRANK CASS

First published in 1995 in Great Britain by
FRANK CASS & CO. LTD.
900 Eastern Avenue, Newbury Park
Ilford, Essex IG2 7HH, England

and in the United States of America by
FRANK CASS
c/o International Specialized Book Services, Inc.
5804 N.E. Hassalo Street
Portland, Oregon 97213-3644

Transferred to Digital Printing 2004

British Library Cataloguing in Publication Data
New Farmers' Movements in India. –
(Library of Peasant Studies, ISSN
0306–6150; Vol. 12)
I. Brass, Tom II. Series
338.10954

ISBN 0–7146–4609–1 (hardback)
0–7146–4134–0 (paperback)

Library of Congress Cataloging-in-Publication Data
New farmers' movements in India / edited by Tom Brass ; preface by
T.J. Byres.
p. cm.
Includes bibliographical references.
ISBN 0-7146-4609-1 : £30.00. — ISBN 0-7146-4134-0 (pbk.) : £15.00
1. Farmers—India. 2. Agriculture—Economic aspects—India.
3. India—Rural conditions. I. Brass, Tom, 1946–
HD1537.I4N48 1994
338.1'0954—dc20 94-31412
CIP

This groups of studies first appeared in a Special Issue on 'New Farmers' Movements in India' of The Journal of Peasant Studies, Vol.21, Nos.3 & 4, April/July 1994, published by Frank Cass & Co. Ltd.

Typeset by Regent Typesetting, London

For Amanda, and Anna, Ned and Miles William (who was born on the day after this book was finished)

Contents

Preface

The so-called new farmers' movements in India began in the 1970s, in parts of Tamil Nadu and the Punjab. Certain 'price and related issues' had become the object of lobbying and rural agitation via non-party movements. These movements, it is suggested, involved 'farmers', rather than 'peasants': the former being distinguished, it seems, by significant market involvement, both as commodity producers and as purchasers of inputs. The issues included, crucially, the prices of agricultural products – the fixing of prOcurement prices being of particular concern; and the demand grew for 'remunerative prices'. The 'other and related' issues encompassed the prices of agricultural inputs, electricity charges, irrigation charges and betterment levies, and the taxation of agriculture, all of which, it was argued, should be lower. Non-repayment and waiving of government loans would also become an issue.

These movements grew in the 1970s, and by the late 1970s they had emerged strongly, too, in parts of Maharashtra, Uttar Pradesh (particularly the west), Karnataka, and Gujarat. They were little in evidence in other states, however. In the 1980s they became a powerful force: employing the distinctive *rasta roko* and *rail roko* (blocking of roads and rail), and *gavbandi* (refusing politicians and bureaucrats entry to villages); and with tens of thousands courting arrest. They peaked in influence and activity in the late 1980s, and have waned since, although a farmers' movement did erupt in Haryana early in 1993. They continue strong in Maharashtra, and retain some presence in western Uttar Pradesh, the Punjab and Haryana. They may well emerge strongly again. That they merit close attention is clear. Already much important work on them has been done in India. This collection is a contribution to the debate on their nature, causes and significance.

The so-called 'new issues', pursued via non-party movements and employing new forms of agitation, have been counterpoised against 'the old issues'. These latter, whose encapsulating slogan was 'land to the tiller' and which were the driving force of previous 'peasant movements', were landlordism, tenancy, rent, and land redistribution; and they were often taken up by the political parties. Of course, peasants had agitated on 'price and related issues', often with considerable success, long before the 1970s, both in the states mentioned and elsewhere. Prices had never previously dominated rural agitation, however, and had never been such a major focus of non-party action. Now they did become dominant.

Already, then, we have four senses in which a new phenomenon is suggested: agency had passed from 'peasants' to 'farmers'; the central focus of rural agitation had shifted from land to prices; the essential agitational form was a non-party one; and distinctive, novel methods of agitation were employed. All of this is controversial, and that controversy is joined in the pages that follow.

During the 1980s there was a fifth, limited, sense in which these movements might be seen as 'new': with a broadening of agenda and ideology, to include the environment and women's issues. This is especially so in Maharashtra. Women's issues seemed, also, to be on the agenda in Karnataka. Certainly, old-style peasant movements had never included such concerns. And by no mean all the 'new farmers' movements' have. But their existence, however limited, has led some to argue that they are part of world-wide 'new social movements', which embrace a new set of post-material values. Such a categorisation is a matter of considerable dispute, whose flavour may be savoured below.

They possess a well-defined ideology, which does vary from region to region, but which, in general, is strongly anti-state (at least the state as presently constituted), is steeped in populist imagery, and has at its core a powerfully stated central tenet of 'urban bias' (the countryside is exploited by the town). The thesis of 'peasant unity' is maintained: whatever divisions exist in rural society are wholly secondary to the exploitation of the whole 'peasantry' by predatory surplus-extracting state. They are, avowedly, non-party movements, which are held to appeal to all cultivators. Cultivators are all now involved in the market. If the movements' demands were met all producers would benefit. Moreover, it is further maintained that agricultural labour, too, would benefit, since the demand for labour would rise and wages could increase too. Theirs is an undifferentiated rural universe. All of this is open to question, and both sides of the debate are represented below.

That these 'new farmers' movements' have much in common is obvious. But that they also embody regional specificities, and that they embrace significantly differing positions on some issues (for example, on the liberalisation of international trade, which is favoured by Sharad Joshi, the leader of the movement in Maharashtra and Gujarat, but in none of the other regional movements; or on whether they should 'enter politics' by contesting seats), need also to be stressed. Both the commonality and the diversity/contradiction need careful analysis. This collection is an important part of that scrutiny. It is the most comprehensive and most incisive treatment to have appeared so far.

T.J. BYRES

Introduction: The New Farmers' Movements in India

TOM BRASS

In March 1993 a number of those carrying out research into the new farmers' movements that had emerged in India during the previous decade took part in a workshop in New Delhi to consider some of the more important theoretical and political issues linked to this process. Among the latter was the extent to which these mobilisations were a response to the exigiences of a globalised neo-liberal capitalism, and in particular the effects on peasant farmers of the change from the development decade of the 1960s to the capitalist crisis of the 1990s, with its accompanying cutbacks in wages and social welfare, its intensified capitalist competition, and its resurgent nationalism(s). Central to this discussion was the role of neo-populism as a mobilising ideology, not least because it pointed to similarities with long-standing forms of agrarian discourse and action, and suggested further that in a very real sense an old pattern – with the addition of some new characteristics – was being repeated.[1]

Emerging from the late 1970s onwards, the farmers' movements operate under different names in specific contexts throughout India (see map). The most important of them are: the *Shetkari Sanghatana* in Maharashtra, led by Sharad Joshi; the *Bharatiya Kisan Union* (BKU), led by M.S. Tikait in Uttar Pradesh, and by Ajmer Singh Lakhowal, Balbir Singh Rajwal and Bhupinder Singh Mann in the Punjab; the *Bharatiya Kisan Sangh* in Gujarat; the Tamil Nadu Agriculturalists' Association (*Tamilaga Vyavasavavigal Sangham* or TVS) in Tamil Nadu, led by Narayanaswamy Naidu; and the Karnataka State Farmers' Association (*Karnataka Rajya Ryota Sangha* or KRRS) in Karnataka, led by M.D. Nanjundaswamy. As all the contributions to this collection testify, it is impossible to ignore or underestimate the powerful effect the farmers' movements have had on local, regional and national politics in India throughout the past decade. Their impact extends from demonstrations, blocking the food transportation system, denying officials access to

---

Tom Brass is at the Faculty of Social and Political Sciences, University of Cambridge, Free School Lane, Cambridge CB2 3RQ.

villages, refusing to pay outstanding bills (tax arrears, electricity dues, bank loans), and withholding crops from local markets (which results in price rises), to an important role in the overthrow of Rajiv Gandhi's Congress government in the 1989 elections.[2]

The contributions to this volume include general considerations of background issues (Brass, Banaji) and also case studies of the more important of the farmers' movements: the *Shetkari Sanghatana* in Maharashtra (Dhanagare, Omvedt, Lindberg), the BKU in Punjab (Gill) and Uttar Pradesh (Hasan, Lindberg, Gill), the *Raitha Sangha* in Karnataka (Assadi), the BKS in Gujarat (Banaji) and – to a lesser extent – the TVS in Tamil Nadu (Lindberg). From the outset emphasis was placed on the fact that significant differences existed between the farmers' movements from each area, due in part to regional economic and cultural variations. The most obvious divergence is on the issue of economic liberalisation, supported by Shetkari Sanghatana but opposed by the BKU in UP and the KRRS in Karnataka. The difference between BKU in UP and Punjab on the one hand, and the Shetkari Sanghatana in Maharashtra on the other, is attributed by Lindberg to the presence in the former of a favourable ecology compared with poor soils and a lack of water in the latter context. Contrasting attitudes towards gender issues are also regionally specific: thus the farmers' movement in Maharashtra adopts a progressive stance on women's issues, whereas the BKU in UP adheres to traditional patriarchal values. Indeed, gender issues are presented by Shetkari Sanghatana and the KRRS as evidence of their progressiveness but, according to Gill, the BKU in Punjab has been unable to secure support from women.

Generally speaking, the workshop agenda sought to cover any or all of the issues connected with or arising from the new farmers' movements. These included the following four general themes: whether or not such movements are in fact 'new', the national/international economic background to these mobilisations, the class composition of the new farmers' movements, and the kind of mobilising ideology used by them.

THE 'NEWNESS' OF THE FARMERS' MOVEMENTS

The first theme adressed questions of definition. What are the new farmers' movements, and are they new? Are there parallels with other forms of (urban) mobilisation elsewhere in the world during the 1980s which come under the general rubric of 'new social movements'? For very different reasons, and drawing very different conclusions, Lindberg,

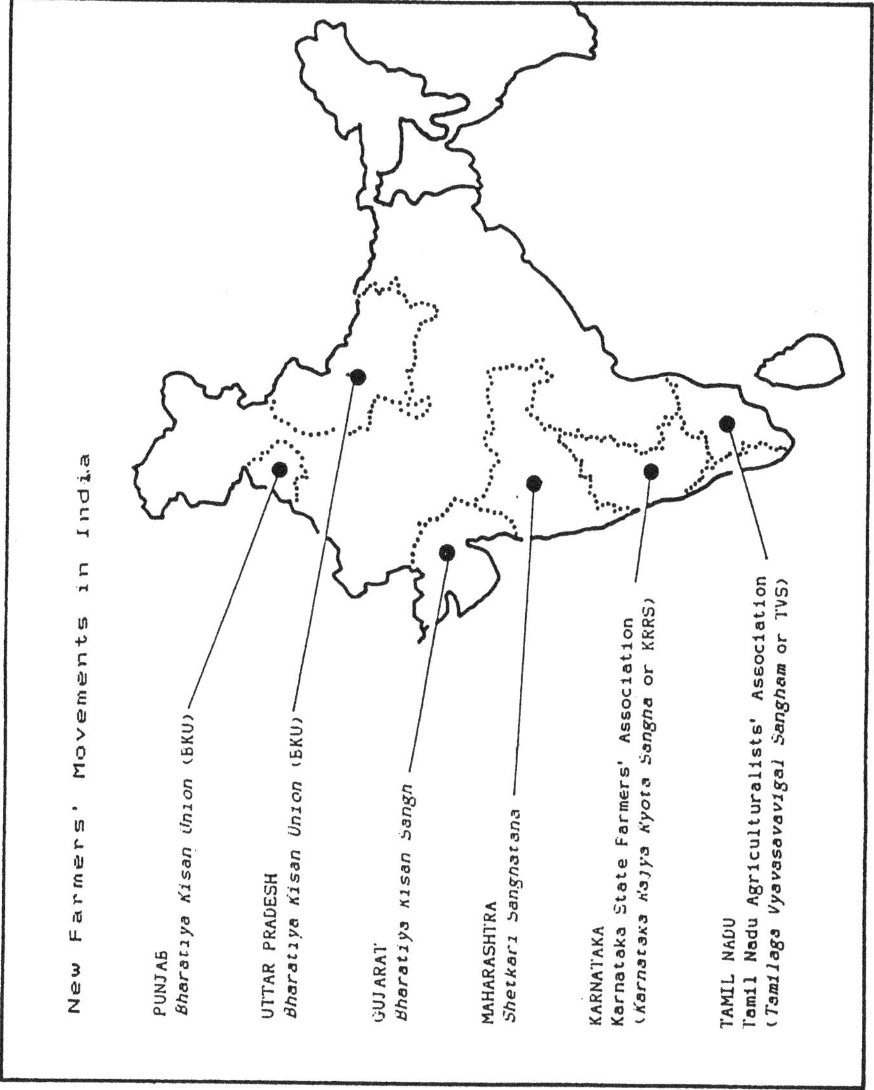
New Farmers' Movements in India
PUNJAB
Bharatiya Kisan Union (BKU)
UTTAR PRADESH
Bharatiya Kisan Union (BKU)
GUJARAT
Bharatiya Kisan Sangh
MAHARASHTRA
Shetkari Sangnatana
KARNATAKA
Karnataka State Farmers' Association
(*Karnataka Rajya Kyota Sangha* or KRRS)
TAMIL NADU
Tamil Nadu Agriculturalists' Association
(*Tamilaga Vyavasavavigal Sangham* or TVS)

Omvedt and Brass agree that the farmers' movements are part of the new social movements that have emerged as a global phenomenon from the late 1960s onwards. Locating his analysis of the farmers' movements within a framework that combines interactionist collective identity formation with a structuralist interpretation, Lindberg eschews his earlier argument that the new farmers' movements in India are rich peasant mobilisations, and maintains instead that they are the response of a mass-based, commodity-producing peasantry to a state whose control over input/output prices affects rich, middle and (to a lesser extent) poor peasants alike. He describes such movements as new, not least because cognitively they draw on a plurality of traditions, are organisationally anarchic or postmodern, and lack a set of fixed criteria for membership. Much of this definition is shared by Omvedt, for whom the farmers' mobilisations in India are also part of the new social movements worldwide: as with the latter, contemporary agitations undertaken by Indian peasants are non-political in form, and characterised by an anti-urban/anti-state/anti-capitalist ideological content.[3]

By contrast, in his first contribution to this volume Brass maintains that the farmers' movements are indeed the same as the new social movements, but paradoxically because neither are in fact new, being much rather the same old class movements articulating the same old class discourses.[4] The claims to 'newness' on the part of the farmers' movements are similarly questioned by Gill and Assadi. The latter shows not only that traditional practices (such as bonded labour, atrocities against backward castes, tribals and women), continue, but also that claims by the KRRS for the a-political nature of its mobilisation are unfounded. For his part, Gill links the rise of the BKU in Punjab and UP to the long history of peasant struggles in the Green Revolution belt of northern India, organised intially by pro-landlord groups and then by political parties of the left, the implication being that in this region such mobilisation is anything but new. He also shows that, although the BKU in Punjab, Haryana and UP has successfully resisted attempts by politicians to utilise the farmers' movement as a vehicle to further their own political careers, it too has nevertheless entered into informal alliances with different political parties in these states.

The problem with many definitions of new social movements which turn on issues such as chronology, organisational modes, and objectives, is that they could apply to almost any kind of historical/contemporary agrarian mobilisation. This in turn raises the awkward question of exactly how 'new' these movements really are: as Lindberg himself notes, not only does land continue to be a live political issue, but action undertaken by Shetkari Sanghatana is based on 'old tactics' employed by farmers in

Maharashtra and historically the issue of prices and the role of the state (the colonial state) have also been targets of peasant mobilisation. Since in the case of India claims for the 'newness' of the social movements of the 1980s made by/about these movements derive largely from what are perceived to be a combination of novel actions/objectives (the relative unimportance of the land question, the participation of women, antagonism towards the state, higher prices for agricultural produce) none of which it seems are actually new, this particular point is of considerable importance.

THE NATIONAL/INTERNATIONAL ECONOMIC BACKGROUND

The second theme adresses questions relating to the historical background and future direction of these mobilisations; in particular, the relationship between the new farmers' movements and the capitalist crisis, the fiscal crisis of the state, the Green Revolution, and the current trend towards neo-liberal economic policies.

The rise of the farmers' movements in northern India is attributed by Gill to the decline in this area of the prosperity generated by the Green Revolution (for a similar point made by Hasan, see below). Increasing market integration of surplus-producing medium- and smallholding peasants made them vulnerable to price fluctuations in regard to both inputs and output. Accordingly, like the other regions of India where such mobilisations have occurred, farmers' demands in Punjab include index-linked agricultural output prices, lower input prices, crop insurance schemes, the ending of bureaucratic corruption, and the imposition of rural quotas for entry into higher education and government employment. By contrast, Banaji links the farmers' movement in Gujarat to a different dynamic, the interpenetration of rural and urban commercial interests, or the economic extension of Bharat into India.

Of particular interest in this regard are the views of the farmers' movement in Karnataka concerning the structure of and the reasons for the continuing underdevelopment of India and its accompanying rural poverty. As outlined by Assadi (and also by Banaji), the KRRS attributes the economic backwardness of India generally – conceptualised as 'weak capitalism' (*badakalu bandavala*) – and its rural sector in particular to Third World underdevelopment structured by the continuing economic dependency of erstwhile colonised nations at the global periphery on their erstwhile western colonisers at the core. The current economic dominance of foreign capital prevents indigenous capitalists from contesting on equal terms, a situation whereby the former exclude the latter both from their own markets and from the technology that would enable them to compete as equals in international markets. To remedy such a situation of dependency, therefore, the KRRS invokes the necessity of a 'khadi curtain', or an all-embracing form of isolationism which, under the guise of protecting indigenous economic and cultural interests from the destructive (= competitive) impact of international capital, is supportive of the accumulation project of the national bourgeoisie, its agrarian counterpart, and through this nationalism.[5]

Although Assadi claims that Shetkari Sanghatana holds a similar view about the nature of Indian economic backwardness, Omvedt disagrees. Thus the argument about 'dependency' as a form of ideological defence against a more competitive international capital, which Assadi attributes to the KRRS in order to protect *rural* interests, is attributed by Omvedt [1994] to a specifically *urban* national bourgeoisie in India engaged in a similar defence of its own economic interests (statism, planning, bureaucracy) against the neo-liberalism of foreign capital on the one hand and, on the other, the economically dynamic farmers' movement in Maharashtra. The latter organisation, argues Omvedt, objects to the emphasis placed by Nehruvian development policies on industrialisation, planning and urbanisation; instead of transferring peasant-produced surpluses out of the rural sector, the Shetkari Sanghatana advocates that these should remain in the villages, where their reinvestment would lead to agrarian capital formation. The irony is that in the wider context of a globalising neo-liberal capitalism, in which Omvedt wishes the Indian farmers' movement to share, neither the small producer nor alternative technology is economically viable: consequently, poor and middle peasants would be the first casualty of the free market policies she advocates.

A further difficulty with the expectation on the part of those such as Sharad Joshi who press for the adoption of neo-liberal economic policies – that output prices would increase while input prices would decline, and that farmers generally would benefit from this difference – is that, once established in India, input-providing MNCs would attempt to reassert a monopoly position and force prices up, while food-providing MNCs competing on equal terms with Indian farmers would undercut them in the market and force all but the most efficient (rich peasants, agrarian capitalists) out of business. This in turn would accentuate the already existing process of peasant differentiation in the villages, and increase both the economic polarity and the political antagonism between landless and propertied. Rather than locating differentiation at an inter-peasant level, however, Omvedt identifies its existence simply at an inter-movement level. Accordingly, her criticism is reserved for those who fail sufficiently to distinguish between the demand for economic liberalisation made by Sharad Joshi and the Kisan Coordinating Committee, and the demands by Tikait and Nanjundaswamy for continued subsidies.[6]

THE CLASS COMPOSITION OF THE NEW FARMERS' MOVEMENTS

The third area of interest concerns the social composition of the new farmers' movements in India, an issue which raises a number of important and complex questions. For example, what kind of following, and why, do these new movements have? Is there any regional specificity to this, or do the movements in Maharashtra, Punjab, and Uttar Pradesh all draw on the same kind of support? How was this support categorised in terms of class: are the farmers' movements composed predominantly of rich peasants, or middle peasants, or a combination thereof? And, most importantly, what was the attitude towards and/or the position in these movements of poor peasants and agricultural workers? If the latter did indeed support the objectives of the new farmers' movements, was this conditional; if so, why, and if not, why not?

On the question of class, it is important to recall that Marxists such as Lenin and Trotsky did not regard the peasantry as a 'class' but as an internally differentiated stratum divided into antagonistic capitalist/proletarian class positions. The extent to which the resulting process of 'depeasantisation' affects the middle peasant – or the degree to which petty commodity production either consolidates or disintegrates – raises in turn the continuing discussion about the applicability to India of the middle peasant thesis and the theoretical/methodological issues which structure this dispute (for the most recent exchanges see, among others, Athreya, Böklin, Djurfeld and Lindberg [1987], Athreya, Djurfeld and Lindberg [1990], Dhanagare [1990], Patnaik [1987; 1988]).[7] This is a debate which is central to any discussion about the social composition (thus political direction) of the new farmers' movements, and unsurprisingly one about which the contributors hold contrasting views.

Dhanagare argues that the Shetkari Sanghatana in Maharashtra is a movement led by and reflecting the interests of rich farmers operating holdings of ten acres or more, on which they cultivate cash-crops such as onions, sugarcane, tobacco and cotton. Criticising the view that the farmers' movements in India are mobilisations of independent, petty commodity producing family farms (= middle peasants), he points out that such claims (made by, among others, Lenneberg [1988] and Rudolph and Rudolph [1987]) are based on unacceptably broad and socio-economically undifferentiated census categories which conflate small agrarian capitalists and subsistence producers.[8] Omvedt, by contrast, maintains that the same movement draws its main support from the poorer eastern districts of the state, and that Shetkari Sanghatana is composed of petty commodity producers or peasants from whom surplus is extracted by state-based power-holders through exchange relations.

Hence the view (see below) that new farmers' movements in India are conduits for the interests solely of rich peasants or kulaks is strongly disputed by Omvedt, who maintains both that peasant family labour is every bit as much the source of wealth as landless workers, and that the latter would benefit from demands for higher crop prices every bit as much as peasant proprietors. Her argument is that the retention in the agrarian sector of capital accumulated there by the utilisation of unpaid family labour in petty commodity production would lead to higher growth in agriculture and generate non-agricultural labour-intensive village employment. Because they fail to impute a value to family labour, Omvedt argues, calculations effected by government price-fixing institutions such as the Agricultural Prices Commission failed to cover production costs incurred by petty commodity producers.[9]

Like that of Dhanagare, the contributions by Banaji, Assadi and Hasan all maintain that in terms of class composition, the farmers' movements are rich peasant organizations. Basing his argument on accounts of Shetkari Sanghatana conventions over the 1982–85 period, Banaji suggests that the Maharashtrian movement is composed of better-off sections of the peasantry. For him, the Shetkari Sanghatana is an example of a rural coalition, or a mass organization led by an agrarian elite. Although the membership of the KRRS in Karnataka is also composed of rich peasants, Assadi points out that the latter nevertheless do not regard themselves as part of the Indian ruling class, and thus perceive themselves as unrepresented by the Indian state. The contribution by Hasan demonstrates how in western UP the BKU finds support among those agrarian capitalists who are surplus-producing farmers operating more than eight acres. She also shows the important role they have in the production of foodgrains in northern India, a point also made by Lindberg with regard to peasant cultivators belonging to the BKU in both Punjab and UP. There are two crucial effects which follow from this. First, surplus-producing farmers in western UP are especially affected by government procurement schemes designed to provide cheap subsidised food for the less well off – in particular the urban proletariat. Accordingly, these farmers object to what they see as artificially low prices for their output, and consequently demand higher (or 'remunerative') prices. And second, the strategic economic importance of their position as food providers to the nation has given these surplus-producers a significant form of leverage over the Indian government.

As already mentioned, Lindberg by contrast sees the new farmers' movements as basically middle peasant movements engaged in conflict about the terms of trade between agriculture and industry. The leadership is socio-economically and politically heterogenous, while the activists are drawn from the ranks of educated sons of farmers for whom there are no urban employment opportunities. A slightly different position is held by Gill, who argues that the farmers' mobilisations in Punjab, Haryana and UP have all attracted heterogeneous support, from every peasant stratum. Initially, therefore, both rich and poor peasants benefited from the Green Revolution; however, the decline in crop prices after the mid-1970s, due to the deteriorating terms of trade between agriculture and industry, had a negative impact on the profits of rich peasants and the deficits of poor peasants, and it was this according to Gill that generated the farmers' movements. Like Lindberg, Gill also points to the fact that the core activists and militants of the farmers' movements in the Green Revolution belt of northern India have been drawn from farmers' sons denied urban jobs linked to their educational attainments and, further, that in Punjab such cadres are also drawn from retired military and bureaucratic personnel with rural backgrounds.[10]

On the question of rural working class support, almost all the contributors note that the new farmers' movements have had nothing to say about the socio-economic conditions and political interests of the rural proletariat, and that in many instances are actually antagonistic to the latter. For example, Gill points out that increasing market integration has brought surplus-producing peasants who purchased labour-power into conflict with their hired workers, a solidarity mediated through the Jat caste identity shared by most farmers throughout the region. Similarly, Assadi observes that landless labourers and poor peasants who migrate from rural to urban areas are categorised by Joshi as 'refugees' from Bharat, yet excluded by him from any prospective coalition reflecting agrarian interests. Not only has the BKU in northern India not been able to attract political support from the agricultural working class, therefore, but the farmers' movements themselves have much rather become a powerful focus for an expression of employer solidarity against attempts by rural labour to improve pay and conditions. Banaji makes the same point rather more strongly, and suggests that both Joshi and Nanjundaswamy are not only antagonistic towards urban industrial workers but show contempt for them. Omvedt holds a very different view on this issue, and argues not only that the term 'looting' applied by Sharad Joshi to the Bharat/India divide is a materialist concept denoting exploitation, but also that he has explicitly linked the receipt by farmers of remunerative prices to payment by them of a higher minimum agricultural wage.[11] Such ideology, she maintains, accounts for the support the Shetkari Sanghatana enjoys among poor peasants, dalits, tribals and workers.

THE MOBILISING IDEOLOGY OF THE NEW FARMERS' MOVEMENTS

The fourth area of interest relates to the nature of the mobilizing ideology utilised by the new farmers' movements. Was this regionally specific, or did it possess components which transcend location? If the latter, what structured this, and why? More generally, how did the public discourse of the new farmers' movements reproduce/reinforce – or even negate – other ideological issues currently topical in India as a whole (for example: the environment, gender, nationalism, ethnicity)? And finally, what links with political parties did the new farmers' movements have, endorse, or reject?

On the question of the mobilising ideology of the farmers' movements in India, most contributors to this volume approach this in terms of the complex interrelationship between populism and class. Since it is not unusual to encounter agrarian movements which have some middle/poor peasant membership, but which nevertheless mobilise on the basis of rich peasant objectives, how such an economic and political contradiction is sustained *ideologically* must be related in turn to the form/content of the mobilising discourse (= populism) which focuses on the presentation/projection of issues and identity in a non-class manner. In the case of the farmers' movements in Maharashtra and Karnataka, for example, all the discursive elements historically associated with populism are present. These include the denial both by the Shetkari Sanghatana and by the KRRS of peasant differentiation and class struggle, opposition to the Nehruvian development project (industry, state), and a corresponding endorsement of Gandhian alternatives (decentralisation, cottage industries, local self-sufficiency, no more external dependency). The importance of being clear about the issues involved is underlined by the fact that, as middle and poor peasants who participate in the farmers' movements are also the providers of labour-power to rich peasants in these same movements, one would expect them to be unstable – not to say potentially antagonistic – partners in such an alliance. Accordingly, if middle peasants both supply labour-power (= workers) and commodify production (= farmers), how is their identity (= consciousness) formed and reproduced in such a context of coexisting/competing contradictions?

The central point here is precisely the question of class versus non-class consciousness, or why (middle) peasants who could just as easily be workers see themselves as peasants (or do they?).

Noting a disjuncture between the rich peasant leadership of Shetkari Sanghatana and the fact that the movement itself attracts a heterogeneous following, Dhanagare argues in Gramscian terms that populism is not a class ideology *per se* but rather a discursive form which enables a dominant class (= rich peasants) to establish and reproduce its hegemony (= class alliance, social block) over the farmers' movement as a whole (rich + middle peasants). Since for Dhanagare populism is not a class ideology, he therefore concludes that the farmers' movements constitute evidence of a growing separation between class and ideology. Much the same point is made by Gill, who notes that in Punjab the BKU has drawn on support from the peasantry as a whole, regardless of differences in religion, caste, gender and class. Although deploying a populist ideology, the economic policies advocated by the farmers' movement in Punjab have nevertheless been designed to benefit rich peasants and farmers.

This is a problematic view, in so far as *any* ideological form which proclaims a common identity based on a notion of 'classlessness' (we-are-all-the-same) in a context where this is palpably *not* the case (we-are-not-all-the-same) cannot but reflect (and thus be to the benefit of) the *class* interests of those whose class position would be revealed (and thus open to attack in the name of *class struggle*) if such a notion of 'classlessness' was absent. In short, an ideological form which licenses the development not so much of hegemony, or the consent to action/policies which may be to the disadvantage of poor peasants, as of a false consciousness (not-of-class-but-of-an-'other'-identity) by either instilling or – where it already exists – reinforcing in them a self-perception as petty commodity producer where in economic terms such an identity is unfeasible. And it is precisely this kind of deflecting role that suggests the possibility of identities/interests not only unconnected with class but also one that can be shared with rich peasants (we-*are*-all-the-same by virtue of being rural-not-urban, peasants-not-workers, Hindus-not-Muslims, Maharashtrians-not-Guraratis, Indians-not-'foreigners'), that populism discharges for an emerging/aspiring agrarian bourgeoisie.[12]

Although he eschews the term 'populism' and opts instead for the concept 'agrarianism', Lindberg concurs with the view about the hegemonic role of the farmers' movements in India: unlike Dhanagare, however, he sees this form of ideological power exercised not by agrarian capitalists over non-capitalist producers but much rather by a combination of rich and middle peasants over the rest of the rural sector. The significance of the latter is that it hints at the kind of political shape a future based on such sectoral hegemony would take. By equating a successful agriculture with the demand by the farmers' movements for a labour-intensive, non-industrial rural production based on family farms, Lindberg overlooks not only the extent to which such a programme is unambiguously populist in its origins, is economically and politically contradictory as long as capitalism remains in place, but also the possibility of an alternative programme based on socialism. That a concept of the peasant family farm is central to the discourse not only of the Shetkari Sanghatana in Maharashtra but also of the Raitha Sangha in Karnataka is clear from the analysis of Assadi. Hence the claim that peasants-as-undifferentiated-cultivators are part of the future is unambiguously populist in tone: in the context of an increasingly global neo-liberal capitalist onslaught, therefore, such a view holds that middle peasants will continue to reproduce themselves economically, and not be subject to 'depeasantisation' as argued by Lenin.

The concept of an opposition between, on the one hand, small-scale 'people's' production and, on the other, large-scale capitalism is central to populism, which regards the state as the mechanism whereby the latter appropriates resources produced by the former. Peasants are forced to pay for industrialisation, which populists maintain is an alien/urban/capitalist phenomenon the cost of which is rural poverty, land shortages, outmigration and the growth of a 'dangerous' proletariat. As argued by Brass, this populist discourse also structures nationalist politics and ideology in Europe and India throughout the nineteenth and twentieth centuries.

In this neo-populist/nationalist discourse, therefore, the city is the locus of negative/(profane) attributes: a large-scale, science-based, polluting industry, protected by a wasteful bureaucracy in the taxing/surplus-extracting state, the revenues of which are used solely for the benefit of an externally-oriented/('treacherous') westernised/('decadent') elite and its potentially/actually politically menacing proletariat ('the mob in the streets'). Behind all the latter, moreover, are to be found the economic and political interests of 'the foreigner'. In short, precisely a combination of agents/institutions/processes that is perceived to undermine petty commodity production, and through this the nation itself.

By contrast, 'the rural' is inscribed by this same discourse with stereotypically positive/(sacred) attributes: the locus of an harmonious/traditional/(atemporal) ethnic/gender/religious/('natural') purity embodied in a small-scale, ecologically sustainable village-level agriculture and artisan production. The latter, however, are condemned to poverty/inefficiency precisely by virtue of the violence/profligacy/('looting') engaged in by their 'other': 'the urban' and its 'foreign' backers.

Brass maintains that at the core of this neo-populist/nationalist conceptual matrix, in which a number of innate identities are symbolically interchangeable (rural = nature = woman = nation) and on which 'popular culture' is based, lies an equally symptomatic – yet politico-ideologically potent – view of 'peasant' as the embodiment of traditional and enduring cultural/religious values. Hence the displacement of a class-differentiated by an undifferentiated concept of 'peasant' in the discourse of the new farmers' movement, ecofeminism and sections of the left, enables – indeed encourages – the recasting of the now-homogeneous peasantry as a (non-economic) *cultural* category, and therefore as a bearer of natural/ahistorical characteristics that can in turn form the basis of an eternal/ever-present (folkloric) national identity and thus nationhood.

Central to populism as a mobilising ideology, therefore, is its implication for other kinds of identity projected in this process: specifically the displacement of class consciousness/struggle by ethnic/national identity/antagonism, the occurrence of which is confirmed in a number of other contributions. Banaji outlines how in Maharashtra Joshi has been unable to prevent the supporters of Shetkari Sanghatana from campaigning for communal organisations such as Shiv Sena and the BJP. In the case of western UP, Hasan shows similarly how a commercial petty-bourgeoisie, linked to the economic growth of the Green Revolution in this area and feeding off the consumer demand generated by this, forms the constituency of the BJP in UP. Since the economic divisiveness of the anti-Mandal agitation threatened to split Hindu unity, the BJP has attempted to restore the latter by (re-) focusing the discourse of 'otherness' and forging a specifically Hindu ethnic/religious/cultural unity on the basis of the Ayodhya issue. Banaji, Lindberg and Hasan all indicate that support for the farmers' movement in this state has been steadily eroded by the communalisation of discourse and conflict on the part of the BJP.

According to Hasan, there are three reasons for this. First, the tacit support for the BJP by Tikait, a point confirmed by Lindberg and Banaji. Second, since the antagonism between landholders and their workers also corresponds to a conflict between high-caste Hindus and Dalits, this in turn has driven farmers into the ranks of the BJP. And third, the BJP has succeeded in capturing the ideologically-potent domain of street festivals; in the latter context it now produces/reproduces high-profile images associated with a Hindu/BJP 'presence', and through this mechanism has contributed to the displacement of economic conflict by cultural struggle. A similar point is made by Brass, who argues that whereas in India the process of agrarian mobilisation for neo-populists such as Gandhi and Charan Singh was largely defensive, a segment of the new farmers' movement has gone on to the offensive, and now regards global free trade as advantageous to the (rich) peasantry. At the level of discourse, this metamorphosis has been matched by an analogous shift in the realm of nationalist/communal ideology on the part of the BJP/VHP/RSS, resulting in a confluence not merely of discourses but more importantly of political action (= self-empowerment) linked to them.

In a similar vein, Hasan shows how class struggle between capital and labour in the agrarian sector of western UP has intensified as a result of farmer consolidation under the BKU, and consequently how the populist discourse of the BKU has shifted the political debate. Accordingly, the potentially divisive impact of antithetical economic demands made by a differentiated grassroots following composed of rich, middle and poor peasants can in this way be deflected into sectoral demands, thereby recasting conflict in terms of a rural/urban polarity. Whereas Gill, Lindberg, Banaji and Hasan all emphasise the importance of caste organisation in sustaining the BKU in UP, there are opposed views on this issue in the case of Shetkari Sanghatana in Maharashtra: Dhanagare maintains that a similarly crucial organisational/recruitment role is discharged by caste/kin identity, but Lindberg denies that this is the case. Gill also indicates that in Punjab the discourse of the BKU has been affected by the rise of Sikh separatism, and how the invocation of Sikh religious idioms in the course of mobilising farmers has alienated Hindu farmers in the state.

Assadi confirms this view, and indicates how the agrarian struggle in Karnataka conducted by the KRRS similarly corresponds to ethnic conflict, a process whereby exploitative economic relationships are represented in terms of caste inequalities. The outcome is the pronounced anti-Brahminism that structures the anti-capitalist discourse of the KRRS. Instead of a political critique of capital in general (foreign + national variants), such a discourse focuses mainly on the non-economic identity of the exploiter, which it identifies either as the 'foreigner' or as the latter's national, high-caste, ally. This ethnicisation of the idioms of economic conflict also permeates working-class consciousness, organisation and struggle, as Brass argues in his first contribution: it is also true of working-class Dalits who, as Omvedt [1993a] shows, similarly resort to anti-Brahminism as a discourse-against. Assadi sees merit in such a development, and argues that by appropriating nationalist symbols/discourse, the farmers' movements have denied these to a bourgeoning Hindu chauvinism, and thus contributed to the struggle against the spread of the BJP. This contrasts with the view of Brass, who maintains that by taking over these symbols and discourse, and projecting caste/communal rather than class identities, the farmers' movements have created a space for and (perhaps fatally) been drawn into the discourse and politics of ethnic identity and nationalism.

URBAN BIAS REVISITED

At the centre of the farmers' discourse, and a crucial aspect of their mobilisation, is the claim about the existence/effect of urban bias, as encapsulated in Sharad Joshi's politico-ideologically powerful slogan 'Bharat versus India'. Dhanagare, Brass and Assadi all question the viability of this distinction, and all provide evidence that theoretically and empirically it is unsustainable. Hasan, Lindberg, Gill and Omvedt, however, all maintain that in terms of resource transfers, terms of trade, pricing policies and so on, urban bias possesses a material as well as an ideological reality.

In a recent review of the debate about 'urban bias', Varshney [1993a; 1993b] has argued that farmer empowerment in India is attributable to the fact that democracy preceded industrialisation, a situation which confers on the rural sector the capacity to exercise an electoral veto on unfavourable (= anti-rural) policy.[13] He makes two points regarding the extent of this rural empowerment: first, the absence of an external obstacle to its consolidation, in the form of the inability of the Indian state to tax agriculture; and second, the presence of an internal obstacle to consolidation, in the form of non-economic fissures (caste, ethnicity, religion).[14]

Noting that since the mid-1970s taxation in India has amounted to 15–17 per cent of GDP, that agriculture is untaxed, and that further revenue from this source could only take the form of direct taxation, Varshney [1993b: 179, 200] nevertheless dismisses the feasibility of taxing agriculture, for three reasons in particular: that such a policy option would result in yet more tax evasion, that for the Indian state to concede farmers' demands for higher prices and then to claw back such gains by means of taxes would further alienate the rural sector, and that, anyway, administrative problems connected with its implementation together with the opposition of politicians would render such a policy unviable. About this view three points can be made. First, the argument that the actual/potential incidence of tax evasion is a sufficient reason for not imposing *additional* taxation could also be used as justification for not having *any* taxation, and is therefore unacceptable. Second, to observe that farmers and their political representatives would be alienated by taxation is tautological: to cite this as a reason for not taxing is to accept the farmers' case (about unequal terms of trade, price differentials, relative supply, and cost escalation), which Varshney clearly does not. *Of course* farmers would object to such a policy, but then this would be equally true of landlords, industrialists and millionaires generally, all of whom could similarly be expected to block/avoid/evade this.[15] Not surprisingly, owners of means of production are (and historically have been) opposed to any kind of measure (expropriation, nationalisation, land reform, income redistribution) that directly or indirectly threatens their property rights.

Much the same kind of difficulty faces the attempt by Varshney [1993b: 202, 205, 208, 210] to explain the failure of the farmers' movements to realise their economic objectives by reference to the fragmenting effect of non-economic identity. In his view, therefore, a combination of religious/caste/ethnic issues has overridden the unifying economic identity of the 'rural sector' in India, in the process placing limits on the politics of farmer empowerment. What Varshney fails to understand, however, is that – as many of the contributions to this volume demonstrate – farmers are unable to cohere around economic issues because, in order to mobilise effectively, it is necessary for them to obtain the support of those categories (poor peasants, agricultural labourers) whose *class* position is not just different from but in economic terms antagonistic to their own. Precisely for this reason, therefore, a necessary condition for such agrarian mobilisation to occur is that its discourse-against focuses on issues and identities unconnected with class divisions. Accordingly, contradictions at the level of the economic require that farmers' discourse project 'otherness' in populist terms, or the 'innate'/'natural' identities of caste, religion, nationality and sector (urban/rural divide). Having recognised the theoretically unsustainable nature of the concept 'urban bias', Varshney is nevertheless unable to explain why this is so. In other words, the fact that both taxation and communalisation are fundamentally political questions to do with *class* and the contradictory effects of capitalist accumulation, an issue which Varshney does not (cannot) confront.[16]

NEW FARMERS' MOVEMENTS, SOCIALISM AND FASCISM

Arising from all these themes concerning the origin and future direction of the farmers' movements in India, their social composition and mobilising ideology, is the related question of why socialism has not thus far found a stronger purchase among poor peasants and agricultural workers, its natural rural constituency in India. The first point to make in this regard is the extent to which the organisational strategy of the new social movements constitutes a shift away from confronting the political issues which socialism attempts to address. Ironically, therefore, in the face of a globalised capitalism – against which any struggle has of necessity to be *international* in its scope – activism and the political focus of the new social movements has tended to move in the opposite direction: that is, exercising power not through capturing the state but rather at the other end of the spectrum (village, neighbourhood, locality), which for the majority of Marxists represents a retreat, amounting to abandoning the field of battle to the enemy.

From different theoretical viewpoints, and drawing different political conclusions, the contributions by Gill, Assadi, Banaji, Omvedt and Brass all demonstrate just how wide a gulf exists between the new farmers' movements and a socialist project. Gill outlines how the impact on the left of the rise of the BKU in northern India has been that peasant organisations linked to the CPI and CPI (ML) have either risked marginalisation or else have had to adopt similar policies. Because the political left ceased its class collaborationist strategy after the Green Revolution, and focused exclusively on organising poor peasants and agricultural labourers, he suggests, rich peasants and farmers were as a result compelled to turn to the BKU as representative of their economic and political interests.[17] Banaji also links the rise of the farmers' movements to the existence of a political vacuum; unlike Gill, for whom it is the left which is responsible for its creation, Banaji attributes this vacuum to the loss of rural hegemony on the part of Congress. Assadi shows that although the KRRS similarly rejects socialism, it nevertheless and paradoxically finds space in its discourse for the socialism of Lohia. The focus of the KRRS is thus on imperialism, which Lohia regarded as having been present since the inception of capitalism. Unsurprisingly, as the structure of such an argument suggests, this 'socialism' is in fact nothing other than a variant of 'dependency' theory in general, and Andre Gunder Frank's version of it in particular. In short, a theory which identifies exploitation as an externally-derived, international relationship, or an oblique form of nationalism.[18]

On the question of the future political direction taken by the new social movements, and in particular the role in this process of intellectuals linked to this project, contributors express even more radically opposed views. For a variety of different reasons, the farmers' movements are perceived by Omvedt, Lindberg and Gill in a positive light, and hence part of the project of modernity; at the very least, they argue, the new farmers' movements in India must be considered as part of a democratic vision. Thus Omvedt and Lindberg see these agrarian mobilisations as harbingers of an alternative economic strategy, whereby agriculture is given preferential status within the existing capitalist structure, while Gill regards the farmers' movement as having made an important contribution to the democratic process by extending the practice of grassroots participation. By implication both Assadi and Gill adhere to a positive interpretation of the role discharged by the farmers' movements, since each perceives as a major political weakness the fact that, rather than transforming themselves into a single, unified *national* peasant organisation, such mobilisation has thus far remained a collection of disparate regionally-specific interest groups.

Omvedt takes an even stronger position and, invoking Marx in support of her view, argues that the anti-capitalist nature of peasant interests is sufficient evidence of the politically progressive character of the new farmers' movements in India. By contrast, Brass points out that anti-capitalism can take two diametrically opposed forms: progressive and reactionary, and in his view the new farmers' movements fall into the latter camp. Omvedt also criticises the left generally for not having addressed environmental issues, and the Indian left in particular for being composed of upper caste intellectuals whose antagonism towards lower castes is mediated ideologically as anti-peasantism.[19] Brass, however, locates the new farmers' movements in the more distinctly undemocratic political tradition of conservative populism, with its emphasis on 'the felt' (= sentimental/emotional) which naturalises both a mystical concept of 'nature' and the ethnic/national/gender identities that derive from this. Taking a critical view of intellectuals framing the discourse associated with the new social movements, he examines the conservative and reactionary form of anti-capitalist/(populist) agrarian nostalgia that (re-) surfaces as nationalism in periods of capitalist crisis, and in particular how this structures the fascist complicity of a significant number of intellectuals connected with the anti- (post-) modern project, aspects of which are now in the process of colonising development studies.[20]

NOTES

1. Words that could apply to the Indian farmers' movements of the 1980s, to the effect that they were mobilisations by 'a class of cash-conscious commercial farmers, producing staples both for the world market and linked to the bustling, competitive petty capitalist life of the expanding small towns of the ... interior' which 'aimed, above all, to restore agrarian profits and to scale down agrarian debts ... [and] assumed that general prosperity could be restored without a thoroughgoing reconstruction of the economic or constitutional order ...', are in fact those used by Hofstadter [1969: 9, 26] to describe the rural supporters of American populism one hundred years earlier. For the link

between the discourse of the farmers' movements in India and that of Russian neo-populism, see the contribution by Brass.

2. It was the National Front government of V.P. Singh which replaced Congress that convened the *Standing Advisory Committee on Agriculture*, chaired by the leader of Shetkari Sanghatana, Sharad Joshi. Its conclusions were set out in an important policy document entitled the *National Agricultural Policy: Views of the Standing Advisory Committee (July 1990)*, and referred to by Omvedt as the manifesto of the new farmers' movement in Maharashtra, on which a number of contributions to this volume make extensive commentary.
3. Elsewhere Omvedt [1993b: xv–xvi] provides her own definition of the characteristics of new social movements. These include non-Marxist concepts of exploitation and opression (appropriation by the state from peasants via the market, oppression of forest dwellers in the form of environmental degredation), the mobilisation of socio-economic categories ignored/undervalued by Marxism (women, dalits, peasants), and a corresponding rejection of class, class politics and ideology together with the vanguard role of the urban working class and its political parties. The extent to which Omvedt has distanced herself from socialist theory and politics was clear from some of the points she made in the New Delhi Workshop during March 1993, where she maintained that there was now no alternative to markets, that anyway socialism with its hierarchies was no better than the latter, that smallscale entrepreneurs were more efficient than workers, and that historically the working class was related to a technicist form of industrial development that was no longer possible. Although it is not possible to consider here the most recent presentation of her arguments [*Omvedt*, 1993b], the latter text will be the subject of a review article in a forthcoming issue of the *Journal of Peasant Studies*.
4. Those who attempt to combine new social movements framework with Marxist categories risk conflating positions/theory which are in fact politically/(polemically) opposed to each other. The problem is that the basic contradiction, between on the one hand a Marxist analysis structured by class, class struggle and (non-) class (false) consciousness ('we-are-not-necessarily-what-we-define-ourselves-as-being'), and on the other hand the open-ended/plural-identity approach of the new social movements' framework ('we-are-always-whatever-we-define-ourselves-as-being'), is not transcended. For Marxism, in short, class is *the* defining identity, of which all other social/cultural/political/ideological forms are but epiphenomenal surface appearances. In the movementist/(postmodern) framework, by contrast, not only is Marxism and class dismissed as part of the unacceptable/irrelevant system of Eurocentric/overarching/'foundational' metanarratives but the plural identities which for Marxism are nothing more than epiphenomena are theorised by, for example, Laclau [1985; 1990; 1992] as non-reducible essentialisms. As some have argued (see Brass [1991] and this volume), the epistemologies structuring these paradigms – to say nothing about their politics – are mutually incompatible. The contradictions involved are not transcended: would a self-proclaimed identity as 'middle peasant', for example, be enough to make petty commodity production a viable economic proposition, particularly when in a (benign – let alone a neo-liberal) capitalist system this would require large and continuing subsidies from precisely that institution – the state – to which such movements are opposed?
5. The concepts 'weak capitalism' and 'khadi curtain' as projected by the KRRS in Karnataka bear out the accuracy of the observation by Walicki [1969: 129], originally made about Russia during the nineteenth century, but equally applicable to the current farmers' movements in India, that: 'Populism ... was not only an ideology of small producers but also the first ideological reflection of the specific features of economic and social development of the 'latecomers' of the backward agrarian countries carrying out the process of modernization in conditions created by coexistence with highly industrialized nations'.
6. With unintended irony, Nanjundaswamy accepts economic liberalisation only so long as the withdrawal of state subsidies is compensated for by higher output prices (see Omvedt, this volume).

7. For theoretically prefiguring texts on the middle peasant thesis and agrarian mobilisation linked to this, see Alavi [1965] and Wolf [1971]. For subsequent contributions to the debate in the Indian context, see among others Charlesworth [1980; 1982; 1985: 268ff.], Hardiman [1981a: 246–50; 1981b; 1984], and Jeffrey [1979].
8. Much the same kind of methodologically problematic procedure is followed by Zamosc [1986] in his analysis of farmers' movements in Colombia. Hence the unproblematic adoption of census landholding categories involves Zamosc following 'the accepted convention, that ... considers units smaller than twenty hectares to be peasant units' [1986: 23]. That the economic interests of those at the top of this category might not be the same as those at the bottom is a question Zamosc never poses. According to the 1960 agricultural census, cultivators owning under 20 hectares accounted for 61 per cent of total output and, more significantly, for half the output of coffee, the principal cash-crop exported by Colombia [1986: 25]. This undifferentiated landholding category would therefore have included not only poor peasants, whose main income derived from the sale of their labour-power, but also small agrarian capitalists producing coffee for the international market.
9. Omvedt is undoubtedly right to claim that in Indian agriculture family labour, and in particular that of women, is a quantitatively significant form of labour-power, and every bit as important as other variants. However, to categorise such workers simply in the form of kinship relations, rather than relations of production based on ownership of or separation from property owned by kinsfolk, is to engage in reification. In circumstances where a farm workforce is composed of family members who are either propertyless, or themselves possess/own insufficient land to reproduce subsistence, but who nevertheless provide or sell their labour-power to the household head, these subjects correspond to wage labour (kinship notwithstanding). Accordingly, in this situation an *economic* relationship that licenses both surplus appropriation and accumulation not merely operates within the peasant family farm itself but is also based ultimately on the private ownership of the means of production inside the peasant family or kin group, and thus corresponds to a *class* relationship that transects the peasant household.
10. Both the fact and the political implications of this important point made by Gill – the participation in the new farmers' movements of military personnel – should not be underestimated. As research carried out by Anand [1940] into the expenditure patterns of retired soldiers in Punjab during the 1934–38 period demonstrates, there is in this region a long history of agricultural investment (livestock, land) by military personnel.
11. Not the least of the problems faced by this argument is who or what would serve to guarantee the payment of minimum wages in the (likely) event of farmers refusing or neneging on this undertaking. The answer is the state, or precisely that institution to which the farmers' movements are opposed and the power of which must in their view be curtailed.
12. As the contribution by Assadi makes clear, such a deflecting mechanism is present in the very criterion for membership of Shetkari Sanghatana itself, where the all-embracing definition of peasant (= shetkari) simply as 'one who works the land' fails thereby to distinguish between rich and poor peasant, capitalist and non-capitalist producer, and manual and non-manual labour. It should be noted, however, that in her contribution to this volume Omvedt interprets this same definition somewhat differently, and maintains that it is evidence merely of the multi-class village-level support which Shetkari Sangatana is willing to rally.
13. It is somewhat curious, to put it no more strongly, that in a collection of essays dealing with the issue of 'urban bias' [*Varshney*, 1993c], no mention is made of the contribution to this debate by Byres [1972; 1974; 1979]. This silence is especially curious in view of the fact that many of the key elements in Byres' argument are conceded at the outset [*Varshney*, 1993a: 5]. Perhaps the most plausible explanation for such an omission is a straightforwardly political one: that Byres' critique, structured by a Marxist framework, is not merely incompatible with but undermines much of the argument contained in the contributions to the collection, all of which comes from a neo-classical economic

position [e.g. *Lipton*, 1993; *Bates*, 1993]. In the case of Varshney, this involves issues of 'choice-making' subjects and institutional constraints [1993b: 202, 207]. Significantly, he shares with Sharad Joshi the perception of the fiscal burden as a 'problem' of unnecessary administrative expenditure [1993b: 202].

14. Given his view that the existence of democratic political structures enables (= empowers) peasants and farmers to exercise pressure for higher prices, it is unsurprising that Varshney [1993b: 210] holds the converse to be true: that is, 'that, *there is no systematic ruralising tendency in authoritarian polities*' (original emphasis). This is a problematic claim, and shows an unfamiliarity with debate about the agrarian question, and in particular Lenin's concept of a Prussian road. The latter's theory of peasant differentiation was itself based on his view that, where the agrarian sector was composed of latifundia or large landed estates, capitalist penetration of agriculture would follow two distinct paths [*Lenin*, 1962: 238–9; 1963: 139ff.]. One of these, known as the Prussian road, entailed a transformation whereby the landlord expropriated the tenants on his estate, either by depriving them of land altogether or (more usually) reducing considerably their usufruct rights while at the same time increasing the levels of rent. The estate was kept intact as a single unit, and the landlord went on to become a capitalist farmer himself. This he did by preserving the pre-existing relationships with his tenants, such as labour-service and debt bondage. Under the Prussian road, therefore, the power of the landlord class in the state is consolidated, and the majority of the peasantry are pauperised. The importance of the distinction between the American and Prussian roads to capitalist development, Lenin argued, was that under the Prussian road, where the estate system and with it the economic and political power of the landlord class remained intact, the peasantry would continue having to pay high levels of rent. Consequently, peasants would be unable to afford to improve agricultural production by adopting new techniques, and since they continued to use labour-service, landlords were under no pressure to install new machinery either. The result was a situation inhibiting the development of the productive forces in agriculture, and with it the continued development of capitalism. Since for Varshney no Marxist theory of the agrarian question exists, however, he is able to claim that [1993b: 211]: 'Unfortunately, there is no good theory of policy change or of conditions under which policies change'. In other words, his is a framework without agrarian class, class formation and class struggle. Because he reifies the concept of political democracy, therefore, Varshney overlooks the extent to which the Prussian path applies not just to India as a whole [*Patnaik*, 1986] or to parts of India, such as Bihar, where owners of large properties continue to defy land ceiling legislation (see Yughandar and Iyer [1993]), but also elsewhere. In the case of Chile, for example, where following the 1973 military coup land was taken away from those who had belonged to trade unions or taken part in land invasions, the ten million hectares expropriated during land reforms of Frei and Allende were once again privatised by the Pinochet dictatorship. Of the estates expropriated prior to coup, some 28 per cent were restored to former owners, a reversal of the land reforms which amounts in this instance to a partial re-Prussification of the development path. In the case of Chile, Varshney avoids having to confront the implications for his argument about 'urban bias' of the latter process by limiting his 'proposed link between democracy, rural empowerment and rural well-being [sic] in the Third World' [1993b: 214, footnote 31] to Chile in the period before 1972.

15. Symptomatically, in considerating the potential/actual role of taxation in India, Varshney makes no mention of the seminal contribution to this debate by Kalecki [1976], who argued that the political unwillingness of the state to directly tax agriculture – a consequence of the class nature of Indian society and the state – would lead to deficit financing and precisely the economic problems that Varshney attempts to address. For more on this issue, see Byres [1994].

16. The fact that the notion of *contradiction* must be inserted into questions about empowerment (of one category/class at the expense of another category/class) seems to escape Varshney. Although acknowledging the importance of including agricultural labour in any consideration of 'urban bias', therefore, he excludes them from his

conceptualisation of 'rural sector' (= peasants, farmers) and then proceeds to argue for a situation of general 'rural well-being' that fails to take into account the antithetical interests of rural workers [1993b: 210, 211, footnote 1].

17. Perhaps a different dynamic may have been at at work here, initiated by peasants rather than by the left. It may well be the case, therefore, that it was because rich and middle peasants themselves began turning to the farmers' movements that groups/parties of the left were then forced to rethink their strategy, and focus solely on the mobilisation of poor peasants and agricultural workers.
18. It could be argued that much of what passes for socialism in India is unduly influenced by – and perhaps nothing other than a variant of – Gandhian nationalism. This would certainly appear to be true of Lohiate 'socialism' in Karnataka, which Assadi counterposes to the Gandhian tendency in the KRRS; as is clear from Lohia [1963: 119ff.] himself, socialism in this instance is elided with Gandhism and, as a 'third way', presented as an alternative to both capitalism and communism. Indeed, the Samyukta Socialist Party, of which Lohia was *de facto* leader, has been described as a populist organisation [*Brass* (1973: 394–95)]. This kind of problem also surfaces with regard to the politico-ideological position of Shetkari Sanghatana in Maharashtra where, according to Omvedt, Sharad Joshi condemns both Marxist and Gandhian politics. yet subsequently accepts the Gandhian model of development.
19. The observation that neo-liberalism has policies about the environment while the left has not is not just incorrect but also fails to take into account the extent to which policies advocated by them address the fundamental question of property relations – but from different ends of the political spectrum. Unsurprisingly, therefore, the free market solutions espoused by those associated with the World Bank [1992: 353ff.] see subsidies as a cause of and the market a solution to environmental degradation. Accordingly, neo-liberalism promotes the privatization of all national/natural resources, and the promulgation of enforcable property rights, whereby all territory, cultivable land, forests, and water currently owned by the state could be bought and sold like any other commodity. As is indeed now already the case, the result of such free market 'solutions' is – and would be – not a decline but much rather an increase in contextually-specific forms of environmental degradation, as metropolitan capitalism sought either to locate hazardous production processes and/or to dump toxic waste connected with this in so-called Third World countries (and not only these) where national property had ceased to be inalienable. The left, by contrast, has made no distinction historically between questions of control/ownership of property of all kinds, and ecologically sustainable planning linked to the common ownership of means of production. In short, for both neo-liberals and marxists the environment is not – and cannot be – regarded as an issue separate from politics and (thus) distinct from the question of property relations.
20. That conservatives themselves lay claim to this anti-capitalist tradition is clear from many sources, not least those written by conservatives themselves. As Nisbet [1966: 26] has observed,

> the indictment of capitalism that comes from the conservatives in the nineteenth century is often more severe than that of socialists. Whereas the latter accepted capitalism at least to the point of regarding it as a necessary step from past to future, the traditionalists tended to reject it outright, seeing any development of its mass industrial nature – either within capitalism or a future socialism – as but a continued falling away from the superior values of Christian-feudal society. It was what the socialists *accepted* in capitalism – its technology, modes of organisation, and urbanism – that the conservatives most despised. They saw in these forces cause of the disintegration of what Burke called the 'inns and resting places' of the human spirit, Bonald, 'les liens sociales', and Southey, 'the bond of attachment' (original emphasis).

The fact, the history and the strength of this claim by the political right on the discourse of anti-capitalism is forgotten by socialists at their peril: by endorsing politically non-specific/undifferentiated forms of anti-capitalist discourse and action, they put the weapons (incorporation, dilution) of the class struggle into the hands of the enemies of socialism.

REFERENCES

Alavi, H., 1965, 'Peasants and Revolution', *Socialist Register 1965*, London: The Merlin Press.

Anand, R.L., 1940, *Soldiers' Savings and How They Use Them*, Lahore: The Board of Economic Inquiry, Punjab.

Athreya, V.B., Böklin, G., Djurfeld, G. and S. Lindberg, 1987, 'Identification of Agrarian Classes: A Methodological Essay with Empirical Material from South India', *Journal of Peasant Studies*, Vol.14, No.7.

Athreya, V.B., Djurfeld, G. and S. Lindberg 1990, 'Identifying Agrarian Classes: Answer to Utsa Patnaik', *Journal of Peasant Studies*, Vol.17, No.3.

Bates, R.H., 1993, '"Urban Bias": A Fresh Look', in C. Varshney (ed.) [1993c].

Brass, P.R., 1973, 'Radical Parties of the Left in Bihar: A Comparison of the SSP and the CPI', in P.R. Brass and M. Franda (eds.), *Radical Politics in South Asia*, Cambridge, MA: MIT Press.

Brass, T., 1991, 'Moral Economists, Subalterns, New Social Movements, and the (Re-) Emergence of a (Post-) Modernised (Middle) Peasant', *Journal of Peasant Studies*, Vol.18., No.2.

Byres, T.J., 1972, 'Industrialization, the Peasantry and the Economic Debate in Post-Independence India', in A.V. Bhuleskar (ed.), *Towards a Socialist Transformation of the Indian Economy*, Bombay: Popular Prakashan.

Byres, T.J., 1974, 'Land Reform, Industrialization and the Marketed Surplus in India: An Essay on the Power of Rural Bias', in D. Lehmann (ed.), *Agrarian Reform and Agrarian Reformism*, London: Faber.

Byres, T.J., 1979, 'Of Neo-Populist Pipe-Dreams: Daedalus in the Third World and the Myth of Urban Bias', *Journal of Peasant Studies*, Vol.6, No.2.

Byres, T.J. (ed.), 1994, *The State and Development Planning in India*, Delhi: Oxford University Press.

Charlesworth, N., 1980, 'The "Middle Peasant Thesis" and the Roots of Rural Agitation in India, 1914–1947', *Journal of Peasant Studies*, Vol.7, No.3.

Charlesworth, N., 1982, 'The Roots of Rural Agitation in India: A Reply to Hardiman', *Journal of Peasant Studies*, Vol.9, No.4.

Charlesworth, N., 1985, *Peasants and Imperial Rule: Agriculture and Agrarian Society in the Bombay Presidency, 1850–1935*, Cambridge: Cambridge University Press.

Dhanagare, D.N., 1990, 'Shetkari Sanghatana: The Farmers' Movement in Maharashtra – Background and Ideology', *Social Action*, Vol.40, No.4.

Hardiman, D., 1981a, *Peasant Nationalists of Gujarat: Kheda District 1917–34*, Delhi: Oxford University Press.

Hardiman, D., 1981b, 'The Roots of Rural Agitation in India, 1914–47: A Rejoinder to Charlesworth', *Journal of Peasant Studies*, Vol.8, No.3.

Hardiman, D., 1984, 'The Roots of Rural Agitation in India, 1914–47: A Comment on Charlesworth's Reply', *Journal of Peasant Studies*, Vol.11, No.3.

Hofstadter, R., 1969, 'North America', in G. Ionescu and E. Gellner (eds.), *Populism: Its Meanings and National Characteristics*, London: Weidenfeld & Nicolson.

Jeffrey, R., 1979, 'Peasant Movements and the Communist Party in Kerala, 1937–1960', in D.B. Miller (ed.), *Peasants and Politics: Grassroots Reaction to Change in Asia*, London: Edward Arnold.

Kalecki, M., 1976, *Essays on Developing Economies*, Hassocks: The Harvester Press.

Laclau, E., 1985, 'New Social Movements and the Plurality of the Social', in D. Slater (ed.), *New Social Movements and the State in Latin America*, Amsterdam: CEDLA.

Laclau, E., 1990, *New Reflections on the Revolution of Our Time*, London: Verso.

Laclau, E., 1992, 'Beyond Emancipation', *Development and Change*, Vol.23, No.3.

Lenin, V.I., 1962, 'The Agrarian Programme of Social Democracy in the First Russian Revolution, 1905–1907', *Collected Works*, Vol.13, Moscow: Foreign Languages Publishing House.

Lenin, V.I., 1963, 'The Agrarian Question in Russia Towards the Close of the Nineteenth Century', *Collected Works*, Vol.15, Moscow: Foreign Languages Publishing House.

Lennenberg, C., 1988, 'Sharad Joshi and the Farmers: The Middle Peasant Lives!', *Pacific Affairs*, Vol.61, No.3.

Lipton, M., 1993, 'Urban Bias: Of Consequences, Classes and Causality', in Varshney (ed.), [1993c].

Lohia, R., 1963, *Marx, Gandhi and Socialism*, Hyderabad: Navahind.

Nisbet, R.A., 1966, *The Sociological Tradition*, London: Heinemann.

Omvedt, G., 1993a, 'Of Brahmins, Sacred and Socialist', *Economic and Political Weekly*, Vol.28, No.44.

Omvedt, G., 1993b, *Reinventing Revolution: New Social Movements and the Socialist Tradition in India*, New York: M.F. Sharpe, Inc.

Omvedt, G., 1994, 'Dependency Theory, Peasants and Third World Food Crisis', *Economic and Political Weekly*, Vol.29, No.4.

Patnaik, U., 1986, 'The Agrarian Question and Development of Capitalism in India', *Economic and Political Weekly*, Vol.21, No.18.

Patnaik, U., 1987, *Peasant Class Differentiation: A Study in Method with Reference to Haryana*, Delhi: Oxford University Press.

Patnaik, U., 1988, 'Ascertaining the Economic Characteristics of Peasant Classes-in-Themselves in Rural India: A Methodological and Empirical Exercise', *Journal of Peasant Studies*, Vol.15, No.3.

Rudolph, L. and S.H. Rudolph, 1987, *In Pursuit of Lakshmi: The Political Economy of the Indian State*, New Delhi: Orient.

Varshney, A., 1993a, 'Introduction: Urban Bias in Perspective', in Varshney (ed.) [1993c].

Varshney, A., 1993b, 'Self-Limited Empowerment: Democracy, Economic Development and Rural India', in Varshney (ed.) [1993c].

Varshney, A. (ed.), 1993c, *Beyond Urban Bias*, London: Frank Cass (also a special issue of *Journal of Development Studies*, Vol.26, No.3).

Walicki, A., 1969, *The Controversy over Capitalism* Oxford: The Clarendon Press.

Wolf, E.R., 1971, *Peasant Wars of the Twentieth Century*, London: Faber.

World Bank, 1992, *Proceedings of the World Bank Annual Conference on Development Economics, 1991*, Washington DC: IBRD.

Yugandhar, B.N. and K. Gopal Iyer (eds.), 1993, *Land Reforms in India – Volume 1: Bihar – Institutional Constraints*, New Delhi: Sage Publications.

Zamosc, L., 1986, *The Agrarian Question and the Peasant Movement in Colombia*, Cambridge: Cambridge University Press.

The Politics of Gender, Nature and Nation in the Discourse of the New Farmers' Movements

TOM BRASS

'It is said that the industrial worker is much better off than the bulk of the rural population and that there is, therefore, much less need for the State to do anything for him than for the rural population. I have noticed that this plea most often proceeds from people who want the State to do nothing either for the one or the other.' An observation made by D.R. Gadgil [1945: 101] in the Banaili Readership Lectures given at Patna University during March–April 1940.

'Nations are products of Nature: History is merely a progressive continuation of animal development'. Alexander Herzen [1956: 178], 'The Russian People and Socialism: An Open Letter to Jules Michelet', 1851.

INTRODUCTION

As elsewhere, the 1980s has witnessed in India a confluence between academic discourse, as projected by the highly influential subaltern studies series, edited by Ranajit Guha, and the political practice of what are termed new social movements.[1] The latter consist not only of regionally-specific farmer's mobilisations but also of environmental movements (composed of tribals and forest-dwellers) and more generally the women's movement, which has played a prominent role in both the ecological and the new farmers' movement. The widespread endorsement of 'resistance' and 'popular culture' in the discourse by/about these

---

Tom Brass is at the Faculty of Social and Political Sciences, University of Cambridge, Free School Lane, Cambridge CB2 3RQ, UK. This article is based on a paper presented in the lecture series on 'Socialism: Recent Pasts, Possible Futures' given at SPS, Cambridge, during November 1991, and subsequently in the JPS/ICSSR Workshop on 'New Farmers' Movements in India', held in New Delhi during March 1993. The writer thanks the Managers of the the Smuts Memorial Fund for a grant towards the cost of attending the New Delhi Workshop.

movements is due in part to the way in which such concepts challenge the notion of passivity, by recognising the voice and action of those historical categories (women, agricultural labourers, tribals, peasants) usually perceived as mute and/or dominated. On the face of it, therefore, such a process can be viewed as politically progressive. It is frequently argued, therefore, both in academic discourse about these movements, and by the spokespersons of the latter, that what is on offer here is nothing other than a radical new agenda, or a complete break with a socialist/nationalist/male past and thus the shape of an entirely new future.[2]

The implication of such an approach is that opposition to the existing social order derives not from class formation, class struggle, and the politics of class, but from a hitherto undiscovered authentic grassroots voice (= 'popular culture') re-presented in subaltern/movement/eco-feminist texts as a *de*politicized discourse untainted by discredited over-arching metanarratives. Like the 'moral economy' position (see Thompson [1991: 184ff.]), primacy is allocated to customs, traditions, culture, and practices as these *already exist* within the peasantry and the working class, a view which contrasts with that of Marxists who have tended to emphasise the backward-looking, politically reactionary and historically transcendent role of much of what passes for resistance based on an already existing 'popular culture' (racism, nationalism, religion). Lenin, for example, warned against the opportunistic espousal/endorsement of spontaneous conflict 'from below' simply because this happened to be taking place, and emphasised instead the importance of party organisation structured by a specifically *political* input into the formation of what would eventually become a consciousness of class.[3]

The argument which follows will make two interrelated propositions. First, that the idioms/agents invoked in furtherance of agrarian mobilisation by new social movements, socialists and ecofeminists in general, and the new farmers' movement in particular, have been those associated historically with the politics of populism/neo-populism and nationalism, in the discourse of which nation = people = peasants = nature. And second, that in the Indian context one significant outcome of this discursive fusion has been to contribute to the reproduction of a politico-ideological space now occupied by the parties and movements of the political right.[4]

I

Neo-populism, Nationalism and 'Popular Culture'

Any consideration of the socio-economic composition and political character of the new farmers' movement in India must necessarily begin by addressing two interrelated issues. First, the way in which the idealisation of peasant society/culture as the essence of nationhood, combined with a suspicious/condemnatory attitude towards science/urbanism/industrialisation, has occupied a crucial historical role in the discourse of the political right. And second, the long-standing debate between populism, neo-populism and Marxism about categorisation of the peasantry and consequently the possibility/desirability of transforming the existing agrarian structure.

Many of the diverse, and seemingly distinct, anti-scientific/anti-modern views considered below possess a common origin in the conservative reaction to the spread of Enlightenment ideas. Historically, the politico-ideological object of conservatism has been the legitimisation of an existing or rapidly vanishing social order by the attempted ideological naturalisation of what are perceived by the ruling class to be its core institutional elements: religion, family, gender, ethnicity, nation, hierarchy and nature itself. All the latter are perceived/presented by the political right as 'naturally-occurring' phenomena, and thus the immutable bases of social existence (= 'being').[5] By elevating 'thinking' above 'being', however, Enlightenment rationalist thought de-essentialises the 'natural'; in the process of challenging what is (or what ought to continue to be), such philosophy has been perceived by a variety of conservative social forces as licensing change, and thus the precursor of revolution. In so far as 'reason' constitutes the antithesis of the 'natural', which it problematizes and historicises, therefore, conservatism is necessarily an anti-rational/anti-Enlightenment philosophy. By contrast, since the political right essentialises traditional institutional social forms as 'natural', the latter concept is as a result not only equated with 'being' itself but also (and therefore) constitutes the basis of conservatism generally and the ideology of counter-revolutionary romanticism in particular.[6] It was precisely because they challenged 'natural' institutions that were specific to national culture (individualism exercised in a particularistic form within a 'given' locality), and threatened to supplant them with new (= 'alien'/'foreign') forms imported from (French, Russian) revolutionary contexts, that conservativism generally has been opposed to the notion of universal (= international) socio-economic categories/processes.[7]

To this conservative pantheon of 'natural' categories can be added the concept 'peasant'. Historically, the opposition of the landlord class to science/urbanism, and the aristocratic reaction against industrialisation generally, derives in a large part from the ways in which these combine to break its power over the peasantry. Thus science/machine-based industrial development offers estate tenants not only alternative (and perhaps better-paid) employment in towns but also the possibility of urban residence, both of which challenge the economic and political dominance landlords traditionally exercise over tenants through the control of land, employment and housing in rural areas. Moreover, once it has migrated to town an erstwhile peasantry, hitherto the embodiment of 'eternal'/ 'natural' rural/national/cultural/religious values, becomes transformed into an urban proletariat (= 'the mob in the streets'), now non-/anti-religious and part of an international working class. In the process it is also reconstituted as a political threat, not only to means of production in the town/city itself but also – and more importantly from the view of the rural landowning class – to agrarian property relations.'[8]

This political divide between on the one hand a materialist/rationalist emphasis on the objective necessity of internationalism, socio-economic change and industrial development, and on the other an idealist/irrationalist commitment to the maintenance/reinvention of an 'imagined community', composed of a peasantry wherein reside indigenous national/cultural/religious values, is itself at the root of the Marxist/neo-populist polemic. All Marxists regard the peasantry as a socio-economic form that fragments into a rural bourgeoisie and a rural proletariat, and for this reason does not itself form a class but is internally divided along class lines.[9] Differentiating the peasantry into rich, middle and poor peasants, Lenin argued that capitalist penetration of agriculture converted the former into a rural bourgeoisie and the latter into a *de facto* proletariat, while middle peasants (or petty commodity producers) were depeasantised.[10] This process was accompanied and accentuated by an increase in the utilisation of machinery and wage labour, the concentration of landownership, and the displacement of small-scale by large-scale production. Consequently, Lenin concluded, in Russia the village community (*mir*) was already disintegrating into its opposed class elements, thereby simultaneously providing capitalism with both a proletariat and a home market.

Combining the economic theory of petty commodity production and the politics/ideology of nationalism, both populism and neo-populism are the mirror image of Marxism. Invoking the conservative values and traditions of a Christian, pre-Petrine Russia against the 'dangerous'/ 'alien' views of the European Enlightenment, the polarities which structured the nationalist/populist ideology of Russian Slavophiles were similar to those structuring the *gemeinschaft/gesellschaft* framework.[11] Against the ideal-type conceptualisation of *gesellschaft* as an 'artificial' large-scale conflict-ridden system associated with European industrialisation, urbanisation, modern government and bureaucracy, Slavophiles counterposed and invoked the desirability of an ahistorical, immanent concept of harmonious/organic small-scale *gemeinschaft*, a predominantly rural and authentically Russian 'community' composed of 'common people'. Whereas *gesellschaft* entails the adoption of rationalistic/calculating (= scientific) and future-oriented universal values that manifest themselves through public opinion, *gemeinschaft* by contrast is based on religion/culture/family, its 'natural' will consequently being the expression of ancient faith, custom and folkloric tradition. Backward-looking and opposed to industrialisation, Slavophile populism was based on the view that each nation could not but follow its own organic laws of development.

Because it threatened on the one hand to expand the urban proletariat and on the other to ruin the small independent peasant producer, the embodiment of traditional religious and nationalist values, Slavophile populists reacted against what was perceived as a foreign (specifically German) capitalist penetration of Russia during the latter half of the nineteenth century.[12] Inverting the Leninist framework, populists maintained that an undifferentiated peasantry reproduced itself regardless of the wider economic system; the uniqueness of Russian development was consequently attributed by them to the presence of a subsistence-oriented rural economy which deprived capitalism of a market. Instead of going down the capitalist path, therefore, populists sought to avoid this altogether, in the process conserving the 'natural'/god-given form of petty commodity production, and with it the ancient cultural traditions of what they regarded as the instinctively egalitarian village community.[13] A corollary of this view is that landlessness is also perceived as 'natural', and thus immutable (which is precisely the argument made by the new farmers' movement in India).[14]

Unlike populism, which was grounded in a liberal critique of the dehumanisation and inequality associated with nineteenth-century capitalist development, neo-populism is a twentieth-century phenomenon opposed not so much to capitalism as to socialism, and in particular to large-scale industrialisation and state collectivisation of peasant smallholders in the Soviet Union.[15] In the neo-populist vision of Chayanov [1966], petty commodity production reproduces itself in the form of the family labour farm, regardless of the presence/absence of feudalism, capitalism or indeed socialism.[16] Unlike Marxist political theory, for which peasant differentiation into small capitalist producers and an agrarian proletariat licenses class-specific revolutionary action designed to capture state power that prefigures a transition to socialism, neo-populism reconstitutes the peasantry as an undifferentiated category that resists socio-economic change, a politically conservative position which does not involve a transition to socialism, entails no expropriation/redistribution of existing property, and hence presents no threat to the continued rule of capital.

For rich peasants the advantage of such a populist/neo-populist discourse is that it enables them to operate politically and ideologically on two fronts: against poor peasants and agricultural labourers as well as landlords and/or international capital. The success of this hinges in turn on the displacement of class categories, whereby agrarian subjects who are defined in terms of ownership of or separation from given means of production are redefined in neo-populist terms simply as 'peasants'/'cultivators'/'farmers', or petty commodity producers in contexts where there is actually great variation in both the relations and the scale of production. Such a discursive fusion permits agrarian capitalist producers to claim not only that all rural inhabitants experience a uniform level of suffering in the face of urban and/or 'foreign' exploitation but also that economic growth is located in and confined largely to towns/cities/industry and/or other nations.[17] By suppressing reference to socio-economic differentiation arising from the process of capitalist development, therefore, rich peasants can challenge landlords and/or imperialism in the name of the peasantry as a whole, which permits them not merely to reinforce and reproduce in discourse shared with poor peasants and agricultural labour the mythic yet politico-ideologically potent image of an homogenous peasantry, but also to claim that they represent thereby the voice of 'the people' (= the peasantry), and thus the nation itself.[18]

Two important consequences follow from this nationalist discourse, each of which is supportive of the neo-populist camouflage adopted by rich peasants. First, that self-empowerment is effected at the expense of a foreign and not an indigenous capitalist class; and second, that 'popular culture' becomes identified unproblematically with the 'voice from below', and action based on this is accordingly deemed to constitute an authentic expression of the democratic will.[19] Consequently, anything and everything associated with its grassroots manifestation automatically becomes the embodiment of democratic expression, and indeed within the new social movements and subaltern studies framework can now be invoked/celebrated as the utterance of the hitherto mute and dominated. The difficulty with this is that once the 'popular' is accepted as an *unmediated* construct (or the 'natural' voice of the people), it follows that what is desirable becomes whatever the 'popular' says is so; in short, a procedure that fails to ask precisely how such views are constructed, by whom, and for what political ends.

In this connection it is perhaps salutary to recall two interrelated points. First, as one observer [*Burke*, 1981] has noted, 'popular culture' is associated historically with the emergence of nineteenth-century European nationalist movements. Hence the importance to the latter of 'reinventing' traditional folkloric concepts linking an ethnically-specific homogeneous 'people' to a particular territory, thereby establishing a politico-ideological claim to its own rightful place/space and simultaneously denying any rival claims to this made by a 'foreign' occupying power. Moreover, as the same source argues [*Burke*, 1981: 217], in the European context the ideology of ethnic 'primitivism' and 'purism' is essentially:

> a label for the assumption that 'the people' really means 'the peasants'. As Herder once put it, '[t]he mob in the streets, which never sings or composes but shrieks and mutilates, is not the people'. The peasants were seen as the true People because they lived close to Nature and because they were unspoiled by new or foreign ways.

As with Slavophile Russian populism, therefore, the discourse of nineteenth-century European nationalism is structured by an idealised/folkloric image/sound of an undifferentiated peasantry, the repository of national culture (embodied in music, language, songs, dress, customs, traditions) and thus emblematic of people/nation/nature, all of which is counterposed to the proletarian/urban 'other'.[20]

The second point concerns perhaps the most telling example of the reactionary provenance of this discourse, together with its political rehabilitation in the name of 'popular culture': Germany during the period 1933–45. In its attempt to undermine the exceptionalist image of German fascism, therefore:

> the right has rethought its analysis of National Socialism in part by borrowing, altering, and often gravely distorting the concepts, methods and conclusions of social history. The right's discourse is filled with pleas to normalize the study of Nazism, to empathize with the little man and to recognize that many aspects of the Third Reich, including its most horrendous acts, were not unique ... It was history from below which first sought to reconstruct non-elite groups' perceptions of fascism.[21]

Of additional significance here is the fact that central to the anti-modern/anti-urban ideological components of German Fascism (as projected in the writings of Alfred Rosenberg and Richard Walther Darré) was the concept of immutable laws of nature reasserting themselves to cleanse the nation, the race, and its soil.[22] Like the 'anti-foreigner' Slavophile populism/nationalism of the nineteenth-century Russian nobility, this idealisation/sanctification of nature (= the environment = the people = the nation) was also based on the romanticisation of a subsistence-oriented smallholding peasantry, projected in politico-ideological terms as the integral embodiment of an ethnically 'pure' German folk culture and the bulwark of a socio-economically atemporal 'natural order' outside history, against which was ranged the town/city, the source of multiple, interrelated and non-Germanic forms of pollution ('Jewish finance capital', socialism, the 'urban mob').

II

In many respects, Gandhian theory and practice in India conforms to the classical pattern of nationalist/populist/neo-populist ideology and politics outlined above with regard to Russia and Europe.[23] On the one hand, therefore, Gandhi promoted class conciliation, endorsed the notion of an ethnically specific hierarchy (based on the Hindu caste system), and advocated a return to traditional cultural and religious values as embodied in village India by an undifferentiated peasantry; on the other hand, he denied progress/modernity, was correspondingly suspicious of all things urban (the locus of 'alien' non-Indian western values), and condemned class struggle.[24] Because of the convenient all-embracing character of this populism, in which an externalised oppression/exploitation/capitalism can be displaced on to an urban/foreign/scientific/Western 'other', the prime movers in the agrarian struggles organised by Gandhi in Bihar and Gujarat during the early part of the century were unsurprisingly the better-off peasants from high castes.[25]

This was the case with regard to the *satyagraha* conducted against European indigo planters in Champaran district, Bihar, where during 1917 Gandhi mobilised tenants against rent increases (*sharabeshi*), illegal levies (*abwabs*), land transfer payments (*salaami*), and the obligation to cultivate the landlord's crops – particularly indigo – on their best land (the *tinkathia* system). The resulting *satyagraha* was led by better-off tenants composed of high-caste Brahmins, Rajputs, Bhumihars and Kyasthas, who were caught between rent enhancements coupled with the declining profitability of indigo cultivation on the one hand, and on the other the need to remove existing institutional obstacles to their growing the more profitable foodgrain and sugarcane crops.[26] Much the same was true of the Bardoli *satyagraha* in Surat district, Gujarat, where, because the rental value of land had increased substantially, and the British administration had decided to raise the level of land revenue, rich peasant proprietors belonging to the Patidar caste who cultivated cotton embarked on a 'no-tax' campaign during 1928.[27]

Significantly, elements of the neo-populist/nationalist discourse which structure Gandhian ideology and 'popular culture' in India have now re-emerged in the print and electronic media.[28] The impact of cinema, and particularly television, has grown in rural India over recent times: by 1988 television coverage extended to include some 62 per cent of the population, and 11 million sets were watched by 90 million people.[29] As important as the reach of television has been the change in both form and content of its presentation. During the 1920s more than 70 per cent of Indian films had a mythological content, and rural existence was depicted in positive terms; after Independence, this mythological focus was replaced by social themes, in which the town was depicted in positive terms, as the source of enlightened values and liberation from the agrestic servitude of a backward-looking and socially anachronistic village existence.[30] From the 1970s onwards, however, this cinematic trend has been reversed: to begin with, not only has the mythological film once again returned to prominence, but it has done this in a way that naturalises (or makes real) the usually highly stylised presentation of Hindu mythology.[31] Similarly, urban India is now recast in politico-ideological terms as the locus not only of a uniformly hostile and corrupt state but also a negative secular/non-familial/alienated form of existence.[32] The latter is in turn counterposed to a similarly recast and idealised concept of the village, the repository of traditional/religious/familial values (at the centre of which is located the potent and interchangable image of the Indian mother and/or *Bharat Mata*, Mother India) now depicted as positive and associated with the purity of an unchanging/ever-present (= authentic) indigenous culture threatened by a specifically urban, western/ 'foreign', greedy and anti-traditional secularism. As will be seen below, the significance of this transformation in the cinematic codes of popular film in India is that they also structure (and thus reinforce) a neo-populist/ nationalist discourse that is shared by the political left, the new farmers' movements, ecofeminism, and now the BJP.[33]

The New Farmers' Movement

The novelty of the farmers' movements which emerged in the Green Revolution areas of India during the late 1970s and early 1980s is generally attributed to a number of characteristics which they are said to have in common. Unlike past anti-landlord movements, led by and reflecting the class interests of rich peasants, the farmers' agitation of the 1980s is regarded as a non-political form of mobilisation, aimed specifically against the state by all peasants who are no longer divided along class lines but are now united as commodity producers, and consequently demanding not land but remunerative prices.[34] A result of the overall commercialisation of production combined with a slowdown in economic growth experienced in these areas of capitalist agriculture, it is argued, is that surplus generating peasants blame the state – as the effective institutional regulator of input/output prices, and through this the economic reproduction of the peasantry as a whole – for adverse terms of trade between industry and agriculture. Hence the opposition to the state on the part of all peasants, and the demand by the latter from the former for 'remunerative prices', or lower costs for inputs (energy, irrigation and credit) and higher returns for output (crops, livestock).

Such an interpretation of the new farmers' movements is faced with a number of difficulties. First, as confirmed by earlier instances in rural India of mobilisation aimed against government on questions of remunerative prices for agricultural commodities and lower taxes, opposition to the state on these issues is not new.[35] Second, land continues to be on the agenda of the new farmers' movement, albeit not in the usual form of an egalitarian redistribution; much rather the opposite, since the demand is for the abolition of land ceilings, or the opportunity for the better-off to extend/consolidate rural property.[36] Third, the balance of the resource flows from the agrarian sector implied in the concept 'urban bias' ignores the existence of substantial direct/indirect subsidies to agriculture by the state.[37] And fourth, the support of not only agricultural labourers but also poor peasants for the new farmers' movements, and with it the multi-class nature of such mobilisation, is questionable; again, much rather the opposite appears to be the case, since peasant proprietors confronting the state over 'remunerative prices' are simultaneously engaged in conflict with their workforce over wage levels and the restructuring of the labour process.[38] Hence the new farmers' movements' antagonism towards the state is itself partial and class-specific: while state intervention on the issue of remunerative prices is perceived as desirable and thus actively sought, there is simultaneously an equally strong opposition by the new farmers' movements to the (actual or potential) implementation by the state of legislation enforcing land ceilings and minimum wages.[39] In short, in these regions of capitalist agriculture rich peasants who support the new farmers' movements want political power exercised through the state not only commensurate with their economic position but supportive of this: that is, the deregulation of state control over land, labour and the price of agricultural produce.

Both the free market philosophy structuring the discourse of the new farmers' movement and the contradictions to which this gives rise emerge most clearly with regard to debate over the propositions formulated by Arthur Dunkel, the GATT Director-General in the period 1980–93, as outlined in the *Draft Final Act Embodying the Results of the Uruguay Round of Multilateral Trade Negotiations*. The latter is endorsed by Sharad Joshi and the farmers' movement in Maharashtra, both because it challenges price-distorting 'urban bias' and state intervention, and because in his view the liberalisation of international trade and the accompanying elimination of agricultural subventions on a global scale would benefit ('heavily taxed') Indian peasants at the expense of ('heavily subsidized') farmers in the US, the EEC and Japan.[40] By contrast, the farmers' movements in Uttar Pradesh and Karnataka (led by Tikait and Nanjundaswamy) are both opposed to the suggestions contained in the Dunkel draft, on the grounds that free trade would permit foreign capital to undermine national economic sovereignty and depress domestic prices of agricultural produce.[41]

This debate about the effect of Dunkel and GATT liberalisation policies on the farmers' movement in India highlights the partial and contradictory position of Sharad Joshi on the interrelated connections between free trade, market competition and the role of the state. To compensate for the low prices determined by 'urban bias', he argues, requires that farmers be permitted to export agricultural produce, irrespective of local and/or national food shortages (a result of which would be to increase existing prices for domestic produce); however, this commitment to free trade is in turn dependent upon state intervention, in the form of tariff protection against foreign competition, to prevent import penetration and a consequent decline in existing prices for domestic produce.[42] The partial nature of this free market philosophy is similarly contradicted by his equivocal attitude towards government subsidies: the latter are to be retained not only for export promotion but also to guarantee the reproduction of existing property relations (for smallholdings which 'are, by their very size and character, uneconomic') and also to raise the level of the productive forces (land consolidation, installation of irrigation, purchase of seeds, hire of machinery).[43] Accordingly, the free market philosophy of Joshi entails a central paradox: the demand for the freedom of farmers to commodify production in response to price advantages on national/international markets depends in turn not only on state provision to these same farmers of export subsidies but also – like Tikait and Nanjundaswamy – on denying foreign capital a similar capacity to engage in free trade (and thus in effect negating GATT).

The political differences over GATT between the *Shetkari Sanghatana* on the one hand, and the BKU and KRRS on the other, should not obscure their agreement about the fundamental issues: all the farmers' leaders blame the Indian government for implementing foreigner-favouring/anti-farmer policies, and all want some form of tariff protection to ensure higher domestic prices. And although seemingly divergent in terms of policy towards Dunkel and GATT, the position of all the farmers' movements nevertheless make reference to and thus invoke the same neo-populist/nationalist discourse. Accordingly, Sharad Joshi maintains that even the 'middle-layer farmer' in India can outcompete the 'foreigner' once the latter is deprived of subsidies, while both Tikait and Nanjundaswamy seek protection for this same smallholding peasant from this same 'foreigner'.[44] The policy of agricultural liberalisation announced by the Namasimha Rao government at the end of March 1993 to coincide with yet another farmers' rally in New Delhi not only constitutes an attempt by the ruling Congress(I) party to gain the support of the new farmers' movements by conceding one of Joshi's principal demands (for export-oriented free trade), but also licenses thereby a more acute process of class differentiation within the new farmers' movements themselves, between the rich peasant beneficiaries of such a policy and those mainly poor peasants for whom it will mean proletarianisation.[45]

These considerations notwithstanding, leaders of and activists in the new farmers' movements deny the importance/existence of class and stress instead the apolitical nature of mobilisation on the part of a rural population (peasants/tribals/women) uniformly exploited by, and thus in conflict with, an 'urban' state. For example, Sharad Joshi – like Gandhi – rejects class struggle within the peasantry, and thus socialism as the outcome, and argues instead not only that all peasants are united as producers and consumers of commodities the prices of which are controlled by the state, but also that higher prices received by farmers for their output will enable them to pay their workers higher wages.[46] Echoing both the Chayanovian concept of a family farm, and also the 'urban bias' thesis of Lipton [1977] and Charan Singh, Joshi maintains that the principal contradiction is no longer found within the agrarian sector (between rich, middle, and poor peasants) but is now located between a powerless, uniformly poor rural population (= *Bharat*) on the one hand, and on the other a powerful, uniformly rich urban population (= India) and its state apparatus.[47]

Accordingly, the peasantry, peasant women and 'women's power' are all identified by Joshi as the major liberating forces in rural India, and the main form of oppression is violence, or 'looting', which he regards as primary and unrelated to property.[48] As is clear from the objectives of the village-level *Laxmi Mukti* ('liberation of housewives') project of inter-gender property transfer developed by the Shetkari Sanghtana in Maharashtra, however, the form taken by women's self-empowerment is in class terms very specific: not only are landless rural women excluded from the programme, but land operated by the peasant household and 'gifted' by men to women is to be cultivated by the latter in a traditional (non-technical/natural/organic) manner solely for the purpose of family subsistence provision.[49] In this way the discourse and practice of the new farmers' movement reinforces the potent mythical image of an ageless/unchanging (= 'natural') subsistence agriculture carried out largely by women, with the object of preserving traditional peasant household production (peasant = woman = nature = *Bharat Mata* = nation).

At first glance, many of the economic demands made by agrarian capitalist producers of the new farmers' movement would appear to have little in common with the rustic traditionalism of Gandhian philosophy.[50] However, this is to overlook the main role of the latter as a mobilising ideology, designed to deflect attention from the process/effects of peasant differentation and thus obtain widespread support in rural areas (the '"us"ness-of-we' as against the '"them"ness-of-they') for what is in fact a class-specific agrarian programme/policy. For precisely this reason, opposition by rich peasants to what they identified as Nehruvian 'socialism' in post-Independence India has generally been framed in Gandhian neo-populist terms: for example, the replacement of Nehruvian 'socialism' by a Gandhian alternative was central to the neo-populist agrarian policy of Charan Singh, political representative and organic intellectual of India's rich peasantry.[51] Claims to the contrary notwithstanding, therefore, the idioms which structure the mobilizing ideology of the new farmers' movements that emerged during the 1980s do not in fact break with this prefiguring discourse.[52] Not only are H.S. Rudrappa, the founder president of the KRRS, and M.D. Nanjundaswamy, its current leader, both staunch Gandhians, but the farmers' movement in Maharashtra has resorted to Gandhian methods of protest and the anti-intellectual 'rustic' ideology projected by M.S. Tikait is a thinly-disguised version of Gandhian/Liptonian 'urban bias'.[53]

In a similar vein, Sharad Joshi not only rejects Nehruvian 'socialism' and advocates a return to the Gandhian model of development but – like Gandhi himself – locates the reasons for this in a specifically nationalist discourse: accordingly, the current existence in India of 'urban bias' is attributed by him to the dual inheritance of the colonial regime, a process of post-Independence industrial growth predicated on the imitation of a 'foreign' lifestyle made possible only by the continued exploitation of the farmer.[54] And like not only Mahatma Gandhi and Charan Singh but also the Russian populists, the main objective of Sharad Joshi is to reconstitute the village community: economically, by retaining within it the surplus otherwise appropriated through 'urban bias'; socially, by providing an employment-generating self-sufficient village economy based on artisan production; and politically, by devolving power from the state to the traditional village *panchayat*.[55]

The New Farmers' Movement and Ecofeminism

Although the economic relationship between ecological concerns and the new farmers' movement are complex and potentially contradictory, at the level of discourse a significant measure of agreement exists. For example, Sharad Joshi blames industrial pollution, industrialisation, and 'urban bias' for declining soil fertility and environmental degradation in India generally and the centuries-old process of appropriation from the farmer. In his view, an ecologically sustainable use of 'appropriate' (= small-scale) agricultural technology would lower production costs and make farmers less dependent on state control over input prices.[56] Much the same kind of arguments are deployed by the influential ecofeminist Vandana Shiva, who not only acts as an adviser to M.S. Tikait but has also addressed the farmers' rally organised jointly by the BKU and the KRRS in New Delhi.[57] When combined with the the views of Sharad Joshi regarding the way in which not only peasants but the environment and women are 'looted' by a 'foreign'/urban/industrial development pattern, therefore, a politico-ideological affinity emerges between the discourse of the new farmers' movement and that of ecofeminism.

Like Sharad Joshi, Vandana Shiva attributes environmental degradation to a specifically urban and western industrial science and technology, and advocates instead the mobilization of women as 'natural' protectors of nature in the context of the traditional Hindu village community.[58] Again like Sharad Joshi, she links women to subsistence production and, like Gandhi, she rejects not only capitalist accumulation but also economic growth generally as 'alien' (= western) impositions on India. Equating the universalising tendencies of science and development with modern western patriarchy, Shiva maintains that all these forces combine to exercise violence not only against nature itself (a manifestation of which is the Punjab conflict) but also against tribals, peasants and rural Indian women ('still embedded in nature'), thereby replicating both process ('violence'/'looting') and target (women/peasants) identified in the discourse of Sharad Joshi; instead, she argues for a reversion to subsistence agriculture that would simultaneously reinstate *prakriti* (= nature/female = source of life), enhance the position of women, tribals and peasants, and (yet again like Sharad Joshi) thereby restore social peace and ecological harmony to rural India.[59]

The compatibility between the analytical approach of Shiva and that of new social movements theory influenced by postmodernism is evident from her positive/negative characterisations: on the one hand, therefore, she advocates a politics of human rights and 'democratic resistance' in pursuit of 'new civic spaces', and celebrates endogeneity/difference/diversity/decentralisation as ends in themselves; on the other hand, she is opposed to the (non-class-specific) state, and rejects development/progress/class/modernity as unacceptable universal categories associated exclusively with a western 'colonial' Enlightenment project.[60]

Similarly, her affinity with nationalism and neo-populism is clear from the way in which she classifies ethnicity and romanticises the agrarian social structure that preceded the Green Revolution. Accordingly, not only is the oppressed nature/female couple equated with ethnicity but for Shiva economic growth *per se* is identified as a form of 'new colonialism' and the Green Revolution is the result of a specifically 'foreign' science, 'foreign' politics, and 'foreign' knowledge produced by 'foreign' expert.[61] Against the externally-imposed, urban-oriented, surplus-extracting, large-scale/high-tech, non-natural, agribusiness of the Green Revolution from which women, tribals and peasants derive no benefit, Shiva counterposes an unambiguously Gandhian vision of small-scale, subsistence-oriented, needs-meeting, survival-guaranteeing natural agrarian structure composed of an undifferentiated peasantry.[62] Indeed, one of her main objections to the Green Revolution is that it disrupted the stability of pre-existing traditional society by eroding tribal and/or peasant 'cultural norms and practices', 'co-operation' and 'mutual obligations'.[63]

Since the romanticized concept of a pristine 'tribal' (itself a colonial invention) is central to this critique, it is necessary to ask: to what historical stage of its development does Shiva wish to restore the 'tribal', and why? Tribal populations throughout India have experienced a continuous process of socio-economic change; those of Gujarat and West Bengal, for example, were already differentiated along class lines by the late 1970s, the unequal pattern of intra-tribal landholding and income distribution being similar to that for the non-tribal population as a whole.[64] Accordingly, better-off tribals in Gujarat and West Bengal benefit disproportionately from welfare provision (thereby intensifying the very differentiation process such measures are designed to prevent), convert tribal land to private property, utilise high yield variety seeds, invest in means of production, and exploit the labour-power of less-well-off tribals.[65]

The New Farmers' Movement and the Left

Significantly, despite being distrusted by the farmers' movement, sections of the left in India also regard it as anti-monopoly capital and thus politically progressive.[66] The way in which the CPI perceives the issue of remunerative prices, and consequently policy towards the new farmers' movement, demonstrates clearly the extent to which its agrarian policy is still anti-feudal/pro-kulak/pro-democracy rather than anti-capitalist/pro-labour/pro-socialist, and thus deeply complicit with the bourgeois nationalism of the Indian National Congress some 40 years after Independence. Rejecting the argument from those to its left that remunerative prices enrich and strengthen kulaks, the CPI instead invokes a resolution passed by Congress at Lahore in 1929 to the effect that it is the inalienable right of the Indian people 'to be free' and 'to enjoy the fruits of their labour'. Reasserting that it is not rich peasants but a combination of landlords/usurers/merchants who are the exploiters and thus the enemies of democracy, the CPI maintained during the early 1980s that remunerative prices would enable farmers to pay minimum wages to agricultural labourers and, further, that the drain of investible resources from rural areas must be reversed since unremunerative prices would eventually ruin marginal, small and middle peasants, and lead to their proletarianisation.[67]

Although it scarcely seems necessary to draw attention to the theoretically and politically problematic nature of the way in which the new farmers' movement is inscribed in such an analysis, the following three points will serve to underline the distance between the CPI and socialism. First, as has been seen above, undifferentiated concepts of freedom and the peasantry have more in common with neo-populism than with Marxism. Second, on the wages question the CPI adopts the discredited 'trickle-down' thesis which overlooks the role of class struggle in determining/maintaining the pay levels and working conditions secured by agricultural labour. And third, the ruination of small/middle peasants – which the CPI wishes to halt – is precisely the effect of agrarian differentiation; that is, again like neo-populists, the CPI adopts a thinly disguised 'urban bias' argument in order to advocate the retention/preservation of an undifferentiated peasant economy which can successfully resist proletarianisation by reproducing itself as an homogenous stratum of petty commodity producers.[68] Ironically, notwithstanding claims that the new farmers' movement is different from the left, both politico-ideological agendas do indeed have much in common; not, however, because the ideas/positions on agrarian change propounded/advocated by the left are connected with socialism, but much rather because they are not.

III

Nationalism Revisited, or Forward to the Past

When combined within a single framework, the neo-populist/nationalist views considered above give rise to the set of politico-ideological oppositions illustrated in Table 1. These politico-ideological oppositions, which structure the discourse not just of/about the new farmers' movements but also that of ecofeminism, the 'popular culture' framework of the new social movements and the subaltern studies series, as well as the analysis by the left regarding agrarian change, are not merely shared with the Hindu chauvinist BJP (*Bharatiya Janata Party*), the VHP (*Vishwa Hindu Parishad*, or World Council of Hindus), and the RSS (*Rashtriya Swayamsewak Sangh*, or National Volunteer Corps), but are in fact more effectively mobilised (and indeed in this form find their authentic expression) from within the specifically anti-socialist, neo-populist, nationalist, and communal discourse of the political right.[69] Along with the scheduled castes and scheduled tribes, it is unsurprising both that women have become an electoral target of BJP activity, and that in Maharastra, Gujarat and Karnataka the BJP has gained political/electoral support at the expense of the farmers' movement.[70]

TABLE 1

		New Social Movements, Subaltern Studies, New Farmers' Movement, Ecofeminism, CPI, BJP/VHP/RSS
('Other')	('loots')	('Self')
West	→	East
Foreigners	→	Hindus
India	→	Bharat
Urban	→	Rural
Industry	→	Agriculture
Science	→	Culture
Development	→	Environment
State	→	Peasants
Class	→	Community
Men	→	Women
(Profane)	→	(Sacred)

This actual/potential electoral shift must in turn be linked to the way in which changes can and do occur in the possession/control exercised over the circulation of specific discursive forms that are shared by competing political groups/parties. Although it is true that no discourse is ever wholly 'owned' by a specific politics, a result of the strong historical link between the political right and religious/nationalist/communal issues is that where such components are currently part of another discourse (remunerative prices + free trade in agricultural produce + female/tribal/peasant/farmer self-empowerment + nationalism + environmentalism + neo-populism + anticapitalism) it becomes possible not just to reappropriate the main individual components themselves (nationalism + neo-populism) but through them to dispossess the current 'owners' – such as the new farmers' movements and the new social movements generally – of the remaining components linked to these nationalist/neo-populist views, and thus to gain control over the whole discourse.

When narratives which emanate from distinct – even formally opposed – political positions, and by virtue of making empowering reference to the same elements are both initially and in their continuation linked discursively, it is the wider socio-economic context together with immediate form taken by the class struggle which confers politico-ideological acceptability. In the case of India, therefore, such a relay-in-statement is made possible not only by the complicity of the political left with nationalism/neo-populism (and hence the absence of a recognisably distinctive alternative, a discourse-against), by the apolitical/anti-political nature of contemporary forms of 'popular culture' and accompanying modes of self-empowerment/resistance (by women, tribals, peasants, as well as the new farmers' movement itself), but also by an overdetermined and unambiguously chauvinist nationalism (in the discourse of which circulate narratives about Ayodhya in general and the events of 6 December 1992 in particular, about communalism and the desirability of a non-secular state, supported by the filmic/televisual resurgence of Hindu epics and the media prominence given to action undertaken by the BJP). Accordingly, where political power entails (paradoxically) a transformation not in the political content of discourse itself but rather in the political control exercised over this, it is not necessary for a group/party of the political right to espouse/project all components of a discourse in order to be able to exercise actual/potential control over the whole discourse itself.[71]

The extent of and similarity between the negative/positive components which structure the politico-ideological discourse of the new farmers' movements and that of RSS is indeed striking, and suggests that a more general reappropriation by the political right would not be difficult.[72] Like new social movements generally and the new farmers' movement in particular, the RSS is opposed to – and claims to stand above – politics, arguing that it belongs neither to the right nor to the left of the political spectrum but takes a '"common man's [sic] approach to economic problems"'.[73] And just as the repoduction of 'urban bias' is linked by Sharad Joshi to the imitation of 'foreign'/'western' patterns of industrial economic growth, so the RSS blames disintegration of national values/culture on a '"[w]esternized" elite who propose capitalism, socialism, or communism as solutions for Indian development'.[74] Like Gandhi, the RSS condemns 'foreign' philosophies because the material development linked to them generates class antagonism that disrupts social harmony.[75]

Instead, the RSS endorses an unambiguously neopopulist/nationalist approach to agrarian change, and – again like Gandhi, Charan Singh and Sharad Joshi – not only supports the cause of 'the small entrepreneur and the yeoman farmer', advocates the abolition of landlordism, but also promotes the concept of village-based artisan production ('cottage industry').[76] The RSS also subscribes to a variant of 'urban bias', in that it opposes co-operative agriculture on the grounds that this presents bureaucrats and politicians with more opportunities to exploit farmers.[77]

It is now possible for the BJP/VHP/RSS to operationalise a potent relay-in-statement, composed of the following politico-ideological matrix.[78] In so far as the Hindu caste system regulated the occupations in which its subject could engage, it can be claimed that it created an 'ecological space' whereby Hindu society was (and could be again) in harmony with 'nature'.[79] Since the environment of India is god-given and hence sacred, ecological destruction offends against Hindu religion, and its perpetrators are thus profaning the sacred.[80] Many of these politico-ideological themes have crystallised around the dispute between Hindus and Muslims over the issue of the temple on the Ram-Janmabhoomi/Babri-Masjid site at Ayodya in Uttar Pradesh.[81] Significantly, in celebrating the sacrifices undertaken to further the construction of a Hindu temple at Ayodya, the discourse of the BJP/VHP/RSS commemorates not only 'martyrs' killed in communal riots but also their mothers and wives.

Within this discursive framework, moreover, the current environmental degradation in India can be blamed on the implantation/operation over a 700-year period of 'foreign' non-Hindu ideas (Christianity, Islam, Secularism) that do not value – and therefore do not conserve – 'nature'.[82] The depletion of natural resources belonging to and emblematic of the nation can then be (re-) presented not only as the result of commercial exploitation by 'foreign' domination and industrialisation, but also (and thereby) as being a threat to and thus against the interests of an authentically indigenous village-based sustainable development structured by the organising principle of caste. Similarly, the actual/potential impoverishment of middle and poor peasant proprietors can be blamed on soil erosion, which is in turn attributable to the environmental degradation that is itself the fault of 'foreigners'.

The role of gender in this chain of signification is especially important. Not only do women themselves have direct experience of oppression (physical assault, dowry deaths), but in the discourse of the political right they discharge both an active and a passive function: they are equated with the role of motherhood-as-racial-preservation and also the last line of resistance against the corrupting values of 'western'/(urban) modernisation.[83] Hence the potency of the combined image of gender-specific/ethnic-specific assault frequently invoked by the VHP, particularly since a Hindu woman raped by a Muslim is also a metaphor for a similarly violent attack by 'foreigners' on a constellation of sacred symbols: the cow (= Mother-Cow/*Gau-mata*), the Hindu mother(land), her/(its) traditional values, and 'nature' itself.[84] Such a view is simultaneously supportive of Hindu nationalism, of a politically conservative form of female self-empowerment, of the ecofeminist argument that environmental conservation is best left to women in the traditional Indian village community, and of the specifically neo-populist concept 'urban bias'.

Finally, in associating exploitation with the 'foreigner', the BJP also reproduces and reinforces the image of capitalism as an unproblematically external phenomenon, a view which annexes the concept of an economically undifferentiated rural population promoted by the new farmers' movement, ecofeminism, neo-populists and the left. In the context of economic liberalisation currently being applied in India, which licenses even more ruthless competition from international capitalism, with an attendant withdrawal of government subsidies, declining prices and shrinking markets, the farmers' movement experiences a twofold pressure: from external (= 'foreign') capital on the one hand, and from the domestic working class on the other.[85] Accordingly, the resulting hostility of the farmers' movement towards international capital reinforces the politico-ideological acceptability of nationalist concepts of 'foreigner' (= 'other'), the same being true of antagonism expressed against workers in analogously communal idioms.[86]

CONCLUSION

Claiming to break with the socialist/nationalist politics/practice of the past, the new social movements (farmers, ecofeminists, tribals, women) which emerged in India during the 1980s have mobilised in support of village community (rural India, or *Bharat*), women as 'natural' protectors of the environment, and an undifferentiated peasantry, against a 'looting', unecological, economically uniform urban industrialism (urban India, or *India*) and its state. However, important components of this discourse, and in particular its structuring principle of an urban/rural divide, are prefigured in and symptomatic of the politics and ideology of neo-populism/nationalism: in Europe from nineteenth-century nationalist movements to twentieth-century fascism, and in India from the freedom movement of Gandhi, through the post-Independence mobilisations of Charan Singh to the communalism of the BJP/VHP/RSS.

In this neo-populist/nationalist discourse, the city is the locus of negative/(profane) attributes: a large-scale, science-based, polluting industry, protected by a wasteful bureaucracy in the taxation/surplus-extracting state, the revenues of which are used solely for the benefit of externally-oriented/('treacherous') westernised ('decadent') elite and its potentially/actually politically menacing proletariat ('the mob in the streets'). Behind all the latter, moreover, are to be found the economic and political interests of 'the foreigner'. In short, precisely a combination of agents/institutions/processes which are perceived to undermine petty commodity production, and through this the nation itself.

By contrast, 'the rural' is inscribed by this same discourse with stereotypically positive/(sacred) attributes: the locus of an harmonious/traditional/(atemporal) ethnic/gender/religious/('natural') purity embodied in a small-scale, ecologically sustainable village-level agriculture and artisan production. The latter, however, are condemned to poverty/inefficiency precisely by virtue of the violence/profligacy/('looting') engaged in by their 'other': 'the urban' and its 'foreign' backers. It is these neo-populist/nationalist politico-ideological oppositions that the discourse of the new farmers' movement, ecofeminism, and elements of the left either endorses or does not challenge.

At the core of this neo-populist/nationalist conceptual matrix, in which a number of innate identities are symbolically interchangeable (rural = nature = woman = nation) and on which 'popular culture' is based, lies an equally symptomatic – yet politico-ideologically potent – view of 'peasant' as the embodiment of traditional and enduring cultural/religious values. Hence the displacement of a class-differentiated by an undifferentiated concept of 'peasant' in the discourse of new farmers' movement, ecofeminism and sections of the left, enables – indeed encourages – the recasting of the now-homogeneous peasantry as a (non-economic) *cultural* category, and therefore as a bearer of natural/ahistorical characteristics which can in turn form the basis of an eternal/ever-present (folkloric) national identity and thus nationhood.

The metamorphosis of 'popular culture' from a passive to an active historical role is linked in part to its being the source of self-empowerment on which grassroots 'resistance' is based. Whereas in India the process of agrarian mobilisation (of nation against colonialism, of peasant against landlord) for neo-populists such as Gandhi and Charan Singh was largely defensive, a segment of the new farmers' movement has gone onto the offensive, and now regards global free trade as advantageous to the (rich) peasantry. At the level of discourse, this metamorphosis has been matched by an analogous shift in the realm of nationalist/communal ideology on the part of the BJP/VHP/RSS, resulting in a confluence not merely of discourses but more importantly of political action (self-empowerment) linked to them.[87]

This in turn can lead to the demobilization of agrarian *class* struggles by transforming/deflecting consciousness of class into (false) ethnic/national consciousness and conflict. Accordingly, organisation/conflict undertaken by agricultural workers and poor peasants against class opponents becomes converted/diverted into a struggle on behalf of nation, against the external and/or internal 'foreigner' (who is to be resisted, and then expelled or killed). By virtue of being resistance in a context where all politically unspecific resistance is regarded as positive (action/discourse-against), however, it remains possible for some to continue to interpret even this kind of mobilisation as progressive.

In these ways, and for these reasons, therefore, not only is the radical new agenda claimed by/for new social movements neither radical nor new, but the complicity of the new farmers' movements, ecofeminism, and sections of the left with what is an historically long-standing neo-populist/nationalist/(communal) discourse about the interrelationship between people/peasants/gender/nature/nation has contributed towards the reproduction of an ideological space which permits right-wing political organisations to reappropiate the Indian past (to undertake 'resistance' in defence of 'popular culture', in other words) with the object of creating an ethnically specific Indian state.

NOTES

1. The subaltern studies project is presented in – but by no means confined to – the collection of texts edited by Guha [1982–89]. For the influence of the latter series, both within and outside India, see Sathyamurthy [1990]. For discussions from different perspectives of new social movements as global phenomena, see Slater [1985], Fuentes and Frank [1989], Eckstein [1989], Foweraker and Craig [1990], Fox [1990], Escobar and Alvarez [1992], Calman [1992], Wignaraja [1993] and Eder [1993]. Although Fuentes and Frank [1989: 184, 187–9] are correct to observe that 'new' social movements are neither new nor comprehensible without reference to class composition, they mistakenly believe that '[i]n the Third World social movements are predominantly popular/working class' and thus overestimate the socialist content and potential of such mobilisation. For a discussion of the divergence between Marxism and the egocentric resource mobilisation theory of collective action that structures much new social movements analysis, see Melucci [1989: 184–92].
2. For more on these points, see my other contribution to this volume, and also Brass [1991]. The claim that it is necessary to break with not only a male/socialist/nationalist past but also industrial economic growth which structures this, and to construct instead a future based on the ecological/social/women's movement is made by, among others, Mies, Bennholdt-Thomsen and von Werlhof [1988].
3. On this point, see Lenin [1961: 349ff.]. Although it was aimed at the politically limited objectives inherent in trade union consciousness, the warning applies with equal force to those who frame their support of 'the oppressed' against imperialism and international capitalism in terms of ethnic/national identity and not class. In short, against

the politically insidious proposition that any oppositional idiom (= 'the-voice-from-below') is always necessarily politically progressive (for an example of which, see Hardiman [1987]).

4. Although in her presentation to the New Delhi workshop Zoya Hasan also noted the impact of the BJP on the support of the BKU in Uttar Pradesh, she argued by contrast that this communal politico-ideological space was a creation of the far right itself.
5. On the core elements and epistemological foundation of anti-Enlightenment conservative philosophy, see Mannheim [1953: 74ff.], Epstein [1970: 103ff.] and O'Sullivan [1976]. Heidegger's enduring and unrepentent complicity with Nazism (Ott [1993]) is one example of this link between an essentialist (to-be-disclosed) concept of 'being' and the anti-modernist ideology of the political right.
6. 'Sociologically speaking', observes Mannheim [1953: 117],

> most philosophical schools which place 'thinking' above 'being' have their roots either in bourgeois revolutionary or in bureaucratic mentality, while most schools which place 'being' above 'thinking' have their origin in the ideological counter-movement of romanticism and especially in the experience of counter-revolution.

7. In this connection it is important to remember that the basis of conservatism is not merely to oppose but also to roll back the possibility of revolution. On this point, O'Sullivan [1976: 10, 11, 12] notes:

> The principal feature of the two centuries which preceded the Revolution had been an increasing tendency to abandon the traditional pessimism about the human condition reflected in the Christian myth of the Fall and in the idea of original sin. A new optimism gradually replaced the old pessimism. This optimism, which had emerged with the Renaissance and then been bolstered by the growth of scientific knowledge, had two consequences. It produced ... a belief that the world is an order which is intelligible to human reason without the need for divine revelation, and is responsive to human will, once reason has comprehended its structure. It is, in fact, nothing more than a huge machine ... which can, in principle be dismantled and reassembled ... The world, in short, now came to be regarded as far more malleable than men had previously considered it to be ... In order to oppose the ideal of radical change it was necessary for conservative thinkers to show ... that the world was by no means as intelligible and malleable as men had come to assume.

An integral theoretical component of this anti-scientific/anti-rational political project has been Romanticism, which recuperated and then celebrated as innate precisely those characteristics which conservatives sought to defend. As Porter and Teich [1988: 5, 7] point out, Romantics had a

> passion for the pre-bourgeois past ... [they] naturally looked within their own nations, seeking to put down new roots in history, in folklore and folksong, in pure, indigenous traditions of language, speech and expression, in bards and ballards. Throughout a Europe recoiling from a French domination which could pretend to advance *universal* progress and rationality, Romantics aimed to uncover national character and even 'racial' continuities through which the past, embodied in living memory, could speak to, guide, and nurture the present. [They] offered avenues a-plenty to make sense of or mask the often distasteful realities of oligarchic societies undergoing traumatic capitalist development, industrialization, urbanization, and proletarianization. They conjured up myths of the glories of the past, the drama of the inner self as hero, spiritual voyages into the religious and transcendental, and communion with the mountains ... [Romanticism] could ally with faith to generate the last great religious 'new awakening' of Western Christendom. Frequently the result was mere escapism. When fleshed out into nationalist and racial fantasies, it might not be so innocent. The Romantics liked to forge solacing ideologies for the developing bourgeois societies they so profoundly despised (original emphasis).

These observations describe much of the discourse not just of Slavophilism but also of the new social movements, the subaltern studies project and ecofeminism, and beyond them all that of the BJP/VHP/RSS.

8. Such misgivings about the 'urban mob' applied in the case of the antebellum American South, for example, where the debates on slavery taking place during the 1840s were structured by an underlying fear of a threat to property relations [*Kaufman*, 1982: 121ff.]. Concerned that an emergent rural proletariat would ultimately demand the expropriation of the Southern landowning class, therefore, anti-abolitionists such as Cardozo and Dew advocated ruling class unity between Northern property owners and Southern planters in defence of slavery in order to counter a potential working-class challenge to existing property rights.
9. References to the non-coincidence of the terms 'peasant' and 'class' abound in the writings of Lenin and Trotsky. On the socio-economic differentiation of the peasantry, see Lenin [1964: 70ff, 172–87].
10. For a consideration of these and connected issues in the Indian context, see among others Patnaik [1986; 1990] and Byres [1991].
11. For the *gemeinschaft/gesellschaft* distinction, see Tönnies [1955]; the similarity between the views of the latter and those of Kireevsky, an important organic intellectual of slavophile nationalism/populism, are outlined by Walicki [1975: 168ff.]. 'German conservatism of the first half of the nineteenth century' Walicki [1975: 174–5] notes, 'was an ideological defence of *Gemeinschaft* against *Gesellschaft* ... slavophile doctrines as a whole provide a more consistent defence of *Gemeinschaft* than those of the conservative German romantics'. Significantly, Tönnies [1955: 69] regarded peasant society in village India as the embodiment of the *gemeinschaft* category; for the influence of his sociological theory, and its place in the philosophical trajectory that culminated in German fascism, see Lukacs [1980: 591–601]. For an example of the way in which current ecological theory invokes Tönnies' concept of *gemeinschaft* in its critique of industrialisation, see Jones [1990].
12. For the link between the espousal by the conservative nobility of Slavophile nationalism and populism, and idealised notions of a subsistence-oriented smallholding peasantry in late nineteenth-century Russia, see Normano [1949: 69ff.], Utechin [1963: 78ff., 128ff.], Wortman [1967], Walicki [1969; 1975; 1980: 92ff.], Kitching [1982: 145ff.] and Frierson [1993]. Slavophilism, argues Walicki [1975: 177–8],

    > was the ideology of the hereditary Russian nobility who were reluctant to stand up on their own behalf as a privileged group defending its own selfish interests, and therefore attempted to sublimate and universalize traditional values and to create an ideological platform that would unite all classes and social strata representing 'ancient Russia'.

    Significantly, both the fear of the urban proletariat as 'the mob in the streets' and the countervailing desirability of the rural artisan in the village commune was echoed in symptomatically pathological utterances by nineteenth century Slavophiles such as von Tengoborski, 'who argued that the development of handicraft helped Russia escape from the "*sore* of the proletariat"' (original emphasis), and Baron August von Haxthausen, who declared that '[t]he commune distinguished Russia from Western Europe ... in that it preserved Russian society from "the cancer of a proletariat"' [*Normano*, 1949: 75, *Petrovitch*, 1968: 208].
13. Malia [1955]. The difference between populists and marxists is summed up by Trotsky [1969: 113] in the following way:

    > Populists regarded all workers and peasants simply as 'toilers' and 'exploited ones' who were equally interested in socialism, while to Marxists a peasant was a petty-bourgeois, capable of becoming a socialist only to the extent that he either materially or spiritually ceased being a peasant ... [a]long that line was fought for two generations the principal battle between the revolutionary tendencies of Russia.

14. See the Marathi periodical *Sujan* for March/April 1992, cited in Guru [1992: 1465].
15. For the origins and political influence of neopopulism, see Mitrany [1951] and Kitching [1982].
16. Critiques of Chayanov's theory of peasant economy point out that it conflates rich and poor peasants, it is an historically static entity abstracted from the national and international economy, it embodies a subjective concept of value, it overlooks the operation/effect of land/labour markets and capitalist competition, and ignores class divisions between/within peasant farms together with a differential capacity to utilise technology (see, among others, Littlejohn [1977] and Patnaik [1979]). Elsewhere it has been argued that it is now possible to trace a common epistemological and politically conservative lineage from the new social movements and subaltern studies project, both strongly influenced by postmodernism, back through the moral economy argument, the 'middle peasant' thesis, and 'resistance' theory, to the neo-populist concepts which structure Chayanovian theory of peasant economy [*Brass*, 1991].
17. This method of focusing on the rural/urban divide with the object of deflecting/diverting the actual/potential development of a consciousness of class among poor peasants and agricultural labourers has a long history in Third World contexts. For example, in Japan during the early part of the twentieth century [*Totten*, 1960: 199], for

    > the villagers, urbanism represented the complex and unknown, the source of ideas subversive of true rustic samurai virtues and a constant temptation to soft living ... A long line of thinkers developed these attitudes into what became known as *nōhonshugi* (agriculture-is-the-base-ism), espoused in the late 1920s and 1930s by such people as Gondō Nariaki (Seikyō) and Tachibana Kōsaburō. The suspicion and fear of urbanism could be built upon by conservative elements in the agricultural villages to combat 'divisive' and 'class' ideas. The landlords emphasized village 'solidarity' *vis-à-vis* the cities and fanned urban–rural tensions ... with the rise of nationalism in Japan *nōhonshugi* gained strength. It came to be thought of as unpatriotic sectionalism for labor and tenant farmers to be organized within narrow class interests.

18. It should be noted that a shift from neopopulist discourse, which attempts to disguise its class origins/interest, to the explicit politics/ideology of class, as in case of the BKU in Uttar Pradesh and Punjab, where the leadership of the new farmers' movement has on occasion resisted attempts to communalise rural struggle, is accompanied by a seemingly progressive – and thus paradoxical – move away from the idioms of communal struggle (see Gupta [1988: 2693]). In such circumstances, however, opposition to communal identity derives not from a principled/progressive politics but much rather from a need to maintain class unity among better-off peasants from different religious/cultural backgrounds (Muslim/Hindu in UP and Hindu/Sikh in Punjab), and thus avoid the risk of a split in the movement along communal lines. Accordingly, not only is the discourse of neo-populism and class each a variant of (bourgeois) mobilising ideology but the presence/absence of each is determined by the exigencies of the class struggle: one is to ensure that working class consciousness is deflected/defused, and the other is to ensure that a bourgeois class consciousness is reproduced.
19. One variant of this position is the cultural ecology of Harris [1966; 1974: 11–32], who argues that because the beef-eating taboo and cow worship are practised by the Hindu population of India, both these cultural phenomena must consequently fulfil (and be an expression of) a 'popular' need. For an example of the extent to which even opposition to 'popular culture' continues to be framed simply in terms 'high/low' culture, rather than politics, see Beik [1993].
20. That this image of the proletarian/urban 'other' still permeates the discourse of the farmers' movements in India is clear from the most recent utterances of Sharad Joshi [*Omvedt*, 1993b: 2709]. At the fifth convention of the Shetkari Sanghatana in October 1993, therefore, Joshi attacked urban workers organised in trade unions for going on strike; he not only urged farmers to withdraw accounts from banks the employees of which were on strike but also advocated that unemployed rural youth be used as strike-

breakers in such disputes, replacing unionised public sector employees in the urban sector who had withrawn their labour.

21. Nolan [1988: 52]. On this point, see also Habermas [1989: 209ff.], Bosworth [1993: 73ff.] and Knowlton and Cotes [1993]. For the reproduction of racist ideas in nineteenth-century North American 'popular culture', see Saxton [1990]. Given that many of the Subaltern Studies, new social movement and ecofeminist texts are structured by postmodern epistemology, it is perhaps significant that the attempt by the political right to 'normalise' (= justify) fascism in the context of the *historikerstreit* has been described as 'postmodern historiography' [*Maier*, 1988: 168ff.]. More generally, the fascist complicity of a significant number of intellectuals connected with the postmodern project, together with the epistemological roots of such collaborationist tendencies in a reactionary form of anti-capitalist/(populist) agrarian nostalgia that (re-) surfaces in periods of capitalist crisis, is examined in more detail in the other contribution to this volume by Brass.
22. On these points, see Bramwell [1985] and Pois [1986]. The words of Darré himself (cited in Mosse [1966: 148–50]) are unambiguous about the nature of the nation/race/ soil/peasant interrelationship:

    > First there was the German peasantry in Germany before what is today served up as German history. Neither princes, nor the Church, nor the cities have created the German man. Rather the German man emerged from the German peasantry. Everywhere one will find primordial peasant customs that reach far back into the past. Everywhere there is evidence that the German peasantry, with an unparalleled tenacity, knew how to preserve its unique character and its customs against every attempt to wipe them out ... One can say that the blood of a people digs its roots deep into the homeland earth through its peasant landholdings, from which it continuously receives that life-endowing strength which constitutes its special character.

    For the important politico-ideological role in German 'popular culture' (art, film) during 1933–45 of this idealised/a-historical image of peasant farming, see Hinz [1980: 111–17] and Welch [1983: 101–51].
23. For example, Fox [1990] equates Gandhian philosophy with socialism and then argues that it amounts to an expression of popular cultural autonomy or resistance to the kinds of colonial domination encoded in Orientalism. Significantly, some of those who write in the Subaltern Studies framework also find in Gandhi the true expression of Indian grassroots tradition, a similar embodiment of the authentic 'voice-from-below' (see, for example, Amin [1984] and Chatterjee [1984; 1981]).
24. Hence the endorsement by Gandhi of the Hindu caste/varna hierarchy as an immutable (and therefore 'natural') social order stemmed from a corresponding rejection of class struggle as a necessary effect of industrial modernization. In his view, therefore, the advantage of the caste/varna system was that in India its 'object ... is to prevent competition and class struggle and class war ... because it fixes the duties and occupations of persons' (cited in Ambedkar [1946: 287–89]). In much the same vein, Bharatan Kumarappa, the Assistant Secretary of the Village Industries Association and a Gandhian who advocated a village-based rural revival, observed [1935: 1–2]:

    > One of the great differences between our Civilization and that of the West is that our Civilization takes its root from rural life while that of the West centres round cities ... The centre of life in our country has always been the village ... Towns and cities were mainly distributing agents of village products, the village being the real producing centre ... Our culture is best understood only when the agricultural background out of which it has arisen is taken into account. That being so, no mere imitation of the West which has developed on lines fundamentally different from our own, can at all fit in with our national heritage.

    This fear the town/city and of the 'urban mob' accords well with the view expressed by the Bombay Pradesh Committee during the late 1920s, whose objective when confronted with increasing militancy on the part of striking mill workers was to '[s]pare no money and no efforts to draw workers away from the communists. They [the workers] ought to be made to understand that the more important struggle [is] between the British government and the people, rather than between capital and labour' (cited in Lieten [1988: 75]).

25. That the agrarian struggles organised/led by Gandhi in Bihar and Gujarat were basically rich peasant movements is clear from, among others, Dhanagare [1975; 1983: 88ff.] and Pouchepadass [1980].

26. On these points, see Brown [1972: 52ff.], Dhanagare [1975: 22–30], Sen [1982: 29ff.] and Das [1983: 57ff.]. Significantly, the indigenous Indian component of the landlord class was not included among the targets of the Champaran mobilisation, and its objectives included neither a redistribution of land to poor peasants nor wage increases for landless workers. One of the main reasons why Gandhi subsequently chose the salt monopoly rather than the land tax as the object of his non-co-operation campaign against the colonial power was precisely his fear that peasants might extend non-payment of rents from British to Indian landlords [*Brown* 1972: 76–77; *Dhanagare*, 1975: 28–29; *Tidmarsh* 1960: 100].

27. Hardiman [1981]; Charlesworth [1985]. It is again significant that, as in the case of the Champaran *satyagraha* a decade earlier, no attempt was made to address indigenous employer/employee relationships:

> Gandhi did not attack the economic basis of the *hali* system nor did he disapprove of the then prevailing serf-master relationship. He simply expected his Patidar followers to be more compassionate towards Dublas and liberalize their conditions of work because ... such compassion would bring more prosperity to Patidar landowners [*Dhanagare*, 1975: 92].

28. The extent to which 'popular culture' in India is permeated by religious/nationalist symbolism can be illustrated by reference to the politico-ideological content of modern bazaar prints featuring Sikh iconography. The traditional prominence given by such popular art to the first and tenth Gurus, Guru Nanak (= the moral power of Sikh religion) and Guru Gobind Singh (= the military power of Sikh nationalism), is now being extended also to Guru Ram Das, because of his status as the founder of the Golden Temple at Amritsar [*McLeod*, 1991: 35–6]. Having come under metaphorical and literal attack from the Indian/ (Hindu) state, the Golden Temple has become the symbol of the combined religious/military/nationalist power of the Sikh Khalsa. In a similar fashion, and for much the same reason, the VHP disseminates popular images of the Hindu God Ram as Warrior King [*Basu et al.*, 1993: 61–2].

29. For the recent expansion in India of the electronic media, see Rudolph [1992] and Manuel [1993]. It should be noted that the antithesis between rural/(= good) and urban/(= bad) outlined below with regard to Indian cinema/television also characterises the distinctiveness of the two most powerful cinematic genres in the 'popular culture' of western capitalism: that is, the contrast between on the one hand the Hollywood western, with its emphasis on the frontier/pioneer achievement (= 'resistance') of the small farmer defending a stereotypically idyllic rural existence against big landowners, railway interests, bankers and businessmen, and on the other film noir, with its fear of the loss of order and the shadowy menace of unseen forces (= 'the mob in the streets') in the American city.

30. Das Gupta [1991: 34, 36, 45ff., 166]. Not only was rural life endorsed in the pre-Independence film of Tamil Nadu, but this was done with explicit actual/symbolic reference to Gandhi himself: for example, heroes/heroines returned to the village from the town in order to carry out Gandhian policy [*Baskaran*, 1981: 109, 116–18].

31. One effect of this 'naturalisation' is the capacity of film stars to project the mythological power of their cinematic persona into political contexts, as evidenced by the electoral success of M.G. Ramachandran in Tamil Nadu and N.T. Rama Rao in Andhra Pradesh. Similarly, the success of the recent cinematic and televisual representations of epics such as the *Ramayana* and the *Mahabharata*, together with the role in this process

of the video casette, serve to reinforce a resurgent Hindu chauvinism [*Das Gupta*, 1991: 165–90, 199ff.; *Datta*, 1991: 2522; ***Rudolph***, 1992: 1494; Basu *et al.*, 1993: 92ff.; *Manuel*, 1993: 243ff.]. For the active participation in the nationalist movement itself by many of the more important actors in the Tamil Cinema of the 1930s, see Baskaran [1981: 102–3]; for the links between cinematic themes and post-1947 regionalist/nationalist politics in Tamil Nadu, see Barnouw and Krishnaswamy [1980: 179ff.] and Lüthi [1993].

32. These combined politico-ideological themes (an explicitly anti-state/anti-urban male hero, justice realised by means of individual revenge, subordinate females, and the idealisation of woman-as-mother in the context and as 'natural' protector of traditional values embodied in the familial unit) are projected not only in films themselves but also in the kinds of (heroic) characters portrayed by major box-office stars such as Amitabh Bachchan, whose roles depict individuals opposed to a corrupt urban officialdom taking the law into their own hands [*Das Gupta*, 1991: 51–3, 240–41]. In contrast to the themes of the commercial cinema during earlier decades, therefore, no attempt is made by the cinematic hero to change the existing (bourgeois) system, only to better his own individual position within this by any means possible (for a similar transformation in the Tamil cinematic roles of M.G. Ramachandran, see Lüthi [1993: 276]). For the existence of similar themes in American film, see Levy [1991]: he shows how the 'small-town' values associated with rural America, which were idealised in films of the 1930s, only to be rejected thematically in films of the 1960s and 1970s, have returned to cinematic prominence once more in the 1980s.

33. Rudolph [1992: 1494] makes the important point that one crucial outcome of extended access to television in India has been the construction of a *national* (as distinct from a regional) Hindu consciousness, uniting Hinduism and an all-India *nationalism* (as distinct from nationalisms) in a way that has not been possible before. Interestingly, he also notes that in the case of the Hindu epic *Mahabharata* the character of 'Draupadi ... is used to articulate feminist sentiments [and] Ram voices environmentalist views while wandering in the forest'.

34. Among those who hold this view are Rudolph and Rudolph [1984; 1987: 333–92], Lenneberg [1988], Gupta [1988], Weiner [1989: 129ff.], Lindberg [1990], and Athreya, Djurfeldt and Lindberg [1990: 314–15]. Interestingly, the slavophile interpretation of 'ancient Russian freedom', which structures the discourse of neo-populism, has a similarly negative political view of the state, one that is inherently conservative and unconnected with the progressive notion of 'republican liberty'. Whereas the latter was associated with freedom *in* politics, itself premissed on active participation, the former by contrast entailed freedom *from* politics, or the 'right to live according to unwritten laws of faith and tradition, and the right to full self-realization in a moral sphere on which the state would not impinge' [*Walicki*, 1980: 96].

35. Thus the 1928 Bardoli 'no-tax' campaign is one example of mobilisation by rich peasants against the attempt by the colonial state to increase revenue in line with land values. Similarly, rich and middle peasant mobilisation in Andhra Pradesh during the 1950s centred not only on landholding but also on tax reduction, better provision of agricultural inputs (irrigation, electricity), and the fixation by the state of remunerative prices for their agricultural produce (National Labour Institute Report [1980]). As is clear from an interview he gave in 1947 to Colin Clark, an economist advising the Indian Planning Commission about development strategy, Gandhi also espoused an earlier version of 'remunerative prices' for peasant farmers. Clark [1984: 63] reported that:

> Gandhi ... proved to be a convinced free-market economist, strongly critical of ... price controls, rationing, and compulsory purchase of farm crops ... The right solution, [Gandhi] said was to raise the price of food, then everyone would have to work harder. The source of India's troubles [he thought] was that the people were thoroughly idle.

The issue of remunerative prices for peasant farmers was also central to Charan Singh's neo-populist programme of the 1960s and 1970s [*Singh*, 1978: 35ff.]

36. For the claim both that in the Green Revolution areas of India land is no longer a

political issue, and that this is one of the distinctively new aspects of the farmers' movements of the 1980s, see Lindberg [1990] and also Athreya, Djurfeldt, and Lindberg [1990: 314]. For the continued importance of the land question in India, see Das [1988: 17]. Adopting a somewhat contradictory position, Rudolph and Rudolph [1984: 284] argue that land redistribution remains an objective of the farmers' mobilisation, but only insofar as it does not threaten existing property relations. For the importance of land as well as marketing and prices as an issue defining the new agrarian movements in Mexico, see Harvey [1990: 41].

37. Between 1981/82 and 1985/86 direct subsidies for items such as food, fertilisers and so on, paid by the Union government to agriculture doubled (from Rs 19,460 million to Rs 41,880 million), an increase which takes no account of the infrastructural expenditure (or indirect subsidies to agriculture) on roads and transportation over the same period [*Mehta*, 1992: 224–5, Table 3]. More generally, from Independence onwards the terms of trade have moved in favour of agriculture [*Chattopadhyay, Sharma and Ray*, 1987: 158–60]. The economic unsustainability of the concept 'urban bias' is echoed in politico-ideological terms by scheduled caste agricultural labourers from Karnataka, who reject it on the grounds that for them the main contradiction remains one between 'private property owners and the non-propertied' in all sectors, and not one between workers in rural and urban contexts [*Nadkarni*, 1987: 150–51]. For the link between neopopulism and 'urban bias', see Byres [1979; 1988].

38. In Karnataka, for example, the farmers' demand for an increase in the price of paddy is strongly opposed by their Dalit workforce, both because it would result in a corresponding rise in the purchase price of rice consumed by poor peasants and agricultural labourers, and because – contrary to the claims made by the farmers themselves – wages would not be increased to meet such price rises. Much rather the opposite: when Dalits challenge farmers to pay them rates stipulated in existing legislation, employers respond by replacing them with externally recruited migrants [*Nadkarni*, 1987: 152]. That is, restructuring the agrarian labour process by recomposing its workforce. For an analogous instance of class struggle leading to workforce restructuring by farmers in Haryana during the late 1980s, see Brass [1990]. For the views of Sharad Joshi on the issue of 'remunerative prices', see Government of India [1991: 14–15, 33–4, paragraphs 37, 84–8]. Joshi himself provides evidence that any link between the receipt by farmers of higher crop prices ('remunerative prices') and the payment by them of higher wages ('trickle down' argument) is problematic when he claims high wage costs as a reason for higher prices: if wage costs are already too high, then any increases in product prices would merely serve to offset these high wages, and consequently would not – as Joshi maintains – be passed on to agricultural workers in the form of wage increases. For Joshi's contradictory utterances on this issue, see Dhanagare [1990: 362, 363].

39. In contrast to the new farmers' movements, by whom the state is perceived as largely negative (denial of remunerative prices, potential/actual implementation of land ceilings and minimum wages legislation), agricultural workers from the scheduled castes in Karnataka regard the state in more positive terms, as provider both of protective legislation and of alternative non-rural employment opportunities. As one of its adherents admitted, the new farmers' movements hostility towards the state is due in part to the fact that 'if the labourers get monetary or material benefits or loans from the government ... they would develop their own activities (like livestock rearing) and would not come for agricultural coolie work. ... [a]griculture would then suffer without coolies' [*Nadkarni*, [1987: 152–3]].

40. Joshi [1993: 3, 4, 6] extols and evaluates the advantages to the farmers' movement of the Dunkel proposals in the following manner:

> it emphasises the importance of rural – urban balance as a structural precondition to a free trade system ... [t]his anti-statism and free marketism has its practical side too. The Indian primary produce is generally in a position of comparative advantage in the international market despite fragmentation of land, low capital forma-

> tion and sustained State repression. The advantage is sizeable in fruit, cotton, some foodgrains and health-foods ... The middle-layer farmer is quietly confident of being able to compete in the international markets if only the Government kept its cotton-picking hands off ... [t]he new epoch of destatisation, liberalisation and globalisation comes like a fresh breeze.

41. The unambiguously nationalist discourse structuring this opposition to the free trade proposals of GATT is evident from the following comments made by peasants attending the farmers' rally in New Delhi:

    > What they [the Indian government] are trying to do to the farming community is selling them to the *foreigners* ... Our leaders have said that the *foreign* paper [Dunkel draft] is an evil design to sell Mother India to *foreigners*. For a kisan, the life support are his land, seed and plough. If the Rao government sells these to the *foreigners* what will happen to the national pride...we are against the Government policies which are not only destroying the farmers's economy in a phased plan but also corroding the country's industry and culture ... We are now self-sufficient in crop production: so why this sell-out to MNCs?' (emphasis added).

    Other proposals made by the farmers' movement and framed in a similarly nationalistic discourse included banning multinational corporations from having access to agricultural land. See 'Farmers against Dunkel Draft', *The Hindustan Times*, 4 March, 1993.

42. On these points, Joshi [*Government of India*, 1991: 36, 42–3, paragraphs 88, 105, 106–7] observes:

    > [A] certain minimum export should be permitted, in the case of commodities which have an international market, irrespective of the supply situation in the domestic market. In cases where the domestic supplies are insufficient, shortfall should be made up by compensatory imports rather than by restriction on exports ... All zonal restrictions on the movement of produce should be scrapped ... the industrial lobbies are for ever active to minimize any exports of agricultural produce with the objective of keeping the domestic prices low.

43. Government of India [1991: 17, 23, 24, 26, 29, 30, 42–3, 49 paragraphs 40, 55, 60, 64, 73, 78, 106–7, 126]. It should be noted that the issue of ownership of crop species and seed varieties is at the centre of the opposition by Tikait, Nanjundaswamy and Shiva to the position adopted by GATT on intellectual property rights. Unsurprisingly, resistance by the new farmers' movement to the threat by transnational agribusiness corporations to patent indigenous seed varieties, and thus establish legal title to an important component of the agrarian productive forces in India, is projected by Shiva [1993a: 555, 557, 560] in nationalist terms: that is, as a challenge by the 'foreigner' both to 'national sovereign rights to biodiversity and patterns of its utilisation' (= 'colonisation'), and to the 'inalienable, cultural rights' of 'traditional' farmers in 'traditional' societies, emphasising thereby the extent to which for Shiva 'nation' = 'nature'. Moreover, the mobilising slogan 'Seed *Satyagraha*' (see Shiva [1993a: 555]) encountered at the farmers' rally of 3 March 1993 asserts this right to control such productive forces in unambiguously Gandhian terms.
44. The extent to which the divergent positions towards GATT are themselves an effect of class differences in the social composition of the new farmers' movements in Maharashtra, Uttar Pradesh and Karnataka remains unclear. For the hostility of the farmers' movement in Karnataka towards the GATT proposals, and the perceived threat to the farming sector in India of pressure from the IMF and the World Bank for the adoption of economic liberalisation policies, see Kripa [1992: 1183], Omvedt [1993b] and the contribution to this volume by Assadi.

45. As demanded by Joshi, Indian peasants will henceforth be permitted to export staple foodgrains, regardless of the domestic situation. Furthermore, agrarian capitalists will now be able not only to import equipment and raw materials duty free, a concession hitherto enjoyed only by export processing zones, but also to sell half the output produced on the domestic market. In keeping with the prognosis of Sharad Joshi, one report characterises the effects of this change in agricultural policy as 'the most significant liberalisation of the country's farm trade ... since independence', and forecasts that Indian farmers, 'could well become internationally competitive exporters'. See 'Farmers Reap Benefit of Indian Reform', *Financial Times* (London), 1 April, 1993.
46. For the views of Sharad Joshi on the issue of agricultural wages and the related question of the fairprice Public Distribution System, see Government of India [1991: 37–9, paragraphs 89–98]. Significantly, by demanding wage increases for hired labour and payment for peasant family labour employed in agriculture, Joshi not only presents himself in a positive manner politically but also (and perhaps more importantly) strengthens his case for remunerative prices linked to higher production costs. As has been noted above, there is no evidence that such wage payments/increases would be passed on to those who actually supply the labour-power; and even if they were, such benefits would be cancelled out by the contraction of the Public Distribution System, another of Joshi's policy recommendations. Unsurprisingly, given his support for the free market and higher crop prices, Joshi is opposed to a Public Distribution System based on state procurement of fixed-price food. At the level of discourse, however, he is able to circumvent this contradiction by maintaining that the main beneficiary of fairprice shops is the urban population, and consequently the Public Distribution System constitutes yet more evidence of 'urban bias'.
47. Hence the observation by Sharad Joshi that '[i]t is a conspiracy on the part of the Indian elite to try to divide Bharat in terms of big, medium and small farmers. There is no line of contradiction between the big and small with regard to prices' (quoted in Nadkarni [1987: 142]). His observation [*Government of India*, 1991: 18, paragraph 42] that '[t]he size of the holding of any family is more directly related to the familial situation than to the economic one' suggests a Chayanovian concept of the peasant family farm, the reproduction of which is determined not by exogenous ('economic') categories such as rent and wages but by the endogenous ('familial') category of the producer/consumer balance. Significantly, the Bharat/India opposition projects not just an urban/rural divide but also the implication that behind the process of urban exploitation of the rural producer lies the 'foreign'/'other' (see, for example, Government of India [1991: 6, paragraph 14]), which in turn licenses the symbolic fusion of Bharat = nation and thus a correspondingly nationalist appropriation of the Bharat/India opposition itself. It becomes possible, therefore, for the Hindu chauvinist BJP to argue that, as all rural inhabitants are the authentic components of *Bharat*, they are consequently the embodiment of nationalism and thus the true inheritors of post-colonial state power. For Joshi's views on the pervasive concept 'urban bias', see Government of India [1991: 3, 6, 45, paragraphs 9, 10, 18, 113].
48. For the position of Shetkari Sanghatana on the desirability of a political alliance between the farmers' movement and the womens' movement, together with Sharad Joshi's reasons for this, see Government of India [1991: 6, paragraph 17] and Omvedt [1986: 2085–6]. It is clear from the latter text, and also from Omvedt [1990a: 238, 246], that the *Sanghatana Mahila Aghadi* activists were predominantly women from middle caste and rich or middle peasant family backrounds who want a better deal under existing property rights, not to change property rights themselves.
49. Guru [1992: 1463–5] and Government of India [1991: 22, paragraph 54]. The acceptability of this intra-household system of property transfer is not unconnected with the ability of rich peasant supporters of the new farmers' movement to use the *Laxmi Mukti* programme as another form of *benami*; that is, to undermine existing agrarian reform laws by evading land ceiling legislation. In a similar vein, Joshi himself justifies opposition to land ceiling legislation not in terms of a capacity on the part of better-off

peasants to retain/consolidate property but in the spuriously progressive framework of gender equality; accordingly, and somewhat perversely, his argument emphasizes that land reform would prevent rural women from becoming proprietors [*Government of India*, 1991: 22, paragraphs 52–3].

50. As noted by one observer [*Baxter*, 1971: 314] about an earlier period, much the same kind of dilemma confronts the parties of the political right: 'The Jana Sangh would like to import western technology and use western capital while barring the entry of western secularism and liberalism. It is doubtful that such a policy can succeed.' (See also Graham [1990: 189–90]).
51. This Gandhian neo-populism is outlined in Singh [1978: 90ff.; 1981: 269ff. 393ff.]. For details about the post-Independence growth in the political influence of the kulak lobby, together with the participation and role of rich peasants in the movements of the 1980s, see among others Nadkarni [1987], Chattopadhyay, Sharma and Ray [1987: 173ff.], Hasan [1989a; 1989b], Prasad [1991], and the contribution by Dhanagare to this volume.
52. For this reason, it is necessary to disagree strongly with the attempt by Rudolph and Rudolph [1984: 330–31; 1987: 357–58] to differentiate the 'old agrarianism' of Gandhi, which they rightly describe as conservative and anti-statist, from what they wrongly regard as the more progressive 'new agrarianism' of the new farmers' movement. For similar attempts to differentiate the 'robust realism' of the new farmers' movements from the backward looking peasant movements of earlier periods, see Dhanagare [1990: 360] and Gupta [1992]. And although they all disagree substantially on the political character of the new farmers' movement, Balagopal [1987a: 1546] and Omvedt and Galla [1987: 1926] deny the presence/importance of Gandhian themes.
53. On these points, see Nadkarni [1987: 142, 226–7], Kripa [1992: 1182–3], Guru [1992: 1464], and Gupta [1992].
54. Hence the complaint by Joshi [*Government of India* 1991: 3, 7, paragraphs 9, 19] that

    > The economic tenets of the Mahatma ... were quickly abandoned. Industrialisation became synonymous with development. Development came to mean native replication of western industrial model ... The nation is reaping the harvest of the anti-Mahatma economics it sowed.

    For the differences between Gandhian and Nehruvian approaches to questions of development and the environment, see Roy and Tisdell [1992].
55. The structure of the Gandhian model of village development envisaged by Joshi [*Government of India*, 1991: 8, 9, 25, 47–9, paragraphs 21, 24–5, 62, 123–30] can be glimpsed from the following programmatic statements:

    > This logic of developmental model makes a major deviation from the model utilised since Independence guided by the 'Mahatma's Talisman'. It bases itself on a flourishing agrarian economic and village autonomy. The Gandhian model does not look upon underdevelopment as either a vicious cycle or a natural state of affairs. It holds that growth is a natural process and can be in fact an enobling and happy experience ... [t]he long-term solution to the problem of rural unemployment can come only from self-employment generated from the surplus that the farmers are allowed to retain ... [t]he control from the state or the centre should be minimized and maximum powers vested in the community fora ... [d]ecentralization of power and resuscitation of village panchayat is an important instrument of the present agricultural policy ... [t]he long-standing tradition has it that the village elders hold a position of respect ...

    This position is very similar to that outlined in the mid-1930s by Kumarappa [1935: 10, 15], who claimed that:

    > [O]ur solution should be one which has room in it both for the profit-motive and for social control. And we believe that such a remedy is to be found in decentralising production and in practising the ideal of Swadeshi. Decentralising means refusing

> to dictate from the centre how things are to be produced and what kind they are to be, but leaving that always to the good sense and initiative of the producer ... our ancient village organization sought to curb the profit-motive, to provide a subsistence to all, so that there are no great inequalities of income, to make villages self-contained and to give first place to personality or things of the spirit. All these objects are ... best served by decentralising production.

Like Joshi and Kumarappa, Charan Singh also wanted to shift investment from heavy industry to employment-oriented artisan production in the village context [*Franda*, 1979: 83]. For examples of the attempt to recuperate a concept of village-based peasant economy for development theory, see Bideleux [1985] and Netting [1993].

56. For the endorsement by Shetkari Sanghatana of natural/organic farming, see Omvedt [1991b]. On the relationship between 'urban bias', environmental degradation, social unrest, and the necessity of 'appropriate' technology, Joshi [*Government of India*, 1991: 11–12, 15, 28, paragraphs 30–31, 37, 72] comments:

> In an old community where for centuries agricultural surplus has been expropriated for medieval luxuries ... and industrial capital accumulation ... land is fragmented and degenerated to low levels of fertility ... the ecology [is] devastated ... [t]he short-sighted rush for industrialization has left the country ... with a seriously damaged life support system – land, water, vegetation. Even before starting to resolve the ecological problems of the bullock-cart era, the nation is facing the problems of industrial pollution. The unbalanced economic policies are threatening to tear the social fabric ... [a]n alternative technology will need to be resorted to ... initiating a real green revolution that would be less dependent on the rapidly depleting petroleum resources ... [i]n order to improve the efficiency of small farms ... it will be necessary to introduce small agricultural implements and machinery along with appropriate technology.

More recently, Joshi [1993: 6] has invoked the ecosystem as a countervailing 'natural' advantage enjoyed by Indian peasants competing in global markets ('third world countries have a natural advantage in natural biodiversity'), to be offset against the highly technified/mechanized productive capacity of farmers in metropolitan capitalist countries.

57. A report in *The Hindustan Times* of 4 March, 1993, about the farmers' rally in New Delhi notes that Vandana Shiva 'who seemed to have earned the respect of senior farmer leaders, said ... "[w]e are here [at the rally] to make the movement sharper. Our goal is to give the farmers' revolution a proper shape and create a political direction and impact"'.

58. For these views, see Shiva [1989; 1990; 1991a; 1991b; 1992a; 1992b; 1993b]. For the political importance and influence of her ideas, see among others Omvedt [1990b: 27ff.], Merchant [1992: 200ff.] and Jackson [1993]. It is important to situate the work of Shiva in the political shift experienced globally by feminist theory over the period from 1970 to the mid-1980s. In its first phase, feminist theory developed a specifically materialist critique of gender difference as a social/historical construct; maintaining that gender subordination/oppression was largely economic, the political solution it advocated was the elimination of masculinity/femininity difference. By contrast, the second phase was characterised by a reactionary form of gender essentialism that not only emphasised gender difference but equated biological female identity with self-empowerment/liberation [*Eisenstein*, 1984]. Like ecofeminism generally, which in Third World contexts is opposed to the devaluation of women and nature by Western culture and accordingly seeks to protect traditional ways of life, the work of Shiva is a product of this second phase. The extent to which her work is structured by this wider project of innateness based on gender essentialism is clear from the following observation by Merchant [1992: 185, 190–92]:

> Many cultural feminists celebrate an era in prehistory when nature was symbolized by pregnant female figures ... which were held in high esteem as bringers-forth of

> life. An emerging patriarchal culture, however, dethroned the mother-godesses and replaced them with male gods to whom the female deities became subservient. The scientific revolution of the seventeenth century further degraded nature by replacing Renaissance organicism and a nurturing earth with the metaphor of the machine to be controlled and repaired from the outside. The ontology and epistemology of mechanism are viewed by cultural feminists as deeply masculinist and exploitative of a nature historically depicted in the female gender. The earth is dominated by male-developed and male-controlled technology, science, and industry. Often stemming from an anti-science, anti-technology standpoint, cultural ecofeminism celebrates the relationship between women and nature through the revival of ancient rituals ... For cultural ecofeminists, human nature is grounded in human biology ... Sex/gender relations give men and women different power bases ... The perceived connection between women and biological reproduction turned upside down becomes the source of women's empowerment and ecological activism. Women's biology and Nature are celebrated as sources of female power ....

For the individualist basis of feminist theory, and hence an inherent epistemological compatibility with the neo-classical economic framework structuring the neo-populism of Chayanov, see Fox-Genovese [1991: 113ff.].

59. Shiva [1989: xiv, xvi, xvii, xviii, 6, 7; 1991a: 11–12]. Her target is encapsulated in the concept 'patriarchal mode of economic development in industrial capitalism' [1989: xvii]. Although considered politically to the left of Shiva (whose work she has influenced: see Mies and Shiva [1993]), Mies [1986: 217ff.] nevertheless ends up invoking as a specifically feminist and alternative perspective of a new society a similarly idealized image of a subsistence-oriented, autarchic peasant society. Interestingly, the World Bank [1992] has also endorsed the concept of women as 'natural' protector of the environment.
60. Shiva [1989: ix, xi–xii, xiv, xv, xviii, xx, 5, 219; 1991a: 11, 15, 233].
61. Shiva [1989: 2, 11; 1991a: 14, 29ff]. For a similar claim that the principal contradiction is no longer between capital and labour, but between on the one hand 'colonised' indigenous peasant women in peripheral Third World contexts, and on the other an exploitative combination of white/male workers and capitalists at the industrialised core, see Mies, Bennholdt-Thomsen and von Werlhof [1988]. For an early invocation by essentialist feminism of woman-as-colonised-subject, see Morgan [1992: 74–7].
62. Shiva [1989: xiv, xix, xvii, 2, 4, 9, 10, 11, 55ff.; 1991a: 47, 49, 94–5]. For her endorsement of 'urban bias', see Shiva [1991a: 178]. This view of rural women in India generally as victims of 'urban bias', together with the women's movement as a response to this, is also advanced by Omvedt [1990a: 231]. For the invocation by Shiva of Gandhian views concerning the non-applicability in Indian conditions of western industrial development, the spinning wheel as reassertion of traditional culture, and a self-sufficient peasantry, see Shiva [1989: xviii, 6; 1991a: 16, 27–8, 236, 238–40, 257, 263]. For the pervasiveness of Gandhian philosophy among gender-specific new social movements in India generally, see Sen [1990: 7]. That the wider object of the *charkha* revival was not only to displace machine-made imports from England with indigenous handspun textiles but also to preserve thereby small-scale artisan-based village production and with it the peasant economy by preventing further outmigration from rural areas (and hence the formation of an urban proletariat, or the feared 'mob in the streets') is clear from Puntambekar and Varadachari [1926: 120ff., 218ff.], a text introduced by Gandhi himself and endorsed by Congress.
63. Shiva [1991a: 171, 173, 175, 185, 191]. Significantly, in support of her views about the traditional and subsistence-oriented nature of peasant society she [1989: 4, 12] invokes both the 'limited good' concept of Foster [1962] and the Chayanovian exegesis of Sahlins [1972]. There are numerous instances from other contexts of a similar ideological convergence between populism and ecology. In the case of Africa, for example, ecological knowledge is equated with traditional knowledge [*Richards*, 1983; 1985; 1986; 1990], a position which in turn licenses a return to the past and thus a reaffirma-

tion of 'nature'. Much the same is true of current attempts to recuperate a romanticised image of the North American Indian as the 'original ecologist', a golden age when the latter subject lived in timeless harmony with nature.

64. About the unsustainability of the tribal/non-tribal distinction, Kosambi [1956: 25] has commented that '[t]he entire course of Indian history shows tribal elements being fused into a general society'. For Gujarat and West Bengal, see Pathy [1984] and Bose [1985].
65. Pathy [1984: 25, 64, 105, 115–16, 118–20, 130, 145, 171]; Bose [1985: 94–5, 101–102, 112–13, 116, 118–19, 121–2]. A similar process of socio-economic differentiation is reported for tribals in the Northeastern Indian states of Assam and Arunachal Pradesh [*Goswami*, 1983: 266–75].
66. For the contributions to the debate about the characterization and the politically progressive/non-progressive nature of farmers'/social movements in India, see among others Rudolph and Rudolph [1984: 328ff.], Nadkarni [1987: 136ff.], Balagopal [1987a; 1987b], Omvedt and Galla [1987], Ray and Jha [1987], Das [1988], Lindberg [1990: 15ff.], Hasan [1989b], Dhanagare [1990], Banaji [1990], Omvedt [1991a] and Mehta [1992: 223ff.]. As an activist involved with the All-Women's Front (*Samagra Mahila Aghadi*) associated with Sharad Joshi's Shetkari Sanghatana in Maharashtra, the contributions to this debate by Omvedt are of particular interest (in addition to the above mentioned texts by her, see also Omvedt [1988; 1989; 1990a; 1991b]). As Ray and Jha [1987: 2229] rightly discern, a consequence of support she initially extended to Sharad Joshi because of his pronouncements on gender oppression is that Omvedt has shifted politically from a Marxist to bourgeois/ (neo-populist) position (that is, a politico-ideological relay-in-statement).
67. All these issues are presented in Sinha [1982: 7, 8, 9, 10, 11, 12–13]. For resolutions of support from the CPI dominated All India Kisan Council, both for the new farmers' movements and their demands for lower taxes and remunerative prices, see All-India Kisan Sabha [1981: 34–9, 49–50].
68. In this connection, it is perhaps worth recalling the warning of Karl Kautsky during the 1880s and 1890s against the trend towards electoral opportunism within German Social Democracy [*Salvadori*, 1979: 48ff.; *Husain and Tribe*, 1984]. Against those like von Vollmar, who wished to build an electoral base among the peasantry, and who – as in the case of the new farmers' movements in India a century later – advocated an agrarian programme of price supports and debt write-offs in order to secure a following among the crisis-ridden small and middle peasantry, Kautsky argued that as ultimately the small peasant farm was an historically doomed institution, no attempt should be made to revitalise it.
69. For the politico-ideological fusion of RSS discourse with that of the BJP and VHP, together with the RSS background of the BJP leadership after 1986, see Anderson and Damle [1987: 228, 230, 235, 236–7] and Basu *et al.* [1993]. Significantly, prior to the emergence there of the Shetkari Sanghatana during the 1980s, M.G. Bokare, now a spokesperson for the RSS-dominated *Swadeshi Jagran Manch*, was an organizer/ theorist of the cotton producers movement in Maharashtra [*Omvedt*, 1993a: 2402].
70. Sarkar [1991: 2057], Nadkarni [1987: 111], Lenneberg [1988: 447], Shah [1991]. To counter the influence of Sharad Joshi and draw support away from the farmers' movement, the BJP in Gujarat has supported the attempt by the BKS (*Bharatiya Kisan Sangh*) to mobilise the peasantry from 1986 onwards. 'In order to mobilise peasants', one observer [*Shah*, 1991: 2923] notes, 'the party took the support of spiritual leaders of different sects, invoked religious symbols and aroused Gujarati sentiments'. Similarly, in Karantaka, where the KRRS participated in the elections for the first time in 1991, it lost the votes of farmers' movement supporters to the BJP over the temple issue (Kripa [1992: 1182]; Manor [1992] and the contributions by Gill and Hasan to this volume). For the inroads made by the BJP into the tribal constituencies of Congress in the 1993 Assembly Elections, see Yadav [1993].
71. In this connection, it is necessary to emphasize two points. First, that just as the BJP can reappropriate nationalist/neo-populist discourse from the new farmers' movement, ecofeminism, new social movements and the left, so this same discourse can in turn be

appropriated – or in the case of Congress (I), reappropriated – from the BJP. Accordingly, the political ascendancy of the BJP might itself change in one of two ways: either the successful annexation of this political discourse by another party/grouping of a similar ideological disposition could lead to the electoral decline of the BJP; or were the BJP to experience an electoral decline for some other reason, this political discourse would then be available for annexation by some other party/grouping of a similar ideological disposition. And second, the neo-populist/communal discourse under consideration here is supportive of nationalism *per se*, and not just the Hindu chauvinist variant currently espoused by the BJP/VHP/RSS: that is, of non-Hindu (or anti-Hindu) regionally-specific nationalism(s) in other parts of India (Punjab, Assam, Tamil Nadu).

72. The increasing rural support for the RSS has been noted by Anderson and Damle [1987: 248–9], who comment:

> Since its formation in 1925 the RSS has attracted support almost exclusively in urban areas, and largely from the salaried lower middle class and smallscale shopkeepers. These are groups whose social and economic aspirations are undermined by inflation, by scarcity of job opportunities, and by their relative inability to influence the political process. The RSS has had little success among the peasantry ... However, as change comes to affect increasingly large numbers of Indians, the revivalist appeals offered by the RSS (and by other groups as well) are likely to become more popular, and there are now signs that the RSS is making some headway in certain rural areas.

73. Anderson and Damle [1987: 81, 103 footnote 50].
74. Anderson and Damle [1987: 72]. For the threat to India of an alien 'consumerism' generated by 'western industrialisation' and more generally by ('foreign') economic imperialism, as conceptualised in the discourse of the RSS-influenced *Swadeshi Jagran Manch*, see Omvedt [1993a].
75. Anderson and Damle [1987: 73–4, 81]. Significantly, in the discourse of the BJP, Muslims are not merely externalized as a passive 'other' ('not-us') but are actively identified with the 'West' ('with-them'): hence the view that 'Muslims always do the opposite of what Hindus do. If the east is sacred to the Hindu, then the Muslim will worship the West' [*Basu et al.*, 1993: 77].
76. Anderson and Damle [1987: 81, 103 footnote 50]. Like the RSS, Sharad Joshi and Kumarappa, the Vice-President of the BJP, Sunder Singh Bhandari, has recently observed that the BJP similarly endorses the process of economic and political decentralisation to village *panchayats* [*Basu et al.*, 1993: 49].
77. Anderson and Damle [1987: 194].
78. On this issue see in particular Sarkar [1991: 2059], who observes: 'The RSS occasionally plugs into a whole range of otherwise radical issues – ecology, world peace, interrelated critiques of western materialistic and monolithic notions of truth that lead to imperialist suppression of non-western identities.'
79. For an exposition of this view, see Dwivedi [1990]. An important prefiguring text in this regard is that by Kumarappa, who observed [1935: 3] that:

> [one of] the basic ideas which underlie our village life and organization [is] to avoid competition and the uncurbed play of the profit-motive, and conversely to promote cooperation. The caste-system distributed the work of society among its various members [thus avoiding] upsetting the whole social equilibrium, as happens today ... The caste system also promoted group loyalty and cooperation, the absence of which is now so evident in us who are city-bred.

80. For the RSS conceptualisation of the 'sacred geography' of India, see Anderson and Damle [1987: 77]. For a Gandhian view equating peasant farming with 'the sacred', see Kumarappa [1935: 2].
81. Symptomatically, the CPI [*Rao and Faizee*, 1989: 3,4ff.] condemns the communalism generated by the temple issue not because it diverts attention from socialist politics but because it endangers bourgeois democracy.

82. On this point, Sarkar [1991: 2059] comments:

> The discourse starts with the unique philosophical concept of tolerance within Hinduism ... This very pluralism and tolerance, however, characterize a single national ethos which is essentially Hindu and to which all immigrant religions have adapted themselves. The notion of an essentially Hindu national ethos came under attack when 'fanatic' Muslim rulers ruled the land and tried to destroy it with 'brute strength'. The British, however, 'planned to subvert the Hindu mind itself'. This was achieved through a seemingly successful mode of western knowledge which ... substituted alien categories of thought for self-knowledge. The perception of a single national ethos was broken up and Indian history was restructured to prove that the nation means simply a geographical space ... [According to the discourse of the BJP/VHP/RSS this] false and alien notion of secularism destroyed the single shared culture and fractured the sense of wholeness, led to communalism and violence, and eventually culminated in partition.

For RSS claims that the Christian and Muslim influences undermine/denationalise India, and further that the disintegration of Hindu society dates from the period of Islamic invasions around the first millenium, see Anderson and Damle [1987: 72].

83. For the racially-specific reproductive role of 'motherhood' in the discourse of the political right, and for the gender-specific appeal of the latter generally, see Macciocchi [1979], Koonz [1987] and Bree [1991]. The potency of this combination of passive/active female roles in the recent communal mobilisation, whereby women take part in the liberation of a male Hindu deity, is noted by Basu *et al.* [1993: 81–2], who comment: 'The reversal of roles equips the communal woman with a new and empowering self-image. She has stepped out of a purely iconic status to take up an active position as a militant.'

84. On the interrelatedness and sacred nature of this Hindu symbolism, see Sarkar [1991: 2057–8, 2061] and Pandey [1991: 2998, 3003–4]. On the same point, Anderson and Damle [1987: 77] note that for the RSS

> [t]he metaphor of the Divine Mother is used to describe both the nation and the 'sacred' geography where the nation resides ... [t]he metaphor offers RSS publicists emotionally-packed imagery to convey their message. The Mother image informs feelings for the homeland, that piece of earth which has nourished and sustained the people through history and is the true setting for the life of the people today; RSS literature is filled with references to the historical desacration of this land. *The division of the subcontinent in 1947 is described as 'rape'. Those who threaten the nation of the 'sacred' geography are portrayed as lustful masculine figures.* In the 1980s, the RSS and its affiliates used the symbol of the Mother-Godess in mass campaigns to inspire loyalty to the country (emphasis added).

Another example of politically reactionary women's self-empowerment in contemporary India is the anti-foreigner movement which took place in Assam during 1979–80. This mobilisation by indigenous Assamese was aimed principally at Muslims coming from Bangladesh after its secession from Pakistan (the 'post-1971 foreigners'), and also against immigrant Nepalis; as well as the disenfranchisement/deportation of the non-Assamese ethnic population, its political demands included the closing of the border between India and Bangladesh. Not only did women play an important role in the movement, but the politically reactionary direction of this gender-specific mobilization passes without comment – either by the authors Barthakur and Goswami [1990] or by the editor Sen [1990] in a collection of texts celebrating female self-empowerment. Not the least of the difficulties accompanying the (active) process of female self-empowerment under the aegis of the political right is that the way in which gender is inscribed in – and takes its ideological structure from – the concept 'nature' means that women in general and rural women in particular are trapped in a discourse that emphasizes female passivity, which in turn places obstacles to the kind of active roles women themselves are permitted to discharge. Like the earth itself, therefore, woman is in ideological terms cast as the passive recepient of (male) seed ('ploughed'), the produce of which she raises and nourishes at considerable cost to herself (= self-denial, sacrifice). In this chain of signification, therefore, female is equated with 'nature'/'seed'/'field', all of which are controlled/owned/(fertilised) by males. On this point, see Dube [1986: 41].

85. Much is made of the fact that the main victims of this economic crisis are not peasant cultivators but the 'trading classes' which profited from the consumer demand generated by the Green Revolution (see, for example, Datta [1991: 2522]). However, such a view overlooks the point that many 'traders' are actually peasant farmers who diversified out of agriculture, yet continue to own rural property (see Banaji, this volume). For the role in Punjab of fundamentalist Sikh gangs in the attempted supression by Sikh farmers of struggles by Hindu agricultural workers for higher wages, see A Correspondent [1987]. For instances of the communalisation of conflict in Karnataka by caste Hindu farmers, see Nadkarni [1987: 149–50, 153–5].

86. It should be noted that nationalist sentiment is fuelled by the different responses of the farmers' movement to economic liberalisation: for Joshi, therefore, it is an effect of Indian farmers' capacity to compete with international counterparts on equal terms, while for Tikait it is an effect of their fears about an inability to do so. Not surprisingly, the BJP is now preparing to capitalise electorally on nationalist anti-foreigner sentiment generated by the current neo-liberal economic climate. As one observer notes,

> ... in the recent meeting of its national executive the [BJP] toyed with the idea of launching an agitation against the Dunkel proposals and the signing of the GATT treaty as a stepping-stone to a widespread 'national economic campaign' which could later be developed into a 'swadeshi' [= 'freedom'] campaign ... [a]ccording to the thinking of a large section in the party, [it] may be able to influence sections of farmer and business interests with its rhetoric of anti-Dunkel 'Swadeshi' ('BJP: Conflicting Pulls', *Economic and Political Weekly*, Vol.29, Nos.1–2, 1–8 Jan. 1994).

87. Claims to the contrary notwithstanding, the outcome of the Assembly Elections held during November 1993 in the four northern states of Himachel Pradesh, Rajasthan, Madhya Pradesh and Uttar Pradesh, as well as in the Union territory of Delhi, confirms the continued electoral consolidation of the BJP, mainly at the expense of Congress [*Yadav*, 1993]. Although defeated in Uttar Pradesh, the BJP vote there nevertheless increased by 1.8 per cent and was spread more evenly throughout the state. Most significantly, in the Upper Doab region of UP, traditionally dominated by the Jat peasant base previously of Charan Singh and now of the BKU, support for the BJP has increased both in terms of vote (+ 2.7 per cent) and the number of seats gained (+ 13). For the first time since Independence, the Jan Sangh and BJP have emerged as a political force in Rajasthan, and the BJP has succeeded not just in capturing tribal constituences from Congress but also forcing other political parties – Congress and Samajwadi – to adopt a communal discourse.

REFERENCES

A Correspondent, 1987, 'Other Side of Punjab Crisis', *Economic and Political Weekly*, Vol.22, No.33.

All-India Kisan Sabha, 1981, *New Peasant Upsurge – Reason and Remedies: Documents and Resolutions, AIKS Meeting November/December 1980*, New Delhi: AIKS.

Ambedkar, B.R., 1946, *What Congress and Gandhi Have Done to the Untouchables*, Bombay: Thacker & Co., Ltd.

Amin, S., 1984, 'Gandhi as Mahatma: Gorakhpur District, Eastern UP, 1921–22', in R. Guha (ed.), *Subaltern Studies III*, New Delhi: Oxford University Press.

Anderson, W.K., and S.D. Damle, 1987, *The Brotherhood in Saffron: The Rashtriya Swayamsevak Sangh and Hindu Revivalism*, New Delhi: Vistaar Publications.

Athreya, V., Djurfeldt, G. and S. Lindberg, 1990, *Barriers Broken: Production Relations and Agrarian Change in Tamil Nadu*, New Delhi: Sage Publications.

Balagopal, K., 1987a, 'An Ideology for the Provincial Propertied Class', *Economic and Political Weekly*, Vol.22, Nos.36/37.

Balagopal, K., 1987b, 'An Ideology for the Provincial Propertied Class', *Economic and Political Weekly*, Vol.22, No.50.

Banaji, J., 1990, 'Illusions About the Peasantry: Karl Kautsky and the Agrarian Question', *Journal of Peasant Studies*, Vol.17, No.2.

Barnouw, E. and S. Krishnaswamy, 1980, *Indian Film*, New Delhi: Oxford University Press.

Barthakur, S. and S. Goswami, 1990, 'The Assam Movement', in I. Sen (ed.) [1990].

Baskaran, S.T., 1981, *The Message Bearers: Nationalist Politics and the Entertainment Media in South India, 1880–1945*, Madras: Cre-A.

Basu, T. *et al.*, 1993, *Khaki Shorts and Saffron Flags: A Critique of the Hindu Right*, New Delhi: Orient Longman.

Baxter, C., 1971, *The Jana Sangh: A Biography of an Indian Political Party*, Bombay: Oxford University Press.

Beik, W., 1993, 'Debate: The Dilemma of Popular History', *Past and Present*, No.141.

Bideleux, R., 1985, *Communism and Development*, London: Methuen.

Bose, P.K., 1985, *Classes and Class Relations among Tribals of Bengal*, Delhi: Ajanta Publications.

Bose, S. (ed.), 1990, *South Asia and World Capitalism*, Delhi: Oxford University Press.

Bosworth, R.J.B., 1993, *Explaining Auschwitz and Hiroshima: History Writing and the Second World War, 1945–1990*, London: Routledge.

Bramwell, A., 1985, *Blood and Soil: Richard Walther Darré and Hitler's 'Green Party'*, Bourne End: The Kensal Press.

Brass, T., 1990, 'Class Struggle and the Deproletarianization of Agricultural Labour in Haryana (India)', *Journal of Peasant Studies*, Vol.18, No.1.

Brass, T., 1991, 'Moral Economists, Subalterns, New Social Movements, and the (Re-) Emergence of a (Post-) Modernised (Middle) Peasant', *Journal of Peasant Studies*, Vol.18, No.2.

Bree, K.M., 1991, *The Women of the Klan: Racism and Gender in the 1920s*, Berkeley, CA: University of California Press.

Brown, J., 1972, *Gandhi's Rise to Power: Indian Politics 1915–22*, London: Cambridge University Press.

Burke, P., 1981, 'The "Discovery" of Popular Culture', in R. Samuel (ed.), *People's History and Socialist Theory*, London: Routledge & Kegan Paul.

Byres, T.J., 1979, 'Of Neo-Populist Pipedreams: Daedalus in the Third World and the Myth of Urban Bias', *Journal of Peasant Studies*, Vol.6, No.2.

Byres, T.J., 1988, 'Charan Singh (1902–87): An Assessment', *Journal of Peasant Studies*, Vol.15, No.2.

Byres, T.J., 1991, 'The Agrarian Question and Differing Forms of Capitalist Agrarian Transition: An Essay with Reference to Asia', in S. Mundle and J. Breman (eds.), *Rural Transformation in Asia*, Delhi: Oxford University Press.

Calman, L.J., 1992, *Toward Empowerment: Women and Movement Politics in India*, Boulder, CO: Westview Press.

Charlesworth, N., 1985, *Peasants and Imperial Rule: Agriculture and Agrarian Society in the Bombay Presidency, 1850–1935*, Cambridge: Cambridge University Press.

Chatterjee, P., 1984, 'Gandhi and the Critique of Civil Society', in R. Guha (ed.), *Subaltern Studies III*, New Delhi: Oxford University Press.

Chatterjee, P., 1986, *Nationalist Thought and the Colonial World: A Derivative Discourse?*, Delhi: Oxford University Press.

Chattopadhyay, B., Sharma, S.C. and A.K. Ray, 1987, 'Rural/Urban Terms of Trade, Primary Accumulation and the Increasing Strength of the Indian Farm Lobby', in B.

Chattopadhyay and P. Spitz (eds.), *Food Systems and Society in Eastern India*, Geneva: UNRISD.

Chayanov, A.V., 1966, *The Theory of Peasant Economy* (edited by Daniel Thorner, Basile Kerblay, and R.E.F. Smith), Homewood, ILL: The American Economic Association.

Clark, C., 1984, 'Development Economics: The Early Years', in G.M. Maier and D. Seers (eds.), *Pioneers in Development*, New Delhi: Oxford University Press.

Das, A.N., 1983, *Agrarian Unrest and Socio-economic Change in Bihar 1900–1980*, New Delhi: Manohar Publications.

Das, A.N. (ed.), 1988, 'Farmer Power: A Symposium on the Growing Unrest in the Countryside', a Special Issue of *Seminar*, No.352.

Das Gupta, C., 1991, *The Painted Face: Studies in India's Popular Cinema*, New Delhi: Roli Books.

Datta, P.K., 1991, 'VHP's Ram at Ayodhya: Reincarnation through Ideology and Organization', *Economic and Political Weekly*, Vol.26, No.44.

Desai, A.R. (ed.), 1980, *Agrarian Struggles in India after Independence*, Delhi: Oxford University Press.

Dhanagare, D.N., 1975, *Agrarian Movements and Gandhian Politics*, Agra: Institute of Social Sciences, Agra University.

Dhanagare, D.N., 1983, *Peasant Movements in India 1920–1950*, Delhi: Oxford University Press.

Dhanagare, D.N., 1990, 'Shetkari Sanghatana: The Farmers' Movement in Maharashtra – Background and Ideology', *Social Action*, Vol.40, No.4.

Diamond, I. and G.F. Orenstein (eds.), 1990, *Reweaving the World: The Emergence of Ecofeminism*, San Francisco, CA: Sierra Club Books.

Dube, L., 1986, 'Seed and Earth: The Symbolism of Biological Reproduction and Sexual Relations of Production', in L. Dube, E. Leacock and S. Ardner (eds.), *Visibility and Power: Essays on Women in Society and Development*, Delhi: Oxford University Press.

Dwivedi, O.P., 1990, '*Satyagraha* for conservation: Awakening the spirit of Hinduism', in J.R. Engel and J.G. Engel (eds.), *Ethics of Environment and Development*, London: Belhaven Press.

Eckstein, S. (ed.), 1989, *Power and Popular Protest: Latin American Social Movements*, Berkeley, CA: University of California Press.

Eder, K., 1993, *The New Politics of Class: Social Movements and Cultural Dynamics in Advanced Societies*, London: Sage Publications.

Eisenstein, H., 1984, *Contemporary Feminist Thought*, London: Unwin Paperbacks.

Epstein, K., 1970, 'Three Types of Conservatism', in M. Richter (ed.), *Essays in Theory and History*, Cambridge, MA: Harvard University Press.

Escobar, A. and S.E. Alvarez (eds.), 1992, *The Making of Social Movements in Latin America*, Boulder, CO: Westview Press.

Foster, G.M., 1962, *Traditional Cultures*, New York: Harper & Brothers.

Foweraker, J. and A.L. Craig (eds.), 1990, *Popular Movements and Political Change in Mexico*, Boulder, CO: Lynne Rienner Publishers, Inc.

Fox, J. (ed.), 1990, *The Challenge of Rural Democratization*, London: Frank Cass & Co.

Fox, R.G., 1990, 'Gandhian Socialism and Hindu Nationalism: Cultural Domination in the World System', in S. Bose (ed.) [1990].

Fox-Genovese, E., 1991, *Feminism Without Illusions: A Critique of Individualism*, Chapel Hill, NC: University of North Carolina Press.

Franda, M., 1979, *Small is Politics: Organizational Alternatives in India's Rural Development*, New Delhi: Wiley Eastern Ltd.

Frierson, C.A., 1993, *Peasant Icons: Representations of Rural People in Late Nineteenth-Century Russia*, Oxford: Oxford University Press.

Fuentes, M. and A.G. Frank, 1989, 'Ten Theses on Social Movements', *World Development*, Vol.17, No.2.

Gadgil, D.R., 1945, *Regulation of Wages and Other Problems of Industrial Labour in India*, Poona: Gokhale Institute of Politics and Economics.

Goswami, M.C., 1983, 'Peasants and Neo-Peasants in Northeast India and their New

Dimension', in J.P. Mencher (ed.), *Social Anthropology of Peasantry*, Bombay: Somaiya Publications.

Government of India, 1991, *National Agricultural Policy: Views of Standing Advisory Committee on Agriculture (SAC)*, Jullundur: Government Printing Press.

Graham, B., 1990, *Hindu Nationalism and Indian Politics*, Cambridge: Cambridge University Press.

Guha, R. (ed.), 1982–89, *Subaltern Studies I–VI*, Delhi: Oxford University Press.

Gupta, D., 1988, 'Country-Town Nexus and Agrarian Mobilization: Bharatiya Kisan Union as an Instance', *Economic and Political Weekly*, Vol.23, No.51.

Gupta, D., 1992, 'Peasant "Unionism" in Uttar Pradesh: Against the Rural Mentality Thesis', *Journal of Contemporary Asia*, Vol.22, No.2.

Guru, G., 1992, 'Shetkari Sanghtana and the Pursuit of "Laxmi Mukti"', *Economic and Political Weekly*, Vol.27, No.28.

Habermas, J., 1989, *The New Conservatism: Cultural Criticism and the Historians' Debate*, Cambridge: Polity Press.

Hardiman, D., 1981, *Peasant Nationalists of Gujarat: Kheda District 1917–34*, Delhi: Oxford University Press.

Hardiman, D., 1987, *The Coming of the Devi: Adivasi Assertion in Western India*, Delhi: Oxford University Press.

Harris, M., 1966, 'The Cultural Ecology of India's Sacred Cattle', *Current Anthropology*, Vol.7, No.1.

Harris, M., 1974, *Cows, Pigs, Wars, and Witches: The Riddles of Culture*, New York: Random House.

Harvey, N., 1990, *The New Agrarian Movement in Mexico, 1979–90*, London: Institute of Latin American Studies.

Hasan, Z., 1989a, *Dominance and Mobilisation: Rural Politics in Western Uttar Pradesh, 1930–80*, New Delhi: Sage Publications.

Hasan, Z., 1989b, 'Self-Serving Guardians: Formation and Strategy of the Bharatiya Kisan Union', *Economic and Political Weekly*, Vol.24, No.48.

Herzen, A., 1956, *From the Other Shore*, London: Weidenfeld & Nicolson.

Hinz, B., 1980, *Art in the Third Reich*, Oxford: Basil Blackwell.

Husain, A. and K. Tribe (eds.), 1984, *Paths of Development in Capitalist Agriculture*, London: Macmillan.

Jackson, C., 1993, 'Women/Nature or Gender/History? A Critique of Ecofeminist "Development"', *Journal of Peasant Studies*, Vol.20, No.3.

Jones, A.K., 1990, 'Social Symbiosis: A Gaian Critique of Contemporary Social Theory', *The Ecologist*, Vol.20, No.3.

Joshi, Sharad, 1993, *Farmers and Dunkel*, Pune: unpublished mss.

Kaufman, A., 1982, *Capitalism, Slavery, and Republican Values: American Political Economists, 1819–1848*, Austin TX: University of Texas Press.

Kitching, G., 1982, *Development and Underdevelopment in Historical Perspective*, London: Methuen & Co.

Knowlton, J. and J. Cotes, 1993, *Forever in the Shadow of Hitler: Documents of the Historikerstreit*, New York: Humanities Press.

Koonz, C., 1987, *Mothers in the Fatherland: Women, the Family, and Nazi Politics*, New York: St Martin's Press.

Kosambi, D.D., 1956, *An Introduction to the Study of Indian History*, Bombay: Popular Book Depot.

Kripa, A.P., 1992, 'Farmers' Movement in Karnataka', *Economic and Political Weekly*, Vol.27, No.23.

Kumarappa, B., 1935, *Village Industries and Reconstruction*, Allahabad: All India Congress Committee.

Lenin, V.I., 1961, 'What Is To Be Done?', *Collected Works*, Vol.5, Moscow: Foreign Languages Publishing House.

Lenin, V.I., 1964, 'The Development of Capitalism in Russia', *Collected Works*, Vol.3, Moscow: Foreign Languages Publishing House.

Lennenberg, C., 1988, 'Sharad Joshi and the Farmers: The Middle Peasant Lives!', *Pacific Affairs*, Vol.61, No.3.
Levy, E., 1991, *Small-Town America in Film: The Decline and Fall of Community*, New York: Continuum.
Lieten, K., 1988, 'The Indian National Congress and the Control Over Labour: The Need for a Passive Revolution', in K. Kumar (ed.), *Congress and Classes: Nationalism, Workers and Peasants*, New Delhi: Manohar.
Lindberg, S., 1990, 'Civil Society Against the State? Farmers' Agitation and New Social Movements in India', Paper presented at the XII World Congress of Sociology, Madrid.
Lipton, M., 1977, *Why Poor People Stay Poor: A Study of Urban Bias in in World Development*, London: Temple Smith.
Littlejohn, G., 1977, 'Peasant Economy and Society', in B. Hindess (ed.), *Sociological Theories of the Economy*, London: Macmillan.
Lukacs, G., 1980, *The Destruction of Reason*, London: The Merlin Press.
Lüthi, D., 1993, 'Krishna and Catir Nãccu: Feature Film as a Political Medium', *Visual Anthropology*, Vol.5, Nos.3–4.
Macciocchi, A.-M., 1979, 'Female Sexuality in Fascist Ideology', *Feminist Review*, No.1.
McLeod, W.H., 1991, *Popular Sikh Art*, Delhi: Oxford University Press.
Maier, C.S., 1988, *The Unmasterable Past: History, Holocaust, and German National Identity*, Cambridge, MA: Harvard University Press.
Malia, M.E., 1955, 'Herzen and the Peasant Commune', in E.J. Simmons (ed.), *Continuity and Change in Russian and Soviet Thought*, Cambridge, MA: Harvard University Press.
Mannheim, K., 1953, *Essays on Sociology and Social Psychology*, London: Routledge & Kegan Paul.
Manor, J., 1992, 'BJP in South India: 1991 General Election', *Economic and Political Weekly*, Vol.27, Nos.24–5.
Manuel, P., 1993, *Cassette Culture: Popular Music and Technology in North India*, Chicago, ILL: University of Chicago Press.
Mehta, U., 1992, 'Indian Agriculture Since Independence', in G. Shah (ed.), *Capitalist Development: Critical Essays*, London: Sangam Books Ltd.
Melucci, A., 1989, *Nomads of the Present: Social Movements and Individual Needs in Contemporary Society*, London: Hutchinson Radius.
Merchant, C., 1992, *Radical Ecology*, London: Routledge.
Mies, M., 1986, *Patriarchy and Accumulation on a World Scale*, London: Zed Press.
Mies, M., Bennholdt-Thomsen, V. and C. von Werlhof, 1988, *Women: The Last Colony*, New Delhi: Kali for Women.
Mies, M. and V. Shiva, 1993, *Ecofeminism*, London: Zed Press.
Mitrany, D., 1951, *Marx Against the Peasant*, Chapel Hill, NC: The University of North Carolina Press.
Morgan, R., 1992, *The Word of a Woman: Feminist Dispatches 1968–1992*, New York: W.W. Norton & Co., Ltd.
Mosse, G., 1966, *Nazi Culture: Intellectual, Cultural and Social Life in the Third Reich*, London: W.H. Allen.
Nadkarni, M.V., 1987, *Farmers' Movements in India*, Ahmedabad: Allied Publishers.
National Labour Institute Report, 1980, 'Post-Independence Peasant Movements in Ryotwari Areas of Andhra Pradesh', in A.R. Desai (ed.) [1990].
Netting, R.M., 1993, *Smallholders, Householders: Farm Families and the Ecology of Intensive, Sustainable Agriculture*, Stanford, CA: Stanford University Press.
Nolan, M., 1988, 'The Historikerstreit and Social History', *New German Critique*, No.44.
Normano, J.F., 1949, *The Spirit of Russian Economics*, London: Dennis Dobson.
Omvedt, G., 1986, 'Peasants and Women: Challenge of Chandwad', *Economic and Political Weekly*, Vol.21, No.48.
Omvedt, G., 1988, 'New Movements', in A.N. Das (ed.) [1988].
Omvedt, G., 1989, 'Ecology and Social Movements', in H. Alavi and J. Harriss (eds.), *Sociology of 'Developing Societies': South Asia*, London: Macmillan.
Omvedt, G., 1990a, 'The Farmers' Movement in Maharashtra', in I. Sen (ed.) [1990].

Omvedt, G., 1990b, *Violence Against Women: New Movements and New Theories in India*, New Delhi: Kali for Women.

Omvedt, G., 1991a, 'Theorists of the Peasantry Should at Least Have Their Feet on the Ground: A Response to Banaji, *Journal of Peasant Studies*, Vol.19, No.1.

Omvedt, G., 1991b, 'Shetkari Sanghatana's New Direction', *Economic and Political Weekly*, Vol.26, No.40.

Omvedt, G., 1993a, 'Of Brahmins, Sacred and Socialist', *Economic and Political Weekly*, Vol.28, No.44.

Omvedt, G., 1993b, 'Farmers' Movement: Fighting for Liberalisation', *Economic and Political Weekly*, Vol.28, No.50.

Omvedt, G. and C. Galla, 1987, 'Ideology for Provincial Propertied Class?', *Economic and Political Weekly*, Vol.22, No.45.

O'Sullivan, N., 1976, *Conservatism*, London: J.M. Dent & Sons Ltd.

Ott, H., 1993, *Martin Heidegger: A Political Life*, London: Harper Collins.

Pandey, G., 1991, 'Hindus and Others: The Militant Hindu Construction', *Economic and Political Weekly*, Vol.26, No.52.

Pathy, J., 1984, *Tribal Peasantry: Dynamics of Development*, New Delhi: Inter-India Publications.

Patnaik, U., 1979, 'Neopopulism and Marxism: The Chayanovian View of the Agrarian Question and Its Fundamental Fallacy', *Journal of Peasant Studies*, Vol.6, No.4.

Patnaik, U., 1986, 'The Agrarian Question and Development of Capitalism in India', *Economic and Political Weekly*, Vol.21, No.18.

Patnaik, U., 1990, *Agrarian Relations and Accumulation: The 'Mode of Production' Debate in India*, Bombay: Oxford University Press.

Petrovich, M.B., 1968, 'The Peasant in Nineteenth Century Historiography', in W.S. Vucinich (ed.), *The Peasant in Nineteenth Century Russia*, Stanford, CA: Stanford University Press.

Pois, R.A., 1986, *National Socialism and the Religion of Nature*, London: Croom Helm.

Porter, R. and M. Teich (eds.), 1988, *Romanticism in National Context*, Cambridge: Cambridge University Press.

Pouchepadass, J., 1980, 'Peasant Classes in Twentieth Century Agrarian Movements in India', in E.J. Hobsbawm *et al.* (eds.), *Peasants in History: Essays in Honour of Daniel Thorner*, Calcutta: Oxford University Press.

Prasad, P., 1991, 'Rise of Kulak Power and Caste Struggle in North India', *Economic and Political Weekly*, Vol.26, No.33.

Puntambekar, S.V. and N.S. Varadachari, 1926, *Hand-spinning and Hand-weaving: An Essay*, Ahmedabad: The All-India Spinners' Association.

Rao, C.R. and S. Faizee, 1989, *Babri Masjid Ram Janam Bhoomi Controversy – Dangerous Communal Situation*, New Delhi: CPI.

Ray, K. and S.K. Jha, 1987 'Assessing Shetkari Sanghatana', *Economic and Political Weekly*, Vol.22, No.51.

Ray, K.C. and C.A. Tisdell, 1992, 'Gandhi's Concept of Development and Nehru's Centralized Planning', in K.C. Roy, C.A. Tisdell and R.K. Sen (eds.), *Economic Development and the Environment*, Calcutta: Oxford University Press.

Richards, P., 1983, 'Ecological Change and the Politics of African Land Use', *African Studies Review*, Vol.26, No.2.

Richards, P., 1985, *Indigenous Agricultural Revolution*, London: Hutchinson.

Richards, P., 1986, *Coping with Hunger*, London: Allen & Unwin.

Richards, P., 1990, 'Indigenous Approaches to Rural Development: The Agrarian Populist Tradition in West Africa', in M. Altieri and S. Hecht (eds.), *Agroecology and Small Farm Development*, Boca Raton, FL: CRC Press.

Rudolph, L.I., 1992, 'The Media and Cultural Politics', *Economic and Political Weekly*, Vol.27, No.28.

Rudolph, L.I., and S.H. Rudolph, 1984, 'Determinants and Varieties of Agrarian Mobilization', in M. Desai, S.H. Rudolph and A. Rudra (eds.), *Agrarian Power and Agricultural Productivity in South Asia*, Delhi: Oxford University Press.

Rudolph, L.I. and S.H. Rudolph, 1987, *In Pursuit of Lakshmi: The Political Economy of the Indian State*, Chicago, IL: Chicago University Press.

Sahlins, M., 1972, *Stone Age Economics*, Chicago, IL: Aldine Atherton Inc.

Salvadori, M., 1979, *Karl Kautsky and the Socialist Revolution 1880–1938*, London: New Left Books.

Sarkar, T., 1991, 'The Woman as Communal Subject: Rashtrasevika Samiti and the Ram Janmabhoomi Movement', *Economic and Political Weekly*, Vol.26, No.35.

Sathyamurthy, T.V., 1990, 'Indian Peasant Historiography: A Critical Perspective on Ranajit Guha's Work', *Journal of Peasant Studies*, Vol.18, No.1,

Saxton, A., 1990, *The Rise and Fall of the White Republic: Class Politics and Mass Culture in Nineteenth Century America*, London: Verso.

Sen, G. (ed.), 1992, *Indigenous Vision: Peoples of India Attitudes to the Environment*, New Delhi: Sage.

Sen, I., 1990, 'Introduction', in I. Sen (ed.) [1990].

Sen, I. (ed.), 1990, *A Space Within the Struggle: Women's Participation in People's Movements*, New Delhi: Kali for Women.

Sen, S., 1982, *Peasant Movements in India*, Calcutta: K.P. Bagchi.

Shah, G., 1991, 'Tenth Lok Sabha Elections: BJP's Victory in Gujarat', *Economic and Political Weekly*, Vol.26, No.51.

Shiva, V., 1989, *Staying Alive: Women, Ecology and Development*, London: Zed Books.

Shiva, V., 1990, 'Development as a New Project of Western Patriarchy', in I. Diamond and G.F. Orenstein (eds.) [1990].

Shiva, V., 1991a, *The Violence of the Green Revolution: Third World Agriculture, Ecology and Politics*, London: Zed Books.

Shiva, V., 1991b, *Ecology and the Politics of Survival*, New Delhi: Sage Publications.

Shiva, V., 1992a, 'Women's Indigenous Knowledge and Biodiversity Conservation', in G. Sen (ed.) [1992].

Shiva, V., 1992b, 'Biodiversity, Biotechnology and Profits', in V. Shiva (ed.) [1992].

Shiva, V. (ed.), 1992, *Biodiversity: Social and Ecological Perspectives*, Dehradun: Natraj Publishers.

Shiva, V., 1993a, 'Farmers' Rights, Biodiversity and International Treaties', *Economic and Political Weekly*, Vol.28, No.14.

Shiva, V., 1993b, *Monoculture of the Mind: Biodiversity, Biotechnology and 'Scientific' Agriculture*, London: Zed Books.

Singh, C., 1978, *India's Economic Policy: The Gandhian Blueprint*, New Delhi: Vikas Publishing House.

Singh, C., 1981, *Economic Nightmare of India: Its Cause and Cure*, New Delhi: National Publishing House.

Sinha, I., 1982, *Some Questions Concerning Marxism and the Peasantry*, New Delhi: Communist Party Publication.

Slater, D. (ed.), 1985, *New Social Movements and the State in Latin America*, Amsterdam: CEDLA.

Thompson, E.P., 1991, *Cultures in Common*, London: Merlin Press.

Tidmarsh, K., 1960, 'The Soviet Reassessment of Mahatma Gandhi', in R. Iyer (ed.), *South Asian Affairs*, Southern Illinois University Press.

Tönnies, F., 1955, *Community and Association*, London: Routledge & Kegan Paul.

Totten, G.O, 1960, 'Labor and Agrarian Disputes in Japan following World War I', in T.C. Smith (ed.), 'City and Village in Japan', a special issue of *Economic Development and Cultural Change*, Vol.IX, No.1, Part II.

Trotsky, L.D., 1969, 'The Three Conceptions of the Russian Revolution', *Writings 1938–39*, New York: Merit Publishers.

Utechin, S.V., 1963, *Russian Political Thought*, London: J.M. Dent & Sons.

Walicki, A., 1969, *The Controversy over Capitalism: Studies in the Social Philosophy of the Russian Populists*, Oxford: Clarendon Press.

Walicki, A., 1975, *The Slavophile Controversy: History of a Conservative Utopia in Nineteenth Century Russian Thought*, Oxford: Clarendon Press.

Walicki, A., 1980, *A History of Russian Thought from the Enlightenment to Marxism*, Oxford: Clarendon Press.

Weiner, M., 1989, *The Indian Paradox: Essays in Indian Politics*, New Delhi: Sage Publications.

Welch, D., 1983, *Propaganda and the German Cinema 1933–45*, Oxford: Clarendon Press.

Wignaraja, P. (ed.), 1993, *New Social Movements in the South: Empowering the People*, London: Zed Books.

World Bank, 1992, *World Development Report 1992: Development and the Environment*, New York: Oxford University Press.

Wortman, R., 1967, *The Crisis of Russian Populism*, Cambridge: Cambridge University Press.

Yadav, Y., 1993, 'Political Change in North India: Interpreting Assembly Election Results', *Economic and Polotical Weekly*, Vol.28, No.51.

The Class Character and Politics of the Farmers' Movement in Maharastra during the 1980s

D.N. DHANAGARE

The new farmers' movement in Maharashtra gathered momentum in the late 1970s and mobilised farmers on a mass scale under the banner of the Shetkari Sanghatana. Since its inception the movement has been under the leadership of Sharad Joshi – a career bureaucrat turned ideologue of farmers – who first articulated the demand for remunerative prices for farm produce with the ideological sophistication it needed badly. Ideologial statements from the leader as also from the Sanghatana have emphasized from time to time the non-class character of the movement; however, the Sanghatana claims that its programmes and agitations have served the interests of all classes in rural India. This study argues that such streaks of populism in an ideology is a form of hegemony exercised by a class of dominant rich farmers over the middle and small producers whose cause the Shetkari Sanghatana – the farmers' movement in Maharashtra – claims to have espoused and whom it has successfully mobilised during the 1980s.

The main thrust of the Shetkari Sanghatana's ideology is on remunerative prices for farm produce, and on the issue of the terms of trade. This has given rise to much speculation about the social forces underlying the peasant ferment in India during the 1980s. It is often argued that only rich farmers and the better-off peasants with substantial landholdings have a marketable surplus, and it is these rural classes who benefit from higher remunerative farm prices, whether for wheat, sugarcane, cotton, tobacco, or any other agricultural produce. Accordingly, it is generally believed that rich farmers, who not only have a marketable surplus but

D.N. Dhanagare is at the Department of Sociology, University of Poona, Pune – 411007 (India). This study was first presented as an endowment lecture at Madras University and was subsequently presented at the XII World Congress of Sociology at Madrid (Spain) in July 1990. Later the author was invited to offer its revised version at a seminar at the Centre for Asian Studies, Amsterdam (The Netherlands) and also at the Department of Sociology, University of Delhi in 1991–92. Finally it was presented at the workshop on 'The New Farmers' Movement organised jointly by the *Journal of Peasant Studies* and ICSSR at New Delhi in March 1993. The author is grateful to Tom Brass, Staffan Lindberg and Partha N. Mukherjee who have commented on the earlier drafts and have offered suggestions.

also form a powerful political lobby, constitute the driving force and are also the main participants in the farmers' movements which have gathered momentum throughout India since around 1978–79.

Some researchers argue that having a vested interest in preserving the existing agrarian order and property relations, rich landowning groups have always tended to avoid violence as a means of collective protest [*Dhanagare*, 1975; *Jain*, 1988]. The logic underlying this argument is simple: these upper echelons of the rural society have more to lose than to gain from a violent mass upsurge and destructive agitations. Historically, participation by rich landowning classes in agrarian movements has taken the form of non-violent protest (passive resistance, *satyagraha* and the like) aimed at securing reformist and/or constitutional change.[1] Barring stray incidents of violence in *rasta-roko* or *rail-roko* agitations in Maharashtra and elsewhere, therefore, the contemporary farmers' movements have confined themselves by and large to this pattern of peaceful protest.[2] Some observers, stressing this relatively quiescent character of the farmers' movements, conclude that the peaceful assertion of peasant power through mass mobilisation in a way defines its class character,[3] an argument that is essentially deductive in form and not wholly untenable empirically.

When the Shetkari Sanghatana in Maharashtra launched non-violent mass agitations in support of the farmers' demands for remunerative prices for onion and sugarcane, tobacco or cotton, left-wing intellectuals were the first to endorse the Shetkari Sanghatana movement and also the first to criticise it as a *kulak* lobby. One of them [*Omvedt*, 1980] commented that 'the moment Sharad Joshi's campaign shifted from onion prices to sugarcane prices in 1980–81, the class form of this peasant movement had become clear'.[4] On the basis of the 1971 Agricultural Census, therefore, it has been argued [*Omvedt*, 1980: 2041–2] that as 83 per cent of all cane in Maharashtra is grown on farms of more than two hectares (itself an underestimation because village records register large landholdings under multiple ownership), and '[s]ince 5 acres of sugarcane requires significant amounts of capital for investment and labour inputs, it is safe to say that over 85 percent of all sugarcane is grown by capitalist farmers'. It is these classes who grow cash crops and sell them in the market who would stand to gain from remunerative prices in ample measure.[5] Here again the argument is logical and deductive but not sufficiently empirical.

The study by Nadkarni [1987] builds its evidence about rich farmers as the class base of the contemporary farmers' movement all over India more inductively. About the class base of the Punjab farmers, for example, Nadkarni says that the Bharatiya Kisan Union (hereafter BKU) leaders are undoubtedly for the rich farmers because they have been the principal beneficiaries of the Green Revolution. Even small and medium farmers have commercialised their production and now have some marketable surplus: in Punjab where they have joined BKU in large numbers, the movement is none the less led and dominated by the rich farmers. Drawing his data from a study by Gill and Singhal [1984: 1728–32], he pointed out that 80 per cent of the Punjab BKU leaders owned more than six acres of land, 49 per cent owned 11 acres, 95 per cent have tube-wells/pump-sets, 84 per cent have wheat-thresher machines and 68 per cent have tractors.[6] Hence the inference is clear: if the leaders of a movement come from the class of rich capitalist farmers, then the social character of the movement could not be very different, although the following of BKU has a mixed class character including small farmers who are led and dominated by rich farmers [*Nadkarni*, 1987: 76].

THE EMERGENCE OF A CLASS OF RICH FARMERS

There is no denying the fact that the rural development strategy adopted and implemented in Independent India has led to the emergence of a class of rich farmers.[7] These do not necessarily exclude absentee landlords of the pre-land-reform era, many of whom managed to retain substantial portions of their tenanted land by force or fraud or by fully exploiting the loopholes in the land reforms statutes.[8] Of course, abolition of absentee landownership has helped the intermediate castes of traditional cultivators to consolidate their position in the rural power structure: the latter have managed to gain control over the state sponsored developmental inputs as well as institutions through which these were channelled. Consequently, even after three decades of land reforms, the pattern of landholding shows a highly skewed distribution.

The data presented in Table 1 clearly show that small and marginal farmers owning up to two hectares of landholdings constituted over 74 per cent of the landholding families, and together held a little over 26 per cent of the cultivated land in India in 1980–81. Conversely the top two strata of landholders – upper-middle holders and large (rich) farmers – whose holdidngs are larger than four hectares (10 acres) are just 11.5 per cent of the total landholding households but control 52.5 per cent of the total cultivated land. Thus, nearly three-quarters of the land-owning rural households have holdings either smaller than or just about the average size (the national average being 1.82 hectares).

In Maharashtra the pattern of distribution of landholdings by size has not been as skewed as it was at the all-India level in the 1980–81 Agricultural Census. For example, the proportion of small and marginal

TABLE 1

DISTRIBUTION OF LANDHOLDERS BY THE SIZE OF THEIR HOLDINGS IN 1980–81

Category of Landholders	Size of landholders	Total Landholding families (in millions)	Per cent	Total Land owned by the category (million hectares	Per cent	Average size of landholding in the category
			Figures for India			
Marginal	Up to 1 ha	50.52	56.5	19.80	12.2	0.39
Small holders	1 to 2 ha	16.08	18.0	22.96	14.1	1.43
Medium holders	2 to 4 ha	12.51	14.0	34.56	21.2	2.76
Upper Medium holders	4 to 10 ha	8.09	9.1	48.34	29.7	5.97
Large (rich) holders	More than 10 ha	2.15	2.4	37.13	22.8	17.24
	TOTAL	89.35	100.0	162.79	100.0	1.82
			Figures for Maharashtra			
Marginal	Up to 1 ha	2.02	29.36	0.98	4.83	0.49
Small holders	1 to 2 ha	1.56	22.67	2.20	10.84	1.41
Medium holders	2 to 4 ha	1.66	24.13	4.66	22.96	2.81
Upper Medium holders	4 to 10 ha	1.34	19.48	8.08	39.08	6.03
Large (rich) holders	More than 10 ha	0.30	4.36	4.38	21.57	14.60
	TOTAL	6.88	100.0	20.30	100.00	2.95

Source: Report of the Agricultural Census in India, 1980–81.

(operational) landholdings to the total holdings in Maharashtra in 1980–81 was 50 per cent and they together controlled just 16 per cent of the total operated area (see Table 2). At the other end of the agrarian social scale, there was a much more even spread of landed property among the upper-middle and large (rich) holders having four hectares or more. In Maharashtra about 24 per cent of the total landholding families belonged to the two top categories in 1980–81, and together they controlled over 60 per cent of the total land. The average holding in Maharashtra is also one-and-a-half times larger than the size of average holding at the all India level. Significantly this average size of the holding for the category of upper-middle holders is larger, and that of the large (rich) landholders' category smaller, than the national averages for the corresponding categories of landholders (see Table 1).

If the time-series data from the 1970–71 agricultural census to the 1990–91 agricultural census of the number of holdings and the area operated by size are examined carefully (see Table 2), then the changes in structure of land control and in the pattern of landholding are more apparent than real. For example, out of the total number of landholdings 30 per cent were larger than four hectares in 1970–71; however their proportion to the total landholdings dropped dramatically to 14 per cent in 1990–91. Correspondingly the area operated and controlled by those 30 per cent landholdings was 76 per cent in 1970–71 and it has come down to 45 per cent controlled by 14 per cent of landholdings in 1990–91. Thus, during the agricultural censuses 1971–91, although the number of holdings with four hectares or more declined dramatically, the area operated by them did not. It can threfore be surmised that the enlargement of the semi-medium landholdings in Maharashtra owning between two to four hectares during 1971–91 censuses (see Table 2) could have been due, at least partly, to the partitioning of landholdings belonging to the top two strata. Because under the provisions of the Ceiling on Land Act, any part of a holding declared as surplus is liable to be acquired by the government for redistribution [*Government of Maharashtra*, 1976: 6432–38A], such land transfers were frequently resorted to by rich landholders with a view to avoid declaring a part of their lands as surplus [*Mehta*, 1975: 71–5; *Dhagamwar*, 1981: 238–9]. Without such transfers and partitioning, or subdivisions of a large number of holdings, it is difficult to explain why the area operated by small and semi-medium categories of landholdings increased in Maharashtra from six to 19 per cent and 15 to 28 per cent respectively during the period covered by the 1971–91 agricultural censuses (see Table 2). Therefore, although the dispersal of landholdings and of the area controlled by them is much better in Maharashtra than it is at the All-India level, it is important to note that the pattern of landhold-

TABLE 2

NUMBER OF OPERATIONAL HOLDINGS AND AREA OPERATED IN MAHARASHTRA DURING AGRICULTURAL CENSUSES, 1971–91

Size Class	Number of Operational Holdings (In lakhs)			Operated Area (In lakh hectares)		
	1970–71	1980–81	1990–91	1970–71	1980–81	1990–91
Marginal (Up to 1.00 ha)	12.42	19.26	32.75	5.77	9.73	16.18
%	25	28	35	3	5	8
Small (1.00 to 2.00 ha)	8.78	15.4	27.27	12.84	23.34	39.83
%	18	22	29	6	11	19
Semi-Medium (2.00 to 4.00 ha)	10.87	16.86	21.26	31.31	48.18	58.8
%	22	25	22	15	23	28
Medium (4.00 to 10.0 ha)	12.29	13.92	11.71	71.17	84.49	68.56
%	25	20	12	36	40	33
Large (10.0 & above ha)	5.14	3.18	1.71	84.7	47.88	25.88
%	10	5	2	40	22	12
Total All sizes	49.50	68.62	94.70	211.79	213.62	209.25
%	(100)	(100)	(100)	(100)	(100)	(100)

Source: Government of Maharashtra, Department of Agriculture, *Agricultural Census – 1990–91 (Maharashtra State)* (Provisional Data for 1990–91) *Census Bulletin*, Pune, Jan. 1993, p.4.

ing distribution continued to be skewed despite the series of progressive land reform measures introduced and implemented in Maharashtra.

Agrarian class structure is a complex phenomenon and the class status of landholding families in rural areas cannot possibly be reduced to or equated with the size of landholding. In determining the class status of rural households, several other indicators – such as per capita holding, per capita income, total income of households from all sources (agricultural plus non-agricultural incomes), and even per capita consumption, as well as patterns of labour utilisation in farm operations, will have to be considered. At the macro-level, all these aggregate data are not available, and even if they were, the adequacy of any one of these indices in the determination of agrarian class status may always be questioned. Treating rural class status as coterminus with size of landholding would therefore be simplistic.

Even accounting for the error of over-simplification, although the data on land distribution patterns do indicate the trend of growing land concentration, such a polarisation does not necessarily result in the emergence of a sharp awareness of common class interests. In Maharashtra, however, almost one out of every four landholding families belongs to one of the two top strata in the rural hierarchy, these families having more than six hectares of land in the 1980s (see the last column of Table 1, and the last two rows for Maharashtra). In straight forward terms, therefore, the situation for the majority of these middle and rich landowning classes is favourable not just in terms of growing cash crops and operating a marketable surplus but also in terms of developing a consciousness of their shared interests. One example of how such class interests were crystallised occurred in Maharashtra during 1986–87, when the state faced a severe drought and an acute scarcity of water. The state government, headed by the then Chief Minister S.B. Chavan, proposed to cut the availability of water supplied through the state-monitored irrigation canals from 12 months to eight months per annum. The intention was to conserve the scarce water resources to supply drinking water to thousands of villages in rural Maharashtra. This proposal was strongly resisted by sugarcane growers from Western Maharashtra, who are the main beneficiaries of the state-provided canal irrigation scheme.

The emergence of dominant class interests in rural India can hardly be disputed. Their political expressions and manifestations may be mediated through caste, kinship and other similar ethnic or primordial identities. The growing political impact of these emerging interests is visible in the steadily rising number of farmers' representatives in legislative bodies in India (see Table 3). The representation of agriculturists as an occupational category has risen sharply from 16.5 per cent in 1952 to over 40 per cent in 1980 among the members of the ruling party in the Lok Sabha (the Lower House of the Indian Parliament). Nadkarni [1987: 24–5] considers even this increase an under-representation, since those in other professions (such as services, trade, teaching, social and political work), who have either an agricultural family background or have themselves acquired some interests in cultivable land more recently, are not included in the category of 'agriculturists' in such a classification (Table 3) based simply on primary occupation. Accordingly, the fact that a powerful farm lobby exists politically and operates at both all-India and regional levels need not be either doubted or debated.

TABLE 3
DISTRIBUTION OF MEMBERS OF THE RULING PARTY IN LOK SABHA BY THEIR OCCUPATION, 1952–80
(Figures indicate %)

Occupation of Members	General Elections and Their Years			
	First 1952	Fifth 1971	Sixth 1977	Seventh 1980
Agriculturists	16.5	39.6	36.4	40.1
Lawyers	36.9	24.1	20.1	20.9
Social and Political Workers	15.6	11.1	24.2	18.9
Other Professions	29.5	23.5	17.9	19.2
Others*	1.5	1.7	1.4	0.9
TOTAL	100.0	100.0	100.0	100.0

**Note*: Others include former princely rulers/chieftains, zamindars, jotedars, etc.
Source: P.A. Pai Panandikar and Arun Sud, *Changing Political Representation in India*, New Delhi: Uppal Publications, 1983, pp.55–6.

With the steady expansion of irrigation and other institutionalised facilities and inputs (credit, seeds, fertilisers and so on), rich landholders in Maharashtra have been able to enlarge their scale of production, generate marketable surplus and gain some – at times even substantial – profits. The fact that agricultural incomes in India are non-taxable strengthens further the position of all cash-crop-growing farm households, more so those of rich capitalist farmers. In Maharashtra this is evident in the well-entrenched position of rich peasants in local power structures, regardless of whether they produce sugarcane, onions, cotton or tobacco. Sugarcane growers, for example, have mobilised resources on a co-operative basis to launch sugar factories: there were as many as 67 co-operative sugar factories in Maharashtra in 1982, since when more sugar co-operatives have been started in the less developed regions of Marathwada and Vidarbha. The major expansion of sugar co-operative factories took place in the 1970s, with the result that the co-operative sugar production in Maharashtra accounts for 32 per cent of the total white sugar production in India.[9] It is this rather unique agro-industrial development, concentrated largely in the Western Maharashtra, that has given rise to the sugar lobby in state politics [*Baviskar*, 1980; *Baru*, 1990; *Attwood*, 1993].

KULAK OR MIDDLE PEASANT MOVEMENT?

Opinions differ about the extent of the sugar lobby's influence on state-level politics and decision-making. Some believe that the sugar barons of Maharashtra run the state, and for all practical purposes sugar co-operatives have a decisive say in state politics [*Lele* 1981: 92–137; 1990: 177–206; *Dastane and Hardikar*, 1984: 70–72; *Baru*, 1990: 84–98]. Such a view of the hegemonic political influence of the lobby, shared widely in Maharashtra, is founded on the assumption that the lobby is cohesive, internally homogeneous and has a unity of purpose. Others who question this assumption [*Rosenthal*, 1972; *Carras*, 1972; *Carter*, 1975; *Baviskar*, 1980: 179–85] argue that the lobby's actual influence is considerable only in so far as patronage distribution and marginal benefits for small farmers and labourers in the form of dividends and jobs are concerned. However, at the level of state politics the sugar lobby hardly operates as a cohesive force. Rather, it is ridden with factional conflicts and competing interests, often mediated by caste, sub-caste, clan or other similar primordial identities.

Critics of the sugar lobby therefore argue that the lobby's actual political influence in state politics is very limited and tends to be vastly exaggerated. Power struggles between castes and classes within the lobby are so frequent that sugar barons appear to be more in positions of than actually in power. Tussles for leadership among individuals often push the 'sugar barons' to form alliances either within or even outside the dominant caste of Marathas [*Attwood*, 1985: 74–5; *Baviskar and Attwood*, 1984: 94–9]. Factions compete and contest for positions ranging from the Board of Directors of a particular co-operative sugar factory to the Chairmanship of a state-level federation of sugar co-operatives, or state or district-level co-operative banks. Comprising the most numerous landowning caste, the Marathas dominate the lobby. However, in order to acquire positions they frequently have to form alliances with other castes and have to accommodate the aspirations of small-scale sugarcane producers.[10] As individuals these farmers' leaders from co-operative sugar factories that constitute the sugar lobby have certainly acquired positions of influence which confer perks and patronage. However, the leader of the Shetkari Sanghatana, Sharad Joshi, claims that as a lobby they are powerless *vis-à-vis* the might of the industrial capitalist class which truly controls factories and also state politics.[11]

Although expressions such as 'sugar lobby' and '*kulak* lobby' are frequently used interchangeably, they do not necessarily coincide in terms of their social compass. The former, though politically powerful, represents a relatively small segment of sugarcane-growing small and big farmers. Through their membership of co-operative sugar factories, these farmers do maintain either direct or indirect ties with the 'sugar lobby' and its barons. To a certain extent the sugar lobby overlaps with the *kulak* lobby which, as a much broader category, consists of peasant producers who turn increasingly to cash-crop farming for market and profit, sugarane production being only one of their priorities, and that only in the perennially irrigated parts of Maharashtra. These farmers constitute one of several 'demand groups', to use the expression of the Rudolphs.[12] As effective mobilisers of unorganised interests these groups rely on *ad hoc* organisational means, and their mode of intervention is outside on the *maidans* rather than within the corridors of power. It is the demand group of agricultural producers, according to the Rudolphs, which has launched successful agitations and has emerged as a distinctive and powerful determinant of state policy in contemporary India.

In the early 1980s Omvedt was inclined to characterise the militant farmers' movement under the banner of Shetkari Sanghatana in Maharashtra as essentially a *kulak* movement, on the grounds that remunerative farm prices would benefit rich farmers more than small and medium level farmers.[13] This class characterisation of the Sanghatana movement has been challenged recently by Lenneberg [1988: 446–7] who raises the following crucial question: if rich peasants or farmers are already strongly represented in the decision-making bodies of government, both at the centre and at state level (ranging from co-operative institutions to village *panchayats* and so on), then 'why do they need or want to protest publicly' for remunerative farm prices [*Lenneberg*, 1988: 446–7]?

In response to her own question, Lenneberg argues that the farmers' movement in general, and Sanghatana in Maharashtra in particular, reflect the political consequences of rural development on the 'middle peasantry'.[14] To say that it is a rich farmers' movement is in her view a distortion, or a deliberate mystification that all 'sugarcane growers' are capitalist farmers. She is particularly critical of Omvedt, whose contention is that 83 per cent of sugarcane supplied to co-operative sugar factories in Maharashtra is grown on farms of two hectares or over. Therefore, an overwhelming majority of even small-scale sugarcane producers must be 'capitalist' farmers (since a five-acre sugarcane plot requires a massive, or at least substantial, capital investment for inputs – seeds, fertilisers, irrigation and so on).

Lenneberg believes that Omvedt's deductions are based on a mistaken interpretation of the agricultural census data of 1971. The former's contention is that, although most sugarcane cultivation is done on holdings over two hectares, the whole area of a holding is rarely devoted by a farmer to a single crop. Since no more than about 11 per cent of the state's cropped area is irrigated, only a small proportion of any holding will be suitable for growing sugarcane. Accordingly, cane is produced usually on between one-quarter and a third of the irrigated portion, and even that on a three to four-year rotation. Hence Omvedt's conclusion that 83 per cent of sugarcane cultivators are capitalist farmers is incorrect.[15]

The stronghold of Shetkari Sanghatana, the farmers' movement in Maharashtra, is primarily in the Nashik, Pune and Ahmednagar districts, where small holdings growing a variety of cash crops overwhelmingly outnumber large farms or landholdings. After a careful scrutiny of cropping patterns at the time of the Agricultural census 1976–77, Lenneberg [1988: 454–6] has pointed out that small and middle-level holdings accounted for between 45 and 60 per cent of the cultivated area under sugarcane, vegetables, wheat and rice in these districts. A major share of cash crops is grown on holdings of less than three hectares, which suggests to Lenneberg that remunerative prices for farm produce would benefit not only rich but also middle and poor peasants, a claim she has attempted to sustain by means of a small-scale survey of those attending the Sanghatana rally in Parbhani during February 1982.[16] Lenneberg has thus advanced a variant of the 'middle peasant' thesis in her explanation of the dynamics structuring the farmers' movement in Maharashtra.

A simple response to the 'middle peasant' thesis is also seen in the recent work of the Rudolphs [1987], who argue that small-scale agrarian producers (middle peasants, in other words) constitute a major demand group in contemporary Indian politics. These peasants have turned increasingly to cash-crop production and have been the principal beneficiaries of the extension of irrigation, the Green Revolution, and modern subsidised inputs channelled through state agencies. The Rudolphs prefer to designate these producers 'bullock-capitalists' rather than rich farmers or capitalist farmers; according to them 'bullock-capitalists' are 'cultivators who rely more on family labour and their own human capital than on wage workers and machines'.[17]

It is interesting to note that both the Rudolphs and Lenneberg have inverted the classical notion of 'middle peasant'. In doing so, the Rudolphs' 'bullock-capitalist'-as-a-middle-peasant comes closer to the

Chayanovian 'family farmer' in terms of self-exploitation and the drudgery of production, but also aspires to being the 'rich peasant' (*kulak*) of Lenin's class model of agrarian society: in short, a producer who attempts to make profits without necessarily employing wage labour.[18] Using very dated statistics (for 1954–72) on the changing pattern of landholdings, the Rudolphs have ventured to place all holders of 2.5 to 14.9 acres in their 'bullock-capitalist' category, believing that 'within this range independent, self-employed, self-funded agricultural producers can be (both) productive and prosperous'.[19] In describing their 'middle peasants' in this manner, the Rudolphs forget that it conflicts with their earlier characterisation of 'bullock-capitalists' as those who benefited from land reforms and the Green Revolution. The fact that small-holding 'beneficiaries' of the Green Revolution who depend substantially on state funding cannot be simultaneously characterised as 'self-funded' is a contradiction which escapes the Rudolphs. Obviously a problematic concept of 'bullock-capitalist' is introduced by them primarily to deny the polarisation/immiserisation thesis. However, their spectrum of 2.5 to 14.9 acres, indicating the boundaries of the 'bullock-capitalist' category without stipulating whether this refers to rainfed land, irrigated holdings, or both, is, in fact, too wide to be convincing. In no less a cavalier manner, Lenneberg has also redefined the 'middle peasant' concept. To her, middle peasants are not 'the self-sufficient, subsistence oriented middle peasant of the theoretical literature, but rather that middling group of small and medium sized landholders who participate actively in the market in an attempt to maximize their economic returns'.[20] Thus, both the Rudolphs and Lenneberg tend to superimpose *capitalist* characteristics on the 'middle peasant' and thus merge 'small/marginal' and 'middle' size landholders into one undifferentiated category.

Any attempt to differentiate agrarian classes and to characterise the new farmers' movement in class terms is for obvious reasons derided by Sharad Joshi, the ideologue of Shetkari Sanghatana. Such attempts are for him no more than a pious devotion to 'the texts' on the part of leftist intellectuals. In an interview with a newspaper correspondent (in 1980) Joshi is on record as saying: 'It is just a conspiracy on the part of the Indian elite to try and divide *Bharat* (in) terms of big, medium and small farmers. There is no line of contradiction between the big and the small with regard to remunerative prices.'[21]

All the same, he admits that big farmers have also been a part of the Sanghatana. But then a real *bagaitdar* – a capitalist farmer – in Maharashtra is for him one who has 20 hectares (about 50 acres) of irrigated landholding: only the latter could be called a '*kulak*' in the context of Maharashtra.[22] After the enactment of land-ceiling legislation, and the subsequent amendments thereon, however, such a definition of 'rich farmer' – *bagaitdar* in Maharashtra – is rather idealistic and unrealistic. Under the provisions of the ceiling legislation in Maharashtra no family of five members is permitted to have a landholding larger than 18 acres, if it is irrigated: the ceiling area for class (a) lands is 18 acres; for class (b) lands 27 acres; class (c) and (d) lands 36 acres, and class (e) lands 54 acres (see Government of Maharashtra [1976: 6428/28A and First Schedule, 6457]). Realising this, Joshi now admits that a peasant holding 18 acres or more of *bagaiti* (that is, wholly or partially irrigated) land, where two or more cash crops are possible, could be considered as a 'big' farmer. Joshi further clarifies that such a big farmer growing sugar cane on the entire plot of 18 acres would earn an income of about Rs 3000 (US$ 100) per month.[23] However, two points need to be noted here: first, Sharad Joshi is referring to the 'agricultual income' only and excludes non-agricultural incomes that a farmer's household earns from other sources. His main contention is that the income of a big farmer in the countryside does not exceed the monthly salary of a junior executive in a city, but such a contention is valid only if gross incomes are considered.[24] Taking into account the payment/non-payment of taxes, and also the differences in cost of living between the city and the countryside, big farmers as defined by Sharad Joshi can still be thought of as enjoying a reasonably comfortable living.

Secondly, and more importantly, in defining agrarian classes in general, and 'rich farmers' in particular, Sharad Joshi opts for a differentiating mechanism based on income, rather than ownership/*de facto* control over the means of production. For obvious reasons he is keen on notionally equating the class status of a big/rich farmer with that of a salaried executive in urban areas. The difficulty with this categorisation by Joshi is that it still remains vulnerable to the assumptions that structure agrarian class distinctions on an income basis. For instance, by leaving a plot of land fallow, not declaring it, or retaining property rights under a *benami* arrangement, a rich farmer may actually receive no income from his farm property, while at the same time retaining ownership/ control of substantial assets in land (a potential rather than an actual source of income). The same applies to a rich farmer who reinvests surpluses in acquiring new means of production: little or no disposable income accrues to him from land owned/operated, but he nevetheless continues to enjoy property rights (a substantial realisable asset) on which is based an expanding accumulation project. Similarly, ownership of land which generates little or no income *per se* may nevertheless confer great material and/or ideological power over workers in its vicinity (frequently interpreted as 'patronage'), a power that in turn generates other forms of non-monetised surplus: for example, the capacity to extract unpaid labour-time from sharecroppers or other potential/actual tenants. For these reasons, it is important to link up class power to the source of income (that is, means of production), rather than to the income *per se* as Sharad Joshi tends to do.[25]

From the data presented in Table 1, it is possible to offer some estimate of the size of the class of big farmers in Maharashtra. In 1980–81 some 300,000 belonged to the category of rich landholders, with an average landholding of 14.60 hectares. In the 1990–91 census the number of rich landholders had declined to 171,000 (see Table 2). However, this may be an underestimation of the actual number because the possibility of subdivision of large landholdings, due to the ceiling legislation, cannot be discounted altogether. The proportion of irrigated land to the total cropped area in Maharashtra (barring Greater Bombay) in 1960–61 was just 2.16 per cent; it increased to 11.82 per cent and 17.13 per cent in June 1982 and June 1990 respectively. In the Western Maharashtra, however, 21.53 per cent of the total cropped area was under irrigation in June 1990 [*Deshumkh*, 1992: 2–4], which is substantially higher than the proportion of irrigated land in other regions of Maharashtra. The latter figure is likely to be even higher in the case of the cropped area operated by large/rich landholders. That this class actively participates in Shetkari Sanghatana campaigns and agitations has been acknowledged by Sharad Joshi himself. The basic question remains one of how to determine the class character of a protest movement like that of the Shetkari Sanghatana. The fact that rich *bagaitdars*/big farmers are strongly represented among the leaders, active workers and supporters of the Sanghatana is not denied by even the 'insiders' of the movement. That they contribute a substantial part of the funds of the Sanghatana is also quite evident. Does all this therefore characterise the new farmers' movement in Maharashtra essentially as a rich farmers' movement? Conversely, Lenneberg and the Rudolphs have endeavoured to show that middle peasants – the 'bullock-capitalists' – aspiring to profit from cash-crop production are the main rank and file element of the Sanghatana. How justifiable would it be, therefore, to project the Sanghatana as a 'middle' peasant movement, as Lenneberg and the Rudolphs have tried to do?

ECONOMISTIC POPULISM OR CLASS?

Broadly speaking there are two ways of ascertaining the class character of a social/protest movement. First, the standardised method in empirical sociology would require 'head-counting', a procedure for empirical verification of the social background of leaders, activist-workers, participants and sympathiser/supporters of a movement. To the best of our knowledge, such a comprehensive survey has not been attempted so far by any researcher for any of the farmers' movements in India. Nor is it within the range of feasibility for an ongoing movement such as the Shetkari Sanghatana. Moreover, the limitations of empirical sociological methods and of inductive inferential logic are too well known to be elaborated on here. This methodology is likely to yield only an outsider's view of a complex reality. The intrinsic worth of this method is, of course, irrefutable, and indeed I am currently engaged in conducting just such a study of the Sanghatana leadership and worker/activists. Although incomplete, my data show that leaders, activists and participants of specific agitations launched by the Sanghatana, and those who laid down their lives for their cause, all came from every stratum of agrarian hierarchy in rural Maharashtra, although most of the leaders seemed to be rich farmers. Hence, induction would not take us very far in determining the class character of the movement. Moreover, statistics on the class status of those who participated in a specific agitation, or a demonstration, of those who were killed in repressive state action or arrested need not necessarily reflect the dominant character of the movement.

The other most obvious method of determining the class character of the movement is to look into its broader ideology and concrete demands, and then to deduce which class interests these tended to serve. The demand of Shetkari Sanghatana is for remunerative prices (support prices) linked to cost of production. Theoretically all farmers – small, medium or large – would benefit from remunerative prices and would have every reason to participate in some measure in support of such a protest movement. As some studies show, even small and medium holders are increasingly turning towards the production of cash crops and to generate a marketable surplus. They would benefit as much as rich farmers from higher prices. In fact, studies on Punjab and Haryana have revealed that even small and marginal holders are increasingly participating in production for the market [*Bhalla and Chadha*, 1983: 39–75]. Lenneberg has also shown similar tendencies of multiple-cropping among the small and medium level farmers in Maharashtra. The broader worldview of 'Bharat versus India' also suggests that better prices would leave profit margins to primary producers which, in turn, would lead to some capital formation. Once the growth process is reversed in favour of rural India, then a chain reaction in the form of better investment in agricultural improvement, rural industrialisation, employment generation, increased purchasing power and higher wages for agricultrual labour could be expected. The Shetkari Sanghatana's broader ideology has strong streaks of populism and, to the letter at least, its economistic ideology is not wedded to specific class interests as such.

If the Shetkari Sanghatana's ideology combines economism with populism, as we have argued all along, then it is necessary to distinguish between the characterisation of a social movement in *class* terms and the determination of its *dominant* class character. According to Laclau, populist ideology has four basic features: (a) its ingrained hostility towards the *status-quo*; (b) a mistrust of traditional politicians; (c) an appeal on the basis not of class identity but rather of 'the people' or 'the masses'; and (d) an anti-intellectual disposition. Usually movements with populist ideologies are produced by what Laclau calls 'asynchronism': that is, a stage of transition from traditional to an industrial society where two opposite tendencies coexist – one favouring change and the other stability.[26]

The populist mystification in the Shetkari Sanghatana ideology can be summed up thus: that there are no exploited or poor people in town (that is, India); that there are no 'exploiters' in villages (that is, Bharat); that all the villagers (implying agrarian producers) have essentially the same interest which assumes an economic form in the demand for remunerative prices for marketed produce; and that the 'Bharat'/'India' divide is absolute, a situation whereby village and town do not share any common interests.[27] The affinity of a movement's ideology with a particular dominant class has been stressed in orthodox Marxism (see, for example, Lefebvre [1968: 69–74], Bottomore [1985: 220–23]). Even if one takes an epiphenomenal view of ideology as a function of a determinate class position, it would still leave open the question as to why small and medium level farmers, who are less likely to benefit from remunerative farm prices, are drawn into the ideological ambit that is dominated by rich capitalist farmers, or *vice versa*. The mobilisation of farmers by the Shetkari Sanghatana has acquired most of the properties of a populist movement, in which there is a growing disjunction between class and ideology on the one hand, and the scope of political action such a movement arouses on the other.[28]

This is, however, not to suggest in analysing a populist movement that the quest for its 'dominant class character' ought to be abandoned. To make some headway in this quest, it is necessary to differentiate between 'class determination of superstructure' and the 'form of existence of classes at the level of these superstructures'. Orthodox Marxism views 'superstructures' as mere reflections of production, and makes class consciousness the basic constitutive moment of class (see, for example, Carver [1982: 21–57]; also Lukacs [1971: 1–26]). Gramsci, and following him Laclau, abandons this reductionist understanding of classes as antagonistic poles of production relations. Both argue that classes exist at the ideological and political level in a process of articulation, and not of reduction, and also that articulation requires non-class content – interpellations and contradictions that constitute the raw material on which class ideological practices operate. Thus, the ideology of the dominant class, precisely because it is dominant, interpellates not just the members of that class but also members of the dominated classes, and potential antagonism between the two is thereby neutralised. Hence, a populist discourse refers primarily to 'people' or 'masses', although class as an historical agent of the people's interests is very much present even in such movements.[29]

The big farmers with substantial holdings who have emerged in Maharashtra, as elsewhere in India, as a dominant class have done so largely as a result of the state policy for rural development; more than any other segment of rural society, land reforms and Green Revolution measures have substantially contributed to the emergence of this class. Why, therefore, do small and marginal as well as middle-level peasants and 'bullock-capitalists' also identify themselves with the movement when it is most likely to be of most benefit to big farmers? Does this, in fact, mean that a class of rich farmers has established its hegemony? An attempt to answer these questions can be made only by first looking into the basic properties of 'hegemony'.

As used by Gramsci, the concept of hegemony implies domination of a class

> not through any special organisation of force but because it is able to go beyond its narrow corporate interests, exert a moral and intellectual leadership and make compromises with a variety of allies who are unified in a social block – of forces [which] represent a basis of consent for a certain order in which the hegemony of the dominant class is created and recreated.[30]

The chief functionaries of the dominant class are what Gramsci called 'organic intellectuals', who mediate between social groups and the world of production and exercise influence both on the state and civil society as a whole. This is where Gramsci goes beyond the definition of the state as an instrument of a class rule as used by Marx, Engels and Lenin.[31]

Such an inter-class alliance, or unification of a social block, is best exemplified by the massive peasant mobilisation achieved by the Sanghatana. Since rich farmers manage to maintain a vertical solidarity with small and medium-level farmers through caste and other primordial links, their dominance as a class permeates the farmers' movement in Maharashtra, but not very visibly. Accordingly, participation in the movement and its agitations is not confined to the rich farmers alone. Whether this class has already become hegemonic in Maharashtra, or is trying to establish its hegemony, is a question which will continue to be debated. It can be argued, however, that the populist form of the Sanghatana's ideological discourse (and its programmatic demands for remunerative prices and so on) is in fact an assertion of that hegemony, and consequently the subjects of political action aroused by such an ideological interpellation cannot be identified simply in terms of class: in short, they symbolise the 'collective wills' which obey specifically formed laws of their own but in an indeterminate manner. Therefore, subjects which exist as a class at the *economic* level do not necessarily manifest this identity at the political livel. Hence, political action initiated by a populist movement draws into its ambit subjects from different class positions who, in ideological terms, realise a superior and transcendent unity.[32]

It is precisely this development of a superior unity that helps a populist movement to deflect roles – of middle and poor peasants – suggesting as Brass points out in the introduction

> the possibility of identities/interests not only unconnected with class but also those that can be shared by them (disadvantaged otherwise in economic terms) with rich peasants (we-are-all-the same by virtue of being rural-not-urban, peasants-not-workers, Hindus-not-Muslims, Maharashtrians-not-Gujaratis [or any other linguistic/cultural group], Indians-not-foreigners) that populism discharges for an emerging/aspiring agrarian bourgeoisie.

Undoubtedly then, at the constitutive moment of that transcendental unity, a class hegemony cloaked in a populist discourse is likely to be diffused.

The very fact that a seemingly dominant class has to raise a populist slogan to enlist support from subordinate, even exploited, classes suggests that dominance can be either partial or total. It is only when it is total dominance that a class can be considered to have attained 'hegemony', although a subsequent development of a genuinely non-class unity cannot be ruled out. It is relevant, therefore, that Balagopal [1987: 1545] talks of a 'provincial propertied class' in Maharashtra, and argues that in class terms the rich farmers form a continuity with the trader, the professional financier, and the property owner in urban areas, in spite of the fact that within their ranks numerous differences and contradictions exist. Significantly the upper sections of the rich landholders' class do not direct their movement against urban traders; rather their agitations are directed against the anonymous 'state'.[33]

> A typical family of this provincial propertied class has a landholding in its native village, cultivated by hired labour, *bataidar*, tenants or

> farm servants and supervised by the father or one son; business of various descriptions in towns – trade, hotels, cinemas, contracts – managed by other sons; and perhaps a young and bright child who is a doctor or engineer – or a professor. It is this class that is most vocal about injustice done to village.[34]

This characterisation of the provincial propertied class by Balagopal is similar to the one offered by Dandekar.[35] What is less convicing in Balagopal's thesis is the apparent paradox: it is precisely this class to which he attributes the divisions between India and Bharat. On this he observes: 'It is the success in incorporating a segment of Bharat into India that has led to the generation of this ideology of Bharat vs. India as an absolute divide'.[36] Although it sounds attractive, this argument does not really stand close scrutiny. If a propertied class has emerged at the provincial (Maharashtra) level either by unifying the interests of the rich landholders in rural areas with those of urban interests (which include industry as well), or by the absorption of the rich former into the latter, it is difficult to understand why one segment should then direct the movement against the other segment of that single, unified propertied class. Balagopal offers no explanation as to why one limb of the body should try to incapacitate the other.

CONCLUSION

It has been argued here that the Shetkari Sanghatana is a movement of that section of the rich farmers which is not absorbed into the class structure of urban/industrial India, and its hostility is therefore directed against the absorbed elements of that propertied class which have joined hands with the industrial bourgeoisie and share with the latter its position but not its power. This explains why Sharad Joshi and Sanghatana workers are critical of co-operative institutions in general, and the leadership of co-operative sugar factories – the sugar lobby – in particular: they are in a sense 'renegades'. The class of rich farmers, which is the sheet anchor of the Sanghatana, does not want to be absorbed into 'India' : rather, its world-view of 'Bharat' is that of opulence in rural areas, to be ushered in through the economism of 'remunerative prices' to the benefit of all sections of Bharat.

Such an ideology of economistic populism produces its own politics and political compulsions. The Sanghatana has wooed practically all political parties in electoral contests, and has taken an anti-establishment stand as well as a pro-establishment stand as the occasion demanded. It has shown an inclination to follow the highest bidder, regardless of the antecedents of political parties or their broader political ideologies. Within a democratic power structure, the politics of populism tend to breed political ambivalence, for which the dominant class that seeks hegemonic position in a movement pays the price. Because tangible gains can be obtained only through practical and pragmatic alliances for power, the Sanghatana's populism, though partially successful, is in the long run most likely to pave the way for class polarisation within as well as outside any movement. In short, the pursuit of power of itself prevents the (dominant) class character of the farmers' movement in Maharashtra from forever remaining hidden under the camouflage of the populist idioms of its ideological discourse.

NOTES

1. For example, I have argued this position in an earlier study [*Dhanagare*, 1983: Chs. V and VI].
2. Gupta [1991]; see also Dhanagare [1988].
3. This has been argued by an eminent observer like Girilal Jain, 'Peasant Agitation in Meerut', *The Times of India* (Bombay), 10 Feb. 1988, p.8.
4. See Omvedt [1980: 2041].
5. Omvedt [1980: 2041–2]
6. Nadkarni [1987: 76–7].
7. This has been stated emphatically by Sen [1962: 166–235]; Desai [1979: 126–42; 1985: 1–38], Mehta [1975: 70–71], and Patnaik [1990: 38–55].
8. For details, see Joshi [P.C.] [1978], Malviya [1955], Thorner [1956], Mehta [1975: 72–5], Rajan [1986] and Damle [1993].
9. See Attwood [1984: 40–41].
10. For example, see Baviskar [1980] and Attwood [1984: 74–5]. It needs to be clarified here that Lele in his earlier work [1981] was of the view that the dominant caste and class in rural Maharashtra, which owes its power to the network of sugar cooperative factories, enjoyed a hegemonic position in the state politics. In a later work, however, Lele [1990] modifies this position to concede that the dominant class power is attenuated considerably by caste factionalism and several other competing interests. Hence, what perpetuates is really the Maratha hegemony, and not class dominance of sugar lobby, in state politics.
11. Sharad Joshi, leader of Shetkari Sanghatana, for example, holds the latter view, and is critical of the 'sugar lobby' (personal discussion with Sharad Joshi).
12. Rudolph and Rudolph [1987: 15]
13. Omvedt [1980: 2041]. It must, however, be stated here in all fairness that Gail Omvedt, a sociologist trained at University of California, is a social activist of Scandinavian and American origin. She has lived and worked in rural Maharashtra (Kasegaon, District Sangli) since 1975. She was first associated with the Lal Nishan Party – a left-wing radical organisation which was initially quite critical of the economistic demands of the farmers' movement (led by Sharad Joshi). However, subsequently Omvedt started working with rural women in the Stri Mukti Sanghatana movement, and also with the Women's front of the Shetkari Sanghatana, perhaps because she found the latter akin to the former. This explains, at least to some extent why her assessment of the new farmers' movement changed through the 1980s. For Omvedt's background see the brief editorial introduction to an article by Omvedt [1992: 116].

14. Lenneberg [1988: 446–7].
15. Lenneberg [1988: 452–3].
16. Lenneberg [1988: 454–6].
17. Rudolph and Rudolph [1987: 2, 333].
18. For the Chayanovian concept of 'family farm', see Chayanov [1987: Chs.2–3], and for the explication of the rich peasant category in Lenin's model, see Lenin [1956: 177–8].
19. Rudolph and Rudolph [1987: 336–47]. Other supporters of this view (that the Sanghatana is a movement of the middle pleasantry) are Ray and Jha [1987: 2229–30].
20. Lenneberg [1988: 459].
21. Joshi [n.d.: 3].
22. See, for example, Joshi [1982: 86].
23. Joshi [1982: 86–8].
24. In comparing the two incomes, however, Joshi [n.d.: 2–3] ignores the fact that the monthly salary of a city-based junior executive is taxable, whereas the big farmers' agricultural income is not.
25. I owe this point to Tom Brass.
26. These characteristics of 'populism' as a form of ideological discourse have been taken from Laclau [1979: 147–9, 152–4].
27. The points have been summed up by Balagopal [1987].
28. I have argued this elsewhere (Dhanagare [1988: 30–31]) in the context of the BKU in Uttar Pradesh.
29. Laclau [1979: 160–67]. A number of issues, that arise from the way the interrelationship between populism and class is being posited here, need further elaboration and clarification. It is not unusual to encounter protest movements having some middle/poor peasant membership which nevertheless mobilise on the basis of rich peasants interests and objectives. How such an economic and political contradiction is sustained *ideologically* must in turn be related to the form/content of the mobilising discourse (= populism) which focuses on the presentation/projection of issues and identity in a non-class manner. For example, the role of gender, nature or nation/ethnicity can and in fact does enter into the neo-populist discourse of the new farmers' movement (see the contribution to this volume by Tom Brass). What is argued here is that the broad ideology of Shetkari Sanghatana has strong steaks of populism that is apparently not wedded to specific class interests as such. However, a growing disjunction between class and ideology (of populism) does not imply that class interests are either non-existent or inoperative in discourse and mass mobilisation of the populist variety. We argue that populism is not a class ideology in *substance*, but the *form* of discourse comes in handy for a dominant class aspiring to establish its hegemonic position. For that matter, any ideological form which, as Brass points out in the introduction,

    > Proclaims a common identity based on a notion of 'classlessness' (we-are-all-the-same) in a context where this is palpably not the case (we-are-not-all-the-same) cannot but reflect (and thus be to the benefit of) the class interests of those whose class difference would be revealed ... if such a notion of 'classlessness' was absent.

30. Bottomore [1985: 201–3].
31. See Gramsci [1976: 12–13]; Axelos [1976: 89–109], and also see Shils [1991: 12–13].
32. This explanation of hegemony as a class alliance is based on Mouffe [1979: 188–95].
33. Balagopal [1987: 1545].
34. Balagopal [1987: 1545].
35. See Mhatre [1983: 31–32].
36. Balagopal [1987: 1546].

REFERENCES

Attwood, D., 1984, 'Capital and the Transformation of Agrarian Class System: Sugar Production in India', in S.H. Rudolph *et al.* (eds.), *Agrarian Power and Agricultural Production*, Delhi: Oxford University Press.

Attwood, D., 1985, 'Peasants versus Capitalists in the Indian Sugar Industry. The Impact of the Irrigation Frontier', *Journal of Asian Studies*, Vol.XLV, No.1.

Attwood, D., 1993, *Raising Cane – The Political Economy of Sugar in Western Indian*, Delhi: Oxford University Press.

Axelos, Kostas, 1976, *Alienation, Praxis and Techne in the Thought of Karl Marx*, Austin, TX: University of Texas Press.

Balagopal, K., 1987, 'An Ideology for the Provincial Propertied Class', *Economic and Political Weekly*, Vol.21, Nos. 36–37.

Baru, Sanjay, 1990, *The Political Economy of Indian Sugar: State Intervention and Structural Change*, Delhi: Oxford University Press.

Baviskar, B.S., 1980, *The Politics of Development: Sugar Cooperatives in Rural Maharashtra*, Delhi: Oxford University Press.

Baviskar, B.S. and D. Attwood, 'Rural Cooperatives in India: A Comparative Analysis of Their Economic Survival and Social Impact', *Contributions to Indian Sociology* (N.S.), Vol.18, No.1.

Bhalla, G.S. and G.K. Chadha, 1983 *Green Revolution and the Small Peasant*, New Delhi: Concept Publishing Co.

Bottomore, Tom (ed.), 1985, *A Dictionary of Marxist Thought*, Oxford: Basil Blackwell.

Carras, Mary C., 1972, *The Dynamics of Indian Political Factions – A Study of District Councils in the State of Maharashtra*, Cambridge: University of Cambridge Press.

Carter, Anthony, 1975, *Elite Politics in Rural India: Political Alliances in Western Maharashtra*, Delhi: Vikas Publishing House.

Carver, Terrell, 1982, *Marx's Social Theory*, Oxford/New York: Oxford University Press.

Chayanov, A.V., 1987, *The Theory of Peasant Economy* (with an Introduction by Teodor Shanin), Delhi: Oxford University Press.

Damle, C.B., 1993, *Land Reforms and Changing Agrarian Relations*, Jaipur: Rawat Publications.

Dastane, S. and V. Hardikar, 1984 *Maharashtra 1984*, Pune: Ramchandra & Co.

Desai, A.R., 1979, *Rural India in Transition*, Bombay: Popular Prakashan.

Desai, A.R., 1985, *Changing Profile of Rural Society in India* (Publication No.7), Bombay: C.G. Shah Memorial Trust.

Deshmukh, B.T., 1992, 'Jalsinchan anushesh' (Backlog of Irrigation, in Marathi), *NUTA Bulletin* (Fortnightly Journal of Nagpur University Teachers' Association), Vol.17, No.1.

Dhagamwar, Vasudha, 1981, 'Problems of Implementing Agrarian Legislation in India', *Journal of the Indian Law Institute*, Vol.23 No.2.

Dhanagare, D.N., 1975, *Agrarian Movements and Gandhian Politics*, Agra: Agra University Institute of Social Sciences.

Dhanagare, D.N., 1983, *Peasant Movements in India, 1920–1950*, New Delhi: Oxford University Press.

Dhanagare, D.N., 1988, 'An Apoliticist Populism', *Seminar*, No.352.

Gill, Sucha Singh and K.C. Singhal, 1984, 'Punjab: Farmers' Agitation, Response to Development Crisis of Agriculture', *Economic and Political Weekly*, Vol.19, No.40.

Government of Maharashtra, 1976, *The Maharashtra Agricultural Lands (Ceiling on Holdings) Act, 1961*, Maharashtra Act No.XXVII of 1961 (as modified up to 5 October 1975), Bombay: The Director, Government Printing & Publications.

Government of Maharashtra, 1993, *Bulletin of Agricultural Census 1990–91*: *Maharashtra State*, Pune: Department of Agriculture.

Gramsci, A., 1976, *Selections from the Prison Notebooks*, London: Lawrence & Wishart.

Gupta, Dipankar, 1991, 'The Country-Town Nexus and Agrarian Mobilisation: Situating the Farmers' Movement in West U.P.', in K.L. Sharma and Dipankar Gupta (eds.), *Country Town Nexus*, Jaipur: Rawat.

Jain, Girilal, 1988, 'Peasant agitation in Meerut', *The Times of India* (Bombay), 10 Feb.

Joshi, P.C., 1978, *Land Reforms in India*, New Delhi: Allied.

Joshi, Sharad, 1982, *Shetkari Sanghatana – Vichar ani Karyapaddhati* (Thought and Method of Working, in Marathi, compiled by S. Mhatre), Alibag: Shetkari Sanghatana

Prakashan.
Joshi, Sharad, n.d., *Bharat Speaks Out*, Bombay: Build Documentation Centre.
Laclau, Ernesto, 1979, *Politics and Ideology in Marxist Theory*, London: Verso.
Lefebvre, Henri, 1968, *The Sociology of Marx*, New York: Pantheon Books.
Lele, Jayant, 1981, *Elite Pluralism and Class Rule: Political Development in Maharashtra India*, Toronto: University of Toronto Press.
Lele, Jayant, 1990, 'Caste, Class and Dominance: Political Mobilization in Maharashtra', in F.R. Frankel and M.S.A. Rao (eds.), *Dominance and State Power in Modern India, Decline of a Social Order* (Vol.II), Delhi: Oxford University Press.
Lenin, V.I., 1956, *The Development of Capitalism in Russia*, Moscow: Foreign Language Publishing House.
Lenneberg, C., 1988, 'Sharad Joshi and the Farmers: The Middle Peasant Lives!', *Pacific Affairs*, Vol. 61, No.3.
Lukacs, Georg, 1971, *History and Class Consciousness: Studies in Marxist Dialectics*, London: Merlin Press.
Malviya, H.D., 1955 *Land Reforms in India*, New Delhi: All India Congress Committee.
Mehta, Uday, 1975, *Agrarian Strategy in India*, Bombay: Vora & Co.
Mhatre, S. (ed.), 1983 *Shetkari Sanghataneche Artha – Shastra* (Economics of Shetkari Sanghatana, in Marathi), Alibag: Shetkari Prakashan, No.5.
Mouffe, C. (ed.), 1979, *Gramsci and Marxist Theory*, London: Routledge & Kegan Paul.
Nadkarni, M.V., 1987, *Farmers' Movements in India*, New Delhi: Allied Publishers.
Omvedt, Gail, 1980, 'Cane Farmers' Movement (Maharashtra – 1)', *Economic and Political Weekly*, Vol.15, No.49.
Omvedt, Gail, 1992, 'Green Earth, Women's Power, Human Liberation: Women in Peasant Movements in India', *Development Dialogue*, 1–2.
Patnaik, Utsa (ed.), 1990, *Agrarian Relations and Accumulation*, Bombay: Oxford University Press.
Rajan, M.A.S., 1986, *Land Reforms in Karnataka – An Account by a Participant Observer*, New Delhi: Hindustan Publishing Corporation.
Ray, K. and S.K. Jha, 1987, 'Assessing Shetkari Sanghatana', *Economic and Political Weekly*, Vol.22, No.51.
Rosenthal, D., 1972, 'Sources of District Congress Factionalism in Maharashtra', *Economic and Political Weekly*, Vol.7, No.34.
Rudolph, S.H. and L.I. Rudolph, 1987, *In Pursuit of Laxmi – The Political Economy of the Indian State*, Bombay: Orient Longman.
Sen, Bhawani, 1962 *Evolution of Agrarian Relations in India*, New Delhi: People's Publishing House.
Shils, Edward, 1991, 'The Virtue of Civil Society', *Government and Opposition*, Vol. 26 No.1.
Thorner, Daniel, 1956, *The Agrarian Prospect in India: Five Lectures on Land Reforms*, Delhi: University of Delhi Press.

New Farmers' Movements in India as Structural Response and Collective Identity Formation: The Cases of the Shetkari Sanghatana and the BKU

STAFFAN LINDBERG

INTRODUCTION

Beginning in the early 1970s the new farmers' movements, or farmers' agitations as they have often been called, have become some of the most important non-parliamentary political forces in various states of India. From one state to another farmers have formed organisations to struggle for better economic conditions in an increasingly commoditised agricultural economy. The main target is the state and its intervention in the agrarian economy, supplying many of the inputs and regulating the markets. Farmers demand lower prices on inputs like seeds, fertilisers, pesticides, lower tariffs on electricity and water, lower taxes, and debt relief. Likewise they demand higher prices for their products of grains, cash-crops, vegetables, milk and so on. 'Farming is not remunerative after the coming of the Green Revolution' is their message, and they claim that the calculations of the Agricultural Price Commission (APC) have not reflected the real costs involved. They also hold that terms of trade between industry and agriculture is increasingly developing in favour of industry and against agriculture.[1]

The movements, which started in Tamil Nadu and Punjab in the early 1970s, later spread to Karnataka, Maharashtra, Gujarat, Haryana, Uttar Pradesh (UP) and some regions in neighbouring states. Today the most important movements are the Shetkari Sanghatana, in Maharashtra, led by Sharad Joshi, and the Bharatiya Kisan Union (BKU) in Western Uttar Pradesh, led by Mahendra Singh Tikait. The Punjab BKU, though very much affected by the conflict in the state, is also fairly strong. The movements in Tamil Nadu and Karnataka were very strong in the 1970s and early 1980s, but have now become fairly weak.

Staffan Lindberg, Department of Sociology, University of Lund, Box 114, 221 00 Lund, Sweden. This article is based on a research project on 'The New Peasant Movements in India' at the Department of Sociology, University of Lund, Sweden. It has received financial support from SAREC, Stockholm and NIAS, Copenhagen. Thanks are due to Tom Brass for his comments and suggestions.

The movements have strong charismatic leaders like, for example, Sharad Joshi and Mahendra Singh Tikait. Though very different in character and style – Joshi is a retired UN official, while Tikait is a Jat peasant and clan leader in Uttar Pradesh – these leaders formulate much of the analysis and take the lead in agitations and other actions. Equally important is the role of intellectuals at various levels, from the academy to the village, who develop the everyday discourse of the movement and defend it against attacks from the outside.

Before the outbreak of communal violence on a large scale in the late 1980s, the peasant unions staged agitations reminiscent of the classic civil disobedience movement. Demonstrations (*dharnas, gheraos*) were truly massive, involving lakhs of peasants and lasting for many days. Roads and railways were blocked (*rasta rokko*), and villages were closed to government officials and politicians (*gavband*). In some states stocks of produce (onions, cotton, tobacco) were withheld from the market, causing steep price rises. The latter type of agitation has, for example, been common in Maharashtra under Sharad Joshi's leadership. Moreover, in some states peasants have refused to pay tax arrears and electricity bills, or to pay interest and amortisation on loans from banks and credit cooperatives. Of late (1990–92), however, the unions have refrained from these types of agitation. One reason for this, according to Sharad Joshi, is that the methods used in the 1970s and 1980s have become ineffective as they have been taken over by the communal forces. He says that 'We were prepared to die one by one for our cause, but they are sending thousands to death. Violence dominates the political scene today, and there is less room for our type of confrontation with the state.'

The central message is the simple and powerful slogan formulated by Sharad Joshi: *Bharat against India*! *Bharat* is the indigenous name for India, with positive connotations, while *India* is the westernised name, symbolising exploitation. They stand for the rural and the urban-industrial populations respectively. On this point Joshi has observed (interview, March 1989): 'The real contradiction is not in the village, not between big peasants and small, not between landowners and landless, but between the agrarian population as a whole and the rest of the society.' Another peasant leader, Gujarat's Bipin Desai, expresses it in the following way:

> The inner core is different ... our struggle is not for issues like electricity tariff or land legislation. We have a wider vision. The whole of the rural economy should be changed. It should not be a field for exploitation as it has been since British rule, a generating centre for the national economy. The surplus should remain in the

> villages, and from this the appropriate growth of village-based industries and development should be made rather than exploiting the villages to create a surplus for urban-based industries which only create unemployment and poverty (quoted by Omvedt [1989: 8–9]).

For the supporters of the movements, the veracity of such pronouncements is confirmed on a daily basis in the form of the opulent living standards of the urban middle classes displayed in or referred to by the media (television, radio and the press). As Mahendra Singh Tikait put it after one of his visits to Delhi: 'Let's talk about land reforms when there is a ceiling on urban property – look at those skyscrapers!'

Union and state governments have been strongly affected by the massive political and economic agitations and demonstrations. The most common reaction has been repression by the police and military, and the peasant movements now count their martyrs in hundreds. Since the farmers are too powerful to be crushed in this manner, such policies have also been combined with negotiations and concessions of a temporary duration.[2] There are strong indications that the farmers' movements played an important role in the overthrow of the Rajiv Gandhi government in the 1989 general elections. In Uttar Pradesh and Haryana, for example, the BKU worked decisively for the National Front opposition, which won an almost complete victory over the Congress. The National Front government later tried to carry out a new policy, involving the moratorium of debts up to Rs 10,000 and the preparation of a new agricultural policy, still incomplete when the government fell in early 1991. There are, however, also many other signs that today almost all political parties have been affected by farmers' agitations, at least on the level of rhetoric. When the new Congress government tried to increase fertiliser prices 40 per cent in July 1991, there was such massive opposition from all political parties that the proposal had to be changed drastically. Similarly, when the same government decided to import wheat in 1992 to keep prices down, it also resulted in countrywide protests by the peasant movements and opposition parties (cf. Lenneberg [1988: 451–2]).

How are we to understand these farmers' movements? Are they related to the so-called 'new social movements', which have emerged globally and especially in the Third World over the last two decades? In India the new farmers' movements have been seen by some observers [*Omvedt*, 1992a] as part of a new wave of movements, which also includes environmental, women's and Dalit's movements. What is the substance of this claim? On a more general level it is important to ask how the new farmers' movements are related to the agrarian and overall economy, to the class structure of rural society, and also to the ideological and political formations in contemporary India. Finally, do we deal with one homogeneous movement, or many different regional movements which differ in important respects?

STUDYING SOCIAL MOVEMENTS – STRUCTURES AND COLLECTIVE ACTION

Social movements are usually defined as organised groups of people mobilised from below in pursuit of goals that challenge the established order, especially that of states and of political parties running of the state. Thus, by definition, social movements are autonomous of the state and their goal is to change society or parts of it or other relations crucial to them. As such, social movements are based on and express social and other conflicts. They differ from local protest groups by being more permanent and also by their potential to appeal to groups of people beyond a particular locality.

It is important to note that this definition represents my perspective in studying the farmers' movements as social movements. It is far from the only possible way. It is, in fact, hard to find a commonly agreed upon definition of social movements. Different forms of collective action, mobilisation from below, mobilisation from above, in various historical contexts (working class, peasant, or fascist movements) have all been called social movements. The definition varies over time depending on who says what in relation to what movement [*Heberle*, 1968: 438–44]. A very early and lasting perspective, however, links the definition to the movements of the industrial working class, which is also the perspective adopted here. A recent development is the definition of so-called new social movements emerging gradually from the 1950s with the civil rights movement, through the student movements, to the women's and environmental movements in the 1970s. Here, a contrast is constructed between 'modernist' and 'postmodernist' movements, in which the latter are said to represent 'the transcendence of "material" or industrial values by a new set of 'postmaterial values' [*Eyerman and Jamison*, 1991: 7]. We will briefly return to this issue in the conclusion of the article.

Social movements are also analysed in quite different ways by various sociologists and historians. One approach is that of the *resource-mobilisation* theorists: for example, the work of Tilly [1975, 1978], Oberschall [1973] and Jenkins [1983]. They concentrate on how movements are able to organise social and material resources and 'stress such "objective" variables as organization, interests, resources, opportunities, and strategies to account for large scale mobilization' [*Cohen*, 1985: 674]. They also seem to 'share' the following assumptions:

(1) Social movements must be understood in terms of a conflict model of collective action.
(2) There is no fundamental difference between institutional and non-institutional collective action.
(3) Both entail conflicts of interest built into institutionalised power relations.
(4) Collective action involves the rational pursuit of interests by groups.
(5) Goals and grievances are permanent products of power relations and cannot account for the formation of movements.
(6) This depends instead on changes in resources, organisation, and opportunities for collective action.
(7) Success is evidenced by the recognition of the group as a political actor or by increased material benefits.
(8) Mobilisation involves large-scale, special-purpose, bureaucratic, formal organisations [*ibid*: 675].

Looking at many typical works within this 'paradigm' one is struck by the fact that they are often concerned with historical movements. In such cases, where the outcome of the movement is known or thought to be known (though it may be understood quite differently from various vantage points), it is hardly surprising that the study of social structures and social change takes precedence over the internal characteristics of a movement. But what about movements that are still growing, and where the outcome is far from clear? We are thinking of movements that do not look like those encountered before, with new types of members, new and perhaps diffuse goals, and with a new definition of the contradictions on which they act.

A Danish political scientist, Thomas Hansen [1991: 45 ff.], has recently written on the shortcomings of going from forms and contents of social structures, structural changes, and social processes to the explanation of collective organisation and action. In such schemes, he claims, analytical levels are transformed into a determinant hierarchy of explanation where collective action is seen as an outcome of the structural changes and social processes, not as a co-determinant of these. Besides ascribing a functional determinacy in a hierarchical manner to social systems, it also tends to leave out the very 'process whereby a social contradiction is turned into a collective action and social change' [1991: 50, my translation]. In a similar manner Hansen also criticises various forms of cultural analysis of social movements, in which cultural continuity is made the major explanatory variable. Culture is not static but part of an ongoing process of change: movements always create their own culture, whether traditional, modern or indeed something else [*Hansen*, 1991: 51–4].

If we want to understand new processes of collective identity formation and action, therefore, we have to go about in a manner which is different from the usual one of making suppositions about the correspondence of movements and transformations in the social structure. We have instead to go into the movements themselves, and examine them in terms of a specific combination of political action, cultural and ideological interpretations, and organisational forms [*Hansen*, 1991: 54–9], and to apply a process-oriented perspective in which movements and societies are seen as constantly moving along a continuum of change and institutionalisation [*Laclau*, 1990]. Social movements are continuously working on and articulating existing social relations and cultural interpretations. They are not just expressions or representations of given classes or social groups or cultural configurations, they also create social conflicts (out of a number of existing or possible contradictions), social relations and culture in a dialectical way. Looking closer at social movements one finds that they are composite phenomena comprising many social relations, world-views and identities, about which there is constant negotiation. In short, they are volatile and changeable structures [*Hansen*, 1991: 60]. It is precisely this potential on the part of social movements to create something new that should be taken seriously. The alternative is to allow traditional movements to 'weigh like a nightmare' on our brains, in which case we will be unable to perceive of the germs of change that new movements may carry.[3]

This emphasis on studying open-ended processes of collective identity formation and action should not be taken to mean that the social structures and social contradictions, in which these processes take place, are equally open-ended. Marx's [1967: 120] classical contention still holds: 'Men make their own history, but they do not make it just as they please; they do not make it under circumstances chosen by themselves, but under circumstances directly encountered, given and transmitted from the past.' What is stressed here, therefore, is only that these circumstances can be defined in more than one way, and also changed in more than one way. Far from relapsing into an idealistic 'everything-is-possible' position, this is to realise only that 'nothing is historically necessary.' The two perspectives outlined above, could be expressed as a contrast between emphasising social structure on the one hand and social interaction on the other. In this study we will attempt to apply both perspectives in order to see what kind of insights can be gained from such a combination into the formation and dynamics of the new farmers' movements.[4]

NEW FARMERS' MOVEMENTS: A STRUCTURALIST INTERPRETATION

A look at the history of peasant movements in India brings out an important feature, which can be interpreted as a historical shift in the patterns of alliance. This shift can be summarised in the replacement of one slogan, 'Land to the tiller!', by another, 'Remunerative prices!'.

'Land to the tiller!' is the slogan of a peasants' movement organised around the major contradiction in a landlord-dominated, class-divided agrarian society – the contradiction between landed and non-landed groups. The demands of a movement acting on this contradiction can be varied, from land reform to rent reduction, and a place to stay (that is, the demand for houseplots). Since Independence, peasant movements in India have primarily been of this 'land-to-the-tiller' type: they have organised land-hungry peasants – that is landless labourers, small tenants, and poor peasants are pre-dominant in the mass base.[5] Landed groups had to form counter-organisations, both in order to defend their interests and in order to wean off small and middle peasants[6] from the influence of such radical movements.[7]

Since the late 1970s, however, the rural political scene in India has been dominated by another type of movement, acting on another contradiction. These movements did not, of course, suddenly spring into existence: many of them are as old as organisations which have experienced renewed activities and recruitment.

These 'remunerative-prices' movements have acted not just on the issue of the price of agricultural produce but also on the price of inputs like fertilisers, electricity, and terms of credit from state-owned or state-sponsored financial institutions. Accordingly, it might be said that these 'new' movements articulate interests which are common to a *commodity-producing peasantry*, or to be more precise, a peasantry which is not only producing commodities but which is also using commodities as inputs. That is, movements based on a peasant economy in which the process of reproduction has to a certain extent been commoditised. As a consequence, the terms of trade between the commodities produced and those consumed (productively or not) have become an essential determinant of the level of reproduction. The peasantry is now linked to a market where to a significant degree price formation is influenced by the state, which in effect regulates the conditions of reproduction of the peasantry. The contradiction on which the 'new' peasant movements act is therefore one *between the state and the peasantry*: it is the state which is seen as the main target of agitation, not the local landlords as in the traditional type of peasant movement.[8]

The relation between the two contradictions outlined above is an interesting one: if the 'old' peasant movements primarily acted on the contradiction between landed and land-hungry groups, and if the 'new' movements act on that between the state and the peasantry, then what is the interrelationship between the two?

When the 'new' movements first emerged in the late 1970s, many observers (see for example Omvedt [1980; 1993]) – including myself – regarded them as 'rich peasants' movements'; that is, the kind of organisation for the defence of landed groups that was mentioned above.[9] However, this interpretation seems to be wrong on two counts. First, it underestimates the mass base of the new movements – their mass base apparently being the middle peasantry – and, second, it also underestimates the degree of structural transformation brought about in Indian agriculture since Independence. One can argue that this transformation has defused some of the dynamite in the land question, and enhanced the level of commoditisation (cf. Athreya, Djurfeldt and Lindberg [1990: 314–15]), thereby bringing about a historical shift in the patterns of political alliances among the peasantry.[10]

These points can be illustrated with data from two Panchayat Unions in Tiruchy District in Tamil Nadu where the two major ecotypes in Tamil Nadu agriculture are represented: that is, what could be called a wet and a dry ecotype (cf. Athreya *et al.* [1990]). In the wet ecotype, land concentration is heavy, sharecropping is widespread, and the level of proletarianisation is high. In the dry area, on the other hand, the distribution of land is much less skewed, the middle peasantry is numerically dominant, and proletarianisation is low. In both areas, the level of commoditisation is high, and it has increased in recent years, as a consequence of the so-called Green Revolution. The impact has been most dramatic in the dry area, where peasants have invested on a grand scale in wells and pumpsets, financed by credit from official institutions.

The history of the peasant movements in this area also fits into the pattern outlined above: until recently peasant mobilisation was mainly a characteristic of the wet area, where the sharecroppers have been active since Independence in fighting for security of tenure and rent reduction, a struggle which to a certain extent also has been successful. The landless labourers have been less active than in other parts of the Tanjore delta, probably because they have better employment opportunities here than anywhere else in Tamil Nadu (due to the extremely high cropping intensity in the area). Moreover, labour gangs function as a kind of *proto-unions*, securing comparatively good wages for their members, both compared to labourers not organised in gangs and compared to other areas in the state (cf. Athreya *et al.* [1990: Ch. 4]).

In 1979/80 this 'old' movement was not very active in the area, but the 'new' movements were there,[11] and the level of activity struck us as higher in the dry area than in the wet one. This impression is also borne out by our survey data, although the difference between the two ecotypes is less than we had expected (see Table 1 below). The table also shows a correlation between membership and class, and although neither very strong nor very neat, it roughly confirms the pattern outlined above: the middle peasantry have rates of membership which are higher than the average in both areas, while the poor peasants rarely are members. In the dry area the capitalist farmers have the highest rates of membership, but since they are numerically weak as a category, this does not contradict the statement that the middle peasantry makes up the mass base of the movement.

TABLE 1
RATES OF MEMBERSHIP IN FARMERS' ASSOCIATION BY ECOTYPE AND CLASS (OWN SURVEY DATA)

Class:	Ecotype: Wet area: % households	% members	Dry area: % households	% members
Landless agricultural labourers	30	0	16	0
Poor peasants	19	6	28	4
Middle peasants	21	20	46	30
Rich peasants	6	16	4	0*
Capitalist farmers	5	2	0	64
Landlords	3	0	0	-
Others	16	25	6	17
Total (all households)		11		17
Total (farming households)		15		20

Note: * *This estimate is uncertain since it builds only on four sample cases.*

To explain this influx of middle peasants into a movement that appears to so many observers as a rich peasant movement, one has to go into the determinants of the class structure and the character of the division of the peasantry into different classes.

An important feature of the middle peasantry, as we have defined them, is that they are a divided group in both the wet and the dry area. The middle peasantry proper, that is, those who reproduce themselves fully and autonomously, thanks to their own labour power, comprise only a small group (24 per cent of all middle peasants in the wet area and nine per cent in the dry area). The majority of the middle peasants are pressed below this level of autonomous reproduction and have to turn to non-farm sources for their reproduction. How should one interpret this? Let me quote from the previous work:

> One way to interpret this finding is to say that there is no middle peasantry to speak of in any of the areas, except those that we have labelled upper middle peasants. We prefer another interpretation: there is a sizeable middle peasantry, especially in the dry area, but it is squeezed so hard that few of them can subsist only on their farming.
>
> The squeeze is exerted by market forces, and is made effective by the significant inroads of commoditization both into consumption and into farm reproduction. In the process the middle peasantry has become more vulnerable to unfavourable fluctuations in the prices paid for consumer goods and farm inputs, and prices received for labour hired out.
>
> In this interpretation, price and market conditions exert a profound influence on the agrarian class structure. But the poor peasants are relatively less influenced by movements in the price of farm produce, since they are not commodity producers to any significant degree. They are, however, affected by market forces to the extent that they use purchased inputs and to the extent that prices of industrial consumer goods affect the real value of the wages they earn from hiring-out. There is, however, a certain fluidity in the class structure, between the different types of middle peasants and even between the middle and the rich peasantry, which is due to the movement of the prices. A more favourable relation between prices received and prices paid might have resulted in more rich and upper middle peasant households. Seasonal and yearly variations in yield induce a similar fluidity.
>
> This fluidity might seem alien to the concept of class, since class has some robust and viscous connotations. A critical reader may conclude from this lack of viscosity that we have not managed to capture the class structure in our area. We prefer another interpretation, namely, that the agrarian class structure is quite fluid, except at the extreme poles ....
>
> The price-induced fluidity in the class structure brings to focus the

> role of the state in the formation of the agrarian class structure. Agricultural prices, both on the output and the input side are to a significant extent administered prices, and thus there is a political element hidden behind the 'invisible hand' of the market [*Athreya et al.*, 1990: 231–2].

It is precisely the contradiction between the commodity producing peasantry and the state over policies affecting the terms of trade between agriculture and industry which potentially unites the middle and rich peasantry with capitalist farmers in the farmers' movements. Moreover, recent studies of agrarian structure and change in India confirm the view that the middle peasants or the family farmers have not been marginalised by the Green Revolution, as predicted by many theorists (see, for example, Harriss [1981], Cain [1981], Attwood [1979], Rao [1972], and Bhalla [1977]). The size and composition of the middle peasantry may vary from region to region, but together with the rich peasants, they make up a considerable part of the agrarian households.[12]

This argument should not be taken to mean that one contradiction has been replaced by another, but that the two contradictions are both actively influencing the shape of the peasants' movements in India today. The land question, as is well known, remains conflict ridden and unresolved in most parts of rural India. Moreover, the sharp contradiction that exists in most areas between agricultural wage labourers and mostly rich peasants and capitalist farmers adds a third important dimension to this 'drama'. Since agricultural wage labour is also supplied by poor and middle peasants, one would expect them to be unstable partners in the alliance mobilised by the farmers' unions [*Athreya et al.*, 1990: 315].

This 'contradiction between contradictions' can perhaps also explain the heterogeneous nature of the peasant movements in India, from the Maoist-inspired uprisings in remote so-called tribal areas,[13] to the onion-growers' protests against unremunerative prices in Maharashtra. To study how movements based on these various 'contradictions' have developed over the past two decades and how they have related to each other, should therefore be an important contribution to the understanding of what the future holds in store for the Indian peasantry and agricultural labourers. In this article, however, the study is limited to some aspects of the new farmers' movements.

AGRARIANISM?

It is tempting to see the farmers' agitations as expressing the type of broad social contradiction, that under certain conditions (the introduction of industrial inputs into small-scale agriculture, combined with administered pricing) and in certain contexts (North America and Western Europe) has become generalised with the commodisation of peasant agriculture. In such situations, the cleavage tends to be one between the peasantry as a whole and the state/urban-industrial interests. As the historical experience from the industrialised countries shows, this is potentially a very stable and generalised social contradiction, which involves the dilemma of an industrialising economy: peasants are expected to produce most of the surplus that is required as investment for industry, while they are left a diminishing role in the economy and the society. The state has often acted as the coordinator of these agrarian policies, implying, in many instances, that the old landlord class has lost much of its previous domination over the state. It is also well known that these changes have led to a broad agrarian mobilisation in the western countries, ranging from 'agrarianism' in the USA to associations, co-operatives, and political parties in the Scandinavian countries.[14]

Are we witnessing the same thing in India now? Rudolph and Rudolph [1987: 334] hold this view: 'When agrarian politics became national in the 1970s and early 1980s, it was not the agrarian radicalism of the rural poor but the demand of independent cultivators and capitalist farmers ["bullock capitalists"] for remunerative prices that rallied agricultural producers generally in support of the new agrarianism.' It is, however, clear that this type of development is not automatically bound to happen in India or the Third World as a whole. Neither is it certain that the economic conditions of the peasants in India or elsewhere in Asia, Africa or Latin America can develop in such a way that the external contradictions to the state and the industrial economy become more important as a basis for mobilisation than the internal differences and contradictions between agrarian classes. Perhaps it is not a coincidence that the new peasant movements in India have had their first strong bases in the dry rainfed areas (the Deccan) or irrigated tracts, where a middle peasantry dominates, while the peasantry in those river-irrigated deltas, which are dominated by big landlords and capitalist farmers, have shown much less interest. In areas dominated by an internal class polarisation of the latter kind, types of politics and alliances other than that practised by the new farmers' movements may still hold sway.

However, the strength of the new movements and the reactions to them by the state may in fact alter this balance between agrarian classes. States do not just react to classes, they may also have a strong impact on class formation itself:

> while states can be shown to be shaped, produced, and determined by class interests, and action, they have also produced class struc-

> tures, transformed them or made them disappear, as when a bourgeoisie or a peasantry has been created by deliberate state policy ... Both of the possible routes of determination must be considered [*Shanin*, 1982: 316].

If the emerging class of middle and rich peasants, as manifested by the new farmers' movements, can bargain successfully with 'the components of the predominantly urban organized economy and society', they may become the 'hegemonic agrarian class' in India [*Rudolph and Rudolph*, 1987: 342]. In this scenario, state policy could then further strengthen the position of these sections of the peasantry *vis-à-vis* other agrarian classes, as has been the case in Western Europe and North America during the last hundred years.

What are the prospects for such a development in India? An attempt to interpret the new farmers' movements with regard to development theory may offer some clues. However, before trying to answer that question, it is necessary to consider the actual mobilisations and collective actions of regionally-based farmers' movements.

SOCIAL MOVEMENTS: COLLECTIVE IDENTITY AND ACTION

Above we have sketched an interpretation of the context of the political economy and class conflicts in which the new farmers' movements have emerged, as well as some current ideas of its potential effects. Let us now turn to an interactionist approach to these movements.

Melucci [1985: 794–5] has suggested that a social movement is

> a form of collective action (a) based on solidarity, (b) carrying on a conflict, (c) breaking the limits of the system in which action occurs ... conflict [is] a relationship between opposed actors fighting for the same resources, to which both give value. Solidarity is the capability of an actor to share a collective identity, that is, the capability of recognizing and being recognized as part of the same system of social relationships. Limits of a system indicate the range of variations tolerated within its existing structure. A breaking of these limits pushes a system beyond the acceptable range of variations.[15]

According to Melucci [1992: 243], the analysis 'should focus on the processes through which actors produce an interactive and shared definition of the goals of their action, studying the fields upon which such action takes place'. He clarifies:

> To speak of goals implies putting accent on ends and on meaning. The notion of a field refers to the possibilities and limits within which goals are pursued; the definition of these goals is something which actors co-produce and is thus neither a representation nor a reflection of structural determinants. This entire process is an active relational process, a process which for lack of better term I call 'collective identity'. Collective identity is an achieved definition of a situation, constructed and negotiated through the constitution of social networks which then connect the members of a group or movement. This process of definition implies the presence of cognitive frames, of dense interactions, of emotional and affective exchanges. What holds individuals together as a 'we' can never be completely translated into the logic of means-ends calculation, or political rationality, but always carries with it margins of non-negotiability in the reasons for and ways of acting together. The important question then becomes how 'we' becomes we. How and why do social aggregates arrive at a definition of themselves as a collective, capable of acting as a group? [*Melucci*, 1992: 243–41].

This approach implies studying how individuals get involved in collective action, how actors construct collective action and unity, and how one can get at the meaning produced out of heterogeneity and pluralism. Melucci suggests that a social movement is the product of continued tensions, negotiations and cognitive processes within a 'multipolar action system' or a 'composite action system', in which widely differing means, ends and forms of solidarity and organisation converge in a more or less stable manner. Instead of studying the product as such (the movement) one should study the process of interaction, negotiation, conflict and compromise among a variety of different actors, which either succeed or fail to produce the unity of collective identity of movements. We are concerned here with networks, or sub-networks, which constitute the submerged reality of movements, before, during and after visible events. 'Networks are the small groups, submerged in everyday life, which require a personal involvement and produce alternative frameworks of meaning. They are networks of meanings, or sign, which put into practice the alternative meanings, which they produce and reproduce. The form of the movement is thus itself a message' [*Melucci*, 1989: 70].

Besides social interaction there is another dimension which is crucial to the formation of social movements. As has been emphasised by Eyerman and Jamison [1991] in a recent contribution to the field of movement studies, a central place in identity formation must be given to knowledge or what can also be called cultural renovation, especially the development of new knowledge about the world, social and material relations, and the political and cultural modes of organisation. In this way intellectuals and intellectual activity are given an important role in identity formation and the rise of social movements. By interpreting the world, by anticipating things, and by formulating new types of knowledge and values based on science, cultural traditions, and so on and spreading this knowledge, they represent an important social force, which acts upon the social formation of new social movements. Utopian and experimental as they may often seem, they nevertheless act upon their contemporary milieu in such a way that not only are there chances that they may give rise to new movements based on these understandings, but they also help to bring about social and cultural conditions conducive to the emergence of new movements. Eyerman and Jamison's book gives several interesting examples of such cognitive processes.

However, this perspective easily leads to the idea that social movements are created by great men or women. It is important to stress that the cognitive praxis and its interaction with social movements, takes place not in the corridors of cultural institutions or learned academies but in a concrete social and historical world that we call society. A situation where economic, political and cultural structures already exist, where classes and cultural groups are already constituted and involved in processes of reproducing and/or changing that very world. It is when the cognitive praxis 'meets' the real world, or the way in which existing institutions and groups react to the emergence and actions of new social movements and their cultural renovation, that the real dynamic of social movements is generated. Eyerman and Jamison have stressed the role of the political culture and mass media in this dynamic: successful movements must define their own political space outside of the established political culture, and they must counteract or adjust in their own way to the definitions clamped on them by the mass media and to the way these mass media create knowledge in the contemporary world.

Central to the cognitive dimension is a sociology of knowledge, which can analyse the ways in which knowledge is constructed. It is the range of epistemological possibilities or opportunities which characterises different social actors which must be understood. How is it, for example, that the same classes of peasants in different parts of India can define the world so differently? In West Bengal and Kerala, under the mobilisation and influence of the communist parties, peasants understand society quite differently from the way peasants, under the mobilisation and influence of the farmers' movements in Maharashtra and Uttar Pradesh understand a very similar reality.[16] Standard views on history, political conditions and cultural and ideological dominance can provide some clues to the analysis, but the full answer to this question is not given by theory but by concrete studies of structures, processes, interaction and the construction of meaning.

The sociological imagination thus needs both an insight into how collective identities are formed and into the social forces making those identities possible. To accomplish that one needs to draw not on one theoretical tradition alone, but on a plurality of traditions. In the following sections we will take a look at what are currently the most active farmers' movements: the Shetkari Sanghatana in Maharashtra, and the Bharatiya Kisan Union in Uttar Pradesh.

CASE STUDY I: SHETKARI SANGHATANA IN MAHARASHTRA[17]

This is the story of Maiah, a 40-year-old woman activist, who had worked as a schoolteacher in Western Maharashtra for many years:

> We went to Yavatmal district in 1980, and at that time we went there for the landless labourers. We had read about their situation. Even my grandfather was a landlord, and we had seen that the exploitation of the labourers gives nothing to them, and how the landlords squeeze them. We had a sort of communist theory that the landlords are the exploiters.
>
> So we went there to work against farmers and for the cause of the labourers. For two years we were working in about 35 villages on the landless labourers' cause, the minimum wages act and all this. All the farmers were against us, that is, me and my husband, threatening to kill us. They said 'You are the ones that have come and now we have to give extra wages.'
>
> While we were doing that work I myself had to buy a small piece of land. It was a great struggle for us just to live in the villages. Whatever extra room there was, was only with the landlords, and they said 'No, no, you don't stay here.' And there was no house to live in, so we decided to buy a small patch of land so that we can build our own hut. I purchased according to the government act and all that. One must have at least three acres, so we purchased near about 5 acres of land.
>
> From whom did I purchase this land? He had 30 acres of land. When I went to his house and saw what he eats and how he sleeps, his mattresses and so on, I realised that he was a very poor man. According to my theory, 30 acres of land, that is, a farmer owning 30 acres of land must be a rich man. But when I really saw, whatever we had read in the books, what I saw on the land was that the people

> owning 30, 40 or 50 acres of land were hardly living an ordinary life of a clerk or even of a 'chaprassi' in the towns and cities. They had a very low standard of life.
>
> At the same time Sharad Joshi was doing his work in Poona. We happened to come across Sharad Joshi at one of his meetings. That meeting was arranged to discuss – what do you call it – EGS, the Employment Guarantee Scheme; that is, bread for the labourers. Sharad Joshi had come there. We were discussing that 2200 calories is essential, and for that much this much wage is essential. Then Sharad Joshi stood up and said: 'Are you talking about hens and pigs, that he requires this much. He is a man, he is a person. He has his cultural life, he has his other entertainment needs. Where is the money that you are thinking of?'
>
> Then my husband thought: 'Here is a man working for the farmers and he is really thinking for the labourers.' And then we met again with Sharad Joshi and we had quite a discussion with him. We realised that the problem is really with the farmers. That is, the farmers don't get enough. Whatever information we had about landlords and labourers, we had some confusion in our minds, no clear vision as such. There was some confusion. There is some disturbance. Whatever is written in that communist ideology and the practical things are two different things.
>
> Then we started working with the farmers, started going to them and asking about their problems, and what prices they get for their crops. And we started to work along with Sharad Joshi. My husband was the first person in Yavatmal district to start Sharad Joshi's work there in 1981.

The Shetkari Sanghatana of Maharashtra is a modern type of organisation and movement. The caste composition is very mixed, and it is hard to find any dominant caste in the movement as a whole, since the Sanghatana is found in widely different regions of the state. The leadership and cadres are drawn from among many different groups, extending from the political left to the right; groups which were originally mobilised in the late 1960s and now participate in a second round of mobilisation. Among them are found urban intellectuals from the Jaya Prakash Narayanan's movement, the Lal Nishan Party and so on. Local activists are often farmers' sons who have studied at colleges and universities, but have returned to take up farming because they could not find a job in the urban economy.

Shetkari Sanghatana has focused its actions on one crop at a time, with the objective of enabling farmers to retain control over a substantial portion of what is harvested. This strategy, which is often thought to have been invented by Sharad Joshi, is in fact an old tactic used by previous peasant movements: it was, for example, used by the cotton farmers of Vidarbha district before Joshi entered the scene [*Sahasrabudhey*, 1989: 28–37]. The particular contribution of Sharad Joshi is that he has applied the strategy with great skill to cover a large area, and has managed to make it into a national issue.

Sharad Joshi is the undisputed and charismatic leader. His leadership is not contested, but the organisation is highly fluctuating from a low of almost no activities to a high of massive and strong mobilisation. The movement is highly dependent on its ability to raise a relevant issue and fight it out. At times when there is no agitation, it is as if the organisation does not even exist.

Thus the organisational form is anarchic or 'post-modern' in the sense that, much like new social movements in the West, it builds structures around actions rather than routine organisation. There is no fixed membership, no fixed rules of organisation, or strict tiers between local, intermediate and top levels in the organisation. Anybody who wears the badge, who participates in agitation, goes to gaol and so on, is a member.

Sharad Joshi is a modern leader whose message is as much directed at the evils of the rural social structure as against urban exploitation. Rural society is seen to be backward because of urban bias, which leaves no surplus for the development of agriculture and rural industries. Joshi has developed a whole world-view around this core, which he has elaborated in a number of speeches and writings [cf. *Dhanagare*, 1990]. His language and ideology is that of economic and cultural reform, with strong reference to previous works in Marathi of social reformers like Jotiba Phule and Ambedkar [cf. *Omvedt*, 1991a]. It must also be seen against the background of social transformations in Maharashtrian society during the last century, where the caste system has been eroded by Harijan and anti-Brahmin movements, and where gender oppression is less pervasive than in North India [*Dhanagare*, 1990]. More recently, this emphasis on cultural reform has taken the form of endorsing anti-Brahmin religious traditions [*Omvedt*, 1991b; 1992b].

At the same time the Shetkari Sanghatana is actively involved in furthering a broad-based process of social transfomation, of which the massive mobilisation of rural women is perhaps the most interesting and novel feature. Nowhere in India, and rarely in the Third World generally, can one find such a large-scale politicisation of women. The normal pattern of feminist politics is that of urban middle-class women working in small groups, supporting peasant and working class women, but rarely generating any major movement as such. In Maharashtra, by contrast, thousands of women have participated in the farmers' agitations, hundreds have gone to gaol, and tens of thousands have held women's meetings on a grand scale, the first taking place in Chandwad in 1986 with more than 150,000 participants [*Omvedt*, 1993]. The main demand of the *Shetkari Mahila Aghadi* (women's front of the Shetkari Sanghatana) is that women should have equal rights to land and property, and there have been attempts to make farmers transfer a part of their land to their wives. So far this has happened only in a few areas, but the women's front attaches symbolic significance to this process, not least because of the increasing incidence of abandoned wives, and question of support or alimony in cases of divorce. Another important issue taken up by Shetkari Sanghatana is violence against women. In these ways the peasant movement has also created a space for women's collective action, although there are extensive discussions between Shetkari Sanghatana, the *Samagra Mahila Aghadi* and other women's organisations over the wish of Sharad Joshi to subordinate the women's front to the goals of the farmers' movement. The Shetkari Sanghatana also receives support from activists engaged in other social movements, such as the Dalits, the Science forum, health-to-the-people, and green movements [*Omvedt*, 1993].

Shetkari Sanghatana is currently one of the most powerful popular groups opposed to the spread of Maharashtra's Shiv Sena in small towns and rural areas. At the moment, however, the communal tide is strong, and there has been a formidable upsurge of these forces recently, which Shetkari Sanghatana may not be in a position to stop.

CASE STUDY II: THE BKU IN UTTAR PRADESH[18]

When compared with the Shetkari Sanghatana in Maharashtra, the Bharatiya Kisan Union of Uttar Pradesh has a very different origin. The movement is confined to four districts of western UP, and is completely dominated by the Jat caste. While farmers of other castes and religions (including Muslims and Christians) have also joined the movement, it is under the traditional caste leadership that has dominated the region economically and politically for a very long time.

From an interactional and cognitive point of view, the most interesting feature of the BKU is its seemingly traditional form and content. The Jat khap organisation (based on clan structure) is the backbone of the movement, with one of the foremost khap leaders, Mahendra Singh Tikait, as leader. Some observers [*Madsen*, 1991; *Hasan and Patnaik*, 1992] claim that it was by using his position in this traditional system that Tikait was able to take over the leadership of the BKU in 1986. Yet the local, district and state units are organised in a modern organisational form (which, as is well known, developed in the transition to a capitalist industrial society in the West starting with the clubs in towns and cities). Formal membership, annual fees, rules, and boards with chairmen, secretaries and treasurers, exist at all levels from the village to the state level. Similarly, BKU members sometimes invoke Arya Samaj[19] and argue against excessive dowry gifts occasioned by marriage; the practice of inter-caste village meetings organised by Arya Samaj may also have prepared the ground for collective inter-caste action. In other ways, however, the ideology of the BKU is highly traditional and parochial, invoking Hindu religious symbols and the virtues of traditional rural society. Social reform has little or no relevance in agitations, and women have no role in the BKU except as housewives and servants. ('The women are standing behind us', is what Tikait replies when asked about women's participation in the movement and women's issues). This is also a reflection of the patriarchal gender relations in Jat society.

The strength of the BKU is very much related to the charismatic leadership of Chaudhari Mahendra Singh Tikait. However, Tikait's dominant position is also a basic weakness: there is a constant conflict below the surface on how to conduct the struggle, what issues to take up, how to relate to political issues and parties and so on. There are even entrepreneurs who use the networks of the BKU for building alternative organisations for more or less personal gains. One important aspect of this dominance of Tikait is the authoritarian claim to represent not only UP, despite the BKU having a strong presence only in its western parts, but also the whole of India: Tikait is the self-styled All-India President of Bharatiya Kisan Union of India. When he summons an All-India meeting, only district presidents and secretaries from UP turn up; it is nevertheless considered an All-India gathering. Discontent with Tikait in many movement sub-networks has not so far lead to any serious split within the BKU as such: it is widely believed that the BKU is nothing without Tikait. Thus, his position seems to prevent the emergence of alternative ideologies and strategies within the movement.

Because it is where the temple struggle in Ayodhya is taking place, the rise of Hindu fundamentalism and politics have been particularly strong in UP. In the recent state elections (May–June 1991) the Bharatiya Janata Party[20] (BJP) was voted into power, which it held up to December 1992. BKU leaders and members stress the non-communal character of the peasant union. Mahendra Singh Tikait also emphasises this point strongly, and it is reported that he very often begins a public meeting by greeting the participants with both a Hindu and a Muslim slogan. In 1991 when asked about their relation to the BJP and the temple issue,

Mahendra Singh Tikait answered: 'We don't participate in those kind of struggles. It is not an important issue for us. So we are strong, and our community is strong, that is all.

A number of interviews with Muslim farmers who are also members of the BKU confirm that the BKU is a multi-communal organisation. These Muslims are not afraid that the temple struggle will split the movement: 'It will not affect the village situation' some claimed. They maintain that the BKU has worked for communal harmony.

There are, however, consistent rumours that, in order to get concessions out of an emerging political force, the BKU indirectly supported the BJP in the last elections. Although in my recent fieldwork no leader or supporter was willing to confirm such rumours, Tikait himself answered in the following ambivalent manner:

> Election is one thing and BKU is another. We don't ask people to vote either this side or that side. People vote according to their conscience, so they can vote any way they want. However, political leaders like Abdul Akadi, who is a muslim leader, made some wrong deals, as a result of which the votes got divided on communal lines. So the muslims voted for Janata Dal, while others voted for BJP. That is a political issue with which we have nothing to do, so it does not affect BKU.

BKU or not, it is quite clear that a number of those involved in the recent demolition of the Babri Masjid in Ayodhya came from those very villages in Western UP where the BKU has a large following.

ONE MOVEMENT OR TWO?

As we have argued above it is possible to see both Shetkari Sanghatana and the BKU as offsprings of the same structural features of the agrarian transformation after independence. They have mostly appeared as non-political mobilisations, and they have also been treated very similarly by intellectuals, journalists and political parties. Most of these observers and commentators are not very sympathetic, seeing them only as spokesmen of the rich peasants and capitalist farmers. An interactionist and regional analysis as outlined above reveals, however, that the farmers' movements in Maharashtra and Uttar Pradesh are indeed very different types of mobilisations. What are the reasons for this difference, and what are the implications for the future mobilisation and impact of the farmers' movements in India?

Important reasons for the differences are of course the political and cultural variations to be found between the regions, and the way social transformations have taken place. There is, however, also a very important difference of ecology and political economy. In UP and Punjab (and Haryana) there are very favourable ecological conditions for the application of the green revolution strategy and a stable agricultural growth. The Indian State is very dependent on the food and cash crops produced in these states for feeding the rest of the country [*Patnaik*, 1991]. It would seem, therefore, that the supporters of the BKU in UP and Punjab are in a strong bargaining position. They have economic resources to fall back on, and their production is crucial to the country as a whole. Very little new thinking on agricultural development has been developed in these unions: they simply ask for the best deal since they are fulfilling the objectives of the green revolution. However, so far their struggles have not met with much success.

The situation in Maharashtra is very different. Because of unstable agricultural growth due to poor soils and lack of water, the Green Revolution has not been much of a success in the state. It is easy to imagine, therefore, that Shetkari Sanghatana's bargaining position would be much weaker than that of BKU in Punjab and UP. Nevertheless, the struggles in Maharashtra have generally been much more successful in achieving their targets.

The agricultural background in Maharashtra is also reflected in the recent thinking of the Shetkari Sanghatana on issues of alternative agricultural development: small-scale and water saving irrigation schemes, new water sharing systems, new bio-technology, as well as rural industrialisation, all form part of their discussions and demands. A report from a large meeting of Shetkari Sanghatana on 17–18 September 1991 notes that:

> Shetkari Sanghatana has found its new direction: it is going to take up the cause of natural/organic farming, of 'self-sufficient agriculture': peasants will refrain from using chemical fertilizers and pesticides, will rely as far as possible on locally-developed seeds. They will do their own primary processing, even if only packaging and winnowing, before bringing any produce to the market. They will produce with a bare minimum of industrial inputs, and they will export (farm products can be India's best earner of foreign exchange, Sharad Joshi argued), and peasants will take responsibility for 'saving the nation' (in this respect) but without importing, without expense on petroleum-based inputs. They will be interested in building links directly with consumers, particularly to the extent

> that a market for organic foods develops in India. They will reserve the option of not going to the market – and women in particular, will cultivate the land that is being given in their names under the 'Laxmi Mukti Campaign' in the traditional manner, without expenses on inputs and with the aim of providing basic family needs [*Omvedt*, 1991b: 2289].

This change from the 'one-point programme' to what has been described by Joshi as a 'battle of production' may still be more of a plan than a real strategy [*Omvedt*, 1992b], but it certainly signifies a shift of emphasis and a profile which is not visible in any of the other new farmers' movements in India today. This suggests that there is indeed a potential for the construction of a variety of social movements among the peasants depending on regional and political characteristics of the peasantry to be mobilised. This variety may also in the long run have important bearings on the development of the agrarian economy as such.[21] This will be discussed below.

PEASANT MOVEMENTS AND DEVELOPMENT ISSUES

One way of understanding the new farmers' movements is to see them as spokesmen for an alternative economic development strategy, in which capitalism and market relations as such are not questioned, but which gives emphasis to agriculture and the rural economy. The message is that if more surplus is left in the rural areas and with rural households, it will be invested in agriculture and small scale industry, thereby creating employment and development for all [*Skarstein*, 1991]. Because of its labour-intensive character, agriculture is presented as a desirable alternative to large-scale industrial development, which provides fewer jobs.

This analysis has been seen by Byres [1979] and others as a variant of populist ideology which has followed in the footsteps of industrialisation and urbanisation the world over for the past 150 years, an expression of people left behind by development. The main targets of this critique are Lipton [1977] and Schumacher [1973]. What this critique tends to forget, however, is that such 'populist' ideas were crucial in the development policies pursued by countries such as China and Tanzania, and also in the development strategies advocated by the ILO in the 1970s [*Kitching*, 1982: 70–84].

Proponents of these views are in good company. Several theories [cf. *Bairoch*, 1973; *Adelman*, 1980; 1984; *Adelman and Taft-Morris*, 1980; *Senghaas*, 1985; 1988] of institutional economics stress the role of agriculture in capitalist economic development, and the conventional view that agriculture should produce cheap food and raw materials, feed urban areas with cheap labour, earn foreign exchange and otherwise be relegated to a dwindling role in the overall economy as capitalist industry and services develop, is now being challenged in a major way: it is the development of agriculture through land reforms, institutional reforms and increased production which is seen as crucial. Even success such as Taiwan and South Korea are seen as examples of how the development of labour intensive agriculture goes hand in hand with successful industrialisation [*Skarstein*, 1991]. On the example of Taiwan, Gunnarsson [1992: 92–3] writes:

> Agricultural modernization gave increased incomes and higher purchasing power to the rural population, thereby enabling it to form a market for industrial goods. The question is how this could happen when agriculture was being so heavily exploited at the same time. The answer lies in the increased productivity resulting from the restructuring of agriculture, chiefly because the land reform was accompanied by a series of institutional changes at the local, regional and national levels, which brought positive effects in terms of diffusion of technology, credits and infrastructure .... .
>
> Perhaps the most important institutional change was the organisation of the so-called Farmers' Associations at the bottom level. The removal of the landlords had left a lacuna with regard to land management and rural credit. If this problem had not been resolved, the land reform would not have been successful. A Farmers' Association was an independent financial association with local management, which organised credit and marketing and helped with the introduction of new technology. Through land reform and its accompanying institutional reforms the marginal cost of land was reduced, which facilitated investment in new technology. Moreover, the incentives reached down to the producers at the bottom level instead of being confined to the big landlords as before.

This line of thinking claims that dynamic agricultural development needs strong organisations and co-operative institutions. In short, the organisation of peasants into autonomous movements which address development issues, press for more efficient administration, credit, infrastructure, and the diffusion of knowledge. Such a view suggests that the farmers' movements must ultimately take the step from agitation to a more positive type of organisation (economic associations, co-operatives and so on) if they are to be successful. The state, on the other hand, must be strong, so as not to yield to the partial interests of the farmers' movements alone, but simultaneously be responsive to farmers' needs; that is, encouraging increased productivity via a combination of price incentives and institutional reforms so as to organise the conditions of production in an efficient way.

Analysed in this perspective, one could say the Indian farmers' movements at least have the potential for this kind of development. At the same time, depending on their class basis and ideological standpoints, they may also prevent the state from carrying through further necessary land reforms, adequate agricultural taxation, new types of irrigation schemes and other institutional changes. In that case we are dealing with a variety of agrarian populism dominated by an emerging agrarian bourgeoisie of rich peasants and capitalist farmers, which mobilise part of the middle peasantry with a rhetoric that hides their real intentions.[22]

The farmers' movements, therefore, are volatile social constructions, which can serve potentially both as promoters of a dynamic agrarian capitalism based on family farms, and also as hindrances to an efficient implementation of such agricultural development. To a large extent this is a class issue, a question of whose interest will ultimately dominate the movements: the middle peasants, the rich peasants, the capitalist farmers, or combinations of these. Whichever class or classes and tendencies prevail is an open question, and depends very much on a number of internal and external factors. It is in this context that the development of the internal discussions and negotiations in the various farmers' movements are crucial for the choices ahead. Since they are regionally specific movements, the outcome will also reflect this difference. For example, the ecological policies now being discussed in Maharashtra may be one such sign of variation.

Equally important in this regard are the policies of the Indian state and international capital, which by setting terms and conditions for the development of the agrarian economy, may determine the way in which peasants/farmers can be mobilised in the future. In fact, it is the interplay between theses forces and the various farmers' movements that in the end will determine the outcome. It is clear, however, that these processes and forces are not bound a priori to favour the interest of rich peasants and capitalist farmers alone. Other outcomes are possible. If, for example, middle peasants cum family farmers can achieve a strong influence in these movements, this would possibly put pressure on the Indian state to pursue policies more friendly to small and intermediate producers rather than to the big capitalist farmers. This in turn could facilitate a scenario of agrarian development not unlike that of Western Europe and parts of the United States, where family farming and its vertical concentration under state agencies, co-operative institutions and agro-industrial capital have become the dominant features (see, for example, Djurfeldt [1983: 152–4]).

CONCLUSION

The New Farmers' Movements in India represent a major change in rural social mobilisation, and must be seen as a response to the structural transformation in the agrarian economy brought about in India since independence. These Farmers' Movements have some features in common with other new social movements across the world in the 1970s and 1980s, but it is a similarity in form rather than in content. Farmers' movements are classically within the mould of popular movements, which, like the working class movements, are formed around a basic class contradiction in capitalist society. The new movements, in contrast, address other issues in contemporary capitalist society, such as gender, the environment, and the crisis of community, urban renewal and re-democratisation. As such, they tend to straddle class borders rather than polarise along them. However, as was shown above, there are several possibilities for alliances between the farmers' movements and these new movements.

An interactionist analysis of the regionally-specific farmers' movements in India suggests that such mobilisations are not predetermined to represent any particular class of farmers or type of agrarian transformation. Indeed, both its class content as well as its impact on agrarian development and transformation are open to considerable variation, depending on a number of factors, including regional ones.

NOTES

1. The best overview of the new farmers movement so far is Nadkarni [1987].
2. An exception to this may be Tamil Nadu, where in the 1970s farmers conducted massive agitations. In the early 1980s M.G. Ramachandran, then chief minister of the state, ordered the police to intervene and disperse demonstrations and mass meetings with brutal force. At the same time he started a political campaign directed against the rich farmers leading the movement. He also gave debt relief and other concessions to poor and middle farmers. Today the farmers are split into several fractions, of which two are registered political parties.
3. This emphasis on identity formation in the study of social movements has been called the identity-oreinted paradigm [*Cohen*, 1985]. For examples of this approach, see Alberoni [1984], Touraine [1984], and Melucci [1985].
4. To many colleagues, I am sure, there would seem to be a mutual incompatibility between on the one hand a structuralist perspective, in which classes and class conflicts take precedence, and on the other hand open-ended processes of identity formation, in which social interaction and ideology play a crucial role. However, the analytical

synthesis formulated here in what I call a process-oriented sociology is an attempt to overcome this duality, in the belief that only such a sociology can capture the complex interplay of various variables. It certainly does not mean that I subscribe to the view presented by, for example, Laclau, that Marxism and class analysis is an irrelevant approach derived from a Eurocentric perspective [*Laclau*, 1985].

5. For an overview see, for example, Sen [1982].
6. The class analysis here and in the following is based on the theoretical and empirical analyses in Athreya *et al.* [1990: Ch. 6]. The main criterion is that of reproductive levels and appropriation of surplus from agricultural production. Poor peasants are defined as those peasants who cannot cover the grain requirements of the household from the income from its farm production. Middle peasants, on the other hand, comprise a range of peasant households, from those who can just about cover this requirement up to those households who are fully reproductive, that is, who able to cover also the non-grain requirements of the household and the cash cost for production itself. Rich peasants are those households who can appropriate a surplus from the farm production, over and above the needs mentioned above (cf. Athreya *et al.* [1990: 196–7]).
7. See, for example, Alexander [1981: 214–15].
8. It should be pointed out that there have been many previous peasant movements agitating for higher prices on their produce, so even in this respect there is a certain historic continuity between peasant movements. However, this does not invalidate the claim that there has been an overall shift towards new peasant movements.
9. It is commonplace to analyse the new peasant movements as mobilizations of rich peasants and capitalist farmers, who have succeeded in winning over middle peasants to their cause. Behind the facade of rural interest, it is argued [*Nadkarni*, 1987; *Banaji*, 1990], is hidden these very particular class interests, which means that the demands of the farmers' agitation actually go against the interests of other rural classes and the economy as a whole. This interpretation is disputed here, in the sense that the 'new' farmers' movements can also represent the interests of middle peasants or family farmers. Whichever tendency dominates will also be of decisive importance for the future development of these movements.
10. Omvedt has, as is well known, completely reversed her earlier position on the new farmers' movements, and now regards them as a progressive mass movement representing also the middle peasants, and the rural economy as whole in relation to the urban-industrial economy [*Omvedt*, 1988, and later works].
11. The 'Tamilaga Vivesayagal Sangam' led by Narayanaswami Naidu. This movement was started in 1966 and launched its first violent agitation in 1972.
12. Vanaik [1990: 206–7] gives a number of references to studies supporting this picture.
13. See CPI(ML) [1986].
14. For this type of agrarian politics or agrarianism see, for example, Hicks [1931], Sorokin *et al.* [1930], Lipset [1950], Crampton [1965], and Gerschenkron [1966]. For a world-wide survey see Esman and Uphof [1984], and Flores [1970]. For studies on agrarian politics in the United States see, for example, Benedict [1953], Block [1960] and McKenna [1974]. For Germany see Raschke [1985]. For the agrarian politics in Eastern Europe before the Second World War see Köll [1992]. Among the more recent treatments there is for example Österud's study [1978] of agrarian structure and peasant politics in Scandinavia, and Gundelach's study [1988] of social movements and social change in Denmark over the last two centuries.
15. Again, in the words of Melucci [1985: 795]: 'These dimensions, which are entirely analytical, enable one to separate social movements from other collective phenomena which are very often empirically associated with "movements" and "protest": one can speak of deviance, regulated grievances, aggregated-mass behaviour, according to which of these dimensions is present or absent. Moreover, different kinds of movements and collective actions can be assessed according to the system of reference of action.'
16. I refer here to the fact that despite differences in the implementation of land reforms and other rural reforms, very similar conditions for the rural economy prevail in these

states. On the peasant movement in West Bengal, see, for example, Bandyopadhyaya [1992]; on the farmers' movement in Maharashtra, see, for example, Dhanagare [1990]; and on the farmers' movement in Uttar Pradesh, see, for example, Hasan [1989] and Gupta [1988].
17. Useful studies of the Shetkari Sanghatana include Omvedt [1988–92], Lenneberg [1988], Sahasrabudhey [1989] and Dhanagare [1990].
18. Useful studies of Uttar Pradesh BKU include Gupta [1988; 1992], Hasan [1989], Hasan and Patnaik [1992], Dhanagare [1991], and Singh [1992].
19. Arya Samaj is one of the religious and cultural reform movements stemming from the 19th century, which like the Brahmo Samaj tried to modernise Hinduism and other social and cultural practices in society. Arya Samaj was founded by Swami Dayananda (1824–83). It tries to unify all sections of Hindu society on the basis of the Vedas, denounces idol worship and the caste system. It has been regarded 'more a school of nationalism than of religion proper' [*Sarma*, 1953: 43–4]. It has been very popular in both Uttar Pradesh and Maharashtra.
20. The political party of the Hindu fundamentalists and activists.
21. It is important to stress that these varieties are here conceived of within a framework of a more or less state guided capitalist market economy, which is to a large extent dominated by international capital. The point stressed here is that there is room for variations not only in form but also in content. We are not dealing with the desirability of one form or the other, but rather with the actual potentialities. It is also my conviction that these variations may have important bearings on the future for poor peasants and agricultural labourers, also beyond the present limitations of capitalist market economies, be it a kind of socialist market economy or something else.
22. Populism is certainly a very elusive term. Populist movements are usually defined as either non-class movements, or popular movements in which the real class content is hidden. Since the term lacks any rigor I prefer not using it. It is clear, however, that most class movements do have an element of 'populism' in them, in as far as they purport to appeal to people outside their own class base. With Gramsci one could perhaps say that they attempt to make their own views and objectives hegemonic. It is also clear that 'populist' movements do not represent one single variety of movement, and that we have to make a detailed assessment of each one of them, what class(es) and alliance(s) they represent, and so on before understanding them fully.

REFERENCES

Adelman, Irma, 1980, 'Economic Development and Political Change in Developing Countries', *Social Research*, Vol.XLVII, No.2.

Adelman, Irma; 1984, 'Beyond Export-Led Growth', *World Development*, Vol.XII, No.9.

Adelman, Irma and C. Taft-Morris, 1980, 'Patterns of Industrialization in the Nineteenth Century', *Research in Economic History*, Vol.V.

Alberoni, Francesco, 1984, *Movement and Institution*, New York: Columbia University Press.

Alexander, K.C., 1981, *Peasant Organizations in South India*, New Delhi: Indian Social Institute.

Athreya, Venkatesh, Djurfeldt, Göran and Staffan Lindberg, 1990, *Barriers Broken: Production Relations and Agrarian Change in Tamil Nadu*, New Delhi: Sage Publications.

Attwood, D., 1979, 'Why Some of the Rich Get Poorer', *Current Anthropology*, Vol.20, No.3.

Bairoch, Paul, 1973, 'Agriculture and the Industrial Revolution', in Carlo M. Cipolla, (ed.), *The Fontana Economic History of Europe. Volume 3: The Industrial Revolution*, London: Collins/Fontana Books.

Banaji, Jairus, 1990, 'Illusions About the Peasantry: Karl Kautsky and the Agrarian Question', *Journal of Peasant Studies*, Vol.17, No.2.

Bandyopadhyaya, Nripen, 1992, 'The Story of Peasant Struggles for Land Reforms in West Bengal', Paper for the Workshop on 'Social Movements, State and Democracy' organized by the Delhi University Group in Politics and the Indian Statistical Institute Sociology Group, New Delhi, 5–8 Oct. 1992.

Benedict, Murray R., 1953, *Farm Policies of the United States 1790–1950: A Study of Their Origins and Development*, New York: The Twentieth Century Fund.

Bhalla, Sheila, 1977, 'Changes in Acreage and Tenure Structure of Land Holdings in Haryana, 1962–72', *Economic and Political Weekly*, Vol.12, No.13.

Block, William J., 1960, *The Separation of the Farm Bureau and the Extension Service. Political Issues in a Federal System*, Urbana, IL: University of Illinois Press.

Byres, T., 1979, 'Of Neo-Populist Pipe-Dreams: Daedulus in the Third World and the Myth of Urban Bias', *Journal of Peasant Studies*, Vol.6, No.2.

Cain, M., 1981, 'Risk and Insurance: Perspectives on Fertility and Agrarian Change in India and Bangladesh', *Population and Development Review*, Vol.7, No.3.

Cohen, Jean L., 1985, 'Strategy or Identity: New Theoretical Paradigms and Contemporary Social Movements', *Social Research*, Vol.52, No.4.

Crampton, John A., 1965, *The National Farmers' Union*, Lincoln, NE: University of Nebraska Press.

Dhanagare, D.N., 1990, 'Shetkari Sanghatana: The Farmers' Movement in Maharashtra – Background and Ideology', *Social Action*, Vol.40, No.4.

Dhanagare, D.N., 1991, 'An Apoliticist Populism: A Case Study of BKU', in K.L., Sharma and Dipankar Gupta (eds.), *Country-Town Nexus*, Jaipur: Rawat Publications.

Djurfeldt, Göran, 1983, 'Classical Discussions of Capital and Peasantry: A Critique', in John Harriss (ed.), *Rural Development. Theories of Peasant Economy and Agrarian Change*. London: Hutchinson University Library.

Esman, Milton J. and Norman T. Uphof, 1984, *Local Organizations. Intermediaries in Rural Development*, Ithaca, NY and London: Cornell University Press.

Eyerman, Ron and Andrew Jamison, 1991, *Social Movements. A Cognitive Approach*, Cambridge: Polity Press.

Flores, Xavier, 1970, *Agricultural Organization and Development*, Geneva: International Labour Office.

Gerschenkron, Alexander, 1966, *Bread and Democracy in Germany*, New York: Harold Fertig.

Gundelach, Peter, 1988, *Sociale bevaegelser og samfundsaendringer* (Social movements and Social Change). Nye sociala grupperinger og deres organisationsformer ved overgangen til aendrede samfundstyper, Aarhus: Politica.

Gunnarsson, Christer, 1992, 'Economic and Demographic Transition in East Asia. Economic Modernisation vs Family Planning in Taiwan', in Michael, Hammarskjöld, B. Egerö and S. Lindberg, (eds.), *Population and the Development Crises in the South*, Lund: Programme on Population and Development in Poor Countries.

Gupta, Dipankar, 1988, 'Country-Town Nexus and Agrarian Mobilization, Bharatiya Kisan Union as an Instance', *Economic and Political Weekly*, Vol.23, No.51.

Gupta, Dipankar, 1992, 'Peasant "Unionism" in West U.P. (India): Against the Rural Mentality Thesis', *Journal of Contemporary Asia*, Vol.22, No.2.

Hansen, Thomas, 1991, 'Protest, frigörelse eller manipulation – om studiet af sociale og politiske bevaegelser i den tredje verden', *Den Nye Verden*, Vol.4, No.24.

Harriss, John, 1985, 'What Happened to the Green Revolution in South India? Economic Trends, Household Mobility, and the Politics of an "Awkward Class"', University of East Anglia, School of Development Studies, Discussion Paper No.175.

Hasan, Zoya, 1989, 'Self-Serving Guardians: Formation and Strategy of the Bharatiya Kisan Union', *Economic and Political Weekly*, Vol.24, No.48.

Hasan, Zoya and Utsa Patnaik, 1992, 'Aspects of the Farmers' Movement in Uttar Pradesh in the Context of Uneven Growth of Capitalist Agriculture', New Delhi: Jawaharlal Nehru University, mimeo.

Heberle, Rudolf, 1968, 'Types and Functions of Social Movements', in David L. Sills (ed.), *International Encyclopedia of the Social Sciences*, London: The Macmillan Company.

Hicks, John D., 1931, *The Populist Revolt*, Minneapolis, MN: University of Minnesota Press.

Jenkins, J. Craig, 1983, 'Resource Mobilization Theory and the Study of Social Movements', *Annual Review of Sociology*, Vol.9.

Kitching, Gavin, 1982, *Development and Underdevelopment in Historical Perspective. Populism, Nationalism and Industrialization*, London: Methuen.

Köll, Anu Mai, 1992, 'Peasant Movements and Democracy in Eastern Europe in the Early 20th Century', in L. Rudebeck (ed.), *When Democracy Makes Sense. Studies in the Democratic Potential of Third World Popular Movements*, Uppsala: AKUT.

Laclau, Ernesto, 1985, 'New Social Movements and the Plurality of the Social', in David Slater (ed.), *New Social Movements and the State in Latin America*, Amsterdam: CEDLA.

Laclau, Ernesto, 1990, *New Reflections on the Revolution of Our Time*, London: Verso.

Laclau, Ernesto and Chantal Mouffe, 1985, *Hegemony and Socialist Strategy*, London: Verso.

Lenneberg, Cornelia, 1988, 'Sharad Joshi and the Farmers: The Middle Peasant Lives!,' *Pacific Affairs*, Vol.61, No.3.

Lipset, Seymour Martin, 1950, *Agrarian Socialism*, Berkeley, CA: University of California Press.

Lipton, M., 1977, *Why Poor People Stay Poor: A Study of Urban Bias in World Development*, London: Temple Smith.

Madsen, Stig Toft, 1991, 'Clan, Kinship and Panchayat Justice among the Jats of Western Uttar Pradesh', *Anthropos*, No.86.

Marx, Karl, 1967, 'The Eighteenth Brumaire of Louis Bonaparte', in K. Marx, F. Engels, and V. Lenin, *On Historical Materialism*, Moscow: Progress Publishers.

McKenna, George (ed.), 1974, *American Populism*, New York: G.P. Putnam's Sons.

Melucci, Alberto, 1985, 'The Symbolic Challenge of Contemporary Movements', *Social Research*, Vol.52, No.4.

Melucci, Alberto, 1989, *Nomads of the Present: Social Movements and Individual Needs in Contemporary Society*, Philadelphia, PA: Temple University Press.

Melucci, Alberto, 1992, 'Frontier Land: Collective Action between Actors and Systems', in Diano, Mario and Ron Eyerman (eds.), *Studying Collective Action*, London: Sage Publications.

Nadkarni, M.V., 1987, *Farmers' Movements in India*, New Delhi: Allied Publishers Private Limited.

Oberschall, Anthony, 1973, *Social Conflicts and Social Movements*, Englewood Cliffs, NJ: Prentice-Hall.

Omvedt, Gail, 1980, 'Cane Farmers' Movement', *Economic and Political Weekly*, Vol.15, No.49.

Omvedt, Gail, 'Capitalist Agriculture and Rural Classes in India', *Bulletin of Concerned Asian Scholars*, Vol.15, No.3.

Omvedt, Gail, 1988, 'The "New Peasant Movement" in India', *Bulletin of Concerned Asian Scholars*, Vol.20, No.2.

Omvedt, Gail, 1989, 'India's Movements for Democracy: Peasants, "Greens", Women and People's Power', unpublished manuscript.

Omvedt, Gail, 1991a, 'Jotiba Phule and the Analysis of Peasant Exploitation', Paper presented at the Seminar on 'Mahatma Jyotirao Phule – An Incomplete Renaissance', Centre for Social Studies, Surat, 9–11 Jan 1991.

Omvedt, Gail, 1991b, 'Shetkari Sanghatana's New Direction', *Economic and Political Weekly*, 5 Oct.

Omvedt, Gail, 1992a, 'Peasants, Dalits and Women: Democracy and India's New Social Movements', Draft of paper for the Workshop on 'Social Movements, State and Democracy' organised by the Delhi University Group in Politics and the Indian Statistical Institute Sociology Group, New Delhi, 5–8 Oct.

Omvedt, Gail, 1992b, 'Interview with Sharad Joshi', unpublished ms.

Omvedt, Gail, 1993, *Reinventing Revolution*, New York: M.E. Sharpe.

Österud, Öyvind, 1978, *Agrarian Structure and Peasant Politics in Scandinavia*, Oslo: Universitetsforlaget.

Patnaik, Utsa, 1991, 'Food Economy in Peril', *Frontline*, 31 Aug. – 13 Sept.

Rao, V.M., 1972, 'Land Transfers in Rural Communities: Some Findings in a Ryotwari Region', *Economic and Political Weekly*, Vol.7, No.40.

Raschke, Joachim, 1985, *Sozialae Bewegungen: Ein Historisch-sytematischer Grundriss*, Frankfurt/Main: Campus Verlag.

CPI(ML), 1986, *Report from the Flaming Fields of Bihar*, Calcutta: Sree Art Press.

Rudolph, Lloyd I. and Susanne Hoeber Rudolph, 1987, *In Pursuit of Lakshmi. The Political Economy of the Indian State*, Bombay: Orient Longman.

Sahasrabudhey, Girish, 1989, 'The New Farmers' Movement in Maharashtra', in Sunil Sahasrabudhey S. (ed.), *Peasant Movement in Modern India*, Allahabad: Cugh Publications.

Sarma, D.S., 1953, 'The Nature and History of Hinduism', in Kenneth W. Morgan (ed.), *The Religion of the Hindus. Interpreted by Hindu*, New York: The Ronald Press Co.

Sen, Sunil, 1982, *Peasant Movements in India*, Calcutta: K P Bagchi & Company.

Schumacher, E.F., 1973, *Small is Beautiful. Economics as if People Mattered*, New York: Harper & Row.

Senghaas, Dieter, 1985, *The European Experience: A Historical Critique of Development Theory*, Dover: NH Berg.

Senghaas, Dieter, 1988, 'European Development and the Third World. An Assessment', *Review*, Vol.XI, No.1.

Shanin, Teodor, 1982, 'Class, States and Revolution: Substitutes and Realities', in H. Alavi and T. Shanin (eds.), *Introduction to the Sociology of Developing Societies*, London: Macmillan.

Singh, Jagpal, 1992, *Capitalism and Dependence, Agrarian Politics in Western Uttar Pradesh 1951–1991*, New Delhi: Manohar.

Skarstein, Rune, 1991, 'Agriculture – Not the Leading but the Crucial Sector in Economic Development. Some Reflections on Experience and Theory', in Olle Törnquist and Karl-Reinhold Haellquist (eds.), *Asian Society in Comparative Perspective*, Papers presented to the 7th Annual Conference of the Nordic Association for Southeast Asian Studies, Mön, Denmark, 1990.

Sorokin, Pitirim A. *et al.* (eds.) 1930–32, *A Systematic Source Book of Rural Sociology*, Minneapolis, MN: University of Minnesota Press.

Tilly, Charles, Tilly, Louise and Richard Tilly, 1975, *The Rebellious Century: 1830–1930*, Cambridge, MA: Harvard University Press.

Tilly, Charles, 1978, *From Mobilization to Revolution*, New York: Random House.

Touraine, Alain, 1984, *The Voice and the Eye. An Analysis of Social Movements*, New York: Cambridge University Press.

Vanaik, Achin, 1990, *The Painful Transition. Bourgeois Democracy in India*, London: Verso.

'We Want the Return for Our Sweat': The New Peasant Movement in India and the Formation of a National Agricultural Policy

GAIL OMVEDT

INTRODUCTION

The new peasant movements in India have acted upon, and theorised, a very different contradiction from the 'class' contradiction focused on by traditional Marxism, a contradiction between peasantry and state-based exploiters, each defined as 'systems' comprising diverse elements.[1] Rather than organising wage-earners against property-owning employers, they have organised entire village communities against the state (with the latter seen as including representatives of the 'state within the villages'). Rather than seeing private property as the basis of exploitation, with peasant-tenant classes posed against landlords or agricultural labourers and poor peasants against capitalist farmers, they have stressed force and domination as a basis for extraction of surplus through exchange relations. And these relations between state-based power holders and the property-holding peasants have been seen not simply as 'distributional' relations of the market or as 'political' relations of the state; they are seen as *economic* relations of exploitation, as exemplified in the most popular slogan of the Shetkari Sanghatana, 'we don't want alms but the return for our sweat'.

The organisations of the movement have established themselves on a regional-linguistic basis: the Shetkari Sanghatana in Maharashtra, the Rayat Sangh of Karnataka, the Vyavasayigal Sangham of Tamilnadu, the Khedut Samaj of Gujarat, the Bharatiya Kisan Union (Punjab) and Bharatiya Kisan Union (UP) (two very different organisations). Here they proposed to organise all sections of rural producers or those whose livelihood is connected with agriculture; thus the Shetkari Sanghatana defines *shetkari* to include agricultural labourers and artisans, while the Rayat Sangh calls itself a 'village' movement rather than simply a 'peasant' movement. The very forms of their agitations in fact reflect the anti-urban, anti-state character of the movement: whereas the typical workers' contribution to the impressive arsenal of non-violent agitational

Gail Omvedt resides in Kasegaon, Sangli District, Maharashtra 415 404, India.

methods in India has been the *gherao* (workers surrounding capitalists and managers), that of the new peasant movement has been the *rasta roko* (blocking roads, or cutting the links between city and village) and the *gavbandi* (forbidding politicians and bureaucrats from entering villages). Both of these can be called forms of delinking city from countryside.

The focus of the movements' campaigns inevitably have centred on Delhi. This has been because of the importance of the central government in determining prices of commercial crops and other agricultural policy, in spite of the fact that agriculture is formally a 'state' subject in the Indian constitution. Thus, while the organisations remained firmly anchored in linguistic-national particularities, efforts at unity on an all-India level began in 1980, with Narayanswami Naidu of Tamilnadu taking the first initiative to form an all-India Bharatiya Kisan Union (BKU) with a flag of its own. This suffered a split in 1982 when a major section protested Naidu's unilateral action in forming a political party in Tamilnadu. Sharad Joshi of Maharashtra then initiated a re-formation on a 'federal' basis under the name of Interstate Coordinating Committee (ISCC, later to be called the Kisan Coordinating Committee or KCC) in October 1982. The powerful Punjab unit of the BKU was part of this, and newly arising organisations were incorporated under the condition that they were non-party, non-violent and secular.

Between 1984 and 1989 this committee provided the loose structure within which the farmers' movement attempted to assert its demands on a national level. A major upsurge centring on Punjabi farmers in 1984 was aborted with Operation Bluestar and the communalisation of the Punjab; for years after that, the Punjab BKU proved incapable of open political organising [*Shiva*, 1989]. Then, following the mass disillusionment with Rajiv Gandhi from 1985 onwards, the break of V.P. Singh from the government and the Congress Party provided a new focus for oppositional movements. The farmers' movement thus entered on a new period of rising agitations that brought its themes and demands to the centre of the Indian political agenda. With the election in 1989 of a minority National Front government headed by Singh, not only was the state committed to debt relief and remunerative prices for peasants but, in addition, a new *Standing Adivisory Committee on Agriculture* (the SAC) was set up to formulate what was to be India's first national agricultural policy ever; its chairman was the most articulate of the farmers' leaders, Sharad Joshi, and he was given the status of a cabinet minister. The new peasant movement, it seemed, 'had arrived'.

The shape of the farmers' upsurge, the nature of the policy put forward by representatives of the movement, and the response of the bureaucracy and other political forces in the country reveal the various aspects of the contradiction between peasantry, state and capital. The way in which the demand for remunerative prices was related both to the problems of agricultural labourers and to wider themes of balanced development show the coupling of what some scholars have called the 'class' and 'populist' aspects of the movement, as the National Agricultural Policy went far beyond issues of prices to offer alternative forms of agriculture and agro-industrial development.[2] Though it was buried after the fall of the National Front government in October 1990, its formulation was an expression of the fact that calls for 'alternative development' were beginning to be heard from a wide variety of social movements and activists in the 1989–90 period. In fact it was the one document of social movements in India of that period that came closest to the seats of power, with themes similar to those expressed by farmers and at least partially realised by state policies in other countries (such as China between 1978 and 1985).

Arguments that the 'new peasant movement' or farmers' movements in India are 'rich farmers' or 'kulak' organisations rest not on assertions about their actual class membership (as Dhanagare and others have noted, they have a high proportion of middle and even poor peasants among them; see Dhanagare (this volume), Lindberg [1992b]) but rather on the belief or assumption that the *demands* they make are in the interest of this narrow section only. This in turn rests on three other assumptions: (1) that the demand for higher crop prices is against the interest of urban and rural wage-labourers and contrary to long-term developmental interests; (2) that only wage labour is a source for accumulation of capital; and (3) a process of lumping together all demands of any section of farmers and of politicians speaking in the name of farmers, to come up with a wide list (higher prices, subsidies to provide lower input prices, higher investment in agriculture and so on) of supposed 'demands of the movement'. In this study we shall argue the following: (1) higher crop prices will benefit wage labourers and lead to higher growth in agriculture and labour-intensive rural industries, while, on the contrary, the development path followed in India which rested on extracting resources from agriculture via the price mechanism and other methods resulted in unbalanced and, ultimately, faltering growth with immiseration of the agricultural economy affecting most of all the rural poor; (2) not only wage labour but, in addition, unpaid domestic labour of women, low-priced natural resources, and market-remunerated labour of 'petty commodity producers' are all part of the arena of capital accumulation; and (3) if we disaggregate the demands of the farmers' movement and note the process by which they developed, we can see a clear distinction.

Between on the one hand those voiced by the most articulate and organised section of the movement, the Kisan Coordinating Committee led by Sharad Joshi, which emphasised prices and included with these a demand for a high minimum legal wage for agricultural labourers; and on the other the programmes put forward by politicians such as Devi Lal, which stressed higher government investment in agriculture, subsidised fertilisers and other inputs, and the eclectic 'shopping list' of demands of leaders such as Tikait of UP.

All of these points become clear in an examination of the process of formulation of, and the debates and struggles regarding, the National Agricultural Policy. Thus this will be the focus of this study.

THE 'NEHRU MODEL': INDUSTRY AND AGRICULTURE SINCE INDEPENDENCE

The thesis of 'peasant unity' is not that there are no contradictions within the village but that these are secondary to the 'main contradiction' between peasantry and state/capital. Whether we see it as 'primary' or 'secondary', the latter contradiction needs some more study. Marxist and radical analyses, in focusing on class relations within the village, have generally neglected the question of relations of exploitation and surplus accumulation from agriculture at a national or international level. For example, it is neo-liberal economists who have pioneered studies on extraction of resources from agriculture by (especially) Third World governments; in their terms, agriculture has been 'taxed' and not 'subsidised' in most developmental policies, not only through direct action to hold down prices by compulsory levies or parasatals and marketing boards, but also through complex systems of regulation and overall financial and monetary policies which have kept exchange rates 'high' to aid industrial imports – but in a way that has penalised the exporters of the primary sector [*Krueger, Schiff and Valdes*, 1991; *Johnson*, 1991]. Marxist theories have rarely attempted to refute these arguments; they have ignored the issues of international trade regimes, prices and government policies to focus only on domination by multinationals. Liberal economists have argued for the need to modify this position, sometimes drastically, but have broadly accepted the arguments, as have, to an increasing degree, the government spokesmen of Third World countries and environmentally concerned agriculturalists [*Mellor and Ahmed*, 1988; *Drèze and Sen*, 1990; *South Commission*, 1990; *Swaminathan*, 1989].

An analysis of India's developmental policy and practice, usually called the 'Nehru model', or the 'Nehru-Mahalanobis model' after the economist who dominated early Indian planning, makes it clear that the framers of the developmental planning effort sought consciously to utilise agriculture for building up the growth of industry. Nehru himself had been dedicated to building a modern, industrial India with a dominating public sector; 'socialism' was something he saw not in terms of the rule of the working class but rather as a rational, managed economy, the antidote to the 'bania' civilisation of the West [*Nehru*, 1960]. In fact Nehru as much as Gandhi operated in terms of a trusteeship notion, the difference being that Gandhi saw private capitalists as potential trustees of mass interests, whereas Nehru believed that this could be done by an elite-managed state. Just as crucial were assumptions of the inherent backwardness of agriculture and the belief that surpluses extracted from agriculture could and should be used for industrial growth, and that even for the modernisation of agriculture itself the technology and impetus would have to come from without. As Sukhumoy Chakravorty has put it in his book on Indian planning:

> In actual fact the planners' strategy boiled down to the traditional thesis, upheld by several contemporary scholars of economic development, that during the early stages of industrialization it was necessary for agriculture to contribute to the building up of a modern industrial sector by providing cheap labour and also cheap food ... while this whole sequence of reasoning was not stated in any plan document, it can be deduced as a corollary from many contemporary discussions [*Chakravorty*, 1987: 21].

But the reasoning was quite evident in the early planners' enthusiasm for reorganising agriculture, as described by Francine Frankel, where the concern to achieve equality seemed to be equally matched by the need to extract resources from agriculture; co-operative and collective forms seemed to make both possible [*Frankel*, 1978: 50–80]. Chakravorty himself implies that the Indian developmental model was a kind of 'incremental' socialist primitive accumulation [*Chakravorty*, 1987: 15]. Of course, in the Indian context collectivisation and the direct extraction of food grains were ruled out; radical land reforms also did not take place, though moderate anti-feudal ones were carried out. The planners, nevertheless, were fascinated by the early Chinese experience, in which co-operatives and state provision of inputs such as credit, fertilisers and pesticides were used to control the peasantry and assure sales of grain to state agencies [*Frankel*, 1978: 125–6]. As commercial crop production began to increase, actual levies were only occasionally imposed, but zoning restrictions and selective imposition of bans on export served as ways of controlling prices. For instance, there was no need for a forced levy of wheat from the Punjab when the wheat produced by Punjabi farmers was overwhelmingly consumed outside the state and the state could prevent private merchants from transporting it: with no incentive for local merchants to buy wheat which they could not sell to local consumers, the state became in effect a monopsonic buyer.

Importing served the same function. The massive import of PL-480 wheat was perhaps necessary to offset the 1966 famine in India; it also certainly served American interests. But along with this it had a major impact in holding down prices not only of wheat but of other foodgrains in India for several years [*Shenoy*, 1974: 29–64]. It was after this that we see the beginnings of the 'Green Revolution', the attempt to stimulate Indian production but in a way that maintained the directive and technological role with the centre through its financing and control of irrigation projects, fertiliser subsidies and seeds. As commercial agriculture developed and productivity increased, though highly concentrated in a few regions, and government procurement increased its significance as the source of supply for the Public Distribution System, the formation of the Agricultural Price Commission (APC) in 1965 attempted to give a formal and rationalistic justification to the prices which the state was imposing.

Along with this growing direct role of the central government in the maintenance of prices and production, other more indirect measures had an equal impact. First, the whole apparatus of the 'licence-permit raj' took away earlier freedoms of the production process from peasant communities and supported their assignment to bureaucratic agencies and industries dependent on the state. Farmers were forbidden to carry on without special permission many of the various types of primary processing common earlier. For example, cotton producers in Maharashtra could no longer separate the seeds from the lint by their traditional methods (or any upgraded version of these) but were compelled to sell the raw cotton to the Cotton Monopoly Purchase Scheme. Cane producers had to get special permission to manufacture jaggery, the traditional low-technology process; indeed the whole structure of pricing and permits favoured the white sugar produced by sugar factories (and even co-operatives here were highly dependent on state loans) and discriminated against many of the more traditional forms in which Indians had consumed sugar. Farmers were not permitted to do their own paddy milling or processing of milk. Thus, a whole structure of state-imposed regulations was erected around rural production, and farmers could neither export nor process except under special licensing which was very difficult to get. So pervasive did the assumption that this was a 'natural' development become that at a 1993 conference in honour of the

Gandhian economist J.C. Kumarappa, when young radicals argued that peasants should not sell any produce outside the village without doing at least some primary processing, the reaction of the institutional Gandhians was totally negative: 'but they have to sell to KVIC!' (the Khadi and Village Industries Commission).

Finally, the overall developmental policy with its artificially high exchange rate for the rupee favoured the development of heavy industry and imports designed as inputs for industry at the expense of exporters, particularly the exporters of the primary sector (but also, in India, the once world-leading textile industry). Translated into the economics of commercial production, this meant an effective lower price for all agricultural products, since the lower price in rupee terms received by any exporters lessened the ability of international prices to put upward pressure on Indian prices.

All this was accompanied by an ideological onslaught of the elite, including university-based upper-caste left intellectuals, against the peasantry. The theme of 'rich and middle peasants' appropriating the gains of development while the 'poor peasants and agricultural labourers' suffered actually began from the Congress, not the left. The reference to 'weaker sections' and the 'rural poor' was also Congress terminology, increasingly spread with Indira Gandhi's authoritarian populism. Marxist intellectuals contributed such terms as 'capitalist farmers' and 'kulak'; but once the caste issue emerged there was a near-universal response from the brahmanic elite arguing that it was the 'affluent OBCs' ('other backward castes', that is, the middle non-Brahman castes) who were the real oppressors of dalits, and that the caste rhetoric was only an ideological cloak for the contradiction between capitalist farmers and agricultural labourers. In fact, the posing by brahmanic and bourgeois interests of non-Brahmans as the main enemies of dalits, and peasants as the main enemies of agricultural labourers, can be said to be a Congress 'divide and rule' tactic which first began to be used in the 1930s.[3]

The APC played itself a major ideological role: its setting of prices was justified as rational and scientific, as providing *support prices* sufficient to cover the cost of production. Leaders of the farmers' movement complained that the APC never made its methodology public [*Joshi*, 1986: 39]; as available documents indicate, the APC initially did seem to try to calculate costs only on the basis of 'paid-out' costs without allowing anything for labour and other inputs provided by the peasant family itself – and when such 'imputed costs' were included they were promoted as a generous measure, but attributed the lowest possible value to peasant domestic labour, that is, the wage level of an 'attached' or bonded labourer.[4] The APC's price was almost always below the free market price, yet by using the term 'support price' the APC and associated intellectuals implied that the basic function of government pricing was to protect the peasants from the market and that the state was providing a better deal than private merchants did.

The terminology of 'subsidies' played a similar role: though in fact fertiliser companies were compensated for selling fertiliser below their own high costs, while irrigation projects sucked up funds that in part provided low-priced water to some farmers but also financed large bureaucracies of engineers and officials (rather than charging farmers at market prices and letting these be included in the costs of production calculations), the impression was easily spread that peasants, especially commercial farmers, were a protected, coddled section whose incomes were kept artificially high. At the same time 'cheap food' became a rallying cry as the remedy for poverty, used to beat down all efforts to contest this complex system of state-dominated production.

IDEOLOGY AND ORGANISATION IN THE FARMERS' MOVEMENT

The leaders of the new peasant movement contested at an ideological as well as agitational level. The most prominent role here was played by Sharad Joshi, a Maharashtrian who had served in Switzerland and France as an official of the Universal Postal Union from 1966 to 1976 and then resigned his job to return to India and experiment with dryland agriculture because, he said, 'visits to over forty countries had convinced me that agriculture was at the root of the poverty of the developing countries'. In 1980 he was drawn into the agitation of onion growers in Pune and Nasik districts of western Maharashtra and began immediately to pose the two major themes of the movement: prices of agricultural products, and the contradiction between 'India' and 'Bharat':

> Before independence it was the British government which took their raw materials for a song, processed the raw materials in London and Manchester, and then sold the finished product at an enormous profit. Today, Pune, Calcutta and Bombay are the London and Manchester. And our current rulers have replaced the British in grabbing the wealth of the country. I do not believe in sophisticated terms like 'class struggle'. You may call it whatever you like. But I call this the struggle between Bharat and India, the fight for liberation by Bharat from India (quoted in Tellis [1980]).

Joshi himself made no humble claims for his theory:

> I make it a point to say that this is an independent system of thought, comparable only with the Marxist system. We share with Marxism the materialist approach, find out errors in Marx where he was not materialist, we also accept the importance of capital accumulation as a generating force; we find his analysis of surplus value incorrect, and therefore we find ourselves in a position to explain Marxism's failure, i.e. why the revolution did not take place in the industrialised countries, why workers have never acted as a class as such. The two reactions to the industrial revolution up to now are the communist and the Gandhian; both are intellectually inadequate. We are definitely making up for the errors in their logic (quoted in Alvares [1985]).

The theme he stressed was that of *exploitation*. 'What is the difference between Bharat and India?', as a Marxist article put it: 'it is the distinction between exploiter and exploited' [*Joshi*, 1985b: 65]. It was explicitly said that the 'Bharat–India' distinction was not one between town and country, that there were representatives of 'Bharat' in the cities ('the pavement dwellers and slum dwellers are the refugees of Bharat in India') and of 'India' in the villages (the 'farmer leaders' who depended on the state for their wealth and power). Thus the schema gave scope for an alliance of rural and urban poor, and even while arguing for an 'all-peasant unity' provided for the existence of dominant and exploiting sections in the villages. The Marathi terminology of Shetkari Sanghatana, in fact, often referred to the 'urban dadas and rural goondas' (urban bosses and rural thugs) as exploiting sections.[5] With regard to agricultural labourers, it was argued that they should get high minimum wages with the proviso that this be incorporated into the cost of production, as a basis for peasant–labourer unity. In fact from the first (1980) conference of Shetkari Sanghatana, when a resolution for Rs 20 minimum wage was passed, the organisation consistently asked for higher minimum wages than representatives of the left and agricultural labourer organisations, and pressed for this on government committees.[6]

In the rhetoric of the movement, 'looter' and 'looting system' were terms used in place of left references to 'capitalists and landlords' or 'capitalist system'. These were not simply more populist in the sense of being readily understood by the masses of people ('looting' seems in fact to be one of the words that has passed into English from the Indian languages); they also had a theoretical point in that the emphasis was on exploition through power and thuggery, not through property holding. The relevance of the concept of 'class' was categorically denied; Joshi tended to use the concept of 'system', arguing, for instance, that Bharat and India were 'systems' which each incorporated diverse and interrelated elements. In this way the conceptual schema admitted hierarchies, diversities and even contradictions in the villages. But while denying class, Joshi insisted that his movement and theory were *economistic*, that the looting of the peasantry was the key part of *surplus accumulation*. The difference from the traditional Marxist interpretation was that this was said to be a process of force and violence, rather than one of (fundamentally peaceful) accumulation based on private property.

As with Marxism, this was seen as a historical and materialistic process. An increase in production and the associated 'accumulation of capital' (technological development) were seen as natural processes, which were associated with increasing human capability and choice, or 'degrees of freedom' in Joshi's terminology. But this natural process was interrupted with an onslaught of violence and plunder, inaugurating a long historical era of the exploitation of producers (primarily peasants) organised as unequal elements of a 'system' rather than a class by non-producers. This has taken different historical forms:

> The new farmers' movement holds that the accumulation of capital in actuality sprang from the exploitation not so much of the metropolitan industrial workers as from the exploitation of the 'third world' colonies ... agriculture with its capacity for physiocratic type of multiplication has been the [main] field of exploitation. Different forms and methods have been used ... for separating the surplus from the agriculturalist, starting from outright robberies. Robbers' bands multiplied to constitute army-like formations and political organizations who fought among themselves mainly for delimiting their ... zones of influence. Extortionate land taxation, slavery and bonded labour were the prominent products of this era. Even the religious institutions developed in a manner such as to facilitate exploitation of the peasantry. The commercial/industrial era brought in a veneer of commerciality ... but the consequences continued to be equally if not more cruel. Cheap primary goods and expensive manufactured goods was the essence of imperialism. Terms of trade proved to be more lethal than all the swords and guns of the earlier epochs. Transcontinental imperialism was replaced by internal colonialism. The former colonies developed dualistic systems ... One exploiter, successor to the bygone imperial regime, another exploited for a second time, this time at the hands of compatriots [*Joshi*, 1985a: 76–7].

Joshi thus argued that even under capitalism the extraction of surplus from agriculture and from natural resources continued to be central, and that while exchange relations and not property relations were the means of exploitation, this was not simply a result of market processes but due to the intervention of the state and its power holders. Even at the level of popular rhetoric the stress was anti-state: 'we're not asking for concessions from the state; we're asking the state to stop exploiting us'. This was sharply distinguished from a position of asking the state to give subsidies, to institute development schemes and provide investment; all these 'schemes', all government planning were seen as a way for politicians and bureaucrats to make profits while creating abject dependence among the peasants.

Finally, the analysis of exploitation was joined to a critique of the developmental model based on extracting surpluses from agriculture to build up islands of heavy industry; instead, remunerative prices would result in leaving the surpluses in the villages, in the hands of farmers (or the village councils which should be given taxing powers) where they would be used for a more labour-intensive, appropriate technology form of development. Thus, there was in fact a powerful logic behind the ideology which had its appeal to small producers and even part of the working class. It remained true, for example, that industrial workers were attracted by the idea of a 'worker–peasant' alliance with the movement even while left intellectuals tried to dissuade them; and rather than worry about whether high prices would 'lower their real wages', saw the issue as 'we're fighting for higher wages; they have a right to fight for higher prices'.[7]

At the *organisational* level, while the Shetkari Sanghatana had none of the armed guards that surrounded the BKU's Tikait, nevertheless military terminology was frequently used (*senapati* or 'general'; *fauz* or 'army') and a firm command structure was held to be a necessity for agitational campaigns. This also reflected the peasant culture of Maharashtra: guns are rarely visible, but a long history of army recruitment, some militant nationalist struggles, and a vivid sense of the heritage of the seventeenth-century king Shivaji and his bands of peasant guerrilla fighters are evocative not only for the large Kunbi-Maratha peasant caste but for all non-Brahmans; even the untouchable Mahars and Matangs have militaristic aspects to their tradition. The geographical basis of the Sanghatana is primarily in the poorer eastern (Vidarbha and Marathwada) regions of the state; in spite of its beginnings in Nasik district and an ongoing presence in irrigated areas it remains weak in the sugarcane districts. Its social base is the wide range (about 60 per cent of the population) of non-Brahman castes, the Kunbi-Maratha 'peasants' and the artisans and specialised farmer-herder 'other backward castes'; upper castes and dalits or ex-untouchables and tribals are also found in its ranks but are under-represented.

On this basis the structure is informal, with a good deal of adhocism and flexibility. There is no formal membership but a badge with the name of the organisation written in white on red ('we're the only farmers' organisation in India with a red badge') and members are expected to vow their loyalty as *paiks* or 'footsoldiers' dedicated to free themselves from subservience and fight for farmers' rights. There are, where possible, village, taluka, district and regional heads, normally appointed from above (occasional efforts to hold elections have not worked; the honesty of activists is instead maintained by the rather small chances to benefit from their positions in the organisation, with many leading activists instead going into debt to carry out their responsibilities). The 'executive' or *karyakarni* consists of these plus in most cases whoever is interested in taking part; most *karyakarni* meetings in recent years have run into hundreds. Above this is a 'high level committee', a kind of politburo consisting of all past presidents of the organisation and its women's wing; Sharad Joshi himself has no formal organisational position.

This has made for an informal but democratic process of consensual decision, though one that can of course be manipulated. In the most controversial decisions Joshi has in a sense appealed over the heads of higher-level activists (who tend to be more 'political' as well as bigger landholders) to a wider mass of activists: these have been mainly in the case of taking up the women's issue and in deciding, at the time of the 1989–90 elections, to oppose the Hindu fundamentalists as well as the Congress (leading activists, with an eye on winning, had tended to want to make an anti-Congress alliance). The December 1989 *karyakarni* meeting, when the decision was taken to allow Sanghatana activists to contest elections on Janata Dal tickets, but with the proviso that this be part of a 'progressive democratic front' of parties opposing both Congress and the BJP–Shiv Sena alliance, was taken at a tumultuous meeting of nearly 900 activists, and afterwards one BJP supporter grumbled about Joshi's manipulation and remembered nostalgically the early days of the Sanghatana when the issues were remunerative prices and 'forty to fifty of us sat together and talked over strategy'. For some other activists though, 'the whole executive (meaning the top leadership) should be lined up and shot, they don't understand Sharad Joshi's thought!' (Discussions, Hingoli, August 1989).

While such an organisational structure and Joshi's mass appeal proved effective at a Maharashtra level, at the all-India level consensus could not be so easily achieved, with diverse state-based organisations with their social and cultural particularities, jealousies about identity and autonomy, and occasional eccentric leaders. In the post-1986 upsurge even the federal structure of the ISCC faced problems. New movements arose in Gujarat and UP. In Gujarat, agitation on peasant issues was initially spearheaded by a BJP-connected farmers' organisation in the north, and representatives of independent peasant organisations in south and central Gujarat then contacted Joshi, affiliated with the ISCC and remained loyal associates. The major section of the Punjab BKU, led by Bhupinder Singh Man and A.S. Rajewal, also provided a core of strength, though the Punjabi farmers were unable to assert themselves very strongly at this time in the face of heavy police rule and Khalistani terrorism. But Karnataka's Nanjundaswamy kept his distance, criticising Joshi as a 'brahman leader of peasants' and talking of a broader 'combining of social and economic issues' to counteract the 'one-point programme' of remunerative prices. However, it was to be Mahendra Singh Tikait of western UP, heading a militant movement in the strategic region around Delhi, who proved to be the primary disorganiser of the farmers' movement.

Tikait's BKU has been one of the most researched of the new peasant organisations.[8] It had its specificities; the clan structure among Jat peasants which provided a fairly egalitarian (among landholders, not in relation to artisan or labourer castes) core to a movement which at its height successfully involved Muslim, Hindu Gujar and other communities; and concurrently a much stronger class/caste divide between landholding peasants and primarily dalit agricultural labourers than elsewhere. The dalits, whose largest section is the Chamars or Jatavs, have themselves had a history of organising, but unlike in Maharashtra there has been no common radical democratic tradition involving both caste Hindus and dalits which could provide a historical social base for unity, and the agricultural labourers in UP remained more alienated then elsewhere from the farmers' movement. Young Maharashtrian activists who had gone to Tikait's 1988 Meerut siege, put the difference in this way:

> We went ticketless, with only 24 rupees between us ... You should have seen the milk and *shirra* (a sweet dish made of wheat) they were getting! And they treat their agricultural labourers so cruelly. They really are rich peasants. Not only that, they have to talk of Ram and Krishna in every sentence they utter. They can't be scientific like us to talk of surplus and capital accumulation (discussion, Kurum, 8 March 1988).

With the rustic, eccentric, proud clan leader Tikait, thoroughly anti-urban and anti-Brahman in his attitudes, and voicing simply whatever demands seemed appropriate at the time, and the articulate and often equally arrogant Joshi, concerned for strategy and a unity of broader forces, the stage was set for a leadership struggle.

'PEASANTS STORM DELHI'

The post-1986 new peasant movement was heavily interlinked with the rise of V.P. Singh and a new opposition to Rajiv Gandhi's Congress Party. Singh, Finance and then Defence Minister in the government, resigned on the issue of the Bofors scandal and, with a trio of helpers that included one dalit, one Muslim and a cousin of Rajiv Gandhi, formed a new oppositional team that created the 'Jan Morcha' or 'People's Alliance'. Among those who responded was Sharad Joshi, speaking at Singh's first mass rally in Meerut in 1987 to assert that 'peasants were looking for a second Mahatma Gandhi to lead a new independence struggle.' And it was Joshi and his associates who began to sponsor the major rallies of Singh in Maharashtra and Gujarat, while UP's Tikait was wooed by his caste fellow and Janata Dal leader Devi Lal, the main political patriarch of the state of Haryana.

Singh on his part began to speak in radical language, claiming that the Jan Morcha was not a political party but a platform for organising movements. He associated himself with independent leaders of workers and peasants such as Datta Samant and Joshi, began to talk of 'social justice' for 'backward castes' (that is, the implementation of the Mandal Commission report which had recommended reservations in education and employment, a major demand of both dalits and the non-Brahman 'backward castes') and held talks with left leaders, including a major Naxalite group beginning to emerge from armed struggle to parliamentary respectability. The Left, he began to say, were his 'natural allies'. In turn its leaders responded, attempting to influence the new formation in what they perceived as a radical direction.

For most progressive intellectual commentators, however, the influence of the social movements on the new political formation made it a potentially dangerous force, with its orientation to demands for higher prices for farmers and reservations for the middle castes, or 'affluent OBCs' as they were referred to. One commentator, describing this elite disdain for the social forces massing behind V.P. Singh, pointed in colourful language to the kind of contradiction the farmers movement was talking about:

> There is, to be sure, a lot of fear behind the sneer. There is fear that the so-called backward classes and harijans will make a determined bid for power at the national level and thus put an end to the elitist rule that has prevailed since 1985 . . . Girilal Jain [then editor of *The Times of India*] has gone to the length of suggesting that only Brahmans can hold India together, while one of his columnists finds in the cohorts of Devi Lal tribes and groups condemned by the

> British as 'Criminals' and therefore capable of 'criminalizing' the political process ... Devi Lal is nothing short of an apparition. He would bring the jats, gujars, ahirs – the narods – to power in Delhi; with them will come the mobilised peasants of the entire Hindi belt and the politically mobilised dalits of Rajasthan and Maharashtra. They will rampage the imperial superstructure built in forty years of independence, with the glitter of five-star hotels and the feasty social and political culture of the English-speaking elite [*Sen Gupta*, 1988].

The new Janata Dal politicians were finding their constituencies in the social movements: Devi Lal was making his claim as the 'farmers' leader'; Ram Vilas Paswan of Bihar staked his claim as a dalit leader, Sharad Yadav as one of the 'backward classes' (and the soon-to-be chief ministers of UP and Bihar, Mulayam Singh Yadav and Lallu Prasad Yadav, also); Maneka Gandhi as an animal liberation and environmental advocate. And finally it must be noted that V.P. Singh himself began to delineate a political identity as a leader of dalits and 'backwards', one that became the centre of his politics after the fall of his government.

But regardless of their social background, politicians wooing constituencies are something quite different from actual movement leaders, and Joshi had consistently refused to recognise even Singh in that fashion, justifying his support only as a need to maintain 'a balance of power among thieves' (*Indian Express*, 1988). There were real differences in the nature of articulation of farmers' interests and demands. Devi Lal took as a major slogan the theme of increasing the investment in agriculture to 50 per cent of the government budget; this in a sense was a typical politicians' (and even left) statist view which stressed action from above; Joshi replied that 'in our opinion that is not an important issue at all. Agriculture is the source of all wealth. So what is ploughed into agriculture cannot be all that important. What is ploughed away is far more important' [*Joshi*, 1990]. Further, interparty factions also illustrated very differing tendencies. Within the Janata Dal in Maharastra Joshi and the Sanghatana found themselves taking the side of state president Mrinal Gore and her mainly urban group (both having their ties with Singh at the national level) *against* the 'rural bosses' of the party (who had their national links with Chandrasekhar and Devi Lal) on some crucial issues, such as the opposition to alliance with the Hindu right parties.[9]

Yet politicians consistently tried to 'speak for' the farmers. This could have been countered by a strong independent force of the movement, and a mass rally proposing to bring five million peasants to Delhi had long been urged by Joshi and others in the ISCC. The main problem after 1986 was to bring Tikait and his allies into this. Tikait resisted, holding his independent rallies which he described as 'kisan panchayats' first in Meerut, where he refused to let Joshi share the platform, then in Delhi itself. These events impressed and fascinated the urban elite (in Meerut because they united Muslim and Hindu peasants in a city which a few months before had been the site of communal riots; in Delhi because there was no molestation of women in a city known for its chauvinism, and because the Congress Party itself was forced to move its own rally in a surrender before 'peasant power'), but they were no substitute for a united movement. Tikait then toured India, insisting that his own BKU was the only centre for peasant unity and that there must be 'one flag, one organization, one leader'.

As this did not get sufficient response, in June 1989 Tikait finally marched into Ambethan, Joshi's village centre, with his armed guard told to leave their guns at the door. A united rally at the Delhi Boat Club was declared under the auspices of the ISCC; it was postponed once again, then finally confirmed for 23 October 1989, Gandhi's birthday.

But it was an ill-fated day. As hundreds of thousands, perhaps over a million, peasants poured into the city, a new drama was enacted. The leaders of the ISCC waited on the platform for two hours with no sign of Tikait and his men. Finally the latter marched in, with Tikait shouting 'come down from the stage'. Women of the Shetkari Sanghatana rushed forward shouting slogans of unity. These had some effect: one photographer caught Tikait beating one of his own men for echoing the appeal (*Navbharat Times*, 3 October 1989). Tikait's men, though, continued to shake the platform; Joshi, a heart patient and feeling a spasm come on, jumped down and went off to the hospital. Total confusion then ensued until the Shetkari Sanghatana and other ISCC groups removed themselves to the other side of the India Gate, and two separate rallies were held. The split in the new peasant movement stood revealed; its independent force was severely weakened.

This was the context in which Devi Lal became deputy prime minister and the most powerful 'spokesman' for farmers' interest. Nevertheless, just before the crucial 1990 Maharashtra state assembly elections, at a huge rally in Nagpur following the Shetkari Sanghatana's 25-day campaign through rural areas combating Hindu fundamentalism in the name of the 'Phule-Ambedkar' tradition, V.P. Singh announced the formation of a new 'Standing Advisory Committee on Agriculture' to be chaired by Joshi. There were already two major committees, an 'Expert Committee for Calculating the Costs of Cultivation in Agriculture' headed by the consistently anti-farmer C. Hanumantha Rao, and a 'high-power committee' headed by Bhanu Pratap Singh, a supporter of farmers' demands.

The SAC was to be given precedence, however; its chair was to have cabinet minister status and it would have the responsibility for formulating a new agricultural policy. Joshi went through the initial proposal from the agricultural ministry and declared it to be useless; the committee then took up the task of drafting an entirely new major policy for agriculture, the first time this had been done in independent India.

THE NATIONAL AGRICULTURAL POLICY

The year 1989 was a turning point throughout the world as Communist regimes in eastern Europe came crashing to the ground. The old models of socialist development which had been under assault for years were now radically revealed as bankrupt. At the same time there was hope that a genuine, even green, democratic socialist force might pose an alternative to capitalist models as well. In India, the defeat of the Congress by a force with socialist pretensions, yet depending on grassroots movements posing different forms of development and backed by the main Communist parties, seemed to offer similar promise.

It was in some ways a year of 'alternatives'. The new social movements were broadening from single-issue and sometimes localised struggles to pose broader alliances [*Omvedt*, 1992]. The Narmada Bachao Andolan, against the building of huge dams on the Narmada river, had brought together a coalition to organise the biggest-ever environmental rally (about 25,000) at the small town of Harsud, which argued for a 'peoples' development in contrast to destructive development. The 'alternative development' theme began to be much debated in Maharashtra, spearheaded by a local environmentalist peasant movement in Sangli district. The fish workers' movement in Kerala made a wider thrust with a march along the coasts of India on the theme 'Protect Waters, Protect Life.'

But 'alternative development' was still a theme not acceptable to the traditional left. Communist parties in particular still focused on heavy industry and reliance on the state as the key to moving towards socialism; their major theme to try to influence the National Front government became that of 'right to work.' Both Communists and socialists, and many NGOs, sought to organise on this, to make it the central political issue.

The major official document which sought to incorporate some form of socialist alternative (and which can thus be contrasted with the National Agricultural Policy) was the Approach Paper to the Eighth Plan put forward by a new Planning Commission which incorporated prominent Socialist-Gandhians. However, the paper, titled 'Towards Structural Transformation', illustrated not so much an alternative structuring of the economy as the limits of traditional Gandhian alternative thinking. The Approach Paper stressed the 'right to work' and sought to actualise employment-generating growth. It also took up Devi Lal's theme of 50 per cent investment in agriculture, and picked up the slogan of 'democratic decentralization'. But decentralisation was not to mean an actual recognition of the autonomous power of lower level political bodies. Instead, what was proposed was 'integrated local area planning' and the 'transfer of resources' from the state to lower level bodies, that is, assuming that the state would go on extracting resources to the top but simply channel somewhat more of them back downwards (and in the process continuing to allow bureaucrats and politicians their share). There was no mention of remunerative prices, and the section on irrigation stressed its expansion and the development of agricultural productivity in arid and semi-arid zones, co-opting some of the rhetoric but completely avoiding the issues raised by those who opposed big dams and 'destructive development' [*Planning Commission*, 1990]. In fact, '50 per cent investment in irrigation' may be argued to be incompatible with a democratic sustainable development, in that almost all such investment up to that point had gone for major irrigation projects and fertiliser subsidies, and there was no reason to think that new investment would be any different.

In contrast to the Approach Paper, the National Agricultural Policy won very little intellectual or bureaucratic support and was not published by government sources at all. Nevertheless it also began with an invocation of Gandhism:

> The Gandhian talisman would be the natural reference point. How do the most deprived and the most oppressed see things? What is their vocation? How is it that despite long hours of back-breaking work they find it impossible to eke out a living? This brings us to the essence of all process of development – application of labour to land, in brief, policy as regards agriculture [*NAP*, 1991: 8].

And the connection of remunerative prices to a balanced development was asserted as a Gandhian model [*NAP*, 1991: 10]:

> The model of development used hitherto can be briefly summarized as follows: surplus from agriculture – capital formation in urban centres – import of technology and machinery – low employment – insufficient effective demand coexisting with low standard of living – external dependence – low rates of growth.
>
> The Gandhian model, on the other hand, works as follows: surplus from agriculture – capital formation in rural centres/

villages – higher agricultural production, investment, wages – self-sufficient villages – development of non-agricultural activities at appropriate levels of technology – massive effective demand for industries – self-sustained cycle of growth and development.

The battle was thus, in effect, joined. We can separate two major aspects of the NAP, the issue of the remuneration for labour in agriculture, which occupied only a small portion of the document but was the centre of greatest controversy, and the whole set of goals and programmes for the development of agriculture and agro-industry over a period of two decades, which represented the proposed alternative development path.

THE REMUNERATION OF LABOUR

Two-thirds of India's workforce, were, as of 1991, still occupied in agriculture, 38.41 per cent of main workers as cultivators, 26.44 per cent as agricultural labourers [*Census of India, 1992*: Table 4.1]. Though many agricultural labourers also had land that they worked, and many poor peasants also worked as labourers, this is probably a fair indication of the degree to which 'family labour' outweighs hired labour overall; it can even be called an underestimate of family labour since all censuses and surveys systematically underestimate women's labour, especially that on family land.

Further, these workers in agriculture were the poorest section of the population. Cultivators and agricultural labourers had the lowest incomes of any broad section of the workforce: in 1981, compared to an average of Rs 10,800 for organised sector workers, cultivators earned an average income of Rs 3,000 and agricultural labourers Rs 1,703 (unorganised sector non-agricultural wage workers earned an average of Rs 4,871 and the non-cultivating self-employed in the unorganised sector earned Rs 5,066) [*CMIE*, 1990: Table 10.1]. Thus the question of the remuneration of labour in agriculture is both a question of the role of crop prices and agrarian wages in overall economic development *and* a direct question of toilers' rights, to struggle for a higher income either through prices or wages. It can be argued that the question of resolving Indian poverty does centre here: in assuring higher income, not 'cheap food' to the poor.

Indeed, the Shetkari Sanghatana rhetoric on prices and wages had consistenly put the issue in terms of rights: *bhik nako have ghamala dam* ('we don't want alms but the return for our sweat') was not only the most popular slogan but in speeches Sharad Joshi constantly spoke the language of rights. In arguments about the minimum wages for agricultural labourers he scathingly attacked the existing practice of trying to compute minimum wage in terms of the cost of living, based on the amount of foodgrain needed to feed a family of five consisting of two workers, with 40 per cent added for other expenditure: 'Are human beings buffalos or something that they only need to eat?'. Not all leaders of the Sanghatana spoke in such language (for example, the more conservative one-time president, Anil Gote, tended to refer to 'the shame that we cannot pay our labourers more'), but it was taken up by lower level activists. Given that a popular national slogan was *jay jawan jay kisan* ('long live the soldier and peasant'). Joshi then suggested taking as a criterion for a minimum standard of living the entering pay of an ordinary soldier. This was apparently Rs 25 by 1987, and this sum was then taken as the demand from 1987 through 1990. Other organisations accepted it, and even Tikait took it up [*Jose*, 1989]. It was much higher than any existing minimum wage law, but when Orissa's chief minister announced a legal minimum wage of Rs 25 in 1990, there was a scathing comment by the Marxist columnist Ashok Mitra in *Economic and Political Weekly* to the effect that no agricultural labour organisation had fought the scorned 'kulak' movement.[10]

The debate over the remuneration of labour in the National Agricultural Policy was simple. The existing practice was to take the wages paid out for agricultural labourers, calculate male family labour at the value of an 'attached labour' and calculate female family labour at a low percentage of this (ten per cent according to Joshi). It was on this basis that the 'costs' to be covered by government-set prices were calculated. The NAP recommended, in contrast, that all labour 'domestic and hired', men and women, be calculated at a legal minimum wage set for agricultural labourers which should, as a minimum, be equal to the entering pay for an army *jawan*, or Rs 25. This was heavily opposed; primarily via Hanumantha Rao's 'expert committee' which recommended that wages actually paid out (to agricultural labourers) be used as the basis. Hanumantha Rao charged that the SAC's position was an unjustifiable one of kulak farmers who wanted to claim the minimum wages while paying out much less to their labourers. This became the main theme of opponents of the NAP, ranging from journalistic commentators and intellectuals to the SAC's member-secretary (the bureaucrat assigned to the committee) who issued a dissenting note claiming, among other things, that for the government to be compelled to buy agricultural products at prices calculated in such a way would involve an annual expenditure of Rs 25,000 crore (about $10 billion at current prices).

The Expert Committee's position had a reasonable look to it, reasonable at least to those conditioned to 'cheap food' and anti-'kulak' arguments: how could those grasping rich farmers ask for higher wages to be calculated in their cost of production while actually paying very low rates? (In fact the committee's survey showed that over much of the country wages were higher than the legal minimum; however, they were in some cases lower, especially for women, and the SAC was indeed asking for raising the legal wages significantly.) In part this was a chicken-and-egg question: farmers could very well argue that they could not afford to pay our higher wages than they were compensated for, and in fact by making 'actual wages paid out' a criterion the government was adding to its bureaucracy, forcing farmers to wait a period of months or a year before surveys confirmed any rise in wages, and exhibiting a strange belief that its own laws were not to be implemented. But there was much more than this wrong with the 'Expert Committee's' position, especially from the point of view of presumed leftists who should have been concerned about the level of remuneration to the lowest paid labour in the land:

(1) It implied that, if the level of wages paid our represented a high rate of exploitation and surplus extraction, the entire resulting surplus was to be extracted from the farmer by the government;
(2) It represented the project of exploiting the male family labour of the peasant household at the same level, that is, extracting surplus above the extremely low standard of living represented by that of the agricultural wage labour; and
(3) It represented the project of super-exploiting the female family labour of the peasant household and, since the household 'head' was not to be paid a family wage, practically forced the woman to go out to work as a wage labourer to supplement the family income.

Besides the issue of return for labour, the other major point of dispute in costing methodology was the calculation of 'managerial costs': both the SAC and the 'Expert Committee' agreed that managerial costs of ten per cent should be added to cost of production, but whereas the SAC wanted them calculated as ten per cent of total cost of production, Hanumantha Rao's committee wanted this to be ten per cent of actually paid out costs. This would have discriminated in favour of the regions with richer farmers (who had more paid-out costs) as compared to the toiling 'middle peasants' (a greater proportion of whose costs were in terms of family labour).

It is difficult to escape the conclusion that the only principle lying behind the 'Expert Committee' recommendations was that of keeping costs, and hence prices, low. Its report argued that its recommendations (evaluating family labour at the rate of casual labour rather than attached labour, including a ten per cent managerial cost) would have the effect of raising the total cost of production by rates ranging from 3.7 per cent to 13 per cent for different crops and regions ('A Costly Controversy', *Economic Times*, 6 August 1990). This was, after all, not much more than inflation levels. On the other hand the SAC's methodology would have raised costs tremendously. But this was only a consequence of the existing very low levels of return to labour in agriculture linked to the current costing methodology and the whole paraphernalia of state intervention in the market. The raising of prices could have been spread out over a period of years once it was recognised in principle that they were too low and that the state had a commitment to raising them as part of its commitment to raising the standard of living of the poorest section of the population. (Further, it would have been compensated by major reductions on fertiliser and irrigation subsidies.) The estimate of the member-secretary that the whole proposal would cost Rs 25,000 crore a year can be taken, conversely, as an estimate of the surplus extracted yearly by means of low prices from agriculture and from the peasants and agricultural labourers who worked in the fields.

It was clear, in any case, from the reactions to the SAC proposals and the way the issue of labour was treated that it was too much to expect from the bureaucracy and most of the intelligentsia of the time to recognise in principle, that the poverty of peasants and agricultural labourers was linked to the economic viability of agriculture, incomes and prices.

THE TRANSFORMATION OF DEVELOPMENT

Prices occupied only a small portion of the NAP. The major part was devoted to a full-ranging formulation of alternatives for agricultural development which inevitably implied a broad alternative pattern for development as a whole. Asserting the need for 'a drastic reordering of the pattern of national priorities,' it outlined future challenges [*NAP*, 1991: 12]:

> The shortsighted rush for industrialisation has left the country, four decades after independence, with a seriously damaged life support system – land, water and vegetation. Even before starting to resolve the ecological problems of the bullock-cart era, the nation is facing the problems of industrial pollution. The unbalanced economic policies are threatening to tear apart the social fabric. The population to be fed is increasing even beyond the worst prognosis. Within a very short period a third of the land actually cultivated

> would need to be diverted from uneconomic agriculture to pastures and forests. A technology package which has, for the time being, given some respite, based as it is on rapidly dwindling petroleum resources, would soon become unfeasible. An alternative technology will need to be resorted to. Despite all these formidable handicaps, a surplus will have to be generated that would ensure increasing standards of living. The NAP faces a really formidable challenge.

Taking, therefore, two decades as a period for planning, and calling for an 'emergency' approach to issues such as the restoration of the topsoil and the impending petroleum shortage, the NAP [1991: 14–16] outlined the following goals:

(1) an achievement of a minimum rate of growth in agriculture of four per cent per year;
(2) raising the minimum recompense for labour in agriculture to that of the lowest strata of organised sector employees;
(3) planned shift of population from agricultural production (not necessarily to the cities, preferably to industrial employment in the villages) so that the proportion of population dependent on agriculture would be reduced to 50 per cent;
(4) restoration and amelioration of the 'life support system' including land, water and biomass; restoration of pasture and forest lands and relieving one-third of the land under plough from exhausting cultivation;
(5) 'initiation of a real Green Revolution' that would be less dependent on petroleum resources; and
(6) giving women, who perform about two-thirds of agricultural work, 'a commensurate recompense and parity on ownership of land and property'.

The framework of these efforts would include (a) the abolition of government policies that 'along with natural economic infirmities of agriculture tend to deny agriculturalists prices and consequently wages', and (b) goals of production that included (1) food; (2) raw materials for the growing non-agrarian sector; (3) creation of exportable surplus for procurement of materials and products from abroad; and (4) creation of further surplus for capital and technology development, and for capital formation in backward and forward linkage activities and other sectors.

Some of these goals seem unexceptionable; few would deny the need to withdraw population from agriculture or provide for a higher living standard. The points about withdrawing land from plough cultivation and moving away from petroleum-based inputs were noteworthy, however, at a time when nearly everyone assumed that to increase production only two methods were open: bringing more land under cultivation or increasing industrial inputs, that is, chemical fertilisers and pesticides and mechanisation. The NAP programme in contrast was for a kind of ecological agriculture. Some agricultural economists did, in fact, argue that India had too much, not too little, land under cultivation; the need for restoring forests was widely recognised and the role of grassland and pasture was only beginning to be admitted by more environmentally conscious scientists. That production could be increased on less land while reducing petroleum-based inputs was, however, more controversial. Joshi in fact had wanted to make some definite statements about the capacity to substitute natural fertilisers and methods for NAP, but found it impossible to get expert testimonial on this issue before the committee. The NAP thus called for stepping up the provision of hybrid seeds and inputs to farmers, but in a way that would step up efficiency of use, and included an integrated strategy involving greater recycling of organic waste, using rock phosphate, tapping biological nitrogen fixation, and greater efforts in bio-gas plants and use of solar energy. Rather than simply 'extending the Green Revolution to the east' as government programmes called for[11] the NAP called for development of diverse strategies in consonance with the requirements of each region and involving more use of biofertilisers [*NAP*, 1991: 21; *Joshi*, 1991]. Further, it called for an end to subsidies for chemical fertilisers, on the grounds that they benefited inefficient fertiliser companies rather than the farmers [*NAP*, 1991: 17–18].

Regarding irrigation, the NAP also called for a change in direction, away from the emphasis 'on surface irrigation and, in particular, on big dams and canal networks'. With an eye particularly to the Gujarat farmers who were enthusiastic backers of the Sardar Sarovar (Narmada river) dam in the belief that it would provide water to drought-stricken peasants, it did not oppose 'big dams' as such, and stated that 'ongoing projects cannot be arrested or postponed'. But it did state that these projects needed to be revised and that future irrigation policy should focus on ground water as the principle source of irrigation and give priority to projects aimed at increasing the percolation of water into the soil [*NAP*, 1991: 22–4].

Along with this were proposals for the development of fisheries, horticulture, animal husbandry and dairying, and poultry, with emphasis on encouraging indigenous stocks; research should also be directed at non-traditional sources of energy and non-petroleum Green Revolution technology, with continual research to improve seeds, fertilisers, pesticides and operational methods seen as necessary. It was noted that present research was 'ivory-tower', without real contact with farmers, and that once farming was made profitable farmers should be able to pay for services and consultancy services: 'all agricultural research institutes should be required to justify their research or at least a good portion of it, on the basis of specific demands made by farmers supported by their willingness to bear a major part of the cost' [*NAP*, 1991: 44]. Support for home packaging and processing units within the village was also stressed. It was also stated that the cost of cultivation need not oblige the government to fix a price that would cover the entire cost; the support price/market interventions should be used as a measure for influencing cropping patterns.

The NAP also took stands on all other major equalitarian issues. The Public Distribution System, it argued, should be revised to 'remove from its scope the upper strata of society' (with a reduction of some 50 per cent suggested) and shops in villages should be managed by village panchayats rather than individual shopowners [*NAP*, 1991: 38–40]. Regarding land, the farmers' movements were not supporters of 'land to the tiller', and the NAP argued that 'employment and reasonable wages and not empty title to a piece of land are the real needs of the labourer' [*NAP*, 1991: 37]. The scope for reducing further land ceilings was said to be exhausted[12] and the usual arguments about the lack of anything comparable in urban areas were made. Nevertheless, it stated that there should be a final resurvey of landholdings and a vigorous implementation (without any compensation if excess lands were not voluntarily disclosed) of existing ceilings. Given that in fact most land struggles are directed either to *benami* (illegally excess) landholdings or to occupations of government lands, with even some radical organisations ready to admit that there was little scope for reduction in the ceilings, this position was reasonable and in fact did represent a 'small producers' tendency within the farmers' movement. The NAP went a step beyond even left organisations of the time by saying that daughters should be treated on a par with sons in inheritance, and that surplus land should either be put at the disposal of village panchayats or, if given to individuals, titles should be transferred in the name of female family members [*NAP*, 1991: 22].

The NAP also called for decentralisation with a more specific statement on community control but with significant differences from the rhetoric of the 'Approach of the Eighth Plan'. Noting the tendency towards concentration of powers at the centre, it argued that the decisions regarding ground level operations 'should be moved as closely as possible to the field'. The centre should be responsible for maintaining buffer stocks, supplying food to deficit regions, research, provision of inputs, export and import, selected processing industries and guidelines on price management, with these functions rationalised under a senior minister. The planning and execution should be shifted to the local community. This required a strengthening of panchayat raj (local self-government institutions), with village councils or panchayats to have taxing powers and to be in control of all village resources:

> The panchayats thus constituted would have the ownership of the entire land vested in them as also specific lands allocated as common, grazing, forest or agricultural lands for their exploitation as such. In many tribal villages shifting cultivation is a fairly common practice. If proper attention is paid for regeneration of the forests, shifting agriculture by itself is not an undesirable practice. While allocating the area of control to the tribal panchayats the area allocated should be extensive enough to permit continuation of the practice [*NAP*, 1991: 29].

This specific support for local community ownership of natural resources was a more radical form of decentralisation than the Planning Commission had backed. Finally, with the stress on ending subsidies (except at the point of consumption) on 'cost effectiveness not only in agriculture but throughout the economy' [*NAP*, 1991: 187], and on deregulation of agriculture support mechanisms, the central approach of the NAP was one that Joshi could claim later as being a 'manifesto for liberalization' (Joshi, interview).

AGRICULTURAL POLICY ISSUES

The fate of the agricultural policy drafted by SAC can be fairly quickly described. Its drafting occupied much of the period from June to September 1990. There was little open public discussion, but themes leaked to the press attracted denunciation: 'Farm plan boon for kulaks'; 'Farmers gain at consumers' expense' and 'Hike in foodgrain prices will check industrial growth' were typical news stories, while the report of the Hanumantha Rao committee received much more favourable response [*Roy*, 1990a; 1990b; *Patnaik*, 1990b]. During the latter part of this period V.P. Singh was coming under increasing pressure, first from Devi Lal, which led him first to proclaim a 'kisan decade' in the 15 August independence speech from the Red Fort, and then to announce the implementation of the Mandal Commission recommendations for reservations for backward castes. The latter led to a massive storm of protest and a student 'movement' that included hundreds of suicide burnings; the storm and the threatened split among 'forward caste' and 'backward caste' Hindus in turn provoked the Hindu rightist party, the BJP, to step up its campaign for the building of a new Ram temple in Ayodhya with a country-wide tour that resulted in riots killing thousands of Muslims and finally ended in the arrest of the leaders and the killing of some Hindus in a police firing at Ayodhya itself. The BJP then withdrew its support and the government fell, to be replaced by an unstable, Congress-supported extreme minority government led by Chandrasekhar as Prime Minister and Devi Lal as, once again, Deputy Prime Minister.

During this last period, Singh had not found time to even meet Sharad Joshi, and the new government worked actively to bury the proposal. In December the 'member-secretary' of the committee issued his dissenting note, which he had insisted on attaching to any publication of the policy. In it he attacked the goals of relieving one-third of land from plough cultivation and vesting income and land ownership in the hands of women as 'lofty views which can merely raise false hopes and damage government credibility'. He also opposed goals of reduction of unemployment and reducing population dependent on agriculture to 50 per cent, argued that tribals and scheduled castes were not neglected, implied that technological packages for improving productivity in rainfed areas did not exist and so had not been adopted hitherto, and gave the estimate of Rs 25,000 crores ($10 billion) as the completely unacceptable cost of government purchase at prices asked for by farmers (*Business and Political Observer*, 4 Dec. 1990).

This open bureaucratic opposition paved the way for a high-level meeting on 8 January 1991 under Chandrasekar, with Devi Lal, an isolated Sharad Joshi, the chairman of the Commission on Agricultural Costs and Prices, the new deputy chairman of the Planning Commission and the member-secretary of SAC. This interpreted the controversy as one between the agricultural ministry and SAC and appointed a new drafting committee, under Devi Lal to 'iron out final changes' (*Economic Times*, 9 Jan. 1991). Instead a much watered-down alternative document was submitted in March 1991 that was welcomed by the Federation of Indian Chambers of Commerce and Industry and most newspaper editorials, and denounced by Joshi as 'a meaningless collection of phrases' (*Economic Times*, 16 April 1991; *The Hindu*, 10 April 1991). The fall of the Chandrasekhar government left even this in the bureaucratic dustbin, and the new Narasimha Rao government that was finally elected in May 1991 had its economic antennae fixed in far different directions than in agricultural policy. 'Liberalisation' and a 'new economic policy' went rapidly ahead but with a foreign and an industrial orientation and, when finally in 1993 the agricultural ministry brought forward a 'draft agricultural policy resolution' of a little over five pages, it was again attacked by Joshi and farmers' representatives as a 'non-agricultural non-policy non-resolution'. The Kisan Coordinating Committee published and circulated the SAC's National Agricultural Policy, including translations in Marathi, Punjabi and Gujarati (there was also an unpublished Kannada version) and at a 300,000 strong rally in the small town of Shegaon on 19 November 1991, the Shetkari Sanghatana announced its adoption as a 'manifesto of the movement'.

The NAP thus had come close to the seats of power but ended as a movement document, along with a new programme for agriculture which stressed (1) experimentation with low-input or no-input farming on part of the family land; this was to be done primarily by women and was called 'Sita farming'; (2) home processing of agricultural products or value-addition; it was argued that no farm products should be taken to market without at least some primary processing or packaging; (3) the establishment of direct producer–consumer outlets; and (4) export agriculture (both of the latter were also to be focused largely on 'natural' farming with highly reduced use of chemical inputs). The fall of the V.P. Singh government and the failure of any official recognition of the NAP had represented a defeat for the farmers' movement, just as it had in different ways for other new social movements, but with the 'new economic policy' of an unstable, minority Congress government, Sharad Joshi claimed a victory: the power of the state to exercise control over agriculture was vanishing. The farmers' movement, he argued in Sanghatana meetings, had always called for the withdrawal of state intervention, 'for the state to stop exploiting us'. Now events beyond the scope of the movement itself were forcing the same result, he noted, much as the British had been forced to grant India independence not simply by the strength of the national struggle as by their sheer inability to maintain control in a changing world. The Shetkari Sanghatana and the Kisan Coordinating Committee thus welcomed 'liberalisation' in principle while condemning many specific government policies (the failure to extend liberalisation to farmers, the import of three million tons of wheat from the US, Canada and Australia, unnecessary loans from the IMF). And the nature of mobilisation shifted to demand the withdrawal of the state rather than any specific policies of intervention by the state. Joshi went so far as to call for full local 'autonomy' and a 'second republic' which would leave the central state only with powers of police and defense, in a rally marking Gandhi memorial day on 30 January 1992.[13]

The extreme anti-state rhetoric was now becoming in part a strategic ploy in a campaign to build up democratic support for economic reforms. This seemed to give an strong ideological character to the ongoing split in the farmers' movement, as the Nanjundaswamy–Tikait group joined campaigns to oppose the entry of multinationals, on the charge that they would capture control of agriculture and farmers through control of seeds resulting from liberalisation and patents. One section of farmers seemed to be seeing the state as the main exploiter, the other capitalism and the market. The two groups held opposing rallies in Delhi in March 1993; which was bigger depended on the politics of the observer (the most objective accounts gave the KCC rally a slight edge, but the Nanjundaswamy–Tikait rally clearly had the most massive backing of Delhi progressive intellectuals).

The split should have been unnecessary. All sections of the farmers' movement were anti-statist and anti-industrial capitalist in their thrust; in fact the Shetkari Sanghatana at the time was probably doing the most of any mass organisation to implement a programme of non-chemical agriculture in which farmers, and not multinationals, would do their own processing and control their own inputs. Nor was it rigidly anti-statist. Anti-statism was a part of the general thrust of the farmers' movement, but while the national agricultural policy called for a good deal of autonomy and powers (including local planning to the village level), it nevertheless left a major role for the state in guidelines, research, provision of services, inputs and so on. What is interesting about the NAP period is that it represented a policy clearly outlining a direction towards ecological agriculture and sustainable development along with its vigorous demands for higher income for peasants and agricultural labourers.

In fact the main issues of the debate show the fallacy of much of the journalistic and academic left characterisation of the so-called 'rich farmers' lobby'. The NAP (and the Maharashtra, Punjab and Gujarat organisations which were its base strength) showed no interest in demanding higher state investment in agriculture, for example; this was pushed by Devi Lal and by the socialist-oriented Planning Commission. Even more significant were stands on the issue of fertiliser subsidy, which has been one of the most costly items in recent years in the Indian budget, and which has been the centre of debate and agitation especially since the proposals for a 'new economic policy'. According to popular left rhetoric, 'rich farmers demand fertiliser subsidies'. Yet Shetkari Sanghatana and the KCC clearly opposed subsidies, and even farmers' organisations in the opposing section, such as Nanjundaswamy's Rayat Sangh, showed no great enthusiasm about the issue and stated that fertiliser subsidies could be withdrawn provided farmers be compensated for higher production costs. Punjabi farmers demonstated on the issue but with the resolution that they would stop using chemical fertilisers; the Maharashtrian farmers in Shetkari Sanghatana areas remained aloof while dissident

Congressmen tried to organise rallies opposing the 'rise in fertiliser prices'. It was rather all the left parties, from the CPI and CPI(M) and the Naxalite Peoples' War Group, to socialists such as the Janata Dal and socialist youth organisations such as Sangarsh Vahini, which took stands opposing withdrawal of subsidies and attempted to mobilise farmers for this. By the logic of the equation, fertiliser subsidies = benefit to rich farmers, *they* should have been called the pro-kulak lobby. A more careful analysis of the fertiliser subsidy issue would suggest that the interests behind them were bureaucratic and political rather than those of any particular segment of the peasantry.

Similarly his vigorous and sometimes overstated support for open market policies brought Sharad Joshi more at odds with the democratic and left parties than he had ever been before. These were busy denouncing liberalisation, the Dunkel Draft and market policies as a sell-out to imperialism. By these standards, Sharad Joshi and the KCC were not simply capitalist farmers but imperialist agents: with the banners at their 31 March Delhi rally describing them as 'Farmers for Feedom' and saying 'dhanyawad Dunkel' (thanks, Dunkel), and with Joshi saying tartly in an interview when asked whether patents would not make farmers slaves of multinationals, that this would be better than current slavery to the Indian state ('If we have to be somebody's slaves we prefer that they be more competent people': see Roychaudhuri and Shankar [1993]), it is perhaps understandable that the left would be alienated and that some commentators would scramble to see how they could make a 'class' distinction between the KCC and the Nanjundaswamy–Tikait group, either by describing the latter as the 'poor peasants' who were demonstrating against multinationals, or by trying to argue that if they were indeed 'rich and middle peasants' then the others were comprador-capitalist farmers 'with feudal tails' [*BM*, 1993.].

But it was at this point that the taken-for-granted 'class categories' were failing to make sense of events. The left in India has been failing to grapple with some important world realities, along with offering no programme of its own for an alternative 'restructuring'. For instance, the Chinese economic reforms after 1978 have been doing, under the name of a 'socialist market economy', much that the new peasant movement and Sharad Joshi have asked for in India, and with a very positive effect on overall economic growth. This success was bringing with it a need to re-think the achievement of China in the earlier period: during the Mao era, land reform and the preservation of minimum health and welfare equality within the commune had been offset by low incomes (resulting from forced production of foodgrains at low prices), drying up of rural sidelines which had been sources of supplements to peasant income, shrinkage and disappearance of once popular local festivals, maintenance of inequalities between communes and a growing gap between urban and rural income to about four to six times in the late 1970s, and vulnerability of villagers to major shocks such as the famine between 1959 and 1962 which killed an estimated 17 to 30 million people [*Matson and Selden*, 1992.]

> If vulnerability accompanied landlessness in India, the equal shares of land Chinese peasants acquired in land reform proved woefully inadequate in protecting them from the depredations of the great leap, giving rise to famine deaths on a scale that has no counterpart in independent India and in any historical conjuncture. Access to land represents the most basic of entitlements in such overwhelmingly agrarian societies, yet at moments of crisis in China even relatively equitable land distribution proved less central to peasant well-being than tax, price and procurement policies that were driven by a push for state-centered accumulation and industrialisation [*Matson and Selden*, 1992: 709].

After 1978, often against the will of a conservative leadership, these policies began to be changed and liberalisation hit the countryside as commune land was divided up and grain prices increased by 50 per cent. As a result foodgrain output grew faster in the 1980s than ever before and non-grain crops did even better; much of the agricultural surplus was invested in small rural industry (the 'township, village and private' enterprises), which became the fastest growing sector in the economy, employing 51 per cent women; real rural incomes doubled or better by 1989 [*Matson and Selden*, 1992; *Byrd and Qingsong*, 1990]. China began to look like a miracle economy, and new speculation that 'a big dragon was following the little ones'.

There were unevennesses, problems of inequality, authoritarian rule, corruption, and ecological destruction linked to all of this. Yet it is equally arguable that much of this has been due not to the reforms as such but to the efforts of the party bureaucracy to hang on to power. Conservatives in the state, fearful of urban protest, have repressed it on the one hand and tried to pacify it on the other, holding back reforms after 1985 with forced procurement at low grain prices, giving rise to rural struggles and warnings that farmers who would not willingly grow grain at such low prices would increasingly turn to non-grain alternatives and China would again become dependent on imports [*Friedman*, 1990; *Putterman*, 1992; *Carter and Zhong*, 1991]. Scholars of China are arguing that the destruction of 'food self-sufficiency' would come about not so much because of the market economy or involvement in export, but because of the contradiction of Third World states trying to maintain low crop prices in an era where farmers really had a choice in what to grow. In any event, whatever the unevennesses, the turn towards a 'socialist market economy' has resulted in a six per cent agricultural and 12 per cent industrial average annual growth rate of GDP (overall nine per cent) in the 1980s, and has also seen increasing Chinese government support for programmes of 'ecological agriculture' that indicates an important turn away from the expensive petroleum-based Green Revolution-type technology that it had adopted in the era of the command economy [*Taylor*, 1992].

The Chinese experience suggests that the Indian farmers' movement, with its rallying cry of 'remunerative prices', was right about a very major point: that higher prices can lead to *local* investment of the surplus accruing to agriculture, and this decentralised investment is far more labour-intensive than either investment by industrial capitalists or the government. Government investment in agriculture has major inefficiencies, offers far-ranging opportunities for corruption, and tends to be concentrated in environmentally destructive megaprojects.[14] Similarly, the low prices and heavy controls on agriculture in the developmental model followed hitherto in India are a major reason for the slow growth of rural non-agricultural activity which Harriss argues in his recent examination of the Indian data to be so crucial for a decline in poverty [*Harriss*, 1992: 205]. This means that higher prices cannot be called simply a class demand of 'capitalist farmers' if their basic effect is to benefit all rural workers. The argument about entitlements [*Drèze and Sen*, 1990] does not deal with this aspect of the stimulus to growth; it concerns distribution rather than production, though it does add an important point, that the poorest should be given access to resources and protection from short-term fluctuations. Thus a public distribution system targeted to the poor (and not financed in such a way as to depress growth, that is, by making farmers pay for the low-priced food via their low incomes) and an employment guarantee scheme, are valuable 'floor' mechanisms. But both, along with a high legal minimum wage, have come to be accepted and voiced by the farmers' movement, while the 'experts' speaking in the name of the rural poor have resisted accepting any arguments about prices.

CONCLUSION

The problem for most Maxists is that issues raised by peasants or farmers have been difficult to fit into conventional frameworks. Notions of differentiation of the peasantry and the leading role of the working class, coupled with assumptions about a progressive development path based on heavy industry and a working class maintained by cheap food, have led to their characterisation as 'kulaks' for demanding higher prices. The framework has also failed to predict other aspects of the Indian movement; one major example is that of fertiliser subsidies, which, contrary to most assumptions, appears to be more a demand of politicians than of the organised farmers' movement. Similarly, the traditional Marxist framework of analysis of religious fundamentalism ('communalism' in India) has taken it as mainly a result of feudal backwardness or a 'retarded capitalism'; this plus the general anti-peasant attitudes of the elite has led to frequent assertions that 'rich peasants' provide a social base for communalism. In fact it seems clear that communalism has spread from the cities (the middle classes, the urban poor *and* the organised working class) to the countryside, and that farmers' organisations have a rather decent record on the issue. Even taking the 'peasant' as a whole it can be pointed out that the farmers' organisation sponsored by the Hindu right, the Bharatiya Kisan Sangh, is considerably weaker among peasants than is its workers' organisation, the Bharatiya Mazdur Sangh, among workers.

The peasantry's opposition to the state has led it to be seen as anti-socialist, and indeed the movement and its leaders have often been consciously opposed to 'socialism'. Yet this is linked to the fact that socialist and Marxist regimes in the Third World as well as eastern Europe have been those that have followed most strongly a developmental policy of fostering heavy industrialisation by extracting surpluses from agriculture, subsidising urban workers through cheap food at the cost of peasants. The real benefactors from the resulting cheap labour have been the controllers of industry and state power, but it has been easy enough for peasants to see organised sector workers and collectivisation policies as their enemy. It has been argued that in China peasants are, properly mobilised, a major force for democracratic and economic rationally [*Friedman*, 1990], while in India the leadership of the farmers' movement centred around Sharad Joshi and the Punjabis and Gujaratis in the KCC has shown its concern for democracy and freedom, has firmly opposed religious fundamentalist forces, and has seen its struggle as an 'economic' one based on a materialistic analysis of capital accumulation. It has also shown an orientation towards an ecologically sustainable development (if an opposition to the extreme environmentalist 'no big dam' type arguments) and has been trying to build the direct producer–consumer relations that are being promoted by 'fair trade' advocates as an alternative to multinational dominated global markets [*Barratt Brown*, 1993]. It has taken firm stands for political decentralisation. This does not make it a pure equalitarian vanguard or a force that by itself can make a revolutionary change: such things do not exist. It clearly has limitations in dealing with intra-village equalities, particularly those of caste. On the whole, along with other 'new social movements',[15] it is a powerful force for what I have called 'reinventing revolution' [*Omvedt*, 1993]; that is, for reshaping the developmental path and restructuring Indian society in an equalitarian, libertarian and sustainable direction. Whether such an outcome will occur, whether forces will unite, whether they will be able to pose a redefined, decentralised socialism as a genuine alternative before the people, depends not simply on the farmers' movement itself but also on the other movements and the initiative and rethinking shown by the traditional intellectuals of the working class movement.

NOTES

1. Marx, though, expresed some very different ideas in his writings on the French peasantry – for example:

   > The roots that small-holding property struck in French soil deprived feudalism of all nutriment. Its landmarks formed the natural fortifications of the bourgeoisie against any surprise attack on the part of its old overlords. But in the course of the nineteenth century the feudal lords were replaced by urban usurers; the feudal obligation that went with the land was replaced by the mortage; aristocratic landed property was replaced by bourgeois capital. The small holding of the peasant is now only the pretext that allows the capitalist to draw profit, interest and rent from the soil, while leaving it to the tiller of the soil himself to see how he can extract his wages ... The interests of the peasant, therefore, are no longer, as under Napoleon, in accord with but in opposition to the interests of the bourgeoisie, to capital [*Marx*, 1972: 132–3].

   This is a clear statement of the *anti-capitalist* nature of peasant interests, thought of course in the nineteenth century the role of the state as lender and extractor of surplus was not visible.
2. The concept of 'class' itself is problematic, but we cannot discuss this in detail here; we may say simply that the 'class' aspect of a movement expresses the way it promotes the interest of a particular section, while its 'populist' aspect expresses the degree to which it seeks to unite other sections as part of a 'people versus power bloc' contradiction [*Laclau*, 1977]. Dhanagare (this volume) follows Laclau in using the term, but whereas Laclau sees populism as at least potentially positive (that is, the working class becomes populist when it unites other sections behind it in opposition to the power bloc), the Indian use of the term is overwhelmingly negative, implying that ruling sections appeal to the masses and that constant and increasingly unfulfillable demands are made on government revenues. Harriss [1992] uses the terms in this sense and argues that the farmers' movement is dangerously populist because it demands nothing but concessions, subsidies, prices and so on. As argued above, this conflates all demands made in the name of farmers or peasants. It may be said that the politicians, including those of the left, who have opposed reduction in any subsidies and supported all demands of organised sector employees upon public revenues are the most 'populist' forces in the negative sense. The most organised section of the farmers' movement, the KCC (and the biggest, judging by the two opposing rallies in March 1993) has shown its readiness to accept withdrawal of fertiliser subsidies, major changes in irrigation pricing recommended by the Vaidyanathan committee, and levying of income tax on agriculture

('Farmers' Representatives Yield Ground on Income Tax,' *Times of India*, 24 Jan. 1992).

3. Thus, for example, Congress leaders such as Rajendra Prasad patronised Jagjivan Ram to established an organization of untouchables (the Depressed Classes League) to counter Ambedkar and an agricultural labourer organisation to counter the radical Kisan Sabha in Bihar, both in 1936. Strikingly, Ambedkar chose to ignore Ram for an effort to ally with the Kisan Sabha. In other respects, we can see high-caste Congressmen taking up 'Harijan work' in the 1930s as a counter to increased mobilisation of non-Brahmans in the Congress [*Omvedt*, forthcoming].
4. For example, N. Krishnaji's articles on the issue of prices and cost calculations take it as ideal that the 'support price' should be above the cost of production (calculated on the basis of existing labourer wages) but below the market price, and he writes that while 'The general consensus is that minium support prices ... must fully cover the average cost of production' the debate is still over whether family land and labour inputs should be included in this:

   > A price covering such a complete cost has been described as a 'forward-looking' floor because it ensures cash income to the farmers over and above the actual money expenditure incurred. Moreover, it is seen to incorporate at least one principle of parity, viz., input return parity, since the family inputs are given the same remuneration that they could notionally earn outside the family farming activity [1992: 71]

   A little reflection will make clear the atrociousness of this framework of thinking: a large section of economists apparently imagined that cost of production could be a serious concept even if it did not pay anything at all to the peasants for their labours, while others could feel it 'forward looking' to give a return to labour at the level of income of what they were ready to call in more 'populist' context, 'bonded labourers.'
5. Balagopal [1987] argues to the contrary, that Shetkari Sanghatana ideology poses 'village' against 'city' as an absolute distinction, and Dhanagare (this volume) reproduces this argument. However, it is factually incorrect. Not only Joshi but common activists refer to exploiters in the villages and treat them as enemies, and see the urban poor as their allies (many have relatives among them). At the level of popular discourse it is mainly the urban middle and upper classes which are identified as 'India'. Further, the rhetoric of 'urban dadas and rural goondas', which functions primarily at the popular level, in the Marathi literature, seems to serve as a kind of equivalent to the Marxist terms 'capitalists and landlords'.
6. In 1987 a new Maharastra state government committee on minimum wages was formed with a Shetkari Sanghatana representative, Bhaskarrao Boravake (who was indeed a rich farmer with a holding of 200 acres in Ahmednagara); it left out any representatives of agricultural labourer organisations, such as Datta Deshmukh (a 50-acre farmer in the same district but a leader of the Lal Nishan Party) who had been on previous committees, and the left promptly protested. But in the end the left party and agricultural labourer organisation demands were for a doubling of the previous wages (to Rs 12, 14, 16, and 20 depending on the zones) while Boravake asked for Rs 25 and resigned from the committee over the issue. While the minimum wages were not necessarily enforceable (in Maharashtra men have very frequently received more while female workers nearly always less), they did commit the government to pay the lowest rate (that is, Rs 12) on employment guarantee schemes. Thus the Rs 25 legal minimum would have had considerable consequences.
7. Two experiences will illustrate this. In late 1987, just before a proposed joint rally of Joshi and the working class leader Datta Samant, I spent a couple of days with friends in the heart of the Bombay textile area. Worker-activists had put up posters hailing the alliance, and when a young activist from a left party which attacked this entered the office he was roundly criticised: 'how do you dare to say Datta Samant is running after Sharad Joshi:? Don't just say it behind our backs, if you dare say it publicly at Shivaji Park ... I don't want to hear any more of this "rich peasant–poor peasant" business': just tell me one thing: are they fighting the state or not?' And in October 1988 at the

time of the Sanghatana's rally in Kolhapur, a district town in southern Maharashtra, the eastern Maharashtrian peasants pouring off the train for the rally were visibly shorter and less well-fed than the workers on the streets of the town; in a party office, similarly, the response of workers was, 'But they *are* poor peasants!'

8. See especially Gupta [1988; 1992], Hasan [1989], Hasan and Patnaik [1993] and Singh [1992]. Other than Singh's, little of this has been based on direct fieldwork in the villages involved in agitation or participant observation of the movement. Friese [1990] gives an analysis in the context of historical background. Comparative discussions are given by Lindberg [1992a; 1992b; 1992c] and Dhanagare [1988], though these do not deal with the historical and cultural differences between UP and other regions such as Maharashtra. For a discussion of the greater overlap of 'class' categories among dalits (scheduled castes) and caste Hindu peasants and labourers in Maharashtra and Karnataka, see Omvedt [forthcoming].
9. The contradiction between Joshi (and other Sanghatana activists) and the rural bosses of Janata Dal in Maharashtra became most severe at the time of the 1990 Assembly elections when Joshi both actively opposed seat adjustments with the BJP-Shiv Sena alliance and fought over the PDF candidacy in some constituencies, forcing at least one rural leader to shift his constituency. Several of the JD candidates who lost (for example, P.K. Patil of Shahada, a longtime foe of the adivasi-based agricultural labourer–poor peasant movement there) blamed Joshi and Mrinal Gore for their loss, for had they been able to make the seat adjustments with the Hindu parties they could have gotten their votes and stood a good chance of winning. Indeed, blocking such an opportunistic alliance very likely helped the narrow Congress victory; an opposition victory would not have benefited the progressive forces but led to a coalition government headed by the Shiv Sena, the worst possible outcome; (see 'United Opposition Could have Won 17 More Seats' in *The Independent*, 14 March 1990).
10. To get a sense of the quality of left intellectual responses to the demand for labour in agriculture to be paid at a rate of Rs 25 a day, see Dantwala [1990], Sethi [1991], Mahanti [1990] and the unremitting anti-peasant commentaries of 'B.M.' in the *Economic and Political Weekly* [*BM*, 1989, 1990a; 1990b; 1990c; 1993]. Thus Sethi [1991: 24], a former Planning Commission member himself, can write that

> 'The Report flouts very economic principle in taking a totally illogical view of the question of minimum wages. It deliberately wants to escalate the cost of agricultural labourer for raising the support price through the inclusion of the statutory wages of farm workers and not the actual wages ... the Report suggests equalisation of all kinds of wages such as for family labour, hired labour, casual labour and all, at the level of statutory wages and not wages actually paid. There is no logic in this ...',

and Mahanti:

> This negative impact will only be heightened by the governmental decision to use the statutory minimum wage ... while fixing support prices ... Add on the fact that the agricultural cost calculations would now include managerial costs ... and the stage for a dramatic rise in support prices is set ... The cost of production now includes items on which the farmers have never had to spend a penny.

11. On 'extending the Green Revolution to the east', see Sunil Jain [1992]. Here World Bank recommendations seemed to be endorsed by left experts such as Hanumantha Rao.
12. This was more or less admitted in the Agrarian Programme of the CPI (ML) (1988), the organisation behind the Indian Peoples' Front in Bihar. The IPF led renewed 'land struggles' in 1992–93, but these mostly won only small gains (a few acres in each village) from mostly *benami* land or occupation of 'commons' land. Similarly, land struggles in Andhra led by another Naxalite group could win only a few thousand acres spread over five districts by taking surplus land of landlords, compared to occupation of a reported 80,000 acres of 'forest land' in one district (Khammam) alone [*Balagopal*, 1990].

13. Most sections of the new peasant movement have made a claim to the Gandhian heritage, particularly in terms of its orientation to a decentralised, village-centred development. The NAP as we have noted emphasised this (though Joshi had generally disassociated himself from the spiritualistic and anti-technology aspects of Ghandi as well as from the language of 'Ram Raj'). Gandhi himself of course had rarely spoken in terms of prices of agricultural products, but the economist most strongly associated with him, J.C. Kumarappa, both argued for remunerative prices and land ceilings [*Kumar*, 1991: 298].
14. For example, a peasant movement in Sangli district in Maharashtra has been opposing a medium (Rs 500 crore) lift irrigation scheme on the Krishna river which is planned to irrigate eight villages totally and 22 partially out of 108 villages in the taluka: in other words, creating islands of green (sugarcane) in a drought-prone sea. Their alternative plan proposes with the same amount of water to provide sufficient water to every family in 60 villages to irrigate three acres for basic needs. The government has been compelled partially to accept this. Most significantly, government engineers have been unable to give a rational justification for the original scheme, to say (1) why only eight villages would be fully irrigated, or (2) why *these* eight villages and not others; and (3) why the feeder canals take the strange zig-zag route proposed. In other words, political criteria and not rational use of water have clearly structured this irrigation 'investment'.
15. Even those admitting the validity of the issues of peasantry versus state/market posed by the farmers' movement often refuse to classify them under 'new social movements', arguing that they do not really oppose the state [*Harriss*, 1992; *Lindberg*, 1992a; 1992b; 1992c]. But neither do the other movements by the criteria they use. My classification of these movements as the same is based on the fact that they broadly represent the interests of exploited sections, either exploited in ways not understood by traditional left analysis or in ways new to the current situation of capitalism. This does not mean they substitute for the vanished revolutionary proletarian vanguard or that they have no regressive aspects.

REFERENCES

Alvares, Claude, 1985, 'The Peasants Rehearse the Uprising', *Illustrated Weekly*, 24 Feb.

BM 1989, 'Agricultural Policy Dictated by the Rich Farmer', *EPW*, 29 May

BM, 1990a, 'Pandering to the Rich Farm Lobby', *EPW*, 27 Jan.

BM, 1990b, 'Economic Policy Making and Coalition Politics', *EPW*, 2 June.

BM, 1990c, 'Search for a Viable Development Strategy', *EPW*, 4 Aug.

BM, 1993, 'New-Look Farm Policy', *EPW*, 10 April.

Balagopal, K., 1990, 'The End of Spring?', *EPW*, 25 Aug.

Barratt Brown, M., 1993, *Fair Trade: Reform and Realities in the International Trading System*, London: Zed Books.

Byrd, William and Lin Qingsong (eds.), 1990, *China's Rural Industry: Development and Reform,* New York: Oxford University Press.

Carter, Colin and Fu-Ning Zhong, 1991, 'China's Past and Future Role in the Grain Trade', *Economic Development and Cultural Change*, Vol.39, No.4, July.

Census of India, 1992, *Final Population Totals. Paper 2 of 1992*, New Delhi: Government of India.

Centre for Monitoring the Indian Economy (CMIE), 1990, *Basic Statistics Relating to the Indian Economy, Volume 1: All India, August 1990*, Bombay.

Chakravorty, Sukhamoy, 1987, *Development Planning: The Indian Experience*, New Delhi: Oxford University Press.

Dantwala, M.L., 1990, 'Agricultural Prices Under Political Pressure', *EPW*, 22 Sept.

Dhanagare, D.N., 1988, 'An Apolitical Populism', *Seminar*, Dec.

Drèze, Jean and Amartya Sen (eds.), 1990, *The Political Economy of Hunger, Volume I,* Oxford: Clarendon Press.

Frankel, Francine, 1978, *India's Political Economy, 1947–1977: The Gradual Revolution*, Princeton, NJ: Princeton University Press.
Friedman, Edward, 1990, 'Deng versus the Peasantry: Recollectivization in the Countryside', *Problems of Communism*, Sept.–Oct.
Friese, Kai, 1990, 'Peasant Communities and Agrarian Capitalism', *EPW*, 2 Dec.
Gill, Sucha Singh, 1990, 'Agrarian Capitalism and Political Processes in Punjab', Paper for Research Project on 'Terms of Political Discourse in India', Bhubaneshwar, Sept.
Gill, Sucha Singh and K.B. Singhal, 1984, 'Farmers' Agitations: Response to Developmental Crisis of Agriculture', *EPW*, 1 Oct.
Gupta, Dipankar, 1988, 'Country-Town Nexus and Agrarian Mobilisation: Bharatiya Kisan Union as an Instance', *EPW*, 17 Dec.
Gupta, Dipankar, 1992, 'Peasant "Unionism" in Uttar Pradesh: Against the Rural Mentality Thesis', *Journal of Contemporary Asia*, Vol.22, No.2.
Hanumantha Rao, C.M., 1989, 'Dispensing with Food Security?', *EPW*, 20 May.
Harriss, John, 1992, 'Does the "Depressor" Still Work? Agrarian Structur and Development in India: A Review of Evidence and Argument', *Journal of Peasant Studies*, Vol.19, No.2.
Hasan, Zoya, 1989, 'Self-Serving Guardians: Formation and Strategy of the Bharatiya Kisan Union', *EPW*, 2 Dec.
Hasan, Zoya and Utsa Patnaik, 1993, 'Aspects of the Farmers' Movement in Uttar Pradesh in the Context of Uneven Growth of Capitalist Agriculture', New Delhi: Jawaharlal Nehru University.
Jain, Sunil, 1992, 'Agriculture: The Lean Season', *India Today*, 10 June.
Johnson, Dale, 1991, 'Agriculture in the Liberalization Process', in Lawrence Krause and Kim Kihwan (eds.), *Liberalization in the Process of Economic Development*, Berkeley, CA: University of California Press.
Jose, George, 1988, 'The Fall of Rajpath: An Eyewitness Account of the Farmers' Demonstration in Delhi', New Delhi: ISI Memo.
Joshi, Sharad, 1985a, *Bharat Speaks Out*, Bombay: Build Documentation Centre.
Joshi, Sharad, 1985b, *Shetkari Sanghatan: Vichar ani Karyapaddathi* ('Thought and Method of Work of Shetkari Sanghatana', Marathi), Raigad: Shetkari Prakashan.
Joshi, Sharad, 1986, *The Woman Question*, Pune: Shethari Prakashan.
Joshi, Sharad, 1988, *Bharat Eye-View*, Ambethan: Shetkari Sanghatana Central Office.
Joshi, Sharad, 1990, 'Balancing Act', *Illustrated Weekly*, 7 Jan.
Joshi, Sharad, 1991a, 'Search for Alternative Technology', Paper for Seminar on 'Sustainable Agriculture', Pondicherry, 12–13 Sept.
Joshi, Sharad, 1991b, 'Answering Before God', *Seminar*, Nov.
Joshi, Sharad, 1992, 'Agro Exports Crucial to Trade Balance', *Times of India*, 7 Feb.
Krishnaji, N., 1992, *Pauperising Agriculture: Studies in Agrarian Change and Demographic Structure*, Bombay: Oxford University Press.
Kumar, Devendra, 1991, 'Kumarappa and the Contemporary Perspective', *Gandhi Marg*, July–Sept.
Krueger, Anne O., Schieff, Maurice and Alberto Valdes (eds.), 1991, *The Political Economy of Agricultural Pricing Policy, Volume 2: Asia* (A World Bank Comparative Study), Baltimore, MD: Johns Hopkins University Press.
Laclau, Ernesto, 1977, *Politics and Ideology in Marxist Theory*, London: New Left Books.
Lindberg, Staffan, 1992a, 'Peasants for Democracy? Farmers' Agitations and the State in India', in Lars Rudebeck (ed.), *When Democracy Makes Sense: Studies in the Democratic Potential of Third World Popular Movements*, Uppsala: AKUT.
Lindberg, Staffan, 1992b, 'Peasants, Communities and the State: Farmers' Movements as Political and Social Processes in Contemporary India', Paper for the International Workshop on 'Social Movements, State and Democracy', New Delhi, 5–8 Oct.
Lindberg, Staffan, 1992c, 'Farmers' Agitations, Civil Society and the State', *Sociological Bulletin*, Vol.41, Nos.1&2.
Mahanti, Tushawar, 1990, 'Economic Ploy', *Economic Times*, 27 Aug.
Marx, Karl, Engels, F. and V. Lenin, 1972, *On Historical Materialism: A Collection*,

Moscow: Progress Publishers.
Matsen, Jim and Mark Selden, 1992, 'Poverty and Inequality: China and India', *EPW*, 4 April.
Mellor, John W. and Raissudhin Ahmed (eds.), 1988, *Agricultural Price Policy for Developing Countries*, New Delhi: Oxford University Press.
Nadkarni, N., 1987, *Farmers' Movements in India*, New Delhi: Allied Publishers.
National Agricultural Policy (NAP), 1991, *National Agricultural Policy: Views of the Standing Advisory Committee*, July 1990, Jullundar: Government Printing Press.
Nehru, Jawaharlal, 1960, *Discovery of India*, London: Doubleday Anchor Books.
Omvedt, Gail, 1992, 'Peasants, Dalits and Women: Democracy and India's New Social Movements', Paper for the International Workshop on 'Social Movements, State and Democracy', New Delhi, 5–8 Oct.
Omvedt, Gail, 1993, *Reinventing Revolution: India's New Social Movements* New York: Sharpe & Co.
Omvedt, Gail, forthcoming, *Dalits and the Democratic Revolution*, New Delhi: Sage.
Patnaik, Ila, 1990, 'Hike in Foodgrains Will Check Industrial Growth', *Times of India*, 3 July.
Planning Commission, Government of India, 1990, 'Towards Social Transformation: Approach to the Eighth Five-Year Plan', May.
Putterman, L., 1992, 'Dualism and Reform in China', *Economic Development and Cultural Change*, Vol.40, No.3.
Rakesh, K.M., 1993, 'Seeds of Discord', *The Week*, 21 March.
Roy, R.K., 1990a, 'Farm Plan Boon for Kulaks', *Times of India*, 14 July.
Roy, R.K., 1990b, 'Farmers Gain at Consumers' Expense', *Times of India*, 25 July.
Roychowdhury, Amit and Shankar, Uday, 1993, 'Farmers Split on Merits of Dunkel Proposals', *Down to Earth*, 15 April.
Sethi, J.D., 1991, 'Reflections on Farm Policy Report', *Mainstream*, 30 March, 6 April.
Sen Gupta, Bhabani, 1988, 'A Different Script', *EPW*, 29 Oct.
Shiva, Vandana, 1989, *The Violence of the Green Revolution: Ecological Degradation and Political Conflict in Punjab*, London: Zed Books.
Shenoy, B.R., 1974, *PL 480 and India's Food Problem*, New Delhi: Affiliated East–West Press.
Singh, Bhanu Pratap, 1992, 'Subsidies Have Not Benefited Farmers', *Times of India*, 23 Jan.
Singh, Jagpal, 1993, *Capitalism and Dependence: Agrarian Relations and Politics in Western U.P.*, New Delhi: Manohar.
South Commission, 1990, *Challenges to the South: Report of the South Commission*, New Delhi: Oxford University Press.
Taylor, D., 1992, 'Sustainable Agricultural Development in China', *World Development*, Vol.20, No.8.
Tellis, Olga, 1980, 'Nasik's Farmers Demand Justice', *Sunday*, Dec.

Abbreviations

EPW: Economic and Political Weekly
BKU: Bharatiya Kisan Union (peasant organisations of UP and Punjab)
BJP: Bharatiya Janata Party, a right-wing party espousing a 'Hindu' identity
APC: Agricultural Price Commission, renamed CACP (Commission on Agricultural Costs and Prices)
CPI: Communist Party of India
CPI(M): Communist Party of India (Marxist) – governing party in West Bengal
CPI(ML): Communist Party of India (Marxist-Leninist) – also known as 'Naxalites' or Indian Marxists
ISCC: Interstate Coordinating Committee
KCC: Kisan Coordinating Committee

Shifting Ground: Hindutva Politics and the Farmers' Movement in Uttar Pradesh

ZOYA HASAN

The decade of the 1980s witnessed the emergence of two interrelated changes in Uttar Pradesh. The first represented an unfolding and crystallization of agricultural transformation initiated in the 1980s, and the second was the growing momentum of surplus-producing farmers as a major political force in UP.[1] Both these developments heightened the growth of a powerful farmers' movement during the 1980s, when farmers mobilised to demand remunerative prices for agricultural commodities and cheaper inputs, demands that raised the broader issue of the terms of trade between the agricultural and industrial sectors.[2] All in all, farmers politics and the agricultural sector have attracted the attention of political parties across a wide spectrum, leading to an increase in the influence exercised by surplus producers over economic policies and the State. The rapidity with which the farmers' movement has gained ascendancy deserves closer analysis.

This study examines the growth and dynamics of the farmers' movement in UP. It explores the political and economic conditions that contributed to the rise of the movement and the ideological and social resources that made it possible. Analysis focuses on the structural contradictions in the polity and economy of UP that generated grievances and thus enhanced the assertion of farmer power and a willingness to act politically through the farmers' movement. The movement, however, has been largely quiescent over the last few years. There are several reasons for this decline. First, class divisions prevented the maintenance of rural unity that was necessary for pushing through public policies in favour of the agrarian sector. Accordingly, the sectorally-based farmers' mobilisation which flourished in the 1980s was unable to transcend its class differences. Second, and more importantly, the intensification of communal politics in UP during the 1990s have undermined a sustained

Zoya Hasan, Centre for Political Studies, School of Social Sciences, Jawaharlal Nehru University, New Delhi-110067, India. For comments and suggestions which have much improved this paper, the author is grateful to Tom Brass, Uma Chakravarthi and Utsa Patnaik, and to the participants in the Workshop on the 'New Farmers' Movements in India' organised by the Journal of Peasant Studies and the Indian Council of Social Science Research, New Delhi, March 1993.

farmers' mobilisation. In short, the farmers' movement has encountered difficulties with the politics of identity (religion, caste, ethnicity).

I

In the forefront of the farmers' movement in UP was the Bharatiya Kisan Union (BKU), formed in 1978, with units established in Delhi, Haryana and western UP. In 1980, the Punjab Khetibari Zamindar Union, a farmers' organisation, was converted into a Punjab unit of the BKU. This gave a big fillip to the movement in north-west India. The UP branch failed to show much activity at the time of its formation. In fact the BKU came to prominence only 1987, when a concerted effort was made to resurrect the organisation in order to fill the political vacuum left by the death of Charan Singh, the leading protagonist of rural interests, Chief Minister of UP, Prime Minister and Minister of Finance in the Janata Dal government (1977–79).

Largely because of the Lok Dal's failure to extract any major concessions from the Congress government on the issue of higher prices for agricultural produce, farmers' politics were in abeyance at this juncture. This was compounded by fissures in the Lok Dal itself, in which two leading factions emerged headed respectively by Ajit Singh, son of Charan Singh, and H.N. Bahuguna, the erstwhile Chief Minister of UP. The revival of the BKU was thus an attempt to fill the vacuum created by the decline of the Lok Dal, and hence an expression of the desire to create a strong organisation for the articulation and assertion of the growing demands of farmers.

Under the leadership of Mahendra Singh Tikait, the BKU captured national attention in the winter of 1988, when its supporters laid siege to Meerut in western UP, in pursuit of demands for higher sugarcane prices, lower farm input prices, waiver of loans, higher rural investment and a lowering of electricity and water rates.[3] Thousands of farmers thronged the Commissioner's office in Meerut for over three weeks, dramatically placing the farmers' demand before government, media and public at large. This was followed by a massive rally in Delhi in October 1988. Both agitations were militant in nature and received widespread support; they lasted for days, roads were blocked, and villages were closed to government officials and politicians. Farmers refused to pay taxes and electricity bills, or to clear their interest on loans from banks and credit co-operatives [*Hasan*, 1989].

It quickly became apparent that the farmers' movement had struck a responsive chord in western UP's rural areas, and captured the imagination of large sections of the rural community. Political leaders of all political parties were anxious to associate themselves with the movement, in order to be seen as champions of the farmers. Both Congress and the Lok Dal tried to jump on to the BKU bandwagon and share its platform. V.P. Singh, leader of the newly-formed Janata Dal, travelled to Meerut to express his support, and Congress leaders from western UP mounted pressure on the government to open negotiations with the BKU. What worried the Congress was the escalation of rural pressure in western UP; this was an area markedly hostile to the Congress from 1967 onwards, when Charan Singh left the Congress to establish numerous rural political formations and alliances so as to challenge Congress supremacy. Several Congress leaders made concerted efforts to associate themselves with the movement because of their concern at the success of the campaign and also its usefulness in embarrassing B.B. Singh, Chief Minister of UP, in the ongoing factional struggle in the UP Congress. Government ministers severely criticised B.B. Singh's inept handling of the agitation and demanded his resignation. Prime Minister Rajiv Gandhi pressed a number of influential national leaders known for their sympathy towards the farmers of north India to negotiate with Tikait.

It was clear from all this activity that the Congress could not afford to ignore the farmers' demands because this would isolate it from the mainstream of rural politics. To be sure the government was anxious to buttress its political standing with surplus-producing farmers, but at the same time it was not prepared to yield to farmers' pressure because the party believed that 'this would disturb the social equilibrium in rural areas besides leading to town and country polarisation' (*Tribune*, 10 Feb. 1988). This kind of ambivalence displayed by the Congress leadership heightened the alienation of farmers from the government. It was compounded by the concessions made by the Haryana government, in the form of an upward revision of sugarcane prices, above those proposed by the Commission on Agricultural Costs and Prices (CACP). Similarly, the Punjab government agreed to lower rates for tubewells and threshers, reduce reconnection charges and line service charges for new connections, and postpone payment of electiricity bills for tubewells [*Gill and Singhal*, 1984]. Gradually, the UP government too became more conciliatory. The most compelling reason for these concessions was the forthcoming Lok Sabha and Assembly elections in 1989. The cabinet reshuffle was used by the Prime Minister to indicate a visible shift in priorities: five ministers were designated to look after Krishi Bhavan, which in itself was significant. This was followed by a package of concessions notable for highlighting a general emphasis on agriculture. One significant feature was the rescheduling of farm loans in the drought affected areas (*Times of India*, 2 Feb. 1989).

At the state level, these policy measures were perceived as a sign of the Centre's willingness to concede farmers' demands. The new Chief Minister, N.D. Tiwari, who had in the meanwhile replaced B.B. Singh, entered into an agreement with Tikait. Several demands made by the farmers' movement were conceded by the UP government: a judicial inquiry into a police firing which killed six farmers in Aligarh district in June 1990, the waiver of electricity bills for 1987–88, the lifting of inter-district restrictions on the movement of agricultural products, the opening of polytechnics in villages, and permission for construction on farm land.

From the standpoint of the farmers, the major gain of the agitations was not the concessions but the emergence of Tikait as a powerful leader with a formidable ability to mobilise the peasantry of western UP. It is important to note that he succeeded in maintaining the momentum of the movement, despite the fact that it did not achieve its major demand of higher prices for sugarcane. Moreover, there was no disillusionment with Tikait, even after the Meerut and Delhi sit-ins were withdrawn. Rather, he succeeded in gaining considerable media attention by dramatically spurning the efforts of political parties to participate in the farmers' movement. The BKU did not allow the Lok Dal or even members of Charan Singh's family to share their platform, despite the fact that this region was the base of Charan Singh's power, and the place where farmers consistently favoured Lok Dal/Janata Dal candidates in elections.[4]

Charan Singh, whom Tikait acknowledged as his mentor, was deeply involved in party politics. He pursued power within the existing system and through the party system, with the object of bringing about a shift in the balance of economic power from cities to the rural areas. He challenged Congress supremacy by constructing an alliance of middle and backward castes, and succeeded in marginalising the Congress in western UP during the 1970s. By contrast, the leadership of the farmers' movement calculated that its effectiveness would be greatest when it acted as a pressure group outside the established party system [*Gupta*, 1988]. Neutrality was perceived as crucial for establishing the credibility of the BKU in the eyes of the government, and also because Tikait had moved farmers' politics on to the streets [*Rudolph and Rudolph*, 1987].

Overall, democratically induced rural pressure exercised by farmers in the 1980s pushed the State and economic policy in their favour, signalling clearly that agricultural prices and higher investment of public resources in the countryside would be the centre-piece of agricultural policy (just as land reforms used to be in the 1950s and 1960s). Furthermore, the existence of political parties with an overwhelming rural base, such as the

Janata Dal, added to the pressure on the Congress to reorient policies in favour of rural development and agriculture. The fact that the majority of UP's legislators have a rural background was another reason why the government took notice of rural mobilisation. Yet another reason for appeasing farmers was the rapid decline in the position of Congress throughout the 1980s. The UP government recognised the need to increase rural investment to appease farmers especially because Congress fortunes in UP were declining so rapidly in the 1980s. However, the concessions offered by government were much below what farmers' groups demanded on the price issue, and were thus were not sufficient by themselves to alter the anti-Congress orientation of western UP farmers.

II

What were the developments in Indian politics and economy that caused the farmers' movement to emerge? What kind of a movement is the BKU? What is the nature of its appeal? An editorial in the *Economic and Political Weekly* attributed the rise of farmers' movements since the late 1970s to the terms of trade having moved against the rural sector (*Economic and Political Weekly*, 8 Sept. 1980).

Although this is an important factor in the rise of farmers' movement, it does not fully explain the specific determination, social support and outcome of the UP movement. To understand that we need to turn our attention to the overall economic and social context of UP itself. As is well known, the impact of the farmers' movement was greatest in those areas of UP where the new agricultural technology brought about a rapid increase in production and incomes. Productivity levels in UP were quite low until the early 1980s, when a major breakthrough in agricultural production was achieved as a result of the introduction of new technology. The most significant improvements occurred in wheat, maize and sugarcane production; average yields increased, for wheat from 15.50 quintals per hectare in 1978–79 to 18.69 quintals in 1984–85, and for maize from 6.85 quintals per hectare to 15.17 quintals in the same period. Fertiliser consumption in the state had risen to 52 kilograms per hectare in 1980–81, and the number of tractors in use to 107 per 1000 hectares [*Westley*, 1986]. All this contributed to an annual growth rate in foodgrain production of 2.79 per cent from 1960–61 to 1978–79, a period during which the average foodgrain yield per hectare was 1068 kilograms [*ibid.*]. The growth rate of UP's economy throughout the 1980s was 3.5 per cent.

Within UP itself the western region, comprising 19 districts, witnessed a markedly faster growth than other parts of the state. Along with

Haryana and Punjab, the region of UP covering Meerut, Agra, Bareilly and Moradabad divisions experienced the largest growth of rural capital investment, processing and small-scale industries in the Green Revolution era. On virtually all the indices of growth and modernisation western UP achieved considerable progress, and by the early 1980s this region was substantially ahead of other regions of the state. The impact of the Green Revolution was greater in this region partly because the western districts were well endowed with canals and irrigation works established at the turn of the century, as a result of which the Doab was transformed into one of the richest tracts during the colonial period. This process of regional growth also manifested itself in the emergence of an infrastructure and the expansion of market towns; commercial farming also gained impetus from the tradition of peasant proprietorship, a prominent feature of the agrarian structure in this part of the state. More importantly, class polarisation between absentee landlords and peasant producers did not occur to the same degree in the western region as it did in the eastern parts of the state.[5]

The UP Agricultural Census of 1980–81 grouped landholdings into five broad categories: marginal holdings of less than a hectare, small holdings of one to two hectares, semi-medium holdings of two to four hectares, medium holdings of four to ten hectares, and large holdings of ten hectares and above. Farmers with semi-medium, medium and large holdings can produce wheat surpluses, and the bulk of these were concentrated in western UP (Table 1). Only a quarter of the holdings in western UP were in the marginal category, compared with 48.7 per cent in the eastern region.[6]

TABLE 1
PERCENTAGE DISTRIBUTION OF HOLDINGS BY SIZE CLASS IN VARIOUS REGIONS OF UTTAR PRADESH

	Size Class in Hectares				
	Up to 1 %	1–2 %	2–4 %	4–10 %	10 and above %
Western	25.0	34.0	39.4	41.3	28.8
Central	18.2	20.5	17.8	13.8	10.5
Eastern	48.7	33.0	27.5	23.2	26.3
Bundelkhand	3.4	7.9	10.9	17.7	30.6
Hill	4.0	4.3	4.4	3.7	3.6
	100.00	100.00	100.00	100.00	100.00

Source: Government of Uttar Pradesh [1981].

A significant change in production technology facilitated rapid increases in output. Although accounting for less than three-tenths of all holdings in UP and 27.3 per cent of the total land area, the western region possessed 74 per cent of all private tubewells, 54.5 per cent of all improved threshing and chopping machines, and 50.1 per cent of all diesel and electric pumps. On average, the number of these modern machines per unit of area was about double the level in the eastern region, with a slightly larger total area and population than the western region [*Government of Uttar Pradesh,* 1986].

An important indicator of the capitalist character of the investment taking place is the concentration not only of physical production and asset formation, but the class-concentration of land itself. Landlords and rich peasants who are becoming agrarian capitalists, respond to profitable conditions by investing more intensively on the land they already have; when this reaches a plateau, they look for more land to augment their farms. This is particularly the case with the rich peasant Jat cultivators who started with a much smaller land base than the ex-zemindars [*Hasan and Patnaik*, forthcoming]. A more rapid process of land transfers from small farms to the well-to-do should be expected in the faster-growing areas, and this is indeed what is revealed by a recent study of land transfers spanning the period 1952–53 and 1982–53 based on a 0.2 per cent sample of Nyaya panchayats in the state [*Shankar*, 1990].

A significant finding of the study was that on average it was the smallest landholders with less than 2.5 acres who had sold land; 7.3 per cent of the land owned by them was sold, compared to around three per cent or less by other size-groups of farmers. In western UP the extent of land transfer was higher than the state average; those with less than 2.5 acres had transferred up to ten per cent, and the landless had transferred 35 per cent of the total land that was sold [*ibid*: 41–4]. Most of these transfers had taken place during the last five years, 1978–79 to 1982–83, out of a total of the three decades covered. The households which became totally landless after transferring land accounted for nearly 42 per cent of the total land transferred.

On the other hand, of the total land that was purchased, some 60 per cent went to owners of more than five acres, of which 28 per cent went to those with over ten acres. There was a net loss of land by those owning below 2.5 acres and a net gain by all others with the largest gains recorded by owners of 10 acres and more [*ibid.*: 44]. The study found that more land transfers had taken place in the post-Green Revolution period than earlier; the trends of net transfer from poorer cultivators to the well-to-do were confirmed by the income and asset-wise analysis, which showed that 56 per cent of total area sold came from farmers with below Rs 10,000 annual income, while 61 per cent of all land purchased was by farmers with over Rs 10,000 income. As usual, the Green Revolution area, in the

TABLE 2
LAND TRANSFER MATRIX IN WESTERN UTTAR PRADESH ACCORDING TO SIZE OF OWNED HOLDING
(Size and Area in Acres)

Sellers	Buyers Less than 2.5	2.5–5	5–10	10 & above	Total
Landless	10.83 (4.25) (17.58)	37.25 (14.58) (26.01)	53.04 (20.76) (26.18)	154.32 (60.41) (47.10)	255.44 (100.00) (34.75)
Less than 2.5	16.62 (22.95) (26.98)	22.46 (30.89) (15.69)	21.88 (30.09) (10.80)	11.76 (16.17) (3.59)	72.72 (100.00) (9.90)
2.5 – 5.0	15.36 (14.78) (24.93)	48.72 (46.88) (34.02)	23.99 (23.09) (11.84)	14.85 (15.25) (4.84)	103.92 (100.00) (14.14)
5.0 – 10.0	6.09 (3.98) (9.88)	22.84 (14.92) (15.95)	73.54 (48.05) (36.29)	50.59 (33.05) (15.44)	143.06 (100.00) (20.82)
10.0 & above	12.71 (8.48) (20.63)	11.93 (7.96) (8.33)	30.16 (20.12) (14.89)	95.09 (63.44) (29.03)	149.89 (100.00) (20.39)
Total	61.61 (8.38) (100.00)	143.20 (19.48) (100.00)	202.61 (27.57) (100.00)	327.61 (44.57) (100.00)	735.03 (100.00) (100.00)

Note: Figures in first parenthesis are percentages of land sold to different categories while figures in the second parenthesis are percentage of land purchases by different categories.
Source: Shankar [1990].

western region of UP, showed a more marked picture of concentration, with 75 per cent of area purchased going to the well-to-do (see Table 2).

Within western UP, the fastest growing districts were Meerut, Muzaffarnagar, Saharanpur, Bulandshahr, Aligarh, Moradabad, Bareilly, Bijnor and Pilibhit, with productivity of major crops ranging from Rs 1,459 per hectare in Bareilly to Rs 2397 per hectare in Muzaffarnagar in 1980–83 (Table 3). Overall, by the early 1980s nearly 42 of UP's 57 districts had productivity levels exceeding Rs 1,000 per hectare, and the majority of these were in western UP. This increase was mainly due to the extensive irrigation and cropping intensity (see Table 4), nearly 85 per cent of the area under wheat in UP is irrigated [*Government of India*, 1992]. Almost the entire area under wheat in Meerut, Muzaffarnagar, Bulandshahr and Aligarh is irrigated. Likewise the intensity of cropping was higher than the average for the country in 1980–81. Similarly, the yields of sugarcane, the most important commercial crop in the state, have improved vastly because of better irrigation and chemical fertilisers. Farmers recorded yields of around 456.55 quintals per hectare in 1982–83. UP accounted for half the total area under sugarcane in the country in 1985–86 and 84 per cent of the area under sugar was irrigated. The western region accounted for 64 per cent of the total sugarcane area in the state in the mid-1970s, and maintained the lead even though important concentrations of cane production exist in the more populous eastern region. Of the total tonnage of sugarcane crushed, as high as 57 per cent was in the western region; it also accounted for 57.5 per cent of sugar produced – owing to a marginally better juice recovery rate.

TABLE 3
DISTRICTWISE AVERAGE AND VALUE OF OUTPUT OF 41 CROPS, 1980–83

1 District	2 Area (000 Hectares)	3 Value of Output (000 Rs)	4 Value per Hectare (Rs)
Agra	463	550901	1189
Aligarh	645	887293	1376
Bulandshahr	577	978641	1696
Etah	473	582062	1230
Etawah	473	537964	1137
Farrukhabad	411	479205	1168
Manipuri	415	480350	1157
Meerut + Ghaziabad	810	1734059	2141
Mathura	430	569934	1325
Moradabad	707	1219688	1725
Muzaffarnagar	515	1234514	2397
Rampur	296	508936	1719
Saharanpur	599	1158756	1934
Shahjahanpur	492	711198	1445
Budaun	560	657000	1173
Bareilly	485	707402	1459
Bijnor	458	901995	1969
Pilibhit	345	601308	1743

Source: Bhalla and Tyagi [1989].

Along with Punjab and Haryana, UP has registered a significant rise in food production, and north India has emerged as the sole area producing a genuine food surplus.[7] Within this region, Punjab–Haryana has recorded a phenomenal 134.4 per cent rise in per capita output, while UP shows a 31.5 per cent increase [*Hasan and Patnaik*, forthcoming]. The share of the northern region in the country's total food production has risen from around one-quarter to two-fifths, thus making a very significant contribution to the urban food economy. Between 1985 and 1988, 98 per cent of the total wheat procurement came from the northern region, while 67 per cent of the total rice total procurement was from this region [*ibid.*].

TABLE 4
DISTRICT-WISE NET CULTIVATED AREA, NET IRRIGATED AREA AND ITS PERCENTAGE IN WESTERN UTTAR PRADESH 1984 (HECTARES)

Districts	Net Cultivated Area	Net Irrigated Area	Percentage of Net Irrigated Area to Net Cultivated Area
1	2	3	4
Saharanpur	380732	279708	73.47
Muzaffarnagar	334889	294892	88.96
Meerut	312685	297621	95.18
Ghaziabad	188220	173682	92.28
Bulandshahr	341074	328376	93.34
Aligarh	390237	364243	93.34
Mathura	308899	225957	84.16
Agra	345700	229834	66.48
Manipuri	283867	240534	84.73
Eatah	295259	247965	83.98
Bynor	344149	213649	62.08
Moradabad	484160	377901	78.05
Rampur	189983	140721	74.07
Bareilly	331120	205465	62.05
Budaun	405903	244308	60.19
Shahjahanpur	347249	253881	73.11
Pilibhit	220824	186045	84.25
Farukhabad	279095	189492	67.90

Source: Statistical Diary, Uttar Pradesh, 1986, Economics and Statistics Division, State Planning Institute.

The bulk of foodgrains procured by the government is used to feed the urban and semi-urban population, as over 60 per cent of fair price shops are located in cities and towns or in their rural periphery, serving a quarter of the country's total population. Government procurement operations are a very important part of total sales of cereals: during the period 1981–85, for example, procurement of wheat and rice amounted to an annual average of 16.73 million tonnes, which made up 16.5 per cent of average annual production of these crops [*ibid.*]. All in all, the public distribution system[8] which has played a crucial role in offsetting inflation and minimising urban discontent, has become increasingly dependent on government procurement of foodgrains from this region. This in turn has boosted the importance of the surplus producing capitalist farmers of the north-western region, and consequently their bargaining position *vis-à-vis* the State and state governments in different regions is much greater than that of farmers in other parts of the country.

III

The economic discontent fuelling the farmer's movement was generally the result of increasing aspirations frustrated by the deterioration in the agriculture–industry terms of trade.[9] The prices of foodgrains relative to manufactured goods rose by 50 per cent from the late 1950s to the mid-1970s [*Mitra*, 1977). From the mid-1970s, however, there has been an adverse flow in terms of trade for the agricultural sector, as reflected in the wholesale prices of agricultural and manufactured products [*Rao*, 1983; *Nadkarni*, 1987]. This means that, though prices of agricultural produce have been rising, they have not kept pace either with those of non-agricultural operations or with rising consumption levels. Although rich farmers were affected because the scale of profits was reduced, middle farmers with modest quantities of surplus to dispose in the market suffered more due to the sharp rise in prices of essential manufactured goods. The worst affected are the poor peasantry, which has to buy foodgrains to sustain itself and has been squeezed by the rise in prices of agricultural as well as non-agricultural commodities. In this context, rich farmers who gained the most from higher output and lower input prices have rallied other sections of the peasantry who objectively may have little or no reason to identify with the demands of the farmer's agitation.

The discontent over prices was located within a more generalised resentment over the large disparity in urban and rural standards of living, especially with regard to public goods and services such as drinking water, energy, roads, communications, health and education. Accordingly, the BKU spokesmen made their case by contrasting the rate of return on their investment in agriculture and that achieved by those engaged in urban occupations in general, and government service, trade and professions in particular.

Ignoring the social differentiation in the countryside, the leaders of the farmers' agitation claimed to speak on behalf of the entire peasantry and tried to give the issues raised by them in the discourse of agriculture-versus-industry, urban-versus-rural. The idea of a basic 'unity' of interests among all agriculturists glossed over the differential impact of material issues. Higher prices affect farmers on an individual basis: consequently the benefits of improvement in terms of trade are cornered by capitalist producers who monopolise commodity sales, whereas the burden of deteriorating terms of trade is invariably passed on to the poorer classes. But then the BKU's agenda was not limited to higher prices. It included a wide range of popular demands from which all farmers might benefit. These were: better facilities for education, roads and employment, and the reservation of jobs for farmers. Though these were popular demands that helped the farmers' movement to marshall broad based support, the BKU did not pursue them with the same vigour as higher prices or loan waiver.

The aspirations of farmers were further heightened by the critical national importance of food surpluses produced in this region. North India has become the main source of food supply for the urban areas. This has given its farmers a bargaining power which their counterparts in western and southern India do not have at the national level. This power has been augmented by the fact that the demands put forward by surplus producers in these regions were increasingly supported by small farmers who, for a variety of reasons, backed these agitations. Such agitations have been more successful precisely in those regions where small and medium farmers have been drawn in to expand the support base. This was the case in western UP where sugarcane was grown by medium as well as small farmers, all of whom have been enthusiastic supporters of the BKU.

TABLE 5
SUGARCANE CULTIVATION BY SIZE-CLASS OF OWNERSHIP HOLDING 1970–71
(% SHARE)

Type of Holding	Size Class (Hectares)	All-India	UP	Mahrashtra
Marginal	0.0–0.5	–	6.8	2.1
Marginal	0.0–1.0	13.7	17.2	6.3
Semi-Medium	2.0–4.0	24.6	27.2	19.5
Medium	4.0–10.0	29.6	26.7	35.3
Large	10.0 and above	15.7	9.6	27.3

Source: All-India Report on *Agricultural* Census 1970–71, 1975.

Cane growers were in the forefront of the BKU's movement for higher price. Since unrest was most pronounced in the sugarcane growing parts of western UP, the BKU focused attention primarily on higher prices of sugarcane and the waiver of loans made to cane cultivators. Their agitation and militancy was strengthened by the structure of cane cultivation in UP (Table 5). Cane is cultivated largely by medium and semi-medium holdings, and also to some extent by rich peasant households. This is evident from the large number of cultivators supplying cane to sugar mills: 25,000 to 30,000 in UP, compared to 3,500 to 4,000 cultivators in Maharashtra [*Baru*, 1990]. The political and economic clout of cane cultivators was considerbly enhanced by the patronage and backing given by Charan Singh to the demand for nationalisation of sugar mills in UP [*Charan Singh*, 1981].

The 1960s and 1970s witnessed further improvement in the bargaining power of the cane grower *vis-à-vis* the sugar mill. This can be attributed to two factors: first, to the increased influence of rich farmers *vis-à-vis* the government; and second, to the emergence of the sugar co-operatives in other sugar cane growing states, a development which in general exercised an upward pressure on cane prices [*Baru*, 1990: 82]. The terms of trade with respect to sugarcane improved in favour of sugarcane cultivators at a compound rate of 0.2 to 0.5 per cent and 3.3 to 3.5 per cent per annum respectively for the period from 1961–62 to 1977–78 [*ibid.*: 173]. Much of this improvement occurred when terms of trade in general have moved in favour of agriculture. As noted earlier, the terms of trade for agricultural commodities, however, have deteriorated since 1976–77. Due to drought, the production of sugar decreased from 36.91 quintals in 1987 to 32.65 quintals in 1988, despite the fact that more sugarcane was crushed in 1988 than in the previous year. Poor rainfall brought down the sucrose content of sugarcane resulting in a recovery rate of only 8.12 per cent in 1988 as against 9.48 per cent in the previous year. As a result, priority was given to the enhancement of sugarcane prices, in order to offset the decline in sugarcane production owing to drought.

There is no doubt the BKU movement evoked a strong, response from a large number of farmers in UP, where several hundred thousand farmers took part in the major protests. The enthusiasm generated by these agitations was impressive, as was the expression of solidarity. But all this activity was concentrated in western UP, most notably in the districts of Meerut, Muzaffarnagar, Aligarh, Bijnor, Moradabad, Ghaziabad, Bulandshahr and Saharanpur. The social base of the farmers' movement was accordingly centred in the districts dominated by Jat peasant proprietors,

Although the farmers' movement mobilised primarily on the basis of rural sector rather than class, economic differentiation is important to an understanding of the politics of the farmers' movement.[10] Class background determines the collective identities of leading actors and, as noted earlier, the BKU articulated the interests of surplus producers (accounting for the bulk of market sales) through highly specific and concrete demands, the interests of small producers being represented only in terms of vague demands for urban–rural parity. A small survey conducted in Meerut and Moradabad provides evidence for the argument that surplus producers who own over eight acres participated most actively in the farmers' movements.[11] This characterisation is further confirmed by a another study, which found that in terms of membership and active participation, the BKU was dominated by rich and middle farmers, and more importantly that every rich farmer household in the five villages surveyed had taken part in the BKU agitation [*Kant*, 1990].[12] Among those surveyed, the supporters of the BKU were large producers with more than eight acres of land and who hired labour to work their farms, while those with less than eight acres depended on family labour.[13] The bulk of the workforce was made up of the landless, who were mostly Harijans and Muslims. Interviews revealed considerable tension between the rural poor and rich Jat farmers.[14] Frequent complaints were voiced about the heavy-handed methods used by the Jats to secure compliance and participation of the poorer sections of the peasantry in the farmers' movement.[15]

The BKU has shown little concern for the specific problems faced by the rural poor, such as minimum wages, employment opportunities, house sites and harassment; minimum wages for agricultural labourers were not even mentioned in the long list of 35 demands put forward by the BKU during the Meerut agitation. For peasant proprietors, the majority of landless scheduled castes are not members of the farming community, and therefore undeserving of notice. In the words of Charan Singh, 'if a man is landless he cannot be called a farmer'. The landless are the agricultural labourers, poor peasants and sharecroppers whose interests are at variance with the farming community, especially the rich peasants [*Byres*, 1988]. It is hardly surprising, then, that the landless agricultural labourers have reacted with apprehension to the consolidation of the affluent peasantry under the banner of the BKU, because they fear it will mean more harassment and oppression for them.

A striking feature of the UP farmers' movement is the low incidence of women's participation in the movement. The stance taken by the farmer's movement articulated in messages such as the abolition of dowry, limiting marriage expenses, discouraging drinking, taking action against husbands deserting or harassing wives, led to some women taking part in the earlier *dharnas* organised by the BKU. But their participation was never an important feature of the movement, in contrast to the prominence of women in various Maharashtra agitations [*Omvedt*, 1990]. Women generally expressed sympathy for the difficulties of farmers, but they were not drawn into the activities or decision-making structures of the BKU. This was largely because of the conservative and traditional attitude of Jats towards women: though women work in the fields, there is no effort to alter the social conditions which hamper their participation in the movement, and no organised attempt to involve them in mobilisations. Many women were thus prevented by the social constrictions arising from the dominant patriarchal norms of the western UP society from participating in politics. Accordingly, the farmers' movement was not the best vehicle for the empowerment of women, since for women to be able to engage in public activity, they must have some control over their lives. In western UP, the autonomy and options of women were limited by social, cultural and religious structures that confined women and dictated a customary social subservience to men in their everyday lives [*Calman*, 1992].

The economic and social contradictions in the BKU movement were obscured ideologically by a kisan ideology which articulated issues in a populist style [*Dhanagare* 1988]. The BKU presented an urban bias view, arguing that the development process is systematically biased against the countryside and that this is deeply embedded in the political structure and bureaucracy which has neglected the legitimate interests of farmers. Such populism emphasised the contradiction between the rural agricultural and urban industrial sectors, rather than the differences between classes in the countryside. In this vein Tikait claimed that his struggle was not confined to the acceptance of the BKU charter of demands, it was also a movement to safeguard the honour, dignity and self-respect of all kisans, irrespective of caste or class (*Navbharat Times*, 8 Feb. 1989). The BKU variety of populism highlighted the moral character of the movement, and is summed up in the following words of Tikait: 'No dispute can ever be solved satisfactorily by legality, it can be settled only through truthfulness. The kisan must go on protesting in the hope that "some day sense will drawn on an insensitive state"' (*Times of India*, 9 Aug. 1989). Within this framework, the farmers' movement was much more than just a protest against the government: it was a crusade that mobilised kisan power in order to convince government about the justness of the farmers' cause and the concomitant primacy of agriculture. The BKU leadership spoke a language that invoked elements of Charan Singh's discourses on agriculture. He deprecated the 'urban bias' of planning and heavy industrialisation, and held it responsible for the diversion of resources away from agriculture. The present leadership, in a somewhat similar vein, blamed the city-based government for the problems faced by the farmers. Hence the imperative nature of the entire farming community mobilising to oppose the privileged position of the urban industrial sector.

The emphasis on developing the rural economy created a political space in which prosperity in the countryside could be promoted by highlighting the common interests of all rural families, from rich capitalist producers to poor peasants. The BKU made much of its concern for the farming community as a whole. In this framework, the well-being of farmers was linked to higher prices for their produce: unremunerative prices affect not just rich peasants but also the small and middle peasants who grow cash crops. All rural producers, then, have a shared interest in demanding the principle of parity of prices, expansion of credit facilities and remission of loans. In short, populism as practised by the BKU promoted the development of a non-class social consciousness by instilling and reinforcing in the ranks of the peasantry the traditional self-perception of an undifferentiated commodity producer.

All this is not to suggest that the BKU's populism succeeded in creating a groundswell of opposition to the Congress government's rural policies. Over the years, the rich and middle farmers of UP, as elsewhere in India, have enjoyed an 'extremely comfortable accommodation with the ruling party' [*Duncan*, 1988: 45], helped in no small measure both by the non-existence of agricultural taxation and by the shelving of serious attempts at land reforms. Further, there was little evidence to show that agriculture suffered from neglect at the hands of the Congress government at the Centre or the state. After all, Congress was the party of India's Green Revolution, and Indira Gandhi was the chief architect of agricultural policies in the 1960s and the consequent boom in agricultural production. Even today the UP government's expenditure on the rural sector is substantial. The net share of agriculture was 51 per cent of the state's national domestic product in 1977–78 [*Westley*, 1986]. Moreover, the rural sector commands considerable influence in the polity. Not only do the majority of UP's legislators come from a rural background, but the mobilisation of farmers has led to an enhancement of rural pressure in the polity and a corresponding boost to the self-confidence of farmers.

The alienation of the surplus producers from the Congress in this context was more political than economic. It gained momentum with the formation and victory of the Janata party in 1977, which foregrounded agrarian ideology and policy. As the new agrarian interests became key players in the Janata coalition, they challenged the Nehruvian project favouring industry, the professional classes and the cities [*Rudolph and Rudolph*, 1987: 335]. The alienation of this surplus-producing rural class from the cultural milieu of urban areas created a major social dichotomy in north India, in that their sense of alienation was heightened by a perception that government was not interested in establishing a rational price regime, principally because of the urban dominated politics.

In several states the farmers' movements went on to pose a serious challenge to Congress dominance. The rural appeal and breadth of their support played a vital part in the defeat of the Congress in Karnataka and Andhra Pradesh Assembly elections in 1982. The Shetkari Sangathana was credited with significantly reducing the margin of victory of many Congress candidates in the 1984 parliamentary elections in Maharashtra, as also in the assembly elections held two months later. The BKU backed the National Front, which won a decisive victory over the Congress in UP in 1989, and thus played a significant role in the overthrow of the Rajiv Gandhi government in 1989.

IV

Despite such wide support and political clout the UP farmer's movement floundered and declined. The most important reason for this decline was the drastic shift in political discourse. Since late 1980s the political agenda in UP has been dominated by Hindutva politics.[16] The national momentum gained by Hindutva paralleled the progressive exhaustion and decline in activity on the farmers' front. Why has this happened?

The political significance and durability of the farmers' movement depended in part on its ability to forge a network of support by transcending the short-term interests of the elites of the movement. The challenge before the farmers' movement was to create the necessary conditions so that a spectrum of rural producers believed they shared economic interests and political outlooks. Initially, the BKU was able to do this. Its early success lay in highlighting a composite picture of the possibilities and influences that could shape agrarian relations: sectoral growth and peasant proprietorship as a counterforce to agrarian radicalism. Tikait's political hallmark was not as much an emphasis on issues and policies shared by everyone as in creating a perception that remunerative prices and low input costs were a collective good for the entire countryside. But in the ultimate analysis these ideological calculations were sufficiently contradictory and ambiguous, and interpretations remained subject to the influence of differing ideologies and interests. The principal constraint stemmed from the nature of ethnic identities and interests. Farmers' politics were very much based on caste, ethnicity and religion which divides the countryside. Rural sectoral interests were overwhelmed by social cleavages. Farmers assertion in this sense was inevitably self-limited [*Varshney*, 1993]. Since it was differentiated and divided on the basis of class, caste, community and religion, rural power articulated by the farmers' movement could not become a cohesive force united in the pursuit of sectoral interests.

At its peak, some observers felt that the BKU movement could negate the communal politics of the Rashtriya Swayam Sevak Sangh–Bhartiya Janata Party–Vishwa Hindu Parishad (RSS–BJP–VHP) combine, as was done in Maharashtra by the Shetkari Sangathana. The Shetkari Sanghatana seemed to many to be the only force capable of halting the growth of the Shiv Sena in small towns and rural areas, and the farmers' movement was the most popular opposition to growing communal forces

[*Omvedt*, 1992]. In UP this impression was fostered by the absence of any communal disharmony in the Meerut agitation of early 1988. This was further borne out by the presence of cross-communal networks, the use of plural religious symbols, and the strong support for the BKU among Muslims. The demographic composition of western UP with a large and visible Muslim presence, contributed a lot to the BKU's cross-community network and need for communal amity The population of Muslims in western UP is higher than their population at the all-India level, and their proportion in districts like Muzaffarnagar, Meerut, Moradabad and Bijnor is particularly high. Consequently, the BKU invested special efforts in promoting communal harmony in Meerut which had been destroyed by the communal massacres in May 1987.

This cross-community support was bolstered by BKU's campaign against the abduction and murder of a Muslim girl in Muzaffarnagar district. This incident snowballed into a major agitation as Tikait marched with thousands of farmers to the banks of the Ganga Canal, and demanded that the government recover Naiyma. Following the recovery of Naiyma's body, hundreds of thousands of farmers gathered near the canal to protest against her murder (*Hindustan Times*, 28 Sept. 1989). This particular agitation helped the BKU to shore up its support among Muslims. As the *Times of India* observed:

> The mere act of thousands of Hindus squatting on the banks of a canal at Bhopa to seek redressal of a Muslim grievance is remarkable in itself. While this does not necessarily mean that communal prejudices are being consciously combated, it does powerfully demonstrate that there is a common code of social morality that guides rural society – a reality that urban politicians are usually unable to grasp (*Times of India*, 9 Aug. 1988).

These anti-communal exertions ultimately did not amount to very much, mainly because of the BKU's general adherence to a strategy and politics based on existing non-economic cleavages of caste, religion and ethnicity. From the very beginning, therefore, the mobilisation of farmers was influenced and bolstered by the communal structure of western UP. The caste distribution of the region, like its communal composition, is unique because of the high concentration of Jats in western UP. The latter comprise nearly 40 per cent of the population in Meerut, Muzaffarnagar, Saharanpur and Bijnor districts of western UP. Because of their numerical preponderance as well as their control over a sizeable proportion of land, Jats dominate both the politics and economy of the region. In the districts where the farmers' movement is particularly strong, the legacy of the *bhaichara* system still prevails among the Jats.[17] The Rajputs and Tyagis in this region also cultivate their own land and consider themselves to be the Jats' equal in status. Many of these peasants are linked by ties of caste and kinship and this helped to establish a rough correspondence between caste and class in western UP: hence the bulk of BKU support comes from Jats and other landholding castes. Caste support, however, is not unique to the BKU: the support of most such movements is located in the landholding dominant castes [*Omvedt*, 1988]. But what distinguishes the BKU from other farmers' organisations is the powerful district-level organisational structure of the Union. The BKU functions on the basis of collective leadership provided by members of 'a community of near equals' [*Gupta*, 1988], inspired by the coparcenary traditions of the *bhaichara* system in the region. The Sisauli Panchayat, the fulcrum of the grassroots decision-making structure, is itself an extension of the Jat *khap* councils, a form of caste panchayat which has existed for five hundred years as the administrative apparatus of the Jat community [*Pradhan*, 1986].[18]

There is no doubt that caste, clan and kinship ties helped in embedding and institutionalising the BKU in the local society and polity of the region. But there were obvious limits to and contradictions in such a pattern of mobilisation. The process of propagating the message through Jat councils might be an effective method in appealing to Jats, but it also deepened existing prejudices and hardened vertical loyalties of caste and community. As a result, the social composition of the BKU's main support base was essentially limited to Jats; accordingly the organisation found it extremely difficult to sustain its support among the backward castes, and even more difficult to build bridges with the lower castes and classes. This failure to transcend communal identity and organisation can explain the problems encountered by the farmers' organisation in sustaining a broad based support across castes and communities.

The farmers' movement in UP ran into difficulties on the issue of caste, especially the policy of reservation for backward caste which was the centre-piece of Janata Dal's strategy to counter the increasing Hindutva influence. Formed in 1989, the Janata Dal government' decided to reserve 27 per cent of government posts in the Central government for the backward castes, in accordance with the recommendations of the Mandal Commission.[19] In addition to this the UP government passed an ordinance to raise the reserved quota for backward castes in the state government by 12 per cent. The reservation policy provided significant new opportunities for social mobility to the backward castes, who were underrepresented in the Central and UP government. Precisely for this reason, the reservation policy was sharply rejected by the upper castes who dominate the bureaucracy and public institutions in India. In the event, the issue of reservations polarised the backward and upper castes in towns and villages throughout the state, and UP broke into an orgy of violence.[20] Everywhere the upper castes mobilised powerful resistance to the Mandal Commission recommendations and this plunged the already split Janata Dal government at the Centre into a serious crisis of survival.

Because it excluded Jats from its purview, the BKU was hostile to the new reservation package. Vehemently criticising caste-based reservation, the BKU countered by advocating an economic criterion for job reservation which would have enabled the dominant castes – including the Jats – to benefit from reservation. The notable feature of the anti-Mandal agitation was its strong support in the western UP districts of Ghaziabad, Mathura, Bulandshahr and Moradabad where the BKU held sway. The BKU backed the anti-Mandal agitation in UP, Haryana and Delhi, which set the stage for the eruption of major conflicts and violence culminating in the fall of the Janata Dal government in October 1990. The disorder in UP from August 1990 to June 1991 contributed to the fall of the Janata Dal government at the Centre as well as in UP: championed and nurtured by the BJP, the BKU, and the Congress, the anti-Mandal agitation played a crucial part in dislodging the Central government. From October 1990 onwards the anti-Mandal agitation slid into communal violence between Hindus and Muslims, intensifying social conflicts and confrontations between various groups and identities.[21]

The anti-Mandal agitation not only made visible all the pre-existing social divisions and tensions but also showed up the fragility of the attempted Hindu unity. Mandal was seen as antithetical to the construction of a composite, unified Hinduism: for the BJP, therefore, the political fallout of Mandal was damaging. As a party that was trying to project the notion of an undifferentiated Hindu society. The issue of caste based reservations was problematic because it undermined the basis of Hindu consolidation, a problem compounded because the BJP had only recently made inroads among the backward castes in north India. The Ayodhya movement launched by the Hindu right very quickly managed to shift the political discourse from economy and reservation to Hindu nationalism and cultural identity, thereby offsetting the divisive impact of the Mandal factor. In this way the caste politics of the Janata Dal was displaced by the communal politics of Hindutva which offered a language and vocabulary for the transformation of caste conflict into religious unity. The appeal of Hindutva's temple movement was strongest in UP because all the three disputed shrines – Ayodhya, Mathura and Varanasi – are located here. The Ramjanmabhoomi controversy has been the most effective source of mass mobilisation in recent times, because of its emotive appeal highlighted by a direct conflict with the Babri mosque, a symbol of Muslim identity. The Ayodhya symbol worked not only because of an intrinsic attachment to Rama in the land of Aryavarta, but also because the symbol simultaneously provided both a rallying counter-ideology against the divisiveness of caste and an incorporating framework that was capable of mobilising Hindus as an undifferentiated community.

The growth area of this movement is western and central UP, where it has made strong inroads into rural areas. In western UP, where growth has been shaped by the commercialisation of agriculture and the rapid expansion of small towns, such as Bulandshahr, Khurja, Aligarh, Meerut, Moradabad, there appears to be a significant coincidence of rapid socio-economic growth and an increase in communalism.[22] Commercial growth predominates over industrial growth, though small-scale industry has expanded phenomenally in the small towns: in the 1970s, for example, the growth of Khurja was due to the rapid growth of the pottery industry. Khurja's economy took off because of rising levels of consumer-oriented demand, both for 'ethnic' pottery and for small inexpensive pottery used in kiosks and tea stalls in small towns, a process which created a new class of small industrial entrepreneurs.

Urban expansion is also connected to the commercialisation of agriculture in western UP. New forms of commercial agriculture closely related to towns have emerged, blurring the dividing line between urban and rural, with agro-based industries dominating and forming a rural-urban nexus. Agriculture and agro-based industries are prominent even in the urban areas, suggesting a close techno-economic link between agriculture and industry which has accelerated the pace of urbanisation. This is why most western UP towns look like overgrown market-towns without a strong manufacturing base. With the rural and urban sectors reciprocally oriented towards each other, and with the growth of a rural middle class, towns are cashing in on the significant increase of the rural elite's purchasing power, fuelled by a consumer boom in the 1980s.

This pattern of combined rural/urban development in western UP is, however, not without its contradictions, which, when accompanied by a general rise in aspirations, have opened up spaces vulnerable to communalisation in the present conjuncture [*Chakravarthi, et al.*, 1992]. There has been a major expansion of the petit bourgeoisie, noted above, which the BJP can now identify as its political base. For example, a new petit bourgeoise among urban Jats which includes traders, shopkeepers, brick-kiln owners – all with strong connections in villages – have been won over by the RSS and BJP. The rise of small towns and Hindu communalism are not directly connected, however: rather, the former has in this region been conducive to the emergence of the latter in that the two histories intersect in significant ways. Accordingly, although neither the growth of a class nor urbanisation per se generate communalisation, their combined development in a specific conjuncture, in which particular forms of political mobilisation and electoral calculation are crystallising, dangerously reorients many kinds of conflicts into Hindu–Muslim antagonisms. In this respect, a significant phenomenon has been the incorporation of hitherto peaceful towns and surrounding rural areas into the ambit of communal violence. As the intensity of communal politics has grown, there has been a marked increase in communal violence and rioting associated with it. The escalation of violence during the *rathyatra*[23] was greatest in UP. More significantly, western UP was the area of maximum concentration. Thus Meerut, Bijnor, Bulandshahr, Saharanpur, Aligarh, Agra and Etah had all major riots – all these were BKU strongholds, clearly affected by communalisation.

Another communal orgnisation, the VHP, has garnered its major support in western UP. Thus the largest number of participants at the Virat Hindu Sammelan[24] hosted by the VHP in June 1990 – the first in UP – came from western UP (*Frontline*, 4–17 August, 1990). Through the activities of such organisations Hindutva ideology has penetrated Jat dominated villages. What is noteworthy is that sustained communal propaganda has fractured the mixed ideological and syncretic traditions of UP.

The Hindu right has gained enormously from its ties with the VHP and the numerous social, cultural and religious organizations associated with the RSS which appear to link the party with the traditional values and concerns of Hindu popular culture. It has used these ties to heighten the friction between the State and the public arena, increasingly dominated by the RSS-VHP through its congregational politics linking the home, the street and the temple [*Chakravarthi et al.*, 1992]. This new style of politics is specifically built around religious festivities requiring public participation and culminating in processions winding through major streets and towns. Congregational politics in UP have filled the streets with festivals, *jagrans* and *yatras*. These celebrations were essential for a takeover of public spaces, previously the domain of the anti-Mandalites through their street theatre, and before that controlled by the *dharnas, gheraos* and *rasta rokos* of the BKU. Hence the methods and appeal of the farmers have been displaced and marginalised by the emotional and political appeal of Hindutva. Its totalising ideology, aggressive chauvinism and the massive communal violence which accompanied its ascendancy in UP politics left little space for other types of struggles and confrontations with the State.

Until 1989 the farmers' movement operated in the public arena with formidable advantages. It could count on the support of political parties because of its avowedly non-party stance. Its steady politicisation since then has diminished its influence considerably. Initially the BKU was caught between the rivalries of different Janata Dal factions: besides, their claim to be devoted to agriculture conflicted with Tikait's claim to be the sole spokesman of UP's farmers. The BKU then found itself arraigned against Yadav, the Chief Minister of UP, who prevented it from holding a kisan panchayat in Lucknow in July 1990 to press farmers' demands on the state government.[25] Tikait was arrested and his supporters lathicharged in Lucknow and Barabanki jail. The BJP leaders were quick to extend full support to the farmers, thus further widening the gulf between farmers and the Janata Dal. This assumed significance in the context of the growing confrontation and turmoil over the Ayodhya issue in the state. Many of the BKU's supporters were clearly attracted to the Ayodhya campaign: indeed, the western districts dispatched a large number of *karsevaks*[26] to Ayodhya. Many of them returned to their districts as heroes who had been able to penetrate the massive security forces deployed to protect the Babri mosque. Some karsevaks were killed in the police firing and became the symbolic fountainhead of mobilisation against the State which was prepared to sacrifice Hindu lives to protect the disputed shrine. Another factor that pushed the farmers' movement more and more towards the upper castes was their shared hostility against Dalits. Frequent Jat–Harijan conflicts in western UP had helped the Bahujan Samaj Party (BSP) to establish a base among the scheduled castes threatened by the social dominance of landed castes in this region.[27] These contradictions might well have encouraged the BKU to combine with the BJP in a trade-off, in order to gain the latter's support in their conflict with the Dalits.

The autonomy of BKU was further undermined by reports of Tikait's decision to enter into an informal alliance with the BJP in the 1991 parliament and state assembly elections in UP. As a result, the BJP performed extremely well in BKU strongholds, in contrast to the major losses suffered by Janata Dal in these areas; it is worth recalling that after his estrangement with the Janata Dal, Tikait warned that without the support of the farmers, the Janata Dal could win no more than a handful of seats in UP (*Frontline*, 14–17 Aug. 1990). So it is not surprising that from a commanding position of 50 per cent of the popular vote in UP in 1989, and a 100 per cent success rate in seats contested, the Janata Dal and Samajwadi Janata party slipped to 37.4 per cent of the popular vote and a success rate of just one-third of the seats contested. By contrast, a combination of ideological activity by the BJP–VHP–RSS combine followed by violence and rioting played a decisive role in the BJP victory in

1991. In western UP, the BJP won 11 of 17 parliamentary seats – all in riot-hit towns, except for Saharanpur and Khurja. In the Rohilkhand region of western UP, the BJP won seven out of 10 seats, again winning in all three riot hit towns – Bijnor, Rampur and Badaun [*Chakravarti et al.*, 1992: 963].

Although the BJP on its own garnered much of this electoral support, the BKU's endorsement helped the party in establishing its credentials among the farmers who might not otherwise have been sufficiently inspired by the BJP's obsession with the Rama Mandir alone. Whereas in the 1991 election there was no indication that agrarian interests could overcome the pull of caste and religious identities, in the past it was from this area, and from the intermediate agrarian classes of western UP, that Charan Singh fashioned a succession of agrarian political formations to provide the Janata Dal with much of its strength in UP. Even the new alliance forged by the Samajwadi party and the BSP in the 1993 assembly elections failed to gain support in western UP which has emerged as the chief bastion of the BJP, in contrast to eastern UP, where this alliance made major inroads in BJP strongholds. To sum up, the election results in western UP indicate that the BJP managed to bring about substantive changes in the political agenda; even though it has not managed to alter the caste–class alliance in the western region of UP, it has managed to change cross-communal networks through a sharpening of Hindu–Muslim polarisation. When these identities begin to dominate the political agenda, they can obstruct a sectoral or even populist construction of rural interests.

It could be argued that voter choices may have very little to do with their preference for higher prices and loans [*Varshney*, 1993]. In other words, a farmer who may have participated in rural price agitation may cast his/her vote on caste, religious or regional consideration. On the face of it, the 1991 election seemed to turn overwhelmingly on the Ayodhya controversy. The crucial issue is whether or not voters supported the BJP simply on emotive-religious appeal, or whether they were favourably disposed to the BJP because of the unprecedented political mobilisation mounted by the Hindu right to highlight the State repression of the karsewa in Ayodhya. Most accounts of elections clearly show that the Hindutva propaganda and its demonisation of the State – and not merely the innate religiosity of people – played a key part in turning the tide in favour of the BJP The second point is the role of the BKU elite in influencing farmers' voting choices. Interviews with the local elite and BKU leaders in Muzaffarnagar district, for example, show that they supported the BJP in order to express their aversion to and repugnance of the Janata Dal's reservation policy and Yadav's refusal to allow the construction of the Ramamandir at the disputed site.[28]

V

Whatever the assessment of the public discourse and the subjective inclinations of the leading actors of the farmers' movement, the objective response to Hindutva was marked by silence; there was no evidence of a counter-campaign to halt its expansion. This does not warrant the conclusion that the BKU is actively supporting the Hindutva politics, but there does seem to be an ambivalence towards it, and a reluctance to confront it.[29] This is not unusual: the ambivalence is shared by all the major political formations. Arguably it could be interpreted as a pragmatic acceptance of the current hegemony of Hindutva in UP, rather than a positive espousal of its politics. Nevertheless, it suggests that the farmers' movement has failed to find an enduring basis in the sphere of social movements or social thinking. An important reason is that the farmers' movement did not contest the social field being taken over by communal politics which was consciously seeking to sharpen religious identities, reinterpret conflicts and reshape institutions. Communal ideologies can flourish in the absence of counter ideologies and movements. The refusal of the farmers' leadership itself to give precedence to their economic interests over ascriptive ethnic identities seriously constrained the sustainability of the movement.

The growth of Hindutva politics and the communal upsurge in UP in the late 1980s and early 1990s has clearly overtaken the farmers' movement. The BKU's politics and strategy might also have increased ethnic energies conducive to a more acute communalisation of political discourse. The adherence to a populist-cum-ethnic register reinforced the space for the growth of the political right. More crucially, such a framework of identity projects and represents issues and interests in a non-class manner, as both the BKU and BJP have done. The BKU has chosen not to construct or present its interests in economic terms. This is because economic interests defined as better prices and subsidies do not affect or benefit all segments equally, and consequently the economic contradictions which in material terms divide rich and poor farmers in the BKU are deflected ideologically by a populism which demands simply a better deal for the countryside from the State. In a similar vein, Hindutva projects an undifferentiated Hindu community oppressed and threatened by the 'pseudo-secularism' of the State and its 'appeasement' of Muslims, and demands a better deal for the Hindu community as a whole. Both ideologies highlight political symbols and forms which generate and reinforce undifferentiated notions of a community of commodity producers or Hindus simply on grounds of being rural-not-urban and Hindus-not-Muslims. In this sense the language employed by the ideologies of agrarianism or Hindutva converge by explicitly placing rural-agrarian in opposition to urban–industrial, or the majority in opposition to minority interests. Both claim to speak for the collective good of the entire agricultural economy/community/nation. Despite the very different ideological provenance of the two movements, the terms of discourse joining together classes, castes and communities shares a political framework which accepts the basic parameters of the present system even as they call for some changes within it.

NOTES

1. 'Surplus-producing' farmers refers to those well-to-do farmers who have a genuine surplus to sell after meeting their own requirements (that is, distress sellers are excluded). These farmers account for the bulk of total sales because they command the bulk of the area under cultivation, and they comprise roughly the top three pentiles of holdings ranked by area.
2. On various aspects of farmers movements see Dhanagare [1988]; Lenneberg [1988]; Nadkarni [1987]; Omvedt [1988; 1992]; and Rudolph and Rudolph [1987]. Farmers have carried out agitations in various states, and staged massive rallies in Delhi.
3. Much of BKU's initial support was built through its advocacy of farmers grievances on electricity supply. The BKU got a shot in the arm after power rates were raised in August 1986, from Rs 22.50 to Rs 30. Added to this were the perennial problems faced by the farmers in dealing with the Uttar Pradesh State Electricity Board. The transformers are often burnt out, and farmers have to bribe officials to expedite repairs. The UP government's insistence that farmers should pay electricity dues or face cuts in power supply generated strong resentment against the government. Tikait quickly seized the initiative, urging farmers to ignore the UPSEB's directive. The non-payment campaign was taken to villages, with BKU activists succeeding in persuading farmers not to pay electricity dues. It is easy to understand why this was so. A regular power supply for tubewells is crucial to the growth of the highly capital intensive agriculture in western UP. Though tubewells are owned and operated by rich farmers, small farmers too have a stake in power supply, because they have to rent tubewells for irrigation. This is the one issue that influenced all the farmers to join the numerous agitations launched by the BKU (*Hindustan Times*, 2 April 1987).
4. The Lok Dal won 85 seats in the 1984 Assembly elections, only nine weeks after the landslide victory of the Congress in the Lok Sabha elections held in the wake of Indira Gandhi's assassination. In 1989 the Janata Dal won the Assembly elections and formed the government in UP.
5. Towards the end of British rule in India the rural economic structure of UP was marked by extreme inequality in the ownership of land and means of production. Inequality in the distribution of landownership was most marked in central and eastern UP. In the central districts 11 per cent of zemindars owned three quarters of the land; the pattern of ownership was slightly less uneven in eastern UP where approximately 11 per cent of zemindars owned 61 per cent of the area. By contrast the great majority in both these areas owned holdings of less than five acres, accounting for four per cent of the land. In comparison, in western UP, about five per cent of large zemindars owned 51 per cent of the land, the 45 per cent of zamindars who had holdings below five acres accounting for four per cent of the land. More notably, western UP was dotted with a substantial class of rich and medium landowners: 36 per cent owned holdings of 5–25 acres and 18 per

cent of the area, while another 13 per cent owned farms of 25–100 acres and 13 per cent of the area [*Singh and Misra*, 1984: 215–17).

6. In 1970–71, 54 per cent of the acreage was controlled by peasants with miminum holdings of 7.5 acres [*Brass*, 1980]. A recent study of Meerut highlights the dominance of capitalist producers and rich peasants, who constituted 7.69 per cent of the households and controlled the largest land area (47–53 per cent). The middle peasants, who formed 20.44 per cent of the households, controlled 39.3 per cent of the land area [*Singh*, 1992].
7. The section on food production is based on Hasan and Patnaik [forthcoming].
8. Through the fair price shops of the public distribution system in cities and towns, foodgrains and some manufactured necessities like sugar and fuel are sold to one quarter of the total population at low prices subsidised by government.
9. According to estimates for the 1980–81 wheat crop, the price index for agricultural products as percentage of that for manufactured products declined from 100.7 per cent in 1974–75 to 87.6 per cent in 1977–80 (*Economic and Political Weekly*, 8 Sept. 1990).
10. Much of the analysis of farmers' movements adheres to the view that is is a movement of the middle peasantry. See Lenneberg [1988] and Omvedt [1992], for an analysis of the Maharashtra farmers' movement, and Rudolph and Rudolph [1987] for the farmers' movements as a whole.
11. A small survey was conducted in two villages in Meerut and Moradabad districts just after the Meerut agitation of January–February, 1988. The village in Meerut had a tradition of peasant proprietorship, while the village in Moradabad had a zamindari background. The stratified sample covered 15 per cent of households for every caste and class in the two villages. I am grateful to Jagpal Singh for his help in carrying out the survey.
12. The domination of the rural rich in the BKU is also stressed by Singh [1992].
13. The table below shows the presence of a high proportion of agricultural labourers in Saharanpur, Muzaffarnagar, Meerut Bulandshahr, Aligarh and Bijnor districts. All these districts have experienced rapid capitalist development.

DISTRICTWISE NUMBER OF TOTAL MARGINAL AND SMALL HOLDINGS (1980–81) AND AGRICULTURAL LABOURERS (1981) (THOUSANDS)

Districts	Total (All Holding Groups	Small (1–2 ha)	Marginal (Below 1 ha)	Agricultural Labourers
Saharanpur	255	49	144	224
Muzaffarnagar	249	45	147	182
Meerut	235	46	138	145
Ghaziabad	161	31	102	63
Bulandshahr	244	52	137	111
Aligarh	252	55	132	129
Mathura	162	37	69	65
Agra	235	52	125	75
Manipuri	347	61	248	50
Etah	319	60	213	64
Bijnor	219	46	117	127
Moradabad	378	77	227	92
Rampur	148	31	92	37
Bareilly	331	61	221	78
Badaun	408	75	274	50
Shahjahanpur	354	65	242	58
Pilibhit	170	36	104	41
Farrukhabad	373	53	284	57
Etawah	287	54	191	58

Source: Statistical Diary, Uttar Pradesh, 1986.

14. Agricultural labourers and rural poor responded to the growing consolidation of the BKU by supporting the Bharatiya Mazdoor Union (BMU), an organisation of agricultural labourers and the BSP. The BSP is a political organisation devoted to the protection and promotion of interests of scheduled castes and backward classes, and in the past the few years has garnered considerable support in UP. The BSP–Samajwadi Party alliance has won 171 seats in the 1993 elections and has formed the government in UP.
15. There has been an intensification of Jat-scheduled caste conflicts in Meerut and Muzaffarnagar in 1989–90. The worst incident took place in Bhopal in Muzaffarnagar, in September 1989, after a labourer refused to work for a Jat farmer belonging to the BKU. The clash ended up in firing which killed 4 persons and injured 24. Jats were backed by the BKU, and scheduled castes by the BMU (see *Hindustan Times*, 28 Sept. 1989).
16. *Hindutva* is a contemporary right-wing movement of Hindu self-assertion, for Hindu rights and Hindu nationhood.
17. *Bhaichara* refers to a system where the management and distribution of land is structured by exclusive customs and traditions of a particular community. The *bhaichara* system prevailed throughout the Jat dominated regions of western UP. In Meerut, for example 40 per cent of land came under *bhaichara* in 1940.
18. Sisauli Panchayat is the main decision making body of the BKU: it meets every month in Sisauli village, Muzaffarnagar district.
19. The Janata party government appointed the Backward Classes Commission in December 1978, headed by Bindeshwari Prasad Mandal, popularly known as the Mandal Commission. The Commission identified castes as socially and educationally backward and recommended reservation of 27 per cent jobs for them in Central government.
20. For details on the anti-Mandal agitation see PUDR [1990].
21. Between the *rathyatra* and the 1991 elections, three phases of tension and rioting can be identified. The first phase, starting in the wake of the anti-Mandal agitation, took the form of tension on the route of the *rathyatra*. This phase ended in considerable rioting when Advani was arrested and some *karsewaks* were killed in police firing. In the first week of November, 34 towns in UP were under curfew along with 36 across the country. The second phase started after the fall of the Janata Dal government, and was followed by another round of violence which lasted from the beginning of December till the end of January 1991. It was concentrated in UP with western UP being the area of maximum concentration. The third phase of rioting began in March 1991 with elections imminent, and continued well until elections in May [*Chakravarti et al.*, 1992]. Similarly, the two months preceding the 1989 elections witnessed riots in 55 places across nine states (see PUDR [1990]).
22. The analysis of the link between commercialisation and communalism in western UP draws upon the research and information I collected along with Uma Chakravarti, Prem Chowdhuri, Pradip Dutta, Kumkum Sangari and Tanika Sarkar [*Chakravarthi et al.*, 1992].
23. *Rathyatra* is a a pilgrimage or largescale procession, the object of which is to put across a religious message. L.K. Advani, President of the BJP, undertook a *rathyatra* in September–October 1990, traversing several states in order to mobilise support for the construction of the Ramamandir in Ayodhya. The course of the *rathyatra* was marked by massive communal violence, culminating in Advani's arrest and the fall of the Janata Dal government in November 1990.
24. Virat Hindu Sammelan is a largescale congregation of Hindus organised at the behest of the Vishwa Hindu Parishad.
25. The BKU's differences with the BJP government emerged because the latter did not allow the BKU to hold its panchayat in Lucknow. The BJP government asserted its

authority twice within a short span of five months, and in effect subdued the BKU. Tikait had to abandon plans to hold the panchayat in Lucknow in order to avoid confrontation (*Statesman*, 10 Feb. 1992).

26. Karseva is the work a devotee is expected to do as a part of his obligation to a religious shrine or place of worship.
27. See note 14.
28. In-depth interviews of the local elite were conducted in Muzaffarnagar district in September 1993. Some of the information and analysis on the growth and impact of the BJP in western UP is based on these interviews. I am grateful to Ajay Kant, Ph.D. scholar in the Centre for Political Studies, Jawaharlal Nehru University for his help in conducting the interviews.
29. Analysis of the relationship between Hindutva and the farmers movement is limited to the period until the 1991 elections. The paper does not analyse developments after June 1991.

REFERENCES

Baru, S., 1990, *The Political Economy of Indian Sugar: State Intervention and Structural Change*, Delhi: Oxford University Press.

Bhalla, G.S. and D.S. Tyagi, 1989, *Patterns in Indian Agricultural Development: A District Level Study*, Delhi: Institute for Studies in Industrial Development.

Brass, P., 1980, 'The Politicisation of the Peasantry in a North Indian State', *Journal of Peasant Studies*, Vol.8, No.1.

Byres, T.J., 1988, 'Charan Singh 1902–97: An Assessment', *Journal of Peasant Studies*, Vol.15 No.2.

Calman, L.J., 1992, *Towards Empowerment: Women and Movement Politics in India*, Boulder, CO: Westview.

Chakravarthi, U., Chowdhury, P., Dutta, P.K., Hasan, Z., Sangari, K. and T. Sarkar, 1992, 'Khurja Riots 1990: Understanding the Conjuncture', *Economic and Political Weekly*, Vol.27, No.18.

Dhanagare, D.N., 1988, 'An Apoliticist Populism', *Seminar*, No.352.

Duncan, I., 1988, 'Party Politics and the North Indian Peasantry: The Rise of the BKD in UP', *Journal of Peasant Studies*, Vol.16, No.1.

Gill, S.S. and K. Singhal, 1984, 'Farmers Agitation: Response to Development Crisis of Agriculture', *Economic and Political Weekly*, Vol.19, No.40.

Government of India, 1975, *All-India Report on Agricultural Census, 1970–71*, New Delhi: Ministry of Agriculture and Irrigation.

Government of India, 1992, *All-India Report on the Agricultural Census*, New Delhi: Ministry of Agriculture and Irrigation.

Government of Uttar Pradesh, 1981, *Agriculture Census in Uttar Pradesh, 1980–81*, Lucknow: Board of Revenue.

Government of Uttar Pradesh, 1986, *Statistical Abstract: Uttar Pradesh, 1983–4*, Lucknow: Economics and Statistic Division, State Planning Institute.

Government of Uttar Pradesh, 1989, *Statistical Diary: Uttar Pradesh, 1988*, Lucknow: Economics and Statistics Division, State Planning Institute.

Gupta, D., 1988, 'Country-Town Nexus and Agrarian Mobilisation: Bharatiya Kisan Union', *Economic and Political Weekly*, Vol.23, No.51.

Hasan, Z., 1989, 'Self-Serving Guardians: Formation and Strategy of the Bharatiya Kisan Union', *Economic and Political Weekly*, Vol.24, No.45

Hasan, Z. and U. Patnaik, forthcoming, 'Aspects of the Farmers Movement in Uttar Pradesh in the Context of Uneven Growth of Capitalist Agriculture', in T.V. Satyamurthy (ed.), *Social Change and Political Discourse in India*, Delhi: Oxford University Press.

Kant, A., 1990, 'Agrarian Mobilisation in Western Uttar Pradesh: A Case Study of the

Bhartiya Kisan Union', M. Phil Dissertation, School of Social Sciences, Jawharlal Nehru University.

Lenneberg, C., 1988, 'Sharad Joshi and the Farmers: 'The Middle Peasant Lives', *Pacific Affairs*, Vol.61, No.3.

Mitra, A., 1977, *Terms of Trade and Class Relations*, London: Frank Cass.

Nadkarni, M.V., 1987, *Farmers' Movements in India*, Delhi: Allied Publishers.

Omvedt, G., 1988, 'New Movements', *Seminar*, No.352.

Omvedt, G., 1990, 'The Farmers Movement in Maharashtra', in I. Sen (ed.). *A Space Within the Struggle*, Delhi: Kali for Women.

Omvedt, G., 1992, 'Peasants, Dalits, and Women: Democracy and India's New Social Movements?' Paper presented at a workshop on 'Social Movements, State and Democracy' organised by the Delhi University Group on Politics of Developing Countries and the Indian Statistical Institute Sociology Group, New Delhi, 5–8 Oct.

Patnaik, U., 1986, 'The Agrarian Question and the Development of Capitalism in India', *Economic and Political Weekly*, Vol.21, No.18.

Patnaik, U., 1992, 'Food Availability and Famine: A Longer View', *Journal of Peasant Studies*, Vol.19, No.1.

Peoples Union of Democratic Rights (PUDR), 1989, *Communal Tensions in India: September–October 1989*, Delhi: PUDR.

Peoples Union of Democratic Rights (PUDR), 1990, *Disputed Passages: Report on Law, Reservations and Agitations*, Delhi: PUDR.

Pradhan, M.C., 1986, *The Political System of the Jats of Northern India*, Bombay: Oxford University Press.

Roy, P.K., 1988, 'Farmers Power', *Frontline*, 20 Feb.–4 March.

Rao, V.K.R.V., 1983, *India's National Income 1950–1980*, Delhi: Sage.

Rudolph, L.I. and S.H. Rudolph, 1987, *In Pursuit of Laxmi: The Political Economy of the Indian State*, Delhi: Orient Longman.

Shankar, Kripa, 1990, *Land Transfers: A Case Study*, Delhi: Gian Publishing House.

Singh, B., and S. Misra, 1984, *A Study of Land Reforms in UP*, Calcutta: Oxford Book Co.

Singh, C., 1981, *Land Reform in UP and the Kulaks*, Delhi: Vikas Publishing House.

Singh, J., 1992, *Capitalism and Dependence: Agrarian Politics in Western Uttar Pradesh 1951–1991*, Delhi: Manohar.

Varshney, A., 1993, 'Introduction: Urban Bias in Perspective', *Journal of Development Studies*, Vol.29, No.4.

Varshney, A., 1993, 'Self-Limited Empowerment: Democracy, Economic Development and Rural India', *Journal of Development Studies*, Vol.29, No.4.

Westley, J.R., 1986, *Agriculture and Equitable Growth: The Case of Punjab – Haryana*, London: Westview Press.

The Farmers' Movement and Agrarian Change in the Green Revolution Belt of North-West India

SUCHA SINGH GILL

INTRODUCTION

During recent years the Green Revolution belt in plains of North-west India – consisting of Punjab, Haryana and western Uttar Pradesh – has been the scene of a large-scale and politically dramatic process of farmer mobilization, under the banner of the *Bharatiya Kisan Union* (BKU). Consequently, existing peasant organisations, such as the *Kisan Sabhas* of the CPI and the CPI(M), and newer ones, such as the *Kirti Kisan Union* of CPI(ML), have either become marginalised or fallen into line with the BKU. Equally significant is the fact that no attempt has been made, both by these and other non-left organisations, to oppose the BKU over issues to do with farmer politics. The resulting autonomy enjoyed by the BKU in party political terms has enabled it to recruit and maintain the support of farmers with widely different political links and views, a characteristic which differentiates the current phase of farmer mobilisation from previous ones. Accordingly, the fourfold object of this presentation is to explore the origins of the present phase of the farmers' movement, to characterise it in terms of its socio-economic composition, to consider its vision of rural society and to examine the limits to this kind of mobilisation.

GENESIS OF THE MOVEMENT

The three factors responsible for the emergence and growth of the farmers' movement in the Green revolution belt are: a long history of peasant struggle (together with an awareness of this tradition), and a combination of both objectively and subjectively favourable conditions for organising and shaping the present movement.

Sucha Singh Gill, Department of Economics, Punjabi University, Patiala – 147002, India.
The author gratefully acknowledges the useful points raised by participants at the JPS/ICSSR Workshop held in New Delhi during March 1993. The study in its present form owes much to the editorial input of Tom Brass.

Prior to the current phase of farmer mobilisation, therefore, peasants in this area were already involved in political activity. For example, in pre-partition Punjab (comprising of a sizeable part of the Indian Punjab and Haryana) peasants were mobilised by the pro-landlord Unionist Party, and in the princely states they were mobilised by the Praja Mandal movement. Similarly, in the pre-Independence era the Zamindara League of Chotu Ram created among the peasantry an awareness of the importance of its own collective strength, while both before and after Independence the Kisan Sabha was organised firstly by the then united CPI and later on by the CPI and the CPM.[1] And as a result of the introduction of the universal adult franchise and the adoption of the Panchayati Raj during the post-Independence period, there was a considerable increase in the power and influence exercised by farmers not only at the level of the village but also the block and the state of Punjab itself.[2]

Much the same is true of farmers in the states of Haryana and Uttar Pradesh. In western UP, for example, the politicisation of the peasantry was well advanced by the late 1970s.[3] Since political power in this region depends on the support of the peasantry, all parties have actively sought this and recruited from among the ranks of petty commodity producers; prominent political leaders, such as Ajit Singh, Devi Lal, Prakash Singh Badal, Gurcharan Singh Tohra, Bansi Lal and Beant Singh are themselves affluent and dynamic farmers. Accordingly, when both the gains generated by and the prosperity linked to the Green Revolution began to decline, these already politicised agrarian producers began in turn to intensify their activity *vis-à-vis* the established power structure; the failure on the part of the ruling party leadership to respond adequately led to the formation of an independent farmers' movement, the BKU.

In economic terms, the farmers' mobilisation under the aegis of the BKU must in turn be located in the material conditions affecting agricultural production in the region after the mid-1960s. The plains of North West India, comprising the states of Punjab, Haryana and Western UP, was the first area in India to adopt the new technology of the Green Revolution. Consequently, the highest level of agricultural development at the All-India level has been recorded in Punjab, Haryana (except for the districts of Hissar, Sirsa and Mahindragarh, and Dadri and Koharu tehsils in Bhiwani district) and most districts in Western UP. These areas generated a per hectare income above Rs 1,250 during 1980–83, and a per annum growth rate in excess of 3.5 per cent throughout the entire 1970/73–1980/83 period.[4]

The success of the Green Revolution in this region was itself made possible by assured and constant irrigation: this was provided initially by water obtained from a canal system harnessed to the river network, and

TABLE 1
LANDHOLDINGS IN PUNJAB, HARYANA AND UTTAR PRADESH BY SIZE, DISTRIBUTION, AND IRRIGATION

	Average Size of Holding *a*	Percent of Holdings 2-10 Has. *b*	Percent of Irrigated to Sown *c*
Punjab	3.82	54.18	86.4
Haryana	3.52	42.21	60.5
Uttar Pradesh	1.01	12.77	57.2
Western UP	n.a.	18.49 *d*	71.0 *e*
All India	1.84	11.84	29.7

Source: Government of Punjab, 1989, *Statistical Abstract of Punjab, 1988*, Chandigarh: Economic and Statistical Organization.

Notes: *a* In hectares, for 1980–81. *b* For 1980–81. *c* For 1983–84. *d* Data refer to 22 wheat producing districts, largely in Western UP, during 1971 (Government of UP, Board of Revenue, Lucknow, quoted in Brass [1980]). *e* Data refer to upper and lower Doab regions during 1976–77 (Government of UP, Board of Revenue, quoted in Hasan [1989]).

subsequently by water obtained as a result of the installation of electric tube-wells and pump-sets. The region as a whole possessed a favourable man–land ratio, and also a relatively large average landholding size (see Table 1). Another factor in this success was the existence of a favourable institutional framework. By legislatively removing a whole range of rent receiving intermediaries, the Indian state created an economically-auspicious context for the peasant proprietor. In addition to irrigation and energy inputs, the Indian state also provided infrastructural facilities such as credit, regulated markets, a rural road network, and agricultural extension and research. Based on HYV seeds, chemical fertilisers, pesticides, weedicides and mechanised inputs (tractors, threshers), the Green Revolution technology was rapidly adopted throughout the region, farmers with larger landholdings doing so quicker than others.

The adoption of new technology increasingly brought farmers within the reach of the market nexus. On the one hand it involved a considerable purchase of inputs from the market (fertilisers, pesticides, insecticides, weedicides, new variety seeds, tractors, threshers, electric motors, pump-sets, electricity, diesel fuel, etc.). On the other hand it increased the quantity of marketed surplus, by extending the area under cultivation, cropping intensity, and crop productivity (particularly wheat, rice, cotton and sugarcane). Moreover, ancillary activities connected with marketing – such as the loading/unloading of produce, cleaning, weighing, stock-taking, storage and transportation – similarly increased. In overall terms, therefore, a consequence of this market integration was that producers became increasingly affected by even small changes in market conditions: the availability of inputs, the fluctuation in the price of the latter, the amount of marketed surplus and the corresponding impact on its price, were all issues in which the farmer now had an interest.

This adoption of new technology was not only a technical factor, it also had implications for and an impact on existing social relations in the sphere of production. One fundamental outcome has been the conversion of agriculture from 'a way of life' into a commercial enterprise, and family labour is increasingly being replaced by hired workers in field operations. Unsurprisingly, large capitalist farmers generally depend on hired labour for most of their field operations, which they themselves supervise; more surprising, however, is evidence which suggests that even small and medium-sized surplus-producing landholders are now purchasing labour-power.[5] Apart from reflecting the nature of agrarian change, the employment of hired labour has also contributed to the importance of the market nexus for agriculture in the region, one effect of which has been to create an arena of conflict between cultivators and workers over wage and work-related issues.

In the initial phase of the Green Revolution, all classes of farmer made considerable gains.[6] This enhanced the economic viability of small producers, and thus contributed to an increased farmer solidarity not only on issues such as input/output prices but also against workers in the eventuality of conflict. Since most of the farmers in the region belong to the Jat caste, the 'community feeling' (*bhaichara*) of Jats is an added factor in this producer solidarity. Generally speaking, therefore, the continuing benefits and profitability of the Green Revolution have generated a high level of economic expectation among a wide section of the rural population in the region.

It proved impossible, however, to sustain the profit levels and related benefits which accrued from the initial stage of the Green Revolution. Data reveal that after 1973/74, the net per hectare income at constant prices for wheat began to decline in all three states. Between 1970/71 and 1980/81, wheat production averaged a negative per annum growth rate of price margin over cost of 17 per cent, 28 per cent and 14 per cent respectively for Punjab, Haryana and UP (Table 2). The main cause of this has been a decline in the net barter terms of trade for agriculture.[7] Since prices paid by the agricultural sector have outstripped prices received (Table 3), the parity between the agrarian and non-agrarian

TABLE 2
NET INCOME FROM WHEAT PRODUCTION, 1970/71 TO 1980/81
(Rupees per Hectare, at 1970/71 Prices)

Year	Punjab	Haryana	Uttar Pradesh
1970/71	328	611	n. a.
1971/72	426	553	504
1972/73	167	n. a.	248
1973/74	589	601	612
1974/75	430	478	n. a.
1975/76	59	331	110
1976/77	124	-109	n. a.
1977/78	72	27	n. a.
1978/79	193	-46	149
1979/80	175	n. a.	78
1980/81	54	n. a.	126
Annual rate of decline of price over cost	17.09	28.18	13.82
Percentage of wheat to net sown area	41.3	26.8	30.4

Source: Agricultural Price Commission data, cited in Swamy and Gulati [1986].

sectors of the economy has been disrupted. Throughout the 1970s, when the terms of trade moved against agriculture, Punjab, Haryana and UP registered an annual increase in cropping intensity of 1.42 per cent, 0.86 per cent and 0.28 per cent respectively. The per hectare wheat yield also registered an increase, of 0.58 per cent, 2.48 per cent and 0.73 per cent annually in these states between 1970/71 and 1980/81.[8] The outcome of this process was a reduction in the profitability of the rich farmer and an increase in the deficits of the poor cultivator, both sets of circumstances combining to produce the objective material conditions necessary for their mobilisation.

TABLE 3
INDICES OF PRICES RECEIVED/PAID BY AGRICULTURE, AND AGRICULTURAL TERMS OF TRADE IN INDIA
(Triannium ending 1971/72 = 100)

	Agricultural Sector		
	Prices Received	Prices Paid	Prices Received/ Prices Paid
1971/72	102.5	105.1	97.5
1972/73	116.9	112.9	103.5
1973/74	145.0	132.3	109.6
1974/75	166.8	166.9	99.9
1975/76	142.4	168.3	84.6
1976/77	157.0	173.2	90.7
1977/78	164.8	181.6	90.8
1978/79	157.1	183.9	85.4
1979/80	185.4	209.3	88.6
1980/81	213.6	244.8	87.3

Source: Tyagi [1987].

The prosperity generated by the initial phase of the Green Revolution, and the consequent substitution of hired workers for family labour, has also created a human reservoir on which the farmers' movement has been able to draw for its mobilisation. The spread of general education has provided opportunities for the children of farmers to complete their schooling, as a result of which a large number of them have been able to enter college and even university. This in turn has produced a large stock of educated youth who aspire to white-collar employment, but for whom there are insufficient such jobs.[9] It is these subjects of rural origin who, not being able to secure white collar employment nor wishing to return to manual labour on the farm, have provided the farmers' movement with some of its core activists and militants. In this they have also been joined by retired army personnel and civilian officials of rural origin.

Evidence for this is confirmed by the educational background of a large number of organisers in the BKU. For example, a study of the Punjab branch of the BKU reveals that in 1982–83 approximately three quarters of all its members were literate, and of these 40 per cent were graduates.[10] This finding has to be evaluated in terms of the 1981 rural literacy rate for the state of Punjab of only 35 per cent.[11] Some 29 per cent of the Punjab BKU organizers were also members – or had in the recent past held membership – of the village panchayats and Panchayat Samities, and twenty per cent were ex-servicemen.[12] Much the same is true of the BKU in western UP, where the leadership is composed of rich farmers, professionals, teachers, ex-army officers and retired government officials.[13]

The origins of the farmers' organisations lie in conflicts within the ranks of the ruling class. Thus both the Uttar Pradesh and Haryana branches of the BKU were founded in 1978 by Charan Singh after he had been ousted from the Desai cabinet, the object of mobilising farmers in this manner being to demonstrate the power and extent of his own support.[14] In a similar vein, the *Punjab Khetibari Zamindara Union* (PKZU), the predecessor of the BKU, was established in 1972 as a result of the efforts of eight prominent politicians, two of whom had been expelled from office: of the latter, one was Secretary of the erstwhile Unionist Party in pre-partition Punjab, while the other was an ex-Akali MLA. Here again the objective was the same: the active role played by Partap Singh Kadian, the ex-MLA, in the farmers' union was designed to facilitate his re-entery into Akali politics.[15]

Once the state branches were formed, however, they operated independently of the political objectives structuring their foundation, and acquired a dynamic of their own based on the prevailing socio-economic conditions. The Punjab branch of the BKU, which had been active from 1972 onwards under the banner of the PKZU and became a separate organisation in 1980, has been engaged in a continuous process of struggle; this culminated in a mass rally during 1984, in the course of which farmers surrounded (*gherao*) the official residence of the Governor of Punjab.[16] Equally, the BKU in Western UP, which became active in 1986, achieved prominence only with the farmers' rallies outside the Commissioner's office in Meerut during 1988 and the Boat Club in New Delhi during 1989. In Haryana, by contrast, the farmers' movement has remained dormant throughout this period, and emerged as a political force only in January 1993 when – with the active support of the BKU branches in Punjab and UP – its own rallies throughout the state vied for public attention with those conducted by the Chief Minister, Bhajan Lal.[17] The BKU branch in Haryana recorded a notable success in June 1993 when, following a protest (*dharna*) in front of the District Court at

Karnal, its demands for improvements in the supply of and lower prices for electricity, together with compensation payments for those killed and/or injured during demonstrations, were conceded.[18] Notwithstanding the intention of politicians to utilise the farmers' organisation as a means of (re-) establishing credibility within their party, the movement has developed independently not only of individual politicians but also of political parties. During the campaigns conducted by the BKU throughout Punjab, Haryana and Western UP, therefore, politicians from the national opposition and ruling parties alike have been denied the opportunity of co-opting such mobilisations for their own advantage.[19]

Another crucial factor in this process has been the shift in the mobilising strategy of the political left. Following the development of a capitalist agriculture in the region, in the course of which rural workers faced a united opposition from producers on issues connected with work and wages, the political left began to organise agricultural labour in separate unions from the Kisan Sabhas of the peasantry.[20] The CPI founded the *Bharatiya Khet Mazdoor Union* (BKMU) in 1968 and the CPI(M) launched the All-India Agricultural Workers Union (AIAWU) in 1982.[21] Even before the creation of the AIAWU, both Communist Parties and some Naxalite groups had already begun mobilising agricultural labour in Punjab on the wages issue.[22] In short, the strategic emphasis of the political left had shifted towards building an alliance between agricultural labour and poor peasants in order to oppose the newly emerging class of agrarian capitalist producer.[23] The earlier strategy of the political left had been to unite both worker and peasant in the same movement against feudal opression and imperialism; however, the development of capitalism and the emergence of a class of rich peasant proprietors and farmers meant that the basis for such peasant + agricultural worker unity ceased, and consequently disappeared from the agenda of the left.[24] It was precisely this institutional vacuum left by both the opposition and the ruling parties – either distrusted or engaged in organising only workers – that the BKU filled.

THE CHARACTERISTICS OF THE MOVEMENT

Although the farmers' movement has eschewed connections with established political parties at the national level, it has nevertheless maintained close links with regional ones.

In Punjab, for example, the BKU has friendly relations with the Akali Dal party, and many activists and supporters of the latter are themselves members of the farmers' movement. From its inception, the movement was courted by Prakash Singh Badal, the Chief Minister of Punjab in the

1977–80 period; during his incumbency the BKU launched two campaigns (*morchas*), one complaining about tractor defects and the other about the short supply of diesel fuel. The inability of the Akali government to accomodate the farmers' demands about fuel prices led to a withrawal of BKU support in the 1980 state elections, and contributed substantially thereby to the resulting Congress(I) victory.[25] The relations between the Akali Dal party and the BKU subsequently improved; the latter made an important contribution to the Akali Dal (Mann faction) victory in the 1989 parliamentary elections, and the BKU faction within the party led by Ajmer Singh Lakhowal played a crucial role in the Akali sponsored boycott of the 1992 assembly and parliamentary polls.

Much the same is true of Uttar Pradesh, where the BKU noticeably failed to launch any campaign against the government of Charan Singh. Although his successor Mohinder Singh Tikait has personally remained aloof from party politics, many of those who support the BKU in Uttar Pradesh have nevertheless retained ties first to the Lok Dal and then the Janata Dal. And in Haryana, where the BKU has maintained its distance from both Congress(I) and the Samajwadi Janata Party (SJP), it has nevertheless received the support of the latter in mobilising farmers against the Congress (I) government from 1992 onwards. As elsewhere, the BKU in Haryana is also opposed to the communists because of their village-level attempts to organise agricultural labour on issues of pay and working conditions.

In keeping with its dual track approach to regional party politics (combining formal opposition with informal closeness in order to maintain its non-party image), the BKU has on the one hand forbidden its officeholders from contesting assembly and parliamentary elections, but on the other allowed its members and supporters to participate in elections for the Panchayats and (in Punjab) co-operative societies. In order to protect itself from political penetration and potential takeover, the BKU operates a similar kind of injunction against party officials. Although leaders of political parties are permitted by the Punjab branch of the BKU to join its membership rolls, therefore, they are constitutionally prohibited from holding elected office in the Union.[26]

Turning to the complex issue of the class composition of the farmers' movement in this region, it is necessary to observe that for over a decade the BKU has been successful in maintaining the support of peasants from a socio-economically heterogeneous background. However, it is equally important to note that this issue is itself the subject of much debate. Some commentators have characterised the farmers' mobilisation as a populist movement: [27] others by contrast have characterised it as a class movement.[28] On the basis of the declared objectives, demands and memoranda submitted at different levels of the BKU in Punjab, Haryana and UP, it is clear that the union is interested in mobilising all rural people regardless of religious, caste, gender and class differences; it wishes in general to build a just society, and in particular its object is to remove the exploitation of and various forms of discrimination practised against village inhabitants. At the level of ideology, therefore, the farmers' movement projects an image of a non-differentiated rural social structure with the dual object of enhancing its appeal and uniting different class subjects throughout India.[29]

The fact that in terms of ideology the farmers' movement wishes to change existing society, makes appeals to 'the rural masses' and not to specific classes, and is not basically anti-intellectual in its orientation, all suggests that it is populist in character.[30] The *practice* of the movement, however, suggests otherwise. In this regard, the appeal of the movement is unambiguously to its capitalist rich and medium farmer membership. Thus the UP branch of the BKU did not include the demand for a minimum agricultural wage until the siege of the Commissioner's office at Meerut in 1988, when it needed the support of rural labour. Even the inclusion of this demand did not attract support from the rural working class, given the extensive and acute nature of the struggle between labourers and peasants together with BKU intervention on the side of the latter. Unlike Karnataka and Maharashtra, where both the *Ryatu Sangh* and the *Shetkari Sanghatana* have been able to draw on the support of Dalit organisations, the farmers' movement in Northwestern India has been unable to attract the support of rural labour.

Equally significant in this regard is the fact that the BKU in Punjab has also failed to secure the participation and support of women. This lack of gender-specific support exists despite the farmers' movement having campaigned to secure an improvement in the social position of women generally, and in particular to eradicate the payment of dowry and the consumption of liquor (both of which are linked to violence against women). On the question of property, the Punjab branch of the BKU has recently shifted its policy in a rather significant manner. Having originally campaigned for a ceiling on urban property equal in worth to 17½ acres of agricultural land, it now advocates the removal of land ceilings altogether. The main beneficiaries of such a policy change, which implies nothing less than the elimination of obstacles to the consolidation/expansion of property rights in both urban and rural contexts, would of course be rich peasants and capitalist farmers.

Other demands made by the farmers' movement are exclusively agrarian in character, and include the following: linking farm prices to a price index with 1967/68 as the base year, lowering farm input prices (for items such as fertilizer, fuel, energy, tractors, building materials and so on), an insurance fund to compensate farmers in the event of natural disaster, the elimination of corruption on the part of government officials, the ending of exploitation by commission agents, the the removal of taxes (*octroi*) on farm products, an entitlement to a retirement pension for all villagers over the age of 55, rural quotas for places in higher education and government service, a free education for the children of farmers owning less than ten acres of land, and generally raising the status of agriculture to that of industry. Although all farmers could be said to benefit from such a programme, those with larger holdings, more productive land, more advanced productive forces and higher output – rich peasants and capitalist farmers, in other words – would undoubtedly gain disproportionately.

The class character of the farmers' movement emerges most clearly in relation to these objectives. The availability and price of inputs, the price of outputs, agricultural insurance schemes, recovering the costs of repairs to the means of production, and the ending of police repression and illegal exactions by petty officials, are in the main issues which address the needs of proprietors whose economic activity derives from owning sufficient (not to say substantial) means of production. About the particular needs of poor peasants, agricultural workers and women, the BKU has generally remained silent (let alone undertaken campaigns in the furtherance of such needs).

Although the farmers' movement led by the BKU resembles a populist movement, therefore, its policies and activities are in reality designed to benefit capitalist rich and medium farmers. The latter are able to count on the support of poor peasants for three reasons in particular: the increasingly all-embracing character of the market nexus, a common opposition to agricultural labour on issues of pay and conditions, and the invocation of ethnic identities in the mobilisation process. When combined with the long history of rural struggles in the region, each of these three factors contributes to (and in ideological terms makes plausible) a powerful notion of peasant unity. In Punjab, therefore, Sikh religious idioms have commonly been invoked for the purpose of mobilising farmers.[31] In UP the clan organisation of the Jats (*khap*) has also been used to generate a sense of 'community', similarly in order to facilitate farmer mobilisation.[32]

VISIONS OF THE FUTURE[33]

By formulating the slogan of 'Bharat versus India', the farmers' movement has signalled its intention to redress what it perceives as being the imbalance in the development strategy of India, a phenomenon associated with the concept 'urban bias'. It is therefore important to understand the manner in which the movement intends to correct this distortion, and the precise nature of its alternative development strategy.

In order to reduce the burden of population growth on the agrarian sector, the BKU plans to set up industries in rural areas and reserve 75 per cent of jobs created in this manner for local village residents. The BKU has also encouraged and helped its members to diversify their economic activity, from cultivation to marketing agricultural products as traders or commissioning agents. To this end the leadership of the farmers' movement set up a company in 1987, the Punjab Kisan Kheti Udyog Limited, with the object of providing fertilisers directly to the agrarian producer.

The Rajewal–Mann faction of the Punjab movement holds the view that the only way in which farmers will obtain remunerative prices is by taking up agro-processing on a massive scale. In keeping with this view, the BKU originally supported, campaigned strongly in favour of and subsequently became disillusioned about the Pepsi project in Punjab. It also strongly advocates the inauguration of a wheat processing plant in Punjab, in order to produce high quality dried and distilled grain for the health food market, an enterprise from which farmers could expect to obtain high returns (Rs 750 per quintal, as against the present rate of Rs 350).[34] To date, the BKU has set up a company to manufacture plywood from eucalyptus trees, unsuccessfully applied for a government licence to operate its own sugar mill, and successfully negotiated an agreement with the Punjab State Industrial Development Corporation to operate three milk processing plants.

The vision of the future held by the BKU is, in short, one which conceptualises the provision of a fair return to farmers, an objective it seeks to achieve mainly through the integration of merchant and industrial capital. The movement is not against capitalist development *per se*; rather it wants to see the farmer cease to be its exploited 'victim' and become instead an integral part (and beneficiary) of this process.

THE LIMITS TO MOBILISATION

Generally speaking, the limits to a mass mobilization such as that of the farmers' movement are set not only by material conditions (input/output prices, market conditions, the economic outlook and so on) but also by subjective factors, such as the kind of idioms used for the purposes of mobilisation (caste, clan, class, religion), and the perspective of those who lead the movement.

The rise of Sikh separatism has unsurprisingly had an impact on the mobilising discourse of the BKU; the demands of the latter have as a result shifted from being concerned exclusively with economic problems to the espousal of issues connected with an independent Sikh state.[35] Because it uses Sikh idioms and symbols in the process of mobilisation, therefore, the BKU in Punjab has so far been unable to obtain the support of Hindu farmers in the state. Similarly, because the UP branch of the BKU organises on the basis of Jat Khap Panchayats, the scope for peasants from other castes occupying high office in the movement has been correspondingly limited. Much the same is true of the way in which the BKU operates in Haryana. The contradictory effect of ethnic and/or religious identity as the basis of mobilisation is that, while it succeeds in establishing the 'otherness' of Dalits who are simultaneously agricultural labourers (thereby reproducing the peasant/worker opposition at the level of ideology), it simultaneously restricts and inhibits the reach of those identified as 'peasants'.

Another limit to the mobilisation process are the splits that have occured in the leadership of the farmers' movement, a development which the Indian government has encouraged by promoting rivalries between individual officeholders. In the case of Punjab, the BKU split in 1988 into two factions: one led by Ajmer Singh Lakhowal, and the other by Balbir Singh Rajewal and Bhupinder Singh Mann. As a result, the level of mobilization declined throughout Punjab, and in the districts of Bathinda and Amritsar the farmers' movement became dormant.[36] Within the Lakhowal faction itself, conflict over policy led to the expulsion of farmers' leaders in Patiala and Sangrur: the latter had extended the support of the farmers' movement to Sikh militants, particularly on the issue of the mass resignation of Panches and Sarpanches during 1991/92 (which resulted in the administrative paralysis of several blocks in the state), and wished to form a united front with Sikh organisations generally with the sole objective of fighting against oppression by the Indian state.[37]

The existence at the All-India level of two Inter-State Coordination Committees (ISCC) for the farmers' movement reflects the existence of a similar split between Tikait of the UP branch of the BKU and Sharad Joshi of the Shetkari Sanghatana. Such developments amongst the ranks of the leadership have unquestionably harmed the farmers' movement by generating damaging personal rivalries and competitive attempts to mobilise the same groups of peasants. The effects of this split are most evident in the divergent positions taken in March 1993 by the BKU and Shetkari Sanghatana on the issue of the Dunkel draft resolution: the latter was endorsed by Sharad Joshi but opposed by Tikait.

CONCLUDING COMMENTS

It is a commonplace that the emergence of or upsurge in farmers' movements occurs in situations where, as a result of the rapid commercialisation of agriculture, cultivators find themselves trapped in market relationships which continuously erode their economic position. Yet these same movements are also products of a specific historical context and a given material reality. This concluding section will consider briefly how these latter elements, outlined above, may shape future developments.

In terms of a positive impact, it can be argued that the farmers' movement has played an important role in the democratisation process. By mobilising a large number of peasants, the BKU has widened the democratic base of political activity and thus added an element of plurality to the political process itself. Paradoxically, the non-party character of the movement has also enabled it to apply pressure on political parties to implement undertakings made to farmers in the course of electoral contests. The mirror image of this rise in organised producer power has has been its negative effect on the struggle by (invariably low caste) agricultural workers. The latter now find themselves opposed by an increasingly powerful and self-confident farming lobby on crucial economic issues such as agricultural pay and working conditions. In an important sense, therefore, the rise of farmer power has not only contributed to the incidence of rural oppression in this region, but also curtailed the emergence of organised labour.

On the question of the future development of the farmers' movement, it is clear that the main organisational issue confonting it is how to effect a transition from disparate, local mobilisations to a single national farmers' movement. Throughout the Green Revolution belt in Northwestern India, the farmers' movement is organised on a regional basis, the scope of state branches coinciding with the provincial or sub-provincial units of political administration. Within a given territory, therefore, farmers have organised themselves with the object of extracting concessions relating to area-specific issues, and in this sense the movement is local in character. The efforts of the movement leadership to build All-India co-ordination committees of farmers' organisations notwithstanding, a recognisably *national* farmers' movement has yet to emerge.

Significantly, the impetus towards an authentically national farmers' organisation derives in part from the limited economic autonomy exercised by the local state apparatus. Since major agricultural policy issues which affect farmers – such as prices, subsidies, the funding of rural development generally, and now the crucial question of free trade and the

Dunkel Draft of the GATT – are all decided by the Government of India rather than state governments, the regionally-specific branches of the farmers' movement are in a very real sense compelled not only to confront the Indian state but to unite in order to do this; that is, the nature of the issues and the circumstances leading to their resolution now make possible (perhaps even necessary) the organisation of a *national* movement. Conversely, the incapacity of localised mobilisation to resolve what are in fact national issues has also contributed to the farmers' movement turning away from what are specifically agrarian questions: in short, it has diverted such movements into regional, caste or communal issues.

At present there are positive signs regarding such a move towards a national farmers' movement. Thus for example, unlike the Akali Dal in Punjab and the Congress (I) and the SJP in Haryana, the Punjab and Haryana branches of the BKU have not so far clashed over the issue of water resources in the region. For the BKU, the solidarity of the farmers' movement takes precedence over potentially divisive interstate disputes. Equally encouraging in this regard is the fact that the BKU branches in Punjab, Haryana and UP have all helped each other in mobilising the peasantry and conducting a common struggle. Such a prognosis is true even of the currently strained relations between M.S. Tikait and Sharad Joshi; personal and policy differences notwithstanding, both share a common vision of agriculture organised on an individual rather than a collective or co-operative basis.

Finally, the current trend towards the liberalisation, privatisation and globalisation of agriculture in India can also be seen as having implications for the future development of the farmers' movement; the latter will be required by its members not just to play a more active role in protecting farmers' interests in such circumstances but also to organise more effectively – along national lines, in other words – in order to do so.

NOTES

1. Singh [1984: 180–327].
2. S.S. Gill [forthcoming].
3. Brass [1980].
4. Bhalla and Tyagi [1989: 149–50].
5. For Uttar Pradesh see Brass [1980: 405], for Haryana see Bhalla [1974: 42–3], and for Punjab see S.S. Gill [1990a: 58].
6. Saini [1976: A-17]. For Haryana, see Bhalla [1974].
7. Tyagi [1987].
8. Swamy and Gulati [1986].
9. K.S. Gill [1983: 301–4].
10. Singh [1990: 52].

11. Government of Punjab [1989: 56].
12. Singh [1990: 56].
13. Hasan [1989].
14. Gupta [1988], Hasan [1989].
15. Singh [1990: 39].
16. Gill and Singhal [1984].
17. *The Tribune* (Chandigarh), 1, 28 and 29 Jan. and 1 Feb. 1993.
18. *The Tribune* (Chandigarh), 29 May and 2 June 1993.
19. Gupta [1988]; Hasan [1989]; Dhanagare [1988a]; Gill and Singhal [1984].
20. Singh [1980: 12].
21. All-India Kisan Sabha [1982].
22. S.S. Gill [1990b: 14–17].
23. Sinha [1980: 160], Surjeet [1986], All-India Kisan Sabha [1982: 22–3].
24. Bhalla [1983].
25. Singh [1990: 83].
26. Bharatiya Kisan Union [1985: 6–7].
27. Dhanagare [1988b].
28. Hasan [1989] categorises the BKU as a rich and middle peasant movement, while Gupta [1988] considers it a rich farmers' mobilisation.
29. Bharatiya Kisan Union [1985].
30. The four characteristics of populism specified by Laclau are: an ingrained hostility to the *status quo*; an appeal to the people or masses rather than to specific classes; a mistrust of traditional politicians; and an anti-intellectual disposition (Laclau [1977], quoted in Dhanagare [1988b]).
31. Singh [1990].
32. Dhanagare [1988b]; Gupta [1988]; Hasan [1989].
33. This section is based on the declaration of demands made by the BKU, and also on a long discussion with Mr Balbir Singh Rajewal at the Kisan Bhavan, Chandigarh, on 1 December 1992.
34. The BKU wishes this project to be part of the public sector, since a major portion of the value added would not accrue to farmers if the plant remained in the private sector.
35. S.S. Gill [1992].
36. Interview with Balbir Singh Rajewal.
37. For details of factional conflict, see the account by the Centre of Communist Revolutionaries of India, 'Report for Punjab: The Struggle Within the BKU', *The Comrade*, Nos.12 and 13, April–Sept. 1992.

REFERENCES

All-India Kisan Sabha, 1982, *Conference Proceedings and Resolutions, 8–11 November 1982*, New Delhi: CPI (M).

Bhalla, G.S., 1974, *Changing Agrarian Structure in India: A Study of the Impact of the Green Revolution in Haryana*. Delhi: Meenakshi Prakashan.

Bhalla, G.S., 1983, 'Peasant Movement and Agrarian Change in India', *Social Scientist*, Vol.11, No.8.

Bhalla, G.S. and D.S. Tyagi, 1989, *Patterns in Indian Agricultural Development: A District Level Study*, New Delhi: Institute for Studies in Industrial Development.

Bhalla, S., 1981, 'Islands of Growth: A Note on Haryana Experience and Some Possible Implications', *Economic and Political Weekly*, Vol.16, No.23.

Bharatiya Kisan Union, 1985, *Bharatiya Kisan Union: Historical Facts* (in Punjabi), Ludhiana: BKU Publications.

Brass, P.R., 1980, 'The Politicization of the Peasantry in a North Indian State: Parts I and II'. *Journal of Peasant Studies*, Vol.7, No.4 and Vol.8, No.1.

Dhanagare, D.N., 1988a, 'An Apoliticist Populism', *Seminar*, No.352.

Dhanagare, D.N., 1988b, 'Subaltern Consciousness and Populism: Two Approaches in the Study of Social Movements', *Social Scientist*, Vol.16, No.11.

Gill, K.S., 1983, 'Employment and Unemployment in Punjab', in R.S. Johar and J.S. Khanna (eds.).

Gill, S.S., 1990a, 'Migrant Labour in Punjab' unpublished mss., Punjabi Unversity. Patiala.

Gill, S.S. 1990b 'Organization of Rural Labour in Northern India with Special Reference to Punjab,' unpublished mss., Punjabi University, Patiala.

Gill, S.S., 1992, 'Punjab Crisis and Political Process', *Economic and Political Weekly*, Vol.27, No.5.

Gill, S.S., forthcoming, 'Agrarian Capitalism and Political Processes in Punjab', in T.V.S. Sathyamurthy (ed.), *Social Change and Political Discourse in India: Structure of Power, Movements of Resistance*, New Delhi: Oxford University Press.

Gill, S.S., and K.C. Singhal, 1984 'Punjab Farmers Agitation: Response to Development Crisis of Agriculture', *Economic and Political Weekly*, Vol.19, No.40.

Government of Punjab, 1989, *Statistical Abstract of Punjab 1985*, Chandigarh: Economic and Statistical Organization.

Gupta, D., 1988, 'Country-Town Nexus and Agrarian Mobilization: Bharatiya Kisan Union as an Instance', *Economic and Political Weekly*, Vol.23, No.51.

Hasan, Z., 1989, 'Self-serving Guardians: Formation and Strategy of Bharatiya Kisan Union', *Economic and Political Weekly*, Vol.24, No.48.

Johar, R.S. and J.S. Khanna (eds.), 1983, *Studies in Punjab Economy*, Amritsar: Guru Nanak Development University.

Laclau, E., 1977, *Politics and Ideology in Marxist Thought*, London: Verso.

Manick, M.S., 1990 'Role of Kirti Kisan Union in Peasant Struggles in Punjab (1978–87)', unpublished MPhil dissertation, Department of Sociology and Social Anthropology, Punjabi University, Patiala.

Saini, G.R., 1976, 'Green Revolution and the Distribution of Farm Incomes', *Economic and Political Weekly*, Vol.11, No.13.

Singh, Master H., 1980, *Agricultural Workers' Struggle in Punjab*, Delhi: People's Publishing House.

Singh, Master H., 1984, *Punjab Peasant in Freedom Struggle*, New Delhi: People's Publishing House.

Singh, K., 1990, *Farmers' Movement and Pressure Group Politics*, New Delhi: Deep and Deep Publications.

Sinha, I., 1980, *The Changing Agrarian Scene: Problems and Tasks*, New Delhi: People's Publishing House.

Surjeet, H.S., 1986, 'Upsurge', *Seminar*, No.267.

Swamy, D.S., and A. Gulati, 1986, 'From Prosperity to Retrogression: Indian Cultivators during the 1970s', *Economic and Political Weekly*, Vol.21, No.26.

Tyagi, D.S., 1987, 'Domestic Terms of Trade and Their Effect on Supply and Demand for the Agricultural Sector, *Economic and Political Weekly*, Vol.22, No.13.

'Khadi Curtain', 'Weak Capitalism' and 'Operation Ryot': Some Ambiguities in Farmers' Discourse, Karnataka and Maharashtra 1980–93

MUZAFFAR ASSADI

The 1980s marked a watershed in the character of farmers' movements in India, when peasants opposed to political opression and bureaucratic corruption began to formulate new agendas and discourses, both about politics, ideology and the state, and also about their own role at different levels of the economy. However, studies by sociologists, economists, and party activists have focused largely on the characterisation of such 'new' social movements in terms of class/caste and 'bullock' capitalists [*Bose*, 1981; *Dhanagare*, 1990; *Lennenberg*, 1988; *Mishra*, 1986; *Nadkarni*, 1987; *Omvedt*, 1980; 1988; *Prasad*, 1980; *Rajashekar*, 1982; *Rudolph and Rudolph*, 1987; Rudra, 1986]. Rather than trying to understand these movements in terms of the totality of the grassroots phenomena involved, or explore the causes for their continued marginalisation from political power, scholars from across the political spectrum have tended to interpret these mobilisations largely in terms of a single issue, such as remunerative prices [*Surjeet*, 1981; 1983; *Swamy* 1987].

Accordingly, this study will focus on grassroots discourse and strategy, with particular reference to the farmers' movement in Maharashtra (the *Shetkari Sangathana*) and Karnataka (the *Karnataka Rajya Raitha Sangha* or the KRRS). The object of such an approach is to understand why the movements have remained marginal, why two formidable organisations have failed to unite and form a powerful All-India movement, and why they have increasingly distanced themselves from each other.

DEFINING PEEASANTS

An important issue for the peasant movement in India is the criterion by which membership is defined: who is a peasant, and why. Invoking the logic of economic individualism, Shetkari Sanghatana defines peasant as

---

Muzaffar Assadi, Department of Political Science, Goa University, Goa – 403203, India.
The writer wishes to thank Sudha Pai, Dipankar Gupta, Shasheej Hegde, D.N. Dhanagare, Ashfaq Assadi for helpful comment on earlier drafts. The study in its present form owes much to the editorial input of Tom Brass.

shetkari or 'one who personally labours on the land', a concept which extends to:

> anyone who is associated with agriculture. As long as a person lives by agriculture, he is a *shetkari*. A member of Parliament would not be considered as a farmer if he did not live by farming. *Shetkari* means one who works the land (*Probe India*, Dec. 1987, p. 16).

This definition is deliberately ambiguous; the concept of work employed here renders equivalent all forms of physical labour (manual, supervisory, managerial), eliminating thereby distinctions between rich and poor peasants.

Unlike its Maharashtrian counterpart, the KRRS does not use a concept of 'work' as the defining criterion, and thus avoids the issue of exploitative relations within the peasantry and between the latter and rural labour. Instead, the farmers' movement in Karnataka invokes government data to support its view that, as lack of irrigation and successive land legislation have made cultivation economically unproductive, the KRRS is a poor peasant mobilisation.[1] Like the Shetkari Sanghatana, however, the KRRS opposes legislative ceilings on rural land while simultaneously advocating limits to the ownership of urban industrial property. As with the Shetkari Sanghatana, therefore, the KRRS definition permits membership heterogeneity; thus by virtue of being rural proprietors, coffee estate owners can participate in the farmers' movement in Karnataka.[2]

Both movements claim that the peasantry is part of the future: the peasant is referred to as 'the real producer', 'the real owner of the country', and 'the harbinger of the new resistance' [*KRRS*, 1986b; n.d.; *Joshi*, n.d.]. The individual peasant is distinct from the 'system', which is viewed as operating against the interests of the former: 'we contribute our labour, but who enjoys the benefit?', 'We milk the cow, but who drinks the milk?', 'Chicken-rearing loans for us, but for whom are the eggs and meat?', are some of the ways in which such 'otherness' is expressed [*KRRS*, 1984d]. Support for womens' issues – such as non-dowry marriage, inter-caste alliances (but not intra-caste marriage), equal property rights and wage parity – is presented as evidence of the progressive character of the movement [*KRRS*, 1983d;1987], as are programmes designed specifically to benefit women: examples of the letter include *Sita*, or organic farming to reduce dependence on costly chemical inputs, *Majkheri Sheti*, or village-level food processing, and *Lakshmi Mukti*, or the division of peasant household property between spouses [*Omvedt*, 1991; *Guru*, 1992].

This future-oriented discourse is marked, however, by ambiguity: a critique of yet a retreat from industrialisation, itself associated with Nehruvian ideas about development, state centralisation, and the perpetuation of agrarian backwardness [*Joshi*, 1985]. As a solution to the problems of industrialisation, the farmers' movements rely on Gandhian alternatives [*KRRS*, n.d.; *Joshi*, n.d.]: the decentralisation of power, support for cottage industries, eliminating external market dependency by means of bio-fertilisers and locally produced goods, and so on. Similarly, a recourse to historically entrenched cultural symbols, figures and concepts that often reinforce prevalent belief also tends to undermine claims about the forward-looking character of the movement, although Sharad Joshi and others argue that its objective is both to close the gap between leaders and the peasantry and to contain the erosion of the farmers' mass base by the new Hindutva mobilisation. To some degree Shetkari Sanghatana has succeeded in halting the spread of Hindu chauvinism in Maharashtra by reinterpreting popular historical figures and cultural symbols, such as Shivaji, Phule, and Ambedkar, and also the Vitobha festivals, thereby limiting the space in which Hindutva ideology can operate.[3] The Maharashtrian farmers' movement has also appropriated from nationalist discourse the concept *Swaraj*/Freedom (*Times of India*, 10 February 1993): if freedom is defined as 'rule by one's own kind' [*Joshi*, n.d: 76], Shetkari Sanghatana observes, then peasants are denied that freedom.[4]

Unlike the farmers' movement in Maharashtra, that in Karnataka has not embraced cultural symbols capable of countering Hindutva ideology. The reason is that to invoke the name of Basavanna (a medieval social reformer) would be to adopt a caste – that is, a Lingayat – identity which the movement has attempted to avoid. Other historical associations, such as Tippu Sultan (a former ruler of Mysore who fought British imperialism) or Shishunala Sharifa (a medieval poet/saint who advocated Hindu/Muslim unity), would have rooted the movement in a different cultural milieu.[5] A consequence of this inability or unwillingness to mobilise historical symbols against Hindutva ideology is that the Raitha Sangha has left a space for communal views to make inroads into its peasant support, thereby weakening the struggle conducted by the farmers' movement.

Like Shetkari Sanghatana, the Raitha Sangha in Karnataka has appropriated nationalist discourse (*Namma Nadu*, 18 October 1985; KRRS [1981; 1984a; 1985c]), comparing existing conditions with those obtaining under colonialism. Accordingly, nationalism and 'peasantism' have become discursively intertwined, culminating in the recent opposition to the Dunkel proposal [*KRRS*, 1993]. Currently, the peasantry of

Karnataka is confronted by two nationalist variants: a culturally-based and *laissez-faire* inclined Hindutva, and one which stresses the economic sovereignty of the Indian state.

THE 'NEWNESS' OF THE FARMERS' MOVEMENTS

The farmers' movements which emerged in India during the 1980s have been characterised as 'new' by observers and participants alike [*Dhanagare*, 1990: 359–61; *Joshi*, n.d.: 72–8; *Shahasrabudhey*, 1986: 6]. This view about 'newness' is based on four claims made by/about the farmers' movements: the latter no longer correspond to the usual image of peasants as 'simple', 'spiritual', 'traditional' and 'passive'; they adhere to a concept of a unified peasantry, undivided by internal antagonisms, and thus are opposed differences based on caste, ethnicity, community, religion; they stress the importance of remunerative prices; and they are apolitical.

On the issue of breaking with tradition, the peasant movements in both Karnataka and Maharashtra have notably failed to break with certain feudal relations and practices. For example, both the Shetkari Sanghatana and the Raitha Sangha have not only not condemned atrocities against tribals and the segregation of Dalits but in some instances the perpetrators of such actions have themselves been their own members (*People's Democracy*, 22 April 1984; *Panchama*, 10 May 1983; 24 December 1983; 20 November 1984).[6] Neither movement has prevented atrocities committed against women in areas where membership is strong, and both have actively continued the practice of bonded labour.[7]

The second claim to 'newness', which involves a denial of peasant differentiation, similarly overlooks the fact that Gandhi advanced this proposition during the anti-colonial struggle in order to prevent the nationalist ranks being split along class lines [*Brown*, 1974: 160–69]. On the issue of a rural 'united front' to wage the peasant struggle, Nanjundaswamy, the leader of the KRRS, simply ignores the reality of class conflict in the countryside, and states [*Natraj*, 1980: 1967]: '[W]e cannot divide ourselves into landlords and landless farmers, and agitate separately, for the agitation will have no strength nor will it carry any weight.' By contrast, Sharad Joshi, who leads the Shetkari Sanghatana, recognises conflict between classes, but – like the KRRS – maintains the necessity of a united front. He observes (*Statesman*, Calcutta, 16 April 1987): 'Though I recognize the conflict between classes in the countryside, I am against dividing the rural side.' The Raitha Sangha has not only provided a platform for the two dominant landowning castes (the Lingayats and the Vokkaligas) but has also ended up systematising the oppression of Dalits and other backward classes.[8] In a similar vein, Shetkari Sanghatana has also ignored the sharpness of rural conflict. Moreover, the denial of peasant differentiation has resulted in splits within the farmers' movements themselves.[9]

The third claim, about the 'newness' of the demand for remunerative prices, is equally questionable. At the All-India level, the case for remunerative prices for agricultural produce was raised by Lohia [n.d.] and the socialists as far back as the 1950s. In Karnataka, the *Hind Kisan Panchayat*, an offshoot of the socialist party, argued along similar lines in the 1960s. However, for Shetkari Sanghatana the issue of remunerative prices remains at the top of its agenda, largely to the exclusion of all other issues (such as relaxing land ceiling laws, the promotion of crop insurance schemes, lifting restrictions on the export of farm produce and the import of agricultural machinery and so on).[10] By contrast, the KRRS has promoted a number of different issues without attributing primacy to any one in particular. The discourse of the Raitha Sangha, which during the initial stages of mobilisation [*KRRS*, 1980] centred on the ending the exploitation of the peasantry, government loan write-offs, as well as remunerative prices, extended in 1982 to include demands for smallscale industrial employment schemes, and changes in state planning/budgeting. Loan write-offs and remunerative prices (for sugar cane), however, have indeed remained important policy objectives for the KRRS; hence its opposition to the government and the sugar factories.[11]

The final claim to 'newness', which relates to the political nature of the farmers' movements, can also be questioned, not least by reference to historical examples of peasant organisations which were non-party yet political in character; Congress itself, for example, operated as a non-party political forum during the colonial era in order to mobilize the peasantry as part of the wider struggle against British imperialism. In Karnataka the initial 'apolitical' (non-party, non-electoral) stage of mobilisation was subsequently reversed, as the KRRS entered the political arena. Between 1983 and early 1984, therefore, it supported opposition attempts to oust the then ruling party [*KRRS*, 1983a; 1984a], and in 1984 it rejected all political parties in favour of a Voter's Forum or *Mathadarara Vedike* [*KRRS*, 1984b; 1984c].[12] The following year the Raitha Sangha sought the support of the various opposition parties against the Cooperative Amendment Act, which would have permitted government attachment and auction of property belonging to loan defaulters [*KRRS*, 1985a; 1985b]. In order to 'capture power for the development of Karnataka and Kannadigas', the Raitha Sangha then formed a political party (*Kannada Desha*) in 1987, but two years later this merged with its parent organisation [*KRRS*, 1989]. In 1990 and 1992, the Raitha Sangha contested the Lok Sabha and Assembly elections under its own banner, but won only two seats in the Assembly.[13]

By contrast, Shetkari Sanghatana has remained aloof from all political parties, because in its view 'whichever party comes to power is going to perpetuate the policy of starving the farmers ... and will not work to get remunerative prices for the farmers' (*The Hindu*, 22 April 1980; *Probe India*, December 1987). Accordingly, Shetkari Sanghatana has adopted a fourfold strategy in the political arena. First, it has sought support from various political parties on the issue of remunerative prices. Second, in terms of electoral strategy it has at different times extended support to different opposition parties, regardless of their ideology: for example, in 1984 and 1985 it aligned with the Congress(S), in 1987 it supported both the Bharatiya Janata Party (BJP) and the Republican Party (*Times of India*, 26 February 1985; 26 March 1986; 28 March 1987; *Deccan Herald*, 21 December 1987; *Statesman*, 18 December 1987). Third, at the national level the Shetkari Sanghatana has attempted to counter the ruling party by aligning itself with V.P. Singh on the grounds that '[he] represents the best hope' and an 'alternative' (*Probe India*, December 1987; *Frontline*, 5–18 March 1988). And fourth, it has contested local level elections in Maharashtra, for the municipalities, the Zilla Parishads, and in the sugar co-operatives.[14]

Each one of the claims to 'newness' made by/about the farmers' movements in Maharashtra and Karnataka, therefore, is found wanting. This in turn raises the question of precisely how the farmers' movements perceive their relationship with/in the wider national and international contexts.

SECTORAL CONTRADICTIONS, OR 'INDIA' VESUS 'BHARAT'

One of the main issues dividing the farmers' movement as a whole has been the different ways the KRRS and Shetkari Sanghatana define sectoral contradiction and the kinds of political alliances to which this gives rise.

For Shatkari Sanghatana, the principal contradiction in Indian society is between 'India' and 'Bharat', distinctions which for Sharad Joshi [n.d.: 2] correspond to 'actual entities'. On this point he observes: 'India ... consists of the urban elite and power, groups, and Bharat consists of the mass of rural people.' However, an ambiguity exists, since this division is also seen by him as 'notional'; consequently, whether this sectoral difference is 'actual' or 'notional' is never fully resolved at the level of discourse. On the one hand, therefore, Joshi argues that 'the chairman of the sugar factory, the director of the co-operative society, even though located within the village, even though they belong to a farmer's family, even though some of them are actually connected with agricultural operations, do not constitute Bharat'. On the other hand, when Shetkari Sanghatana organised a 'public limited company' of farmers, as in Wardha during 1992–93, this same director of the cooperative now becomes – as an elected representative – part of 'Bharat'. But those elected representatives who belong to political parties are designated by Shetkari Sanghatana as part of 'India', notwithstanding the fact that in terms of background and class position these subjects are no different from others (landlords, rich peasants) categorised as part of the 'rural' sector.

Although Shetkari Sanghatana recognises that theoretically 'India' could exist within 'Bharat', the 'India'/'Bharat' opposition corresponds to the urban/rural dualism and echoes the concept 'urban bias' associated with the work of Lipton [1980]. According to Shetkari Sanghatana, the rural sector in India has remained poor, backward and dependent (see below). Those who migrate from rural to urban areas – artisans, landless labourers, middle and small peasants – are categorised by Joshi [n.d.: 5] as 'refugees' and perceived as doubly exploited – both in the home area and also in the urban context. Despite their displacement and exploitation, such 'refugees' from 'Bharat' are not regarded by the Shetkari Sanghatana as dependable allies in any coalition designed to achieve a radical transformation. A serious attempt to forge an alliance with trade union organisations, particularly the powerful *Maharashtra Kamgar Union*, has also proved futile (*Indian Express*, 15 March 1982; *Statesman*, 30 March 1982). Instead, the Shetkari Sanghatana has courted members of other political parties and petty bourgeois elements engaged in commerce, transportation and construction (*Times of India*, 2 April 1993).

Similarly attributing rural backwardness to 'urban bias', the Raitha Sangha of Karnataka characterises itself as a 'village movement'.[15] At different intervals, it has advanced criticisms of anti-farmer biases in government policy [*KRRS*, 1986a; 1988a; 1988b; 1992], identifying no less than 25 instances of 'urban bias' in the 1983 budget allocation alone [*KRRS* 1983]. However, with the exception of urban intellectuals, with whom the Raitha Sangha has conducted serious dialogue before formulating strategy, the farmers' movement in Karnataka has shown little concern for urban categories, preferring instead to enter into a dialogue with language movements and the Dalits.[16]

FARMERS' MOVEMENTS AND THE STATE

Except for passing references to its role in 'colonizing the villages' or as 'mass power' (PNRS [1981]; *Prajavani*, 4 November 1985), the socio-economic structure of the Indian state has not been the object of in-depth political analysis by the KRRS.[17] Government at all levels – local as well as national – is simply perceived as an instrument of international capital in particular and industrial capitalism generally, and thus necessarily oppressive to and exploitative of peasants. Rejecting a transition to the *laissez-faire* policies advocated by Dunkel and GATT [*KRRS*, 1993], the Raitha Sangha envisages a fourfold, positive role for the state: first, as a government of and by the peasantry itself; second, to free agriculture from the control exercised by agribusiness transnational corporations; third, to allocate sectoral priority to agriculture over industry; and fourth, to check further encroachment on agriculture by industry and the urban sector.[18]

Although similarly criticising the state for its anti-peasant policies and denying the ruling class status of the rich peasantry, the farmers' movement in Maharashtra – unlike its counterpart in Karnataka – supports a *laissez-faire* programme and thus argues for minimum state interference. Shetkari Sanghatana has also actively collaborated with the state apparatus; in 1989, for example, Sharad Joshi accepted the Chair of the Standing Advisory Committee on Agriculture, from which position he has advanced 'Operation Ryot', or his views about remunerative prices linked to economic liberalisation. Using this platform provided by the state, he argues [*Government of India*, 1991], would enable the movement to suggest the 'restructuring of priority areas for state action', to demand a 'divorce from the regime of statism and welfarism', to ensure the 'minimization of state activity', thereby 'economizing administration costs', and, finally, to make 'state intervention in the price market more formal and strict'. Like the KRRS, however, Shetkari Sanghatana regards the Indian state as a device of the industrial capitalist class, whereby an 'entire armoury of economic, fiscal, budget and monetary instruments are deployed ... to keep the prices of agricultural produce at a level which does not cover their real cost of production' [*Joshi*, 1984: 1]. For the farmers' movement in Maharashtra, therefore, the elimination of state interference requires policies such as cutbacks in the administrative apparatus and the consequent freeing of agricultural trade from bureaucratic bottlenecks, a reduction in direct and indirect taxation, the liberalisation of raw material and capital imports, a lifting of restrictions on the export of agricultural goods, and the withdrawal of subsidies. The result of this policy shift – a reduction in state control, in other words – would be that the pattern of agricultural production, distribution, and trade generally, would be decided on by the peasantry itself.

THE FARMERS' MOVEMENT AND THE THEORY OF WEAK CAPITALISM

Questions concerning the role of the Indian state in the discourse of the farmers' movements necessarily raise a wider issue: the role of India's peasants in the world capitalist system.

In the case of the Raitha Sangha, a mainly Gandhian ideology, with its emphasis on rural reconstruction, peaceful agitation, and class collaboration, was soon combined in an interesting fashion with a theory of Third World 'dependency'; that is, a view of capitalist underdevelopment structured by relations between a dominant core and weak periphery.[19] Among the many reasons for the adoption of this ideological framework is the fact that the KRRS has had to accomodate different ideological tendencies (Lohiate, Gandhian); without its Gandhianism, for example, the farmers' movement in Karnataka would have experienced a further loss of support.[20] Generally speaking, the Raitha Sangha attributes underdevelopment in former colonial nations such as India to structural backwardness caused by the subordination of indigenous/(Indian) capital to western or international capitalism [*KRRS*, 1984d].

For the Raitha Sangha, therefore, this system of dominant/subordinate linkages, which ensures a *de facto* continuation of economic colonialism beyond the cessation of colonial rule, is sustained by two interrelated factors: on the one hand the capacity of foreign capital to undermine indigenous producers in former colonies by means of cheap imports manufactured with advancing productive techniques, whilst on the other simultaneously denying these same indigenous producers access to the technical knowledge necessary for increasing output. In effect, the farmers' movement in Karnataka finds itself trapped in a situation which prevents indigenous producers from competing with foreign capital on equal terms. According to the KRRS, a consequence of this link is the reproduction of a dependent and thus a weak capitalism (*badakalu bandavala*) which is unable to challenge either the former colonial masters or western capitalism.

With the passage of time, ambiguities have surfaced with regard to this theorisation of the nature of external exploitation. The KRRS has now moved from a position whereby western capitalism is castigated for its exploitative character and Indian capitalism is perceived as correspondingly *badalaku* or weak, to one in which the latter has been reconceptualised as *hondanike*, or comprador capitalism. In this respect, the farmers' movement in Karnataka can be said to have moved away from a Gandhian ideology and closer to a Marxist one.

Extending this kind of analytical framework inwards, the Raitha Sangha equates capitalists in Indian society with upper castes generally and Brahmins in particular, the result being that the discourse of the farmers' movement in Karnataka has a pronounced disposition towards anti-Brahminism. The argument on this issue takes the following form: through a denial of education and a fair distribution of property, the upper castes/capitalist class in India have perpetuated the spirit of *badakalu bandavala*, or weak capitalism, and – together with foreign capital – are jointly responsible for India's current underdevelopment. The outcome is accumulation at the expense of the Indian masses (of which the farmers' movement is a part), a process which involves two forms of bondage: that of producers (*utpadakara jeetadalu*), mainly the peasantry, and that of consumers (*balakedarara jeetadalu*), which refers mainly to industrial workers and salaried employees.[21] According to the Raitha Sangha, the Indian capitalist class maintains the peasantry in a state of perpetual bondage by means of mechanisms such as anti-rural planning biases, non-remunerative prices, inflated input costs, loans and debts. In a similar vein, urban employees and industrial workers are maintained in bondage as consumers, by means of revisions in wages and dearness allowances. Both these exploitative forms of bondage (*utpadakara jeetadalu, balakedarara jeetadalu*), in the opinion of the farmers' movement, combine to reproduce the situation of *badakalu bandavala*, or India's backward agrarian economy. This vicious circle, it is argued, has to be broken before an egalitarian society can be created.

While endorsing egalitarianism in this manner, however, the farmers' movement in Karnataka has strongly distanced itself from any suggestion of socialism, preferring instead to stress the relevance of a Gandhian model of development, with its emphasis on democratic decentralisation and rural reconstruction. Accordingly, the KRRS proposes a form of egalitarianism founded on what it has termed a 'Khadi Curtain', or the equal relationship between India and Western capitalism that would replace current – and unequal – forms of exploitation.[22] The scepticism of the Raitha Sangha towards socialism has also surfaced in the context of its analysis of imperialism. When it formed the *Kannada Desha* in 1987, the farmers' movement in Karnataka explored four variants of imperialism – linguistic imperialism, intellectual imperialism, produce imperialism, and 'loot' imperialism – without making any reference to what Lohia [n.d.: 172–235] once termed 'cultural imperialism'. However, the Raitha Sangha has subsequently moved closer to Lohia's understanding of imperialism; unlike orthodox Marxists, Lohia conceptualised it as a process which accompanied the growth of capitalism from the very beginning.[23] Accordingly, the farmers' movement in Karnataka feels that by challenging all these variants of imperialism (Lohia's included), it would contribute towards the construction of an egalitarian society.

Like its counterpart in Karnataka, the farmers' movement in Maharashtra subscribes to a concept of externally-derived exploitation which is approximately the same as the core/periphery model of dependency theory. For Shetkari Sanghatana, therefore, economic backwardness results from the exploitative linkages between nations. On this point, Sharad Joshi [n.d.: 77] observes:

> the commercial/industrial era brought in a veneer of commerciality to conceal the crudity of feudal techniques. But the consequences continued to be equally if not more cruel. Cheap primary goods and expensive manufactured goods were the essence of imperialism. Terms of trade proved to be more lethal than all the swords and guns of the earlier epochs. Transcontinental imperialism was replaced by internal imperialism. The former colonies developed dualistic systems by subdividing themselves into two entities. One exploiter – successor to the bygone imperialist regime, another exploited for the second time at the hands of compatriots.

Structural backwardness is attributed by Shetkari Sanghatana to mechanisms such as the unfavourable terms of trade,

> procurement levies in the periods of scarcity at prices well below the prevailing open market ... [the flooding] of domestic markets with products imported at prices far exceeding the internal market, [and the dumping of] huge quantities of products received as gifts or aid, [plus] prohibitions on inter-district and inter-state movements [of produce] [*Joshi*, n.d.: 77].

For this reason, the reordering of the terms of trade by means of remunerative prices remains the principal item on the agenda of the farmers' movement in Maharashtra.[24]

According to Shetkari Sanghatana, such a reordering of the terms of trade depends on the Agricultural Price Commission fixing the prices for agricultural produce so as to take into account the costs incurred by producers for cultivation, wages, transportation, inputs, management, repairs, depreciation, rent and capital [*Joshi*, 1984: 2]. Only when this programme of remunerative prices finally becomes a reality, therefore, will structural weakness and agrarian backwardness be eliminated and the corresponding endemic problems, such as rural poverty, unemployment and outmigration, be solved.

There is ambiguity in this position also: although the farmers' movement in Maharashtra blames international capital at the centre of the global economy for the unremunerative prices received by Indian peasants at its periphery, it has no intention of delinking the latter from the former. The reason for Shetkari Sanghatana not wishing to separate 'Bharat' from 'India', and ultimately from western capitalism, is quite simply the many benefits which peasants derive from 'India' and the link with the international economy: for example, government aid and programmes such as PL 480 and the Green Revolution. Hence the contradictory elements in the discourse of the farmers' movement in Maharashtra: on the one hand opposing the state, yet on the other welcoming the liberalising measures enacted by the state, such as delicensing, withdrawing agricultural subsidies, eliminating barriers to the import of capital and raw materials, permitting free competition and so on (*Indian Express*, 24 January 1992; Joshi [1985]). Like the farmers' movement in Karnataka, therefore, what the Shetkari Sanghatana wants is essentially a better deal within the existing world capitalist system.

CONCLUSION

The marginality of the farmers' movement in Maharashtra and Karnataka from political power, and the fact that each has increasingly distanced itself from the other, is due in part to the many ideological/strategic ambiguities as manifested in the multiplicity of contradictory features in their discourse. These extend from claims by/about the 'newness' of this type of agrarian mobilisation, through the basic definitions of who is a peasant, what the social composition of 'Bharat' and 'India' is and why, and by implication who is to be included/excluded from membership of and/or in alliances with the farmers' movements, to the different positions on the state and its liberalising policy, and beyond that to the linkages with international capitalism itself.

On the latter point, both the KRRS and Shetkari Sanghatana adhere to a view of national and agrarian economic backwardness premissed on the existence of 'weak capitalism' (*bandakalu bandavala*) imposed by foreign capital on ex-colonies at the periphery, or by the 'external dependency' of the latter. The solution advocated by the farmers' movements is neatly encapsulated in the terms 'Khadi Curtain' and 'Operation Ryot': the former invokes Gandhian notions of resistance against colonialism/(neo-colonialism), while the latter formulates a strategy for indigenous capitalism. Both have as their object the elimination of inter-national exploitation and – through this – establishing egalitarian relations (non-exploitative terms of trade based on remunerative prices).

NOTES

1. See KRRS [1983b; 1985c]. According to the Raitha Sangha, small subsistence producers constitute 83.3 per cent of total landholders in the state, a category which includes all those who possessed land below two-and-half hectares. To sustain its argument about the absence of a rich peasantry, the KRRS pointed to the existence in the state of only five per cent of irrigated land.
2. There were instances in parts of Karnataka of coffee estate owners not only leading the peasant movement but also appropriating the benefits it secured. Officially, the KRRS is vehemently opposed to the participation in the movement of large landholders.
3. For example, in order to demonstrate caste/communal solidarity and thus oppose attempts to divide farmers along caste/communal lines, Shetkari Sanghatana held a rally (honouring Shivaji and Dr Ambedkar) in Jalagaon on 18 April 1988.
4. The denial of freedom is perceived as a negation of political and economic alternatives, of an ability to determine prices, to market produce, and to choose strategy options. There will be no *Swaraj*, argues Shetkari Sanghatana, unless these 'rightful' freedoms are conceded, and in particular a free market.
5. Muslims do not constitute a large proportion of the agrarian population of Karnataka. In 1984, for example, they accounted for only ten per cent of agricultural labourers and seven per cent of landholders with more than twenty acres [*Government of Karnataka*, 1986]. This is the reason why, until recently, villages in this state have remained free of communal strife.
6. In places such as Sakleshpur, Dalits have been attacked by the members of the Raitha Sangha for not accepting lower wages for agricultural work or manifesting opposition to residential segregation. In Dasarahalli sanctions were imposed on Dalits for refusing to carry out their traditional function of *Aarathi*, and in Suligelele for not joining the movement. Of these events, a Dalit journal observes: 'Harijans are not allowed to walk on the streets of the [high caste] Vokkaligas. They have been threatened with dire consequences for continuing to deal with shopkeepers, and their cattle have been prevented from entering the villages' (see *Panchama*, 10 May 1982, 20 October 1982, 5 November 1982, December 1983, November 1984).
7. The persistence of debt bondage relations in KRRS strongholds is described thus: '[Raitha Sangha] leaders who have received loans for purchasing fertiliser and seeds instead lend this money to Dalits or rural workers as cash advances for agricultural labour in their fields. [Peasant movement] leaders charge interest on these loans, and wages paid to their workers are adjusted downwards accordingly. This bondage continues until the debts are repaid' (*Panchama*, Special Issue, Nov. 1983).
8. There are numerous instances of oppression against Dalits: for example, forcible evictions, encroachments, and setting fire to Dalit housing (see *Panchama*, Oct. 1981, Oct. 1982, Nov. 1982 and July 1983).
9. In Karnataka, the Raitha Sangha split in 1983, with the Bellary peasantry under Revana Siddayya forming a separate Association of Peasants and Agricultural Labourers (*Raitha – Raitha Koolikarara Sangha*), while in Maharashitra Anil Ghote, once a staunch supporter of Sharad Joshi, parted company from the latter to form his own organization.
10. About this, Sharad Joshi has observed (*Probe India*, Dec. 1987): 'I work to correct the terms of trade. This is quite different from espousing the farmers' cause. If any farmer comes to me for anything other than this, I don't even listen to him. If somebody comes and says that his land has been taken, or that he is indebted, or he has problems with water or subsistence, I don't even care ...'
11. The focus of KRRS agitations were the privately-owned sugar factories (Thungabadra in Shimoga, and Chamundeshwari and Salarjung in Mandya). In 1981–82 the Raitha Sangha demanded from the sugar factories a price of Rs 238 per tonne, but settled for Rs 220. In 1983 it demanded Rs 422, at a time when the government had fixed the price at Rs 180; as before, the KRRS settled for Rs 220 per tonne.

12. The Forum met with little success electorally, receiving barely above five per cent of votes cast.
13. The Raitha Sangha fought in eleven constituencies for the Lok Sabha election, and in 111 constituencies for the Assembly election.
14. See *Indian Express*, 28 Nov., 4 Dec. and 10 Dec. 1991. The Hinganghat municipality controlled by Shetkari Sanghatana was won by the Hindu chauvinist Shiv Sena in the 1991 election.
15. In an interview with the writer on 6 July 1988 at Bangalore, Najundaswamy – who leads the farmers' movement in Karnataka – called the latter a 'village movement'.
16. Intellectuals whose arguments have been deployed by the Shetkari Sanghatana include V.N. Dandekar, A.S. Kholan, and C. Subramanian. Vandana Shiva has been instrumental in formulating anti-Dunkel arguments advanced by the farmers' movement in Karnataka, while she and S. Bandopadhyay have assisted it in mobilising arguments against the plantation of eucalyptus trees. The work of Ashok Mitra, however, is strongly opposed by the Shetkari Sanghatana.
17. Since most of the rich peasant activists interviewed by the writer did not regard themselves as part of the ruling class, they did not perceive the Indian state as representing their interests. Nanjundaswamy himself objected to the use of the term 'state' because of its Marxist connotations.
18. In pursuit of its anti-Dunkel/anti-GATT 'seed satyagraha', the KRRS has ransacked the Bangalore office of Cargill Seeds India Pvt., Ltd, as well as a warehouse owned by Cargill in Bellary, and served notice to quit on 11 agribusiness multinationals (*Indian Express*, 31 Dec. 1992; *Udayavani*, 2 Jan. 1993).
19. For 'dependency' theory, see among others Amin [1974; 1977], Baran [1970], and Frank [1978; 1980: 230–44]. Ideologically, the Raitha Sangha operates with a combination of Gandhianism and what Fuentes and Frank [1987] call 'linkages', or a process whereby a national economy delinks from the world capitalist economy.
20. The rest of this section is based on information gathered in the course of interviews with the leadership and activists of the farmers' movement in Karnataka.
21. It must be noted in passing that the definition of 'masses' used by the KRRS is itself inconsistent. In 1980 this term referred only to the peasantry, but from 1982 onwards it was extended to include the industrial working class and salaried employees as well. Significantly, however, the concept 'masses' as used by the Raitha Sangha excludes landless agricultural labour.
22. The concept 'Khadi Curtain' was elaborated by Nanjundaswamy in an interview with the writer in July 1988 and, as its name implies, both opposes western cultural hegemony and capitalist development and – in order to establish national parity with erstwhile colonial masters at the international level – simultaneously encompasses an alternative to this based on what might be called a 'discreet isolationism'.
23. On this point Lohia [n.d.: 182–3] observed: 'imperialism not only appears at the first stage of capitalism but also goes on developing with it ... Imperialism and capitalism have developed jointly throughout the history of capitalism'.
24. The nature of this linkage has been made explicit by Sharad Joshi: '[O]nce remunerative prices are given, then there would be an automatic feedback. This would ensure better wages for farm workers. A chain of processing units could be set up in the rural areas to strengthen the rural economy. This will prevent further fragmentation [of the rural economy] by providing alternative sources of remunerative employment. Migration will halt' (*The Hindu*, 22 Dec. 1980).

REFERENCES

Amin, S., 1974, *Accumulation on a World Scale*, Vols.1 and 2, New York: Monthly Review Press.

Amin, S., 1977, *Imperialism and Unequal Development*, New York: Monthly Review Press.

Baran, P., 1970, 'On the Political Economy of Backwardness', in R.I. Rhodes (ed.), *Imperialism and Underdevelopment*, New York: Monthly Review Press.

Bose, P., 1981, 'Farmers' Agitation', *Seminar*, No.257.

Brown, J., 1974, 'Gandhi and the Indian Peasants, 1917–22', *Journal of Peasant Studies*, Vol.1, No.4.

Dhanagare, D.N., 1990, 'Shetkari Sanghatana: Farmers' Movement in Maharashtra', *Social Action*, Vol.40, No.4.

Frank, A.G., 1978, *Dependent Accumulation and Underdevelopment*, London: Macmillan.

Frank, A.G., 1980, 'Development of Crisis and the Crisis of Development', *Economic and Political Weekly*, Vol.15, Nos.5–7.

Fuentes, M., and A.G. Frank, 1987, 'Ten Theses on Social Movements', *Economic and Political Weekly*, Vol.22, No.35.

Government of India, 1991, *National Agricultural Policy: Views of Standing Advisory Committee on Agriculture*, Jallundar: Government Printing Press.

Government of Karnataka, 1986, *Backward Class Commission Report*, Vol.II, Bangalore.

Guru, G., 1992, 'Shetkari Sanghatana and the Pursuit of "Laxmi Mukti"', *Economic and Political Weekly*, Vol.27, No.28.

Joshi, S., n.d., *'Bharat' Speaks Out*, Bombay: Build Documentation Centre.

Joshi, S., 1984, 'Scrap APC [Agricultural Prices Commission] Demand Farmers', unpublished paper presented at the Gandhian Studies Institute, Rajghat.

Joshi, S., 1985, *Economics of Rajiv*, Pune.

Karnataka Rajya Raitha Sangha (KRRS), 1980, *Charter of Demands*, Shimoga: KRRS.

Karnataka Rajya Raitha Sangha (KRRS), 1981, *Letter to the Chief Minister*, Shimoga: KRRS.

Karnataka Rajya Raitha Sangha (KRRS), 1983a, *Shasana Sabah Chunavane Raitharige Riluvalike Patra*, Shimoga: KRRS.

Karnataka Rajya Raitha Sangha (KRRS), 1983b, *Bhoo Sudharane Nanthara Nava Zamindari Virudda Raitha Sangha Karyakrama*, Shimoga: KRRS.

Karnataka Rajya Raitha Sangha (KRRS), 1983c, *Baragalavanne Mareterua Budget*, Shimoga: KRRS.

Karnataka Rajya Raitha Sangha (KRRS), 1983d, *Vivaha Samhite*, Shimoga: KRRS.

Karnataka Rajya Raitha Sangha (KRRS), 1984a, *Ella Pakshada Shasakarugala Virudda Dharani Gerau*, Shimoga: KRRS.

Karnataka Rajya Raitha Sangha (KRRS), 1984b, *Mathadarara Abyarthi Hege? Yaru? Hege Aikeyagabeku*, Shimoga: KRRS.

Karnataka Rajya Raitha Sangha (KRRS), 1984c, *Mathadarara Vedike Pranlike*, Shimoga: KRRS.

Karnataka Rajya Raitha Sangha (KRRS), 1984d, *Karnataka Raitha Hortada Ashottaragalu*, Mandya: KRRS.

Karnataka Rajya Raitha Sangha (KRRS), 1985a *Karala Kanoon Eke Radhdhagabeku*, Shimoga: KRRS.

Karnataka Rajya Raitha Sangha (KRRS), 1985b, *Letter to the Chief Minister*, Shimoga: KRRS.

Karnataka Rajya Raitha Sangha (KRRS), 1985c, *October 2rinda Raithara Briath Padayatre Aramba*, Shimoga: KRRS.

Karnataka Rajya Raitha Sangha (KRRS), 1986a, *Baragalavanne Marethirua Budget*, Shimoga: KRRS.

Karnataka Rajya Raitha Sangha (KRRS), 1986b, *May 27 1986randu Raitha Hutatmarige Sradhanjali*, Shimoga: KRRS.

Karnataka Rajya Raitha Sangha (KRRS), 1987, *Haliyaldalli Nadedha Mahila Samaveshadalli Thegedukonda Nirnayagalu*, Shimoga: KRRS.

Karnataka Rajya Raitha Sangha (KRRS), 1988a, *Reaction to the Budget*, Shimoga: KRRS.

Karnataka Rajya Raitha Sangha (KRRS), 1988b, *Raithara Brihat Samavesha*, Mudigera: KRRS.

Karnataka Rajya Raitha Sangha (KRRS), 1989, *9/12/89randu Shimogadalli Nadedah Rajya Samitia Theermanagalu*, Shimoga: KRRS.

Karnataka Rajya Raitha Sangha (KRRS), 1992, *Raitha Virodhi Vidhana Saudhakke Echharike Kodalu*, Shimoga: KRRS.
Karnataka Rajya Raitha Sangha (KRRS), 1993, *Rastravyapi Beeja Satyagraha Raitharinda Dehali Muttige*, Shimoga: KRRS.
Karnataka Rajya Raitha Sangha (KRRS), n.d., *Sanghatakaru Madbekada Vicharagalu*, Shimoga: KRRS
Lennenberg, C., 1988, 'Sharad Joshi and the Farmers: The Middle Peasant Lives!', *Pacific Affairs*, Vol.61, No.3.
Lipton, M., 1980, *Why Poor People Stay Poor*, New Delhi: Heritage.
Lohia, R.M., n.d., *Fragments of a World Mind*, Calcutta: Maitreyani.
Mishra, V., 1986, 'The Peasant Question', *Frontier*, Vol.18, No.49.
Nadkarni, M.V., 1987, *Farmers' Movements in India*, Ahmedabad: Allied Publishers.
Natraj, L., 1980, 'Farmers' Agitation', *Economic and Political Weekly*, Vol.15, No.47.
Omvedt, G., 1980, 'Maharashtra Cane Farmer's Movement', *Economic and Political Weekly*, Vol.15, No.49.
Omvedt, G., 1988, 'New Movements', *Seminar*, No.352.
Omvedt, G., 1991, 'Shetkari Sanghatana's New Direction', *Economic and Political Weekly*, Vol.26, No.40.
Ponnampet Nadu Raitha Sangha (PNRS), 1981, [untitled], n.p.p.
Prasad, P.H., 1980, 'Rising Middle Peasants in North India', *Economic and Political Weekly*, Vol.15, Nos.5–7.
Rajashekar, G., 1982, 'Shimoga Raitha Chaluvaliya Thathvika Niluugalu', *Rujuvathu*, No.8.
Rudolph, L., and S.H. Rudolph, 1987, *In Pursuit of Lakshmi: The Political Economy of the Indian State*, New Delhi: Orient.
Rudra, A., 1986, 'Surrender to Kulak Lobby', *Frontier*, Vol.18, Nos.8–9.
Shahasrabudhey, S. (ed.), 1986, *The Peasant Movement Today*, Delhi: Ashish.
Surjeet, H.K., 1981, 'Upsurge', *Seminar*, No.267.
Surjeet, H.K., 1983, 'Marxism and the Peasant Question', *The Marxist*, Vol.1.
Swamy, D.S., 1987, 'Economic Retrogression of Farmers during 1970', *Marxist Today*, Vol.2, No.1.

The Farmers' Movements: A Critique of Conservative Rural Coalitions

JAIRUS BANAJI

The farmers' movements in India have been represented by a variety of organisations, of which the most important have been the Shetkari Sanghatana in Maharashtra, the Bharatiya Kisan Union (BKU) in Punjab, an organisation of that name in UP, the Bharatiya Kisan Sangh (BKS) in Gujarat, and the Karnataka Rajya Raitha Sangha (KRRS). Unlike the more straightforward, class-based movements of earlier decades, both before and after independence, these movements have been defined by a relatively articulate leadership, extraordinary skills in holding the attention of the media, a systematic use of 'ideology', and agitational methods which, though innovative, reflect the wider influence of the urban labour movement with its strong tradition of public protest. Indeed, if the 1980s was a period when organised workers in India faced sharp attacks both on the shopfloor and in the labour market, it is precisely in this period that the farmers' movements emerge, as if the retreat of organised labour was being compensated by an advance of rural militancy. However, appearances notwithstanding, leaders like Sharad Joshi and M.D. Nanjundaswamy have no interest in forging links with the urban labour movement, and exude, if anything, a strong contempt for organised sector workers.[1] The ideological legacies are not those of labour reformism (contrast the 'rural syndicates' in Brazil),[2] nor is the link with the anti-landlord peasant movements of the past in any sense apparent. What these movements clearly do reflect is the loss of Congress hegemony in the rural areas in the course of the 1980s,[3] but why this has occurred and how far the explanations lie in factors peculiar to particular states are not issues which have so far been investigated in any systematic way.

In what follows I shall begin with some early evidence on the base of the agitations, then go on to summarise reactions which can broadly be described as responses from the left. The general claim on the other side is that the farmers' movements are a new type of 'peasant' movement and that this is a progressive struggle because the 'peasantry' is the largest

---

Jairus Banaji is involved in research for the Internatonal Union of Food, Agricultural, Hotel, Restaurant, Catering, Tobacco & Allied Workers' Associations (Asia/Pacific). He resides at 31B, Sun and Sea, 25 JP Road, Versova, Bombay 400 061, India.

exploited class in the country (it is claimed) and its interests are potentially those of all exploited and oppressed groups everywhere in India.

THE SOCIAL BASE

It is worth starting with Praful Bidwai's report on the first convention of the Shetkari Sanghatana, one of the earliest accounts of that organisation.[4] Bidwai noted:

> A broad consensus emerged today on the second day of the three-day convention of the Shetkari Sanghatana against making any distinction either between landless labourers and landowning peasants or between big and small peasants operating irrigated and unirrigated plots respectively. The gathering – predominantly composed of rich and middle peasants – heard vituperative attacks upon all those who make such a functional distinction as well as on 'India' (i.e. cities and towns) as opposed to 'Bharat' (countryside). The convention ... also appeared to be of the view that the question of paying even minimum wages to farm labour cannot be raised until the farmers are paid what the Sanghatana defines as remunerative prices for their produce. Several speakers even claimed that not only the small peasants but even the landless are actually better off than the big farmers.

While the convention was attended by 'peasants belonging to different layers', Joshi's call for a cane price of Rs 300 per tonne seems to have struck a special chord among the *bagaitdars* or owners of irrigated holdings in the talukas of Niphad, Baglan, Malegaon, and Kalwan in Nasik.

The Sanghatana's second convention at Parbhani was covered by Purandare (in February 1984). He pointed out 'The attendance at the convention showed that there was less response from the poorer classes and particularly from Marathwada, where the convention was held. It was difficult to locate landless farm hands among the delegates.' Indeed, 'One of the topics for discussion at the meet was "Participation of farm labourers" in the Shetkari Sanghatana's work. The discussion as such never took place. Only Mr Sharad Joshi dwelt on the subject for a few minutes.' But 'middle farmers' had clearly gathered in some numbers and were being asked by Joshi to boycott the grain markets, although, according to the reporter, they themselves had 'only modest quantities of surplus foodgrains'. Moreover, 'In Maharashtra, there are nearly 6.5 million farm labourers (as per the 1981 census). If the foodgrain output is reduced, prices will go up and this section will itself be compelled to purchase foodgrains at very high prices ...'.[5]

At the third convention (at Dhule), D.V. Hegde of *The Nation* quoted Joshi as saying, 'My support comes from all sections, but peasants with 3 to 3.5 acres of land ... support me most', and added 'However, after talking to many farmers at Dhule, this correspondent found that, though the Sanghatana drew support from all sections of farmers, it is mainly agriculturists owning 5 to 15 acres of land and growing commercial crops who constituted its solid base'. The demand for implementation of the Minimum Wages Act for agricultural labourers was made, characteristically, by leftwing observers at the conference, but 'it was not spelt out what the Sanghatana would do to bring about minimum wages for agricultural workers'. '[The] medium and rich peasants who have benefited from advanced technology and intensive farming and who have acquired greater economic clout are now demanding a greater say in the political affairs of the state. The two-day conference of the Shetkari Sanghatana amply demonstrated that.'[6]

These three accounts, spread over 1982–85, are consistent in depicting the social base of the movement as the better-off sections of the peasantry. What Joshi had managed to do was capture a section of the traditional rural support for Congress and build a coalition of rural interests by also attracting smallholders. As Purandare noted in 1987:

> 'There is no denying that the sanghatana has established its roots firmly in rural Maharashtra despite the fact that its leader is a non-Maratha. This is because a section of the leaders of well-to-do and middle class farmers within the Congress are supporting the sanghatana. The other sections of small holders and farm-hands are attracted to it for various social and economic reasons. They regard the sanghatana as the only body capable of redressing their immediate grievances. The sanghatana thus has assumed a typical *mixed-class* character.[7]

The Shetkari Sanghatana thus implies a more general model of *mass organisations led by sections of the rural elite*. Sharad Patil, who was associated with the movement till 1985, would later claim

> S[hetkari] S[anghatana] is definitely the biggest mass organisation of Maharashtrian peasants; but its leadership is also definitely that of rich peasants. I can cite names of their top leaders: Madhavrao More, Ramchandra Patil, Narendra Ahire, Bhaskarrao Boravke, Anil Gote etc are all rich peasants. SS workers openly complain that their 'Saheb' has use for the ordinary peasant workers only at the time of mass struggles, but when elections come he shoves them aside to make way for rich peasant candidates, even from the ruling Congress.[8]

Until 1984, the Punjab-based BKU (Bharatiya Kisan Union) was probably the best organised and most powerful agrarian lobby in the country. Although most observers claimed that the group behind the early 1984 agitation were 'mostly big landowners',[9] Bharat Bhushan's fine description of the movement noted at the time that

> The BKU leadership comes from the middle farmers and their support base is in middle and small farmers, i.e. those with land-holding sizes of 3 to 25 acres. BKU support is very high in the districts of Ludhiana, Patiala, Ropar, Sangrur, Bhatinda and Hoshiarpur ... It is also worth noting that the BKU does not have the support of landless labourers nor does it have any conception of what will happen once BKU's demands are met.[10]

Although another writer described the Punjab BKU as a 'platform of rich landowners', he was careful to note the difference between it and the Akali Dal. He seemed to agree that the wealthiest landowners were supporters not of the BKU but of the Akali Dal.[11] The BKU 'never talks of land reforms or ceilings on holdings. While talking in the name of the entire peasantry, it confines itself to serving the interests of the 20 per cent upper crust.' On the other hand, the pro-Akali landlords adopted a more aggressive stance *vis-à-vis* agricultural labour. Also, like Sharad Joshi and Nanjundaswamy of the KRRS, it was the Akali landed interest that articulated the ideology of an urban/rural divide, 'painting all urbanites as the enemies of the rural people'. 'It is highly significant that Sikh industrialists are totally opposed to this section of the Akalis.'[12]

The base of the Jat-dominated BKU in West UP looks again like a coalition of rural strata. 'Mr Tikait's BKU draws support mainly from those Jat ranks which gave muscle to Mr Charan Singh's Lok Dal. The bulk of them, prosperous farmers owning tractors and tubewells, are driving from far and near to Meerut every day.'[13] Others wrote that Tikait had 'galvanised thousands of well-to-do peasants',[14] or that he drew the 'bulk of his support from relatively wealthy farmers'.[15] However, during the Meerut satyagraha (in 1988) Tikait claimed. 'The average holding per farmer gathered here today is between 4 and 7 acres, which is hardly any evidence of prosperity'.[16] The solution lies in the peculiar institutional underpinnings of the BKU, which was 'consciously conceived as a Jat organisation based on providing a share in leadership to all sub-divisions of the Jat community'.[17] Reorganised in 1985 on the basis of the *khaps* (that is, 'clans' or 'panchayats'), 'the subordinate leadership of the BKU came to consist of the choudharies of the various "khaps". This re-organisation cut across the different sections of the Jat peasantry in one swift move and brought in even the poorest of the Jat farmers into the ideological ambit of the BKU.' Thus the BKU articulated the economic demands of the rich peasantry but 'would be able to organise the other sections too to fight for them'. Secondly, Tikait was careful to appeal to both Muslims and Gujars as the largest minorities in western UP and for a while at least, consciously promoted communal harmony.[18] Thus in the late 1980s it was possible that he would emerge as a 'leader whose support base cuts across caste and community boundaries'. 'A major consequence of this would be an increase in the political hegemony of the rich farmers of UP and this would continue to be a major threat to the landless agricultural workers of the area.'[19]

In Gujarat large landowners have lined up behind the Bharatiya Kisan Sangh in most districts of the north and centre, and the Khedut Samaj in the south. The chief difference between these organisations is a political one: the Khedut Samaj was part of the Inter-State Coordination Committee controlled by Sharad Joshi,[20] whereas the BKS has been dominated, politically, by the RSS and BJP.[21] However, the social base of both organisations is the Patidars. During the violent agitation of March 1987, it was reported that the organisers received 'strong support from the areas dominated by the Patels, a rich community ...'[22] 'While the leadership of the Sangh remains obscure [i.e. RSS-controlled, J.B.], it is certain that the bulk of the cadres belong to the affluent and intermediate caste of Patidars, particularly the Kadva Patidars who dominate in Mehsana and Sabarkantha' in North Gujarat.[23] The Khedut Samaj, likewise, is a 'political union of the dominant peasant castes of rural Gujarat', chiefly the Patidars, who, in the south, have based their prosperity largely on the sugar co-operatives.[24] When Joshi visited Gujarat early in 1987, he was reported to have told the Khedut Samanvay Samiti (or Khedut Samaj) that he wanted 'more mobilisation of "backward class" farmers in Gujarat – not just Patels'.[25] On the other hand, the BKS was said to have the backing of an estimated five lakh farmers at that time.[26]

REACTIONS FROM THE LEFT

The Communist Parties would eventually end up supporting the farmers' agitations, though without much enthusiasm and despite their own earlier criticisms.[27] But on the broad left the current of opinion was decidedly critical.

> Large and medium farmers form the backbone of the farmers' lobbies. Because their land is generally better irrigated, they produce most of the marketable surplus ... Since big farmers have come to control State legislatures, they have exempted themselves from paying income tax and enjoy huge subsidies from the States' irrigation departments and electricity boards.[28]

'Tikait speaks only for the Jat kulaks . . . this section has always controlled the political balance in the area . . . even the left parties have not yet found it convenient to attack a movement that is outspoken in its advocacy of the rural haves and [that has] totally ignored the lot of the poor and the landless.'[29]

> [T]hese farmers' agitations are not the by-product of the impoverished rural scene but offspring of the green revolution . . . In this the big farmer is the boss and not, of course, the day labourer . . . And it is largely because of the failure of the Left to dig in and build powerful movements of the rural poor that the rich farmer holds sway and claims to speak on behalf of the entire kisan community . . . Not only the Congress, even the Left parties are anxious to be on the right side of the farmer bosses.[30]

Or finally,

> the rural mass is not homogeneous or undifferentiated . . . those who own land and those who do not are virtually inimical to each other. Obviously Sharad Joshi cannot represent the whole of 'Bharat' which, according to him, is rural India and discriminated against by the government. He has systematically promoted the myth of the India–Bharat divide. The myth, for obvious reasons, has not taken root among the rural poor.[31]

The basic point is a fairly obvious one. The interests of the new rural elites are scarcely compatible with those of the rural poor. The most vulnerable groups in the countryside are those 'who have to actually purchase foodgrains from the market on a net basis'.[32] A victory for the farmers' movements would be a direct blow to these sections, apart from enormously strengthening the hand of employers against workers.

These are issues on which Sharad Joshi has been consciously evasive. The main thrust of his attack has been on the state as the representative of industrial capital.[33] To give his politics the appearance of a reasoned stance, he revives a crude version of Physiocratic theory, arguing that 'historically surplus comes from the primary producer, that is, the farmer and not industrial workers'.[34] To give it a wider political significance and purpose, he has claimed that 'the concept of remunerative prices [is] the fundamental premise for any poverty eradication'.[35] Obviously, the idea is that rural welfare as a whole depends on the profitability of the farm sector. That is, a 'peasant' employing labour will only pay higher wages if he/she can afford to do so. Again, the further assumption is that as the profits of farming increase, landholders will not substitute capital for labour but translate some indeterminate portion of profits into higher wages for farm workers, increased rural welfare, and so on. Given the harsh reality of the Indian countryside – the boycotting of entire communities in village after village, the dismal oppression inflicted on migrant workers by Joshi's associates in the Khedut Samaj[36] – all this seems like a fairy story.

Nor have the Dalits been inclined to buy it. B. Krishnappa, President of the Karnataka Dalit Sangharsh Samiti, told M.V. Nadkarni in an interview in 1985: 'Any strengthening of farmers on a majority caste basis poses a threat to the economic interests and security of the oppressed minorities particularly at the village level ... Dalits do not accept the view that once prices improve, agricultural wages too improve.' Krishnappa pointed out that in Shimoga district itself, both paddy and sugarcane prices had much more than doubled in the preceding decade, but wages remained practically the same. Dalits, according to Krishnappa, were also opposed to the demand for abolition of procurement levies, and anything that adversely affected the public distribution system. He stressed the need for extending it in rural areas along with employment guarantee schemes, so that the dependence of Scheduled Castes on farmers and traders in times of distress could be reduced. Dalits, he said, do not accept the ruralist ideology of 'Bharat versus India' expounded by Sharad Joshi, though undoubtedly the rural sector and the rural poor needed more attention. Ironically, the only hope of rural Dalits was in escaping to urban areas, away from the caste oppression prevailing in rural areas, he said. Finally,

> Dalits have a different perspective about the nature and role of bureaucracy too. Krishnappa said that a bureaucracy committed to an implementation of programmes for alleviation of poverty is in the interest of the poor, and any agitation which demoralises such a bureaucracy or restricts their access to the rural poor is anti-people. To regard bureaucracy as a whole as an enemy is erroneous, he felt.[37]

Thus the Dalits have refused to be drawn into the Kannada Desha, a party floated by Nanjundaswamy in 1988,[38] and conversely, as a recent report notes, 'Dalits [in Karnataka] have even earned the hostility of ... political groupings such as the Raitha Sangha which resents the Dalits' lack of enthusiasm for the Sangha'.[39]

THE LIMITS OF 'PEASANT' POWER

The farmers' movements have had several important features in common. The first and most important of these is that their social base has been drawn from relatively cohesive dominant castes – Jats in Western UP, Patidars in Gujarat, Marathas in Maharashtra. In so far as these are landed castes, the movements have been isolated from landless labour not just for economic reasons (employers/workers) but due to caste factors, above all in states where there is undeniable tension between caste Hindus and Dalits (notably Maharashtra).[40] Secondly, the support base of the various organisations has usually been concentrated in limited regional strongholds. Joshi, strong in Vidarbha and the north (Nasik and so on), has failed to gain any significant hold in southern Maharashtra, the proverbial fiefdom of the sugar barons.[41] Tikait failed to expand into east UP. Gujarat has always been partitioned by distinct and rival organisations, despite their common background and objectives. In Joshi's case, the failure to penetrate the sugar country of southern and western Maharashtra proved a fatal weakness when the Sanghatana's political calculations backfired and plunged the entire organisation into a deep crisis in the course of 1990. As Joshi admitted, the comparative stability of the Congress(I), following the Assembly elections, was due to its 'deep-rooted sugar cooperative network in Western Maharashtra'.[42] For the BKU, likewise, failure to extend beyond the Jat strongholds in West UP has meant rapid degeneration into casteist (anti-reservation) and communal politics,[43] and deepened the internal strains in the organisation.

A third feature, this time of the evolution of the movements, has been their inability to resist the blandishments of power, and the consequent tendency to draw individual organisations into alliances which only have fractured both their internal unity and the political coherence of the movement as a whole. The illusion that the Indian 'peasant' can actually throw up a coherent and viable political alternative for the country has been permanently shattered by the various manoeuvrings and factional struggles of the period after 1987.[44]

Finally, we may note that the conflict between private profitability and public good is invariably resolved in the former's favour, even to the detriment of the 'long-term' interests of the rural population. The most striking expression of this, and one fraught with massive implications for the future of agrarian capital, is that as recently as September 1993, the Gujarat-based BKS mobilised a mammoth rally of four lakhs, demanding reduction in electricity rates. The largest contingent, it is reported, came from the north Gujarat region, said to be 'one of the worst affected by the hike in power rates due to the fast depleting subsoil water level'.[45] But this alarming ecological crisis has been brought on precisely by the excessive pumping of groundwater and the resultant decline of water tables in areas which have seen the fastest expansion of energised water extraction mechanisms.[46] Having transformed large parts of Gujarat into a desert, with characteristic foresight the large farmers are now asking the state to subsidise further investments in heavy motors, so that the water tables decline even faster and they are forced to solve their problems ultimately, with the large-scale destruction threatened by the Sardar Sarovar Project.

Although by 1989 it was said that the farmers had 'emerged as a major third force' in Indian politics,[47] it is worth emphasising that they simply failed to make any significant political impact. They were, on the contrary, incorporated into the political system and their fragmentation further consolidated.

The history of the farmers' movements can be divided into two main phases distinguished by rather different styles of agitation and by a progressive loss of unity and deepening crisis in the period after 1988. Starting in 1981 around the struggles of tobacco growers, the earlier agitations had been local and frequently violent, with the state unleashing considerable repression. After the notable lack of success of Tikait's Meerut satyagraha early in 1988, the style became notably less confontationist, more theatrical in some ways, and centred largely on Delhi, the seat of bureaucratic power. The key development was the decision to seek wider political alliances, starting with Sharad Joshi's flirtation with V.P. Singh[48] and the tensions this began to produce in his relations with Tikait.[49] These escalated so abruptly that by February 1988 Joshi was openly attacking Tikait for the failure of the Meerut agitation and for choosing to ignore the Inter-State Coordination Committee controlled by him, and by August Tikait was planning to compete for rural support in Vidarbha.[50] Relations were strained throughout 1989[51] (Tikait's attempt to form a national-level organisation of farmers at a meeting on May 22 was denounced by Joshi as 'illegal')[52] and finally exploded at the disastrous 'kisan panchayat' on 2 October that year.[53] Of course, Tikait's credibility dropped sharply and in the following year he was rapidly losing ground in the rural areas, especially among the minorities.[54] The BKU was instrumental in bringing the BJP to power in UP in 1990. Indeed, the BJP government was said to have 'swept to power with the unstinted support of Mr Tikait and his men'.[55] According to another reporter, 'In the recent elections the villagers got the impression that he [Tikait] was supporting the BJP, and voted accordingly ...'.[56] By late 1992, it was reported that Tikait's despotic methods had provoked a 'virtual vertical split in the BKU'.[57] So much for a 'new' movement.

For Joshi, too, the temptations of power proved disastrous. Faced with the rapid erosion of his base by the expansion of the Shiv Sena into rural Maharashtra,[58] Joshi correctly redefined all priorities and made the 'struggle' against communalism (the Shiv Sena, not so much the BJP)[59] the prime task. The Lok Sabha elections of late 1989 were a severe blow to the Shetkari Sanghatana, not least because they demonstrated Joshi's inability to command the political loyalty of his own supporters, who actively campaigned for the Sena/BJP combine.[60] In the Assembly elections of 1990, it was Pawar who held the Sena at bay in rural Maharashtra, but the erosion of the Sanghatana's base in Vidarbha was still evident.[61] By early 1990, the Sanghatana faced a serious crisis, with charges of corruption, calls for the dissolution of the organisation, and Joshi's offer to resign,[62] and in October that year it lost its main organiser, who broke away to form a separate organisation called the Kisan Manch.[63]

These examples illustrate the inability of the farmers' movements to throw up a genuinely independent politics. By the early 1990s, some of the leading organisations either began to crack up or display signs of a serious internal split. Ideologically, the 'new' 'peasant' movement became less coherent than ever. Nanjundaswamy's political ambitions nurtured a split in the Raitha Sangha, with a section of the activists alleging that 'the Kannada Desha was formed without the consent of bonafide farmers' and accusing him of 'politicising the whole movement against the objectives of the Raitha Sangha'.[64] With a clear sense that he was losing ground, Nanjundaswamy turned to 'anti-imperialism', launching a purely xenophobic campaign against multinationals in agribusiness.[65] The rhetoric was crudely left-wing, the political understanding closer to the Swadeshi Jagran Manch (controlled by the RSS) with its 'second war of economic independence'. Meanwhile, Joshi's new line for the Shetkari Sanghatana veered to extreme neo-liberal stances, with sharp attacks on the state and a clear intuition of the new alliance between Free Traders and peasant capitalists based on food processing,[66] agro-exports, and contract farming;[67] or, as one writer described it, 'The new direction of the Shetkari Sanghatana that is being bandied about is a well-thought out action plan to catapult Indian agriculture from the confines of the domestic arena to the lucrative world markets'.[68] Shetkari Solvent, a company recently started by Joshi at a capital cost of several crores of rupees,[69] is a clear indication of the new front along which agrarian capital is expanding, with visions of an *integrated* rural capitalism in which peasant entrepreneurs flourish both independently and in contract with domestic and international agribusiness.[70]

GENERAL CHARACTERISATIONS

Both in the article cited earlier and in his book, M.V. Nadkarni has taken the position that since rural labourers and many small farmers are net buyers of food and, of course, form the poorest sections of rural society, the farmers' movements 'cannot be considered as having a mass character in an overall perspective. But they cannot also be said to be movements of a few landlords or big farmers'.[71] The aim of these struggles has been to 'increase the political clout of surplus farmers'. This analysis is surely correct, as far as it goes. By contrast, Gail Omvedt argues that the farmers' movements are historically progressive class-based movements of the peasantry, and that, objectively at least, they are aimed at ending the exploitation of the countryside by a destructive, ecologically insatiable urban industrial capitalism. This almost romantic picture of the farmers' movements ignores both their profound shortcomings (their neglect of, if not active hostility to landless labour, their incorporation into bourgeois politics with often disastrous consequences, their authoritarian leadership styles, their anti-modernist ideologies which can sometimes degenerate into fascist rhetoric[72] or 'feudal' violence) and their willingness to be accommodated within the system once governments are seen to consolidate rural interests.[73] There is clearly more 'materialism' in Nadkarni's analysis than in Omvedt's, but neither of them locates the farmers' movements in the context of underlying changes in the nature of Indian capitalism. In 1989 the distinguished human rights activist K. Balagopal suggested that the true class base of the farmers' movements was a new 'provincial propertied class' whose business activities integrated urban and rural enterprises and whose interests straddled the division between town and countryside. 'It is this class that is most vocal about injustice done to "villages".'[74] There is a precise image of this sort of capitalism in Boyack's recent work on the new business community (or class) which has developed from the prosperous peasantry or dominant landed caste (Kammas) of the canal-irrigated villages of coastal Andhra, families with 'very large' and 'large' holdings of upwards of 50 acres. This group is characterised by 'significant investment in business enterprises, *both rural and urban*' (emphasis added – JB). Boyack refers to a 'sharp increase in the number of rural business-cum-agricultural households (as well as to) diversification in the type of investments made by them', and thus to the 'interpenetration of business and agriculture, and of rural and urban property interests'.[75] In Gujarat, likewise, another author has emphasised the 'integration of rural wealth and urban enterprise' in the state, and noted 'Agricultural surplus is being diverted in a big way into industries'.

> Agro-based industries are proving very attractive for those with investible surplus. Most of the sugar factories, oil mills and of course the dairy and other cooperative ventures are dominated by *patidars*. In the recent industrial expansion in powerloom, chemi-

> cals, light engineering and other sectors, especially in South Gujarat, the involvement of the *patidars* is considerable. Through all these processes a substantial and well-integrated class *with both urban and rural interests* has grown in Gujarat.[76]

The conclusion that seems to follow from these accounts is that the 1970s and especially the 1980s saw the consolidation of a new *sector of capitalism between the large corporate groups and the traditional rural and commercial elites*. Contrary to the imagined division between 'Bharat' and 'India', this layer of capital is powerful in both, and represents, if anything, an extension of rural power into urban enterprise and politics. Moreover, however we characterise this new class (entrepreneurs of peasant origin?), farmers' movements do not exhaust their political options and are surely not even the primary means by which they organise or pursue their interests. To grasp the significance of such movements, we have to locate them in the wider context of an emerging rural capitalism for which they are simply one of several forms of intervention. Why such movements have emerged in some states and not in others, and why even within particular states their influence is concentrated is specific regions are factors which depend on the overall relationship between the new capitalism and local politics.[77]

To conclude, from the standpoint of society as a whole, the farmers' movements are essentially conservative movements that seek to reinforce the existing property rights and consolidate a broad-based and diversified rural capitalism where rural industrialisation is not left to the large business groups.[78] Sharad Joshi, for example, is opposed to agrarian reforms and 'fiercely opposes the class struggle of agricultural labourers against their rural exploiters'.[79] The *kheduts* behind the Gujarat agitation of 1987 wanted removal of the ceiling on agricultural and urban land, lifting of the ban on farmers buying land more than eight kilometres away from home, exemption from the stipulations of the Minimum Wages Act (including withdrawal of cases against employers not complying with the Act), and 'implementation of the Rs 8000 crore inter-state Narmada Project on a war footing'.[80] Tikait's 31-point charter included scrapping of the land ceiling laws and of the legislation on minimum wages.[81] Gail Omvedt herself wants an end to the 'cheap food policy',[82] and that in a country where the rural poor are crucially affected by the price of foodgrains![83] The curious idea that 'Indian farmers are competitive under world conditions'[84] rests, of course, on the unspoken assumption of an *unlimited* exploitation of agricultural workers.

Meanwhile, rural violence continues with horrifying atrocities against Dalits, who are mostly farm labourers.[85] But as Balagopal has pointed out, the increasing incidence of rural violence reflects not the submissiveness but the struggle of the Dalits against oppression at the hands of caste Hindus/landed castes. With the electoral successes of the Bahujan Samaj Party in UP and the emergence of strong grassroots organisations like the Karnataka Dalit Sangharsh Samiti, it is new coalitions around these sectors of society, and not landowners' agitations, that offer real possibilities for the revival of a strong democratic movement in the country.

NOTES

1. Nanjundaswamy, in an interview with *Sunday*, 1 April 1984, p.28: 'You know, I can't resist a laugh every morning at 10.00 a.m. when the entire literate mass of Bangalore city set out promptly to their offices on two-wheelers and four-wheelers to destroy the country and promptly return at 5.00 p.m. They are the real anti-socials. They are the ones who have reduced this country to a third-class nation.' Sharad Joshi, in an interview with the *Free Press Journal*, 29 September 1985: 'When I drive to my farm from Pune city, I pass this line of companies – Atlas Copco, Garware, and so on – all with red flags fluttering – representing workers whose incomes even the biggest farmer would be envious of.'
2. Moraes [1970]. The Peasant Leagues appeared to one writer (Maria Helena Moreira Alves) as a 'system of rural unions'. They were ruthlessly dismantled by the dictatorship [*Alves*, 1985].
3. Rahman *et al.*, *India Today*, 30 Nov. 1987, observe: 'the growth of farmers' organisations has been at the cost of traditional Congress (I) hegemony in rural areas'. Compare Bidwai [1982], explaining why the Shetkari Sanghatana gained its initial base in the Nasik area: 'the fragmentation of the Congress party organisation in the district between 1977 and 1981 produced not only conditions within which the traditional leadership of the *bagaitdars*' co-operatives could be bypassed, but also a power vacuum – which the Sanghatana filled'.
4. Bidwai [1982] in a series of two articles in the *Times of India*.
5. Purandare [1984].
6. Hegde [1985].
7. Purandare [1987]; emphasis added.
8. Patil [1988: 8]. Sharad Patil seems to have been associated with the movement till 1985. I was clearly wrong to attribute the phrase 'lamb in the stomach of the tiger' to him, as he has confirmed in a letter dated 10 Feb. 1994, where he says he does not know who the author is.
9. So R. Venkatachary in the *Deccan Herald* (Bangalore), 27 March 1984, compare *Indian Express*, 11 Sept. 1984, 'The BKU is headed by large farmers, not marginal farmers or landless labourers'.
10. Bhushan [1984: 70].
11. 'The dominant section of the Akali Dal consists of capitalist landlords . . .', for example, Prakash Singh Badal [*Chawla*, 1987].
12. Chawla [1987].
13. Janak Singh in the *Times of India*, 11 Feb. 1988.
14. Arindam Sen Gupta in the *Sunday Observer*, 7 Feb. 1988.
15. *India Today*, 29 Feb. 1988.
16. Interview with Shekhar Ghosh, *Imprint*, March 1988.
17. This and the following citations are from Bhushan [1988].
18. See especially Nanda [1989] and Gupta [1988: 2694].
19. Bhushan [1988].
20. 'The Gujarat Khedut Samaj considers their organisation as almost a part and parcel of the Shetkari Sanghatana. Both the organisations are in fact together and they [the

Khedut Samaj – JB] listen to me with as much attention as Maharashtra farmers do', Joshi told *Debonair* in June 1988 (p.20).

21. See Bhatt [1987a], especially 'The Samaj and the BKS do not see eye to eye primarily because the farmers' organisation, whose leadership comprises a fair number of former Jana Sangh and RSS members, does not want to play second fiddle ... they do not regard each other with much cordiality.'
22. Ashraf Sayed in *Times of India*, 21 March 1987.
23. Editorial, 'Towards Caste War', *Times of India*, 24 March 1987.
24. Breman [1990], with the description of the Samaj on p.598.
25. Reported in *Frontline*, 18 April/1 May 1987.
26. *India Today*, 30 Nov. 1987.
27. Support: 'The CPI and CPM have come out in support of the 'just' demands of the agitating peasantry in U.P.' (*Times of India*, 19 Feb. 1988), 'The two CPs and the BJP lent support to the demand for remunerative prices for farmers being projected by the BKU agitation' (*Times of India*, 2 Nov. 1988). Earlier criticisms: for example, about the KRRS, 'A feeling among Marxist circles is that the agitation is being backed by rich landlords who are trying to use poor farmers to get good returns for their produce' (*Economic Times*, 3 Oct. 1982); about the Punjab BKU, 'according to Avtar Malhotra (state secretary of the CPI), "it should not be forgotten that the BKU is basically a kulak organisation ... It is anti-town and anti-worker"', cited Bhushan [1984: 72].
28. *Statesman*, 8 April 1984.
29. Editorial, *Telegraph*, 4 Feb. 1988.
30. Nikhil Chakravarty in *Times of India*, 28 Feb. 1988.
31. Ketkar [1985].
32. Nadkarni [1985].
33. 'The government exploits the farmers in rural areas to pay for the development of the industry and industrialisation of the country', Hegde [1985: 15] reporting Joshi's views.
34. Joshi in an interview with Rajni Bakshi in the *Illustrated Weekly of India*, 18 Jan. 1987.
35. Interview with Bakshi, see note 34.
36. Breman [1985] and Breman [1990], see also note 20 above.
37. Cited from Nadkarni [1985]. The latter continues, 'Inspite of all the differences and suspicions, the attitude of the Dalits towards farmers' movements cannot be construed as one of total animosity'.
38. See Murthy [1988].
39. Nair [1993: 912], who notes that the Dalit Sangharsh Samiti has 'built up a formidable base in nearly every taluk of Karnataka' (p.911).
40. For the latest round of violence against Dalits (this time in Marathwada), see Badrinath [1994]. The farmers' movements have been seen as reactions to the erosion of power suffered by the forward castes. This is particularly clear in the analysis suggested in one editorial written during the Gandhinagar agitation early in 1987. Noting the support extended to the BKS by the Patidars, this argued,

    > In a way, the farmers agitation can be regarded as a rural (but delayed) manifestation of the backlash against the consolidation of gains of the KHAM (an alliance of Kshatriya, Harijan, Adivasi and Muslim) strategy put in place by the Congress first in 1980. The urban reaction came by way of the anti-reservation agitations of 1981 and 1985 when the Patidars began realising the full implications of loss of political power. And though Mr Amarsinh Chaudhary jettisoned part of Mr Solanki's pro-backward policy package, there was no going back on the changed caste composition of the assembly ... What is happening now is that the BJP is capitalising on the acute sense of disillusionment among the intermediate castes' (*Times of India*, 24 March 1987).

    Nadkarni [1985] reports a similar analysis for Karnataka:

    > There is a strong view in Karnataka, which leaders of the Dalit movement also share, that farmers' movements here were meant, *inter alia*, for restoring the dominance of landowning castes, a position they had enjoyed since the formation of the State in 1956 till 1971. They lost this dominant position after Devaraj Urs staged a

silent revolution with the suport of Mrs. Indira Gandhi, through which backward minority communities and Scheduled Castes and Tribes came to the fore in State politics.

In Maharashtra, caste factors probably account for Sharad Joshi's reluctance to contemplate any serious organisation of agricultural labourers.

41. About Joshi's rally in Kolhapur, held on 2 October 1988, it was said, '... the contribution from South Maharashtra which still remains the stronghold of the sugar barons was conspicuously low' (*Indian Express*, 3 October 1988). In December 1989 Joshi was reported to have 'denied that his clout in Vidarbha and Nasik, the one-time strongholds of the Sanghatana, had been captured by the [Sena/BJP] combine', V. Kulkarni in the *Independent*, 28 December 1989. About the Pune panchayat which was held in March 1991, Agashe said, 'One reason why the sugarcane growers from south Maharashtra failed to turn up was the Sanghatana's continued failure to penetrate the sugar barons' citadel ... Farmers from even the traditional Sanghatana strongholds of Vidarbha and Marathwada did not turn out in large numbers ...' (*Independent*, 10 March 1991).
42. Reported Agashe, *Independent*, 3 March 1990.
43. Especially *Hindu*, 18 September 1990, 'Tikait said it was shameful for the farmers that when the late Charan Singh had not liked the recommendations of the Mandal Commission [his son should be in a government] which had virtually unleashed a caste war for political reasons by deciding to implement the Mandal recommendations', compare also *Times of India*, 19 July 1990. Again, in an interview with *Sunday Observer*, 4 Aug. 1991, Tikait was asked, 'Isn't it true that Muslim farmers are drifting away from the BKU', and replied, 'Yes, the Muslims have got a bit alienated. It's because they have a feeling we were supporting the BJP in the elections.' See also note 54 below.
44. Note especially the disastrous kisan panchayat held at the Boat Club lawns in New Delhi on 2 October 1989, when Tikait almost hurled Joshi off the platform in front of two lakh farmers! For a vivid report see *Statesman*, 3 Oct. 1989.
45. *Times of India*, 29 Sept. 1993.
46. See Bhatia [1992] for Gujarat and Rao [1993] for Karnataka.
47. Ketkar in *Economic Times*, 18 Sept. 1989, 'The Congress concedes that the farmers have emerged as a major third force ...'.
48. *Indian Post*, 6 Sept. 1987; 7 Nov. 1987; *Indian Express*, 14 Nov. 1987 for references to this, especially to Congress attempts to 'tackle the combined threat of V.P. Singh and the Shetkari Sanghatana leader Sharad Joshi'.
49. *India Today*, 30 Nov. 1987.
50. *Indian Express*, 27 Feb. 1988, with the headline 'Joshi Lambasts Tikait', *Indian Express*, 28 August 1988, with the statement, '... the differences between Mr Joshi and Mr Tikait depend on the issue of association of politicians with farmers' organisations. The BKU leader feels that the organisation (sic) should be non-political ...'. Of course, the careful posture of apoliticism did not stop Tikait from finding his political hero in Devi Lal (*Statesman*, 30 May 1990, 'Tikait wants Devi Lal as P.M.').
51. See, above all, *Times of India*, 29 April 1989.
52. *Times of India*, 26 May 1989.
53. See note 44 above.
54. S.K. Tripathi in *Indian Express*, 10 July 1990.
55. *Times of India*, 1 Sept. 1991.
56. Amit Agarwal in the *Times of India*, 5 Aug. 1991.
57. R. Bhushan in *Indian Express*, 22 Nov. 1992.
58. Note that the Sena used Joshi's movement to expand its rural support, compare especially *Times of India*, 13 December 1986, where the Sewagram 'rail roko' was said to have 'received the full support of the local Shiv Sena units' (The reporter, Prakash Joshi, continues, 'According to observers here, the Shiv Sena has proliferated in Parbhani district, which was hitherto under the influence of left parties. According to rough estimates, the Sena has started 300 branches in villages which have a *large number of unemployed youths* ...'; emphasis added – JB). In December 1986 Feroze

Chandra described the Sena as 'poised to make its first foray into the hinterland of Maharashtra', *Deccan Herald*, 21 Dec. 1986. In November 1988 a *Times* reporter noted the 'growing influence of the Shiv Sena in rural Maharashtra', *Times of India*, 24 Nov. 1988. A year later Joshi 'spoke of the danger posed by communal forces who were trying to spread the division in the cities to the villages', *Times of India*, 11 Nov. 1989. The following month the *Independent* claimed 'Joshi admitted there was a threat from the Sena to the Shetkari Sanghatana. The Sena had spearheaded the spread of communal feelings in the area, wasting the Sanghatana's work in the state since the last ten years', reported Kulkarni, *Independent*, 28 Dec. 1989. Also see note 61 below.

59. See Agashe in the *Independent*, 24 Nov. 1989, 'Joshi offered to reconsider the Sanghatana's stand towards the BJP if the latter snapped its ties with a "parochial and uncultured" outfit like the Sena after the Lok Sabha elections'. Vijay Javandhia, president of the Kisan Coordination Committee, told *Onlooker*, 1/15 Dec. 1989, 'The BJP, though communal, is not criminal. We have supported them in the past.' Compare Agashe, *Independent*, 3 Feb. 1990, reporting that according to Joshi, 'despite its Hindu chauvinism, the BJP needs to be distinguished from the Sena'.
60. 'I shall fight against communalism all alone even if Sanghatana workers are busy electioneering' (Joshi quoted by Agashe in the *Independent*, 10 March 1991) was a tacit admission that his own ranks were campaigning for the saffron alliance. Indeed, Joshi admitted the loss of his cadre to the Sena when he told Agashe that youth in their teens or early twenties were 'probably returning to the Sanghatana fold following [their] disillusionment with the Sena', *Times of India*, 16 Dec. 1991.
61. Evidently, Joshi stated 'As for the saffron alliance, the performance of the BJP and Sena in *Vidarbha* and Bombay has exceeded my expectations', cited Agashe, *Independent*, 3 March 1990 (emphasis added – JB)
62. See especially *Independent*, 10 April 1990, 'Sanghatana Facing Serious Crisis', and Anand Agashe's later reports in *Independent*, 10 March 1991 and *Times of India*, 16 Dec. 1991.
63. See *Times of India*, 9 Oct. 1990, 'Sanghatana Splits', and the fuller report by Agashe, *Independent*, 14 Oct. 1990 (about Anil Gote).
64. See M.D. Riti, 'Voices of Dissent', *Ilustrated Weekly of India*, 27 August 1989.
65. *Economic Times*, 13 July 1992, 'Cargill Complex Damaged in Farmers' Attack', *Economic Times*, 18 July 1993 (listing companies scheduled for attacks), and *Economic Times*, 20 December 1993, 'Farmers to Intensify Stir against MNCs'. The background, of course, was the widespread opposition to the Dunkel Draft.
66. The food processing industry is on the verge of considerable expansion, see *Ministry of Food Processing Industries* [1993]. It also accounts for 12.3 per cent of the foreign investments approved since the liberalisation in July 1991, see *Business World*, 20 Oct. 1993, p.26 (the largest volume of investment after power and oil).
67. See P.K. Surendran, *Times of India*, 25 Feb. 1993, 'Farm Lobby for Agro-unit'. For Joshi all this appears to have signified an abandonment of the famous one-point programme. A report in the *Indian Express*, 21 Sept. 1991, cited him as saying that the situation in 1979 when the Sanghatana was launched to demand remunerative prices for agricultural produce had drastically changed as the successive governments after Mr V.P. Singh hiked the remunerative prices (sic) of almost all the agricultural produce.
68. N. Karunakaran, *Indian Express*, 6 Nov. 1991, who also notes that according to Joshi, 'Exports ... ought to be sustained irrespective of the supply situation in the domestic market'.
69. Surendran, *Times of India*, 25 February 1993, an investment of over six crores.
70. Watts [1992: 92–93] describes some of the households involved in contract farming as a 'substantial middle peasantry' or 'prosperous middle peasantry'. Also see Korovkin [1992] on Chile.
71. Cited from Nadkarni [1985], compare Nadkarni [1987].
72. Such as Sharad Joshi inciting unemployed rural youth to break strikes, see Omvedt's admiring account of the Aurangabad convention of the Sanghatana in Omvedt [1993].
73. Omvedt's conception fails to explain why these movements have either not surfaced in, or totally ignored, the drought prone areas [*Nadkarni*, 1987] where the bulk of farmers

are dependent on the market for purchase of foodgrains on a net basis, see Harriss [1983: 87], where she notes 'the labouring peasantry is significantly dependent upon the market for the purchase of all cereals ...'. Are these sections not part of the 'peasantry'? Omvedt also wants to give her 'peasant movements' an anti-capitalist character, when it is crystal clear that Sharad Joshi stands not for the overcoming of capitalism but for its extension and more rapid development. With agribusiness controlling the conditions of capitalisation of agriculture, Omvedt suggests that the *whole* peasantry is exploited by capital, which is thus identified mainly with multinational-controlled agribusinesses: 'Today the *real* agrarian capitalist is not the 20-acre farmer hiring labour to seek the standard of living of a low-grade bank employee, but the agrobusinessman marketing seeds and fertiliser' [*Omvedt*, 1991: 2290; emphasis added – JB]. In more abstract terms, Omvedt envisages the growth of agricultural capitalism involving the 'growing exploitation of the peasant *as a peasant producer*' [*Omvedt*, 1987]. But the *theoretical* reasoning is spurious, since it divorces the idea of exploitation from labour and the labour process. In particular, her position is not equivalent to the idea that peasant labour is being *subsumed* into capital through the extension of capitalist control over the production and labour processes of the grower, as, for example, in (some or most forms of) contract farming, since the 'exploitation' she has in mind is mediated through the market (and state regulation of the market) and bears more resemblance to models of 'unequal exchange' than to the Marxist theory that exploitation by capital works through extension of control over the *labour process* (though the labour itself, the base for valorisation, may be of diverse types – unfree, independent commodity production and so on. The substantial peasants who control the sugar co-operatives are themselves *owners* of capital and *produce* capital, in part by seeking as far as possible to subsume the labour of a large mass of dispersed cane growers; they are not 'peasants' exploited *by* capital, but a distinct layer of capital in competition with sugar producers elsewhere in the world and with the international layer of capital represented by corporate-controlled agribusiness.

74. Balagopal [1987].
75. Boyack Upadhya [1988: 1376ff., 1433ff.]
76. Das [1988; emphasis added – JB]. Das describes the group as 'neither exclusively rural nor by any means "middle peasant" in character'.
77. The farmer-capitalists of Andhra have abstained from extra-parliamentary agrarian struggles. In Gujarat the movements reflect strong control by powerful groups of large landowners, who have the backing of equally powerful Opposition parties. By contrast, the Shetkari Sanghatana has consistently failed to penetrate the Congress base in western Maharashtra, and Joshi has frequently had to attack the 'sugar barons', see *Indian Post*, 20 Jan. 1988, *Indian Express*, 3 Oct. 1988.
78. Corporate restructuring is of course pushing the industrial revolution deeper than ever into the Indian countryside, with ultra-modern, hi-tech plants with small to medium workforces with no previous union traditions. But this movement is dominated by the large business groups, including existing and new international firms.
79. Patil [1988: 8].
80. Bhatt [1987b].
81. *Times of India*, 28 Feb. 1988.
82. Omvedt [1991: 2289].
83. See Nayyar [1991: 175ff.] on the impact of food prices on rural poverty.
84. Omvedt [1993: 2708].
85. See Balagopal [1991].

REFERENCES

Alves, M.H.M., 1985, *State and Oppositon in Military Brazil*, Austin, TX: University of Texas Press.

Badrinath, K., 1994, 'Bearing the Brunt: A Tale of Two Villages', *Frontline*, 11 Feb., pp.10–14.
Balagopal, K., 1987, 'An Ideology for the Provincial Propertied Class', *Economic and Political Weekly*, Vol.22, Sept., pp.1545–6.
Balagopal, K., 1991, 'Post-Chundur and other Chundurs', *Economic and Political Weekly*, Vol.26, Oct., pp.2399–2405.
Bhatia, B., 1992, 'Lush Fields and Parched Throats: Political Economy of Groundwater in Gujarat', *Economic and Political Weekly*, Vol.27, Dec., pp.A 142–170.
Bhatt, T., 1987a, 'Is the Congress Losing Ground in Gujarat?' *Telegraph*, 31 March.
Bhatt, T., 1987b, 'Kisan Sangh Exploits Political Vacuum in Villages', *Telegraph*, 1 April
Bhushan, B., 1984, 'Punjab: Politics and the Farmers' Agitation', *Business India*, 2 July.
Bhushan, B., 1988, 'Tikait's Gains from BKU Stir', *Times of India*, 19 Feb.
Bidwai, P., 1982, 'All Distinctions Go, says Sanghatana', *Times of India*, 3 Jan.
Bidwai, P., 1982a, 'Era of Defiance Ushered in', *Times of India*, 11 Jan.
Boyack Upadhya, C., 1988, 'The Farmer-Capitalists of Coastal Andhra' *Economic and Political Weekly*, Vol.23, July, pp.1376ff., 1433ff.
Breman, J., 1985, *Of Peasants, Migrants and Paupers: Rural Labour Circulation and Capitalist Production in West India*, Delhi: Oxford University Press.
Breman, J., 1990, '"Even Dogs are Better Off": The Ongoing Battle Between Capital and Labour in the Cane-fields of Gujarat', *Journal of Peasant Studies*, Vol.17, No.4, pp.546–608.
Chawla, S.S., 1987, 'To Power Through Land', *The Hindu*, 29 Oct.
Das, A., 1988, 'Power and Politics in Gujarat, II', *Times of India*, 26 Jan.
Gupta, D., 1988, 'Country-town Nexus and Agrarian Mobilisation: BKU as an Instance', *Economic and Political Weekly*, Vol.23, Dec., pp.2688ff.
Harriss, B., 1983, 'Relations of Production, Exchange and Poverty in Rainfed Agricultural Regions', *Economic and Political Weekly*, Vol.18, Sept., pp.A 82ff.
Hedge, D.V., 1985, 'Joshi Bides His Time', *The Nation*, 3 Feb.
Ketkar, K., 1985, 'Sharad Joshi – in Dubious Battle', *Economic Times*, 10 Feb.
Korovkin, T., 1992, 'Peasants, Grapes and Corporations: The Growth of Contract Farming in a Chilean Community', *Journal of Peasant Studies*, Vol.19, No.2, pp.228–54.
Ministry of Food Processing Industries, 1993, *Food Processing Industries in India. Investment Opportunities*, New Delhi.
Moraes, C., 1970, 'Peasant Leagues in Brazil', in R. Stavenhagen (ed.), *Agrarian Problems and Peasant Movements in Latin America*, New York, pp.453–501.
Murthy, S., 1988, 'The Peasant Revolt', *The Week*, 3–9 Jan.,
Nadkarni, M.V., 1987, *Farmers' Movements in India*, New Delhi
Nadkarni, M.V., 1985, 'Troubled Farmers: Their Stir for Better Times', *Deccan Herald* (Bangalore), 6 Oct.
Nair, J., 1993, 'Badanavala Killings: Signs for the Dalit Movement of Karnataka', *Economic and Political Weekly*, Vol.28, May, pp.911–12.
Nanda, R., 1989, 'BKU's Impact on Communal Front', *Times of India*, 30 July.
Nayyar, R., 1991, *Rural Poverty in India*, Bombay: Oxford University Press.
Omvedt, G., 1987, 'The "New Peasant Movement" in India', typescript.
Omvedt, G., 1991, 'Shetkari Sanghatana's New Direction', *Economic and Political Weekly*, Vol.26, Oct., pp.2287–91.
Omvedt, G., 1993, 'Farmers' Movements: Fighting for Liberalisation', *Economic and Political Weekly*, Vol.28, Dec., pp.2708–10.
Patil, S., 1988, 'Liquidating Marxism', *Frontier*, 23 April, p.7–10.
Purandare, B.M., 1984, 'Farmers' Stir May Hit Economy Hard', *Times of India*, 25 Feb.
Purandare, B.M., 1987, 'Sanghatana Sings "Song of Bharat"', *Times of India*, 13 Sept.
Rao, D.S.K., 1993, 'Groundwater Overexploitation Through Borehole Technology', *Economic and Political Weekly*, Vol.28, Dec., pp.A 129–34.
Watts, M., 1992, 'Peasants and Flexible Accumulation in the Third World: Producing Under Contract', *Economic and Political Weekly*, Vol.27, July (Review of Political Economy), pp.90–97.

Post-Script: Populism, Peasants and Intellectuals, or What's Left of the Future?

TOM BRASS

'Those freed from the past are chained to reason; those who do not enslave reason are the slaves of the past' – Georges Bataille [1985: 193].

INTRODUCTION

Arising from reflections on points made in the New Delhi workshop discussion concerning the relationship between the new farmers' movements in India and more generally the role of intellectuals and grassroots party activists in such mobilisations, this concluding essay considers the political implications of the form taken by much current intellectual/academic/activist opposition to modern capitalism, and in particular that linked to populism and its essentialist view of 'nature'. The object of this postscript, in short, is to aim a (Marxist) discourse-against at another, seemingly progressive (populist) 'discourse-against'.[1]

Claims about the persistence of petty commodity production notwithstanding, it is clear that globally the economic base of 'peasant economy' is subject to constant erosion by a neo-liberal capitalism, and that consequently the majority of peasants are now no more than part-time/full-time providers of labour-power for a world-wide industrial reserve army of labour.[2] Ironically – but unsurprisingly – this trend towards economic globalisation, or the attempt by capital to impose the law of value on an international scale, has been (and continues to be) accompanied both by the rejection on the part of peasants, farmers' movements and intellectual/academic circles alike of the universal categories associated historically with a socialist future, and by a corresponding retreat into the national/regional/local/ethnic particularisms/identities which characterise populism. Although the latter appears progressive in political terms, it is argued here that many currently-

---

Tom Brass is at the Faculty of Social and Political Sciences, University of Cambridge, Free School Lane, Cambridge CB2 3RQ.

fashionable forms of intellectual/academic/activist opposition to international capitalism derive their epistemological and political roots not from a forward-looking, progressive/modern anti-capitalism which seeks to transcend bourgeois society, but much rather its opposite: a backward-looking, romantic anti- (or post-) modern form of 'discourse-against', located in agrarian nostalgia and reactionary visions of an innate 'nature' that are supportive of conservatism, nationalism and even fascism.

In part, this retreat from socialist ideas has been justified in academic/intellectual circles by reference to the supposed unfeasibility/undesirability/unworkability of socialism itself. Because class struggle is generally regarded as a process waged largely – albeit unsuccessfully – from below, there has been a corresponding tendency to underestimate both the capacity and willingness of the colonial and post-colonial ruling classes in rural India to protect their interests by waging class struggle from above. Traditionally, the latter has taken two forms. First, violence by landlords, their private gangs, and the state, directed against the left in general and in particular its grassroots support among poor peasants and agricultural labourers. And second, the attempt from above to divide potential/actual political opponents by communalising the agrarian struggle.

Instead of opposing attempts to undermine class struggle by undermining communal identities invoked 'from above', however, sections of the Indian left have themselves invoked communal identity 'from below'. By not only supressing class issues in the name of a spurious peasant unity but also directly or indirectly communalising the agrarian struggle, the CPI/CPM/CP (ML) have – like their political opponents – also contributed to the undermining of a socialist project. Ironically, therefore, the parties on the Indian left have long adhered to precisely that mobilising discourse (operating through existing ideology/identity) which many of those critical of socialism now wish them to adopt.

THE GLOBAL RESTRUCTURING OF 'PEASANT ECONOMY'

The seemingly unstoppable expansion of capitalism, and the continuous renovation of the new international division of labour itself, in the form of relocation/restructuring and workforce recomposition (in terms of national/ethnic/regional/gender identity), raises an important theoretical question about the way we analyse capitalism, both in terms of its past and its future. This in turn leads us back to the unjustly neglected work of Rosa Luxemburg [1951] regarding the limits to capitalism, and in particular her views about the way in which non-capitalist formations are vital to the existence and further reproduction of capital. She argued that the basic contradiction facing capitalist accumulation was the inability of consumption to keep pace with production. In other words, the necessity on the part of capital to keep down the living standards of the working class necessarily placed a limit on the demand for its own commodities.[2a] However, in the short term a countervailing mechanism exists in the form of the ability of capital to unload part of its production on to populations outside the closed capitalist system; that is, capitalists can still find market outlets in non-capitalist contexts. But, she argued, the very process of capitalist expansion eventually destroys this safety valve, as increasingly acute competition for markets means that even non-capitalist contexts are ultimately incorporated into (and thus become a part of) capitalism. In the long term, therefore, this initial tendency toward crisis cannot be avoided.

The significance of Luxemburg's views about the relation between the non-terminal nature of capitalist crises (in the short term) due to the ability of capital to reproduce itself through access to hitherto untapped sources of cheap labour-power in non-capitalist contexts, and current theory about the globalisation of the industrial reserve army concern three developments. First, the contribution of rural populations driven off the land in so-called Third World contexts to the expansion of the global industrial reserve army of labour. Second, the role in this process of ex-socialist and actually existing socialist countries which are now being incorporated into the new international division of labour. And third, the impact of export-oriented industrialisation policies on crises of overproduction.

First, since the global pattern of agrarian transformation suggests that the major portion of Third World peasantries have no future simply as subsistence cultivators, what then are the implications for development theory of their economic role as part-time/full-time providers of cheap labour-power in what has been described by Fröbel *et al.* [1980] as the new international division of labour?[3] According to the latter view, post-war economic development has been characterised by a shift in production from the metropolitan capitalist countries, initially to the newly industrialising countries (Hong Kong, Korea, Singapore, Taiwan) and subsequently to yet other national contexts (China, Vietnam, Thailand, Malaysia). It is not so much that permanent work both in manufacturing and agriculture is declining (which is what some observers claim), rather that the same kinds of jobs are still being done, but now by casual labour. In other words, it is not the work that is declining so much as the pay and conditions of those who do it. This continuing process of restructuring/recomposition/relocation – and with it the globalisation of the industrial reserve army of labour – has been made possible by the breakdown in 'traditional' agrarian structures, the development of transportation and communication technology, the fragmentation of the labour process, and the deskilling of the workforce.[4] Significantly, many of the workers employed in the world market factories and export processing zones that characterise the new international division of labour come from rural backgrounds, driven from the land as 'peasant economy' ceases to be viable.[5]

Second, as the examples of in what are now *de facto* or *de jure* ex-socialist social formations (Russia, Eastern Europe, China, Vietnam) demonstrate, the new international division of labour applies not only to the relations between metropolitan capitalist countries and newly industrialising countries but – and perhaps more importantly – to the relations between the latter and other less developed countries. These are now engaged in what amounts to a Dutch auction, whereby governments attempt to undercut one another in terms of the cheapness and compliant nature of the workforce they are able to deliver to international capital. Accordingly, it can be argued that the labour-power of peasants in actually existing and ex-socialist countries is now being mobilised to give new life – and prolong the existence of – the world capitalist system. The extent of this paradox may be illustrated by the fact that both actually-existing and ex-socialist countries will be at the centre of the two main regional political economies now in the process of formation. One of these corresponds to the Pacific rim, and will involve the access by US and Japanese capital to the labour reserves of China. The other will be located in Europe, and will entail a similar access by European and other capitals to the labour reserves of Russia and Eastern European nations.

And third, the development of an authentically global capitalist economy, in which all countries adopt export-oriented production and simultaneously depress the living standards of their own workers in order to become more competitive, raises once again Luxemburg's thesis about the systemic limits to the realisation of surplus-value and the collapse of capitalism. Sooner or later, a situation is reached in which everyone is producing for export to populations who have had their own consuming power cut back in order to achieve the same end (that is, the realisation of a classic overproduction crisis).[6] It is significant, therefore, that – although not identified as such – not only is overproduction at root of farmers' grievances worldwide, in that the political slogan 'remunerative prices' is nothing other than a demand for prices higher than those which the free market 'awards', but more generally the trend towards globalisation has been accompanied by the resurgence in many contexts of nationalism and even fascism. Not only has the political right made gains throughout Europe, Russia and North America, therefore, but even in those cases where its electoral support has not increased it has nevertheless extended its influence in terms of defining the agenda of other ('moderate'/'democratic') political parties.[7]

It might be expected that, after the experience of the 1930s and its lessons concerning the link between fascism and national identity, there would be vigorous opposition to such developments, especially from Marxists, even from non-Marxist intellectuals and from the academic community generally. However, the opposite seems to be the case, in that much intellectual discourse not only condemns the kind of arguments about universals and internationalism which historically have been mobilised so effectively against the political right but now actually subscribes to methods (deprivileging, decentring, a-political deconstruction) and concepts (the 'plurality of the social', the acceptability of any/all forms of identity, an a-political process of empowerment/resistance) which make it difficult – if not impossible – to criticise the epistemological basis of such politics.

THE PRIVILEGE OF BACKWARDNESS OR THE BACKWARDNESS OF PRIVILEGE

The list of left scholars worldwide who have abandoned socialism (either directly, or indirectly by discarding its basic tenets) because of perceived difficulties with socialism itself is now very long. It extends from those in the UK associated with the journal *Marxism Today*, whose 'designer socialism' emphasises revolutionary form (style, consumerism) at the expense of revolutionary content, and who have not only made their peace with neo-liberal capitalism but now regard the latter ('new times') as a victory for the workers, to the genuinely confused.[8] There are also other reasons for such changes of political position, which have more to do with the prevailing intellectual fashion within academic contexts.

Recent events in Eastern Europe have been widely interpreted as the atavistic resurgence of long-supressed national/ethnic identities, or the reaffirmation of a 'natural' social order ('nature' reasserting itself). Consequently, the absence/demise of socialism is attributed by many ex-socialists as well as non- or anti-socialists to its unfeasibility, unworkability, undesirability, or to a combination of all these.[9] It is necessary, therefore, to ask the following three questions: why has this move away from socialist views taken place, why in so many instances have socialist views been replaced with populist ones, and what is the role of intellectuals in this transformation?[10]

Although the subject of much debate, populism encompasses a number of recognisable characteristics: generally speaking, therefore, it expresses antagonism towards the large scale, and more particularly towards politics, class, capitalism, socialism, and the state; by contrast, it endorses the small scale, and especially the idea of common interests ('the masses', 'the people') operating on the basis of grassroots/local initiatives.[11] In so far as it advocates micro-level empowerment of non-class (national/ethnic) identities on the basis of romantic anti-capitalist ideology realised by means of ('everyday forms of') resistance to the state acting in the interests of large/foreign/finance capitals, therefore, populism not only creates a space for but in some instances actually licenses nationalism and/or fascism.[12]

The idealised or romantic anti-capitalism of populist theory, however, is opposed not to capitalism *per se* but only to big business and/or foreign capital; for this reason, therefore, populism is not just compatible with an indigenous/(small-scale) capitalism but is also nationalist in its (political) orientation. The latter notwithstanding, populism operates with an anti-party-political framework ('above politics'/'non-political') which amounts to a 'refusal of politics'. Accordingly, it constitutes an attempt to de-politicise opposition to the state apparatus by capitalising on and the mobilising of 'resistance' without at the same time adressing the question of the class/classes which rule through this institution. Significantly, this 'refusal of politics' characterises not only populism but also much post-modern theory as well as the approach of new social movements.[13]

The importance of populism, and one of the reasons for its political acceptability, is that its anti-capitalism is regarded as a socio-economically progressive project. Unfortunately, it is usually forgotten that political opposition to and the rejection of capitalism as an economic system historically has taken – and, as populism generally and the farmers' movement in India in particular demonstrate, still can take – two opposing forms. On the one hand, therefore, anti-capitalism may involve the progressive 'going-beyond' of Marxism, which argues for both the desirability and possibility of socialism (the expropriation of property, its control by the working class through and by means of state power, and the harnessing of the means of production/distribution/exchange for social rather than private ends). On the other hand, anti-capitalism can also take a reactionary form, or the regressive 'going-back' to a pre-/non-capitalist 'golden age'.[14] The latter form of anti-capitalism entails a process of empowerment/resistance based on non-class identities (nationalism, ultra-conservatism, fascism), and is based on two distinct visions of 'nature': the first (and merely conservative) operates with a concept of 'nature' which is harmonious, while the second (and more openly fascistic) operates with a concept of a violent 'nature', or nature as 'red-in-tooth-and-claw'.[15]

In terms of constituency, because populism is anti-Marxist, and thus denies the existence/importance of class and class struggle, it claims as a consequence to be able to speak pluri-vocally, in the name of all socio-economic classes and interests within a given national context. In this way, and for this reason, populism not only focuses on an external enemy (foreign/international capital) but in the process discovers a spurious unity (= ideologically sanctifies) amongst a plurality of socio-economically differentiated components of 'the nation' – or amongst a plurality of nations, as Billig notes with regard to the new nationalisms of Rorty (see below) – and gives a (false) concreteness to 'nationhood'/'nationality'. Missing from this endorsement of 'plurality' is the element of contradiction, or the incompatibility between what are the opposing political views which arise on the basis of irreconcilable economic positions.

The difficulty with this endorsement by populism of diversity/difference is that the latter lies at the root of much conservative thinking.[16] Once the premiss of plurality is conceded, then it becomes possible to apply it to spheres beyond the 'cultural'; in short, it can now be argued that the uneven distribution of means of production, of wealth and power, is nothing more than a recognition of this principle at work. It should be recalled also that the apartheid system in South Africa was consecrated ideologically precisely by the principle of ('separate') development based on ethnic/racial/tribal 'diversity' and 'difference'.[17] This same principle structures the political programme of the Hindu chauvinist BJP in India, and also the claims to territorial sovereignty advanced by the contending parties to the conflict in ex-Yugoslavia.

The link between the resurgence of populism and the current territorial expansion of capitalism is not difficult to identify. In a context of a globally rampant neo-liberal capitalism, therefore, what is a universalising (economic) process necessarily licenses as its (politico-ideological) antithesis the invocation of the particularistic. Accordingly, throughout the so-called Third World (but by no means confined to it), this process of economic change is experienced ideologically as a cultural de-naturing, or a threat to religion, kinship, family, community, region, and nation. Consequently, in order to preserve all the latter against capitalist development, a rejection of capitalism defines itself against not only the economic aspects of this universalising tendency but also against its ideological manifestations (the pervasiveness of a western/modern/Enlightenment 'other'). Unsurprisingly, therefore, the specific form of anti-capitalism associated with the current spread of international capitalism manifests itself as a defence of the particular, or that which-is-specific-to-us (the '"us-ness"-of-"we"', the capitalist other's 'other'). Accordingly, in the absence of a specifically socialist project (see below), or in cases where such a project is under attack or in retreat, the internationalisation of capitalism licenses mobilization/resistance which is based not on class but on national/ethnic identity – or precisely that '"us-ness"-of-"we"' which, by denying class, creates a space for the romantic anti-capitalist 'above-politics' politics of populism which is nevertheless compatible with continued accumulation by indigenous/national capital.

Equally problematic in this regard is the claim by populism that, if nothing else, it has at least a politically progressive programme of action. Designed to achieve empowerment at the grassroots, therefore, populist action in so-called Third World contexts is undertaken not by political parties but rather by non-party/'apolitical' non-government organisations (NGOs).[18] Guided by the latter, such action takes the form of de-politicised mobilisation ('popular participation') or resistance by the 'people' or 'masses', and its object is merely to restore the *status quo ante* ('redemocratisation'). However, such organisational initiatives are not just contradictory but also irredeemably reformist, doing no more than work within the limits imposed by (an international) capitalism to which populism is in theory opposed.[19] In terms of politics, this kind of micro-level activity is at best of limited value: hence NGOs create the impression not only that problems are being solved but further that they can be solved locally, thereby diluting antagonism towards the existing class structure and diverting mobilisation away from other, large-scale and thus more effective forms of action.

The difficulty here is that in order to claim the accomplishment of grassroots empowerment based on resistance, it is necessary to deny what is interpreted as the passivity of 'victimhood'. Those who merely contrast the (positive) activity of resistance with (negative) passivity, and unproblematically endorse every/all variants of the former simply because they negate the latter, fail to notice that in its undifferentiated form ('action-against'), the process of resistance/empowerment subsumes radically different political solutions.[20] Hence the denial-of-victimhood requires in turn not merely the dissolution of analytical categories based on or leading to conflict (class, struggle) but much rather their inversion: accordingly, those social relationships hitherto regarded as forms of opression/exploitation can now be celebrated as evidence of empowerment/resistance.[21]

The process of historiographical revision which results from this inversion entails, amongst other things, the relativisation of slavery and fascism.[22] Despite many claims to 'newness', such revisionist theory is in fact both traditional and politically conservative. The appropriateness of the latter designation stems from revisionist epistemology: it invites us to change our perceptions (negative → positive) of – and hence to accept – the system in question (slavery, colonialism, capitalism, fascism). Furthermore, in so far as the existing is represented as the desirable, not only is there no need to change it but such situations are now actively to be sought. Not the least important issue raised by this kind of ontological transformation is the role played by the academy and its intellectuals in the current process of 'rethinking' politics generally, and in particular the spread of postmodernist views regarding the (im-)possibility/(un-)desirability of development.

There are a number of reasons for the shift in the current intellectual climate and the form this has taken. To begin with, for specifically material reasons the academy itself is extremely sensitive to changes in political power.[23] Linked to this is the theoretical/political effect of the contraction in academic employment: the postmodern method of deconstruction is politically expedient in a conservative or reactionary climate, since it renders valid anything and everything intellectuals have to say about a text – any text – and thus makes it possible for one thousand interpretations to bloom where only ten operated previously. Furthermore, postmodernism means that academics no longer have to be oppositional, nor do they have to represent views other than their own.[24] In other words, it legitimises not just a much wider range of theory but also the politically 'safe' views that are supportive of its practitioners' employment prospects within the academy.[25]

In the field of development studies, for example, much current non-/anti-Marxist theorising about the subject of agrarian change is divided between economists who mathematise it and non-economists who deny its possibility.[26] Into the latter category fall postmodernists, for whom Marxism is the main target, and who instead identify/endorse a process of 'resistance'/'empowerment' based on plural identities that celebrate 'diversity', 'difference', and 'choice'.[27] As Petras suggests, therefore, the change in political climate generally has produced a corresponding change in the views which prevail inside the academy.[28] Accordingly, if conservative ideas are once again academically in vogue, then it is not because the ideas themselves are intrinsically right (= theoretically acceptable) but rather because the times are right (= politically acceptable), in both senses of the term.[29]

Emanating from linguistic/literary theory and rapidly colonising the social sciences, postmodernism encompasses much of the populist discourse which permeates (among others) the Subaltern Studies project, and the theory about new social movements, 'everyday forms of resistance' and popular culture.[30] The influence of its methodological and theoretical impact on political practice cannot be overestimated. A form of radical conservatism which denies the fixity of meaning (or the theory of the floating signifier), postmoderism licenses an anti-universalistic, indeterminate, decentring and thus a relativistic interpretation of social existence, in which no particular identity or political view is – or can ever be – privileged. From within a postmodern epistemology, therefore, it is possible not merely to deny the necessity and/or desirability of changing an existing or traditional political order but also to espouse/endorse fascism with a clear conscience. Thus it cannot be without significance that a number of those closely linked to the postmodern project have also exhibited/espoused fascist political beliefs.

Despite eschewing metanarratives, it is evident from a number of examples that postmodern theory can be – and in the case of its application to so-called Third World contexts is – a discourse not just of nationalism but also, and ultimately, even of fascism. Two opposed views exist concerning the origins of this discourse, and the reasons for its impact on development theory. According to Petras [1990], postmodernism ('indeterminacy') is a Trojan horse that has entered development discourse from western capitalism. He attributes the decline of the organic intellectual and the coterminous ascendancy of the institutional intellectual to the funding of the latter by overseas agencies and research organisations, in the course of which neo-liberal, conservative and even fascist agendas emanating from the political right in metropolitan capitalist countries have been transferred to so-called Third World contexts, amounting to an ideological process justifying the accompanying economic recolonisation.[31]

By contrast, Ahmad [1992] has suggested that the postmodernisation of the intellectual is due to the opposite cause: the transfer of what is actually a traditional form of cultural nationalism from Third World colonial/ex-colonial contexts to metropolitan capitalist contexts through a process of privileging the migrant intellectual ('the figure of exile'), a point which applies with particular force to many of those who have contributed to the Subaltern Studies project.[32] The philosophy of Rorty is yet another example of the epistemological link between postmodern theory and what has been termed the 'new' nationalism.[33] For Rorty, therefore, a 'commonsense' ethnocentrism is both inevitable and at the centre of his own postmodern discourse. Since what he defends/endorses/celebrates is a socially non-specific notion of 'democracy', the locus of which is (an equally unspecific) 'society', because in his discourse the latter concept is theoretically interchangeable with 'nation', Rorty's philosophy is a defence of 'nationhood'/'nationalisms'.[34]

As the recently-disclosed fascist sympathies/links of a number of prominent intellectuals (Heidegger, Blanchot, de Man, McLuhan) who either prefigure or are associated with the postmodern project suggest, the latter is compatible not just with nationalism *per se* but also with its most reactionary form.[35] Although postmodernism's complicity with fascism is deemed 'uninteresting' by one commentator [*Harvey*, 1989: 357], it is impossible to dismiss the political and theoretical significance of this connection quite so easily.[36] In the case of Heidegger and McLuhan, for example, such complicity derives from the same cause: not only do both share a common anatagonism towards technology, but each espouses much the same kind of agrarian populist belief in a mythical/folkloric concept of 'primitive'/'natural'/(unspoiled) man.[37] In the case of McLuhan, the politically reactionary provenance of this anti-modernism/anti-capitalism is clear from his nostalgia for the lost tradition of the aristocratic/agrarian American South, which he contrasts favourably with the commercial/industrial utilitarian capitalism of New England.[38] In so far as he endorsed a policy of national self-sufficiency based on agriculture and small-scale industry, such views possessed for McLuhan a programmatic status.[39]

At first sight, the inclusion of the academically unfashionable work of Marshall McLuhan in the postmodern pantheon may be surprising.[40] Although not identified as such, however, many of the extremely fashionable views currently associated with the high priests of postmodernism such as Lyotard and Baudrillard are in fact prefigured in texts by McLuhan. For example, an opposition to metanarratives in general and Marxism in particular, and also the view about the impossibility/undesirability of representing the 'other'.[41] Of equal significance in this connection is the fact that, for McLuhan, the form of the electronic media is more important than its content in determining meaning, a theory which directly anticipates the view about 'hyperreality' now held by Baudrillard.[42]

Moreover, in keeping with postmodern theory, McLuhan operated with a concept of ideological indeterminacy, he deprivileged 'high' culture by erasing the boundary between it and the 'popular', and more generally focused on culture/consumption/ideology at the expense of the economic and production.[43] Similarly, his affinity with the populism of new social movements is evident from the way in which he condemned the corruption of the modern, eschewed politics for specifically 'non-political' ecological concerns, and his views about the desirability of decentralization to the smallscale.[44] For Heidegger, a universally objectifying (= 'inauthentic') technology similarly represents a negation not only of the subjectivity (= 'authenticity') of 'being' but also and with it of 'nature' and ecology.

Of particular significance in this regard is the fact that the object of

McLuhan's interest in technology in general and specifically the electronic media was to understand their dynamics in order to prevent them from bringing about the kind of social order he feared.[45] Unsurprisingly, therefore, McLuhan's concept of 're-tribalisation' by means of the electronic contraction of time/space, was itself premissed on the recuperation of an idealised version of a small-scale pre-literate society ('tribal culture') in which oral communication between individuals would be possible once again.[46] In a similar vein, Heidegger [1969: 50] laments the appearance of television antennae on peasants' dwellings, a view which suggests that – as with McLuhan – against modern technology (= 'artificial'/industrial/urban) is counterposed an ahistorical, romanticised concept of immanent (= 'natural'/rural) 'being'.[47]

The real importance of postmodernism, and its accompanying populist ideology, lies in its theoretical impact on political practice: it forbids socialism, encourages bourgeois democracy and nationalism, and allows fascism. Where agricultural labour is concerned, the consequences of such an approach are clear. In admitting that 'the complexity of drawing such a [postmodern] portrait makes it difficult to measure the changing fortunes – or rather the immiserisation – of agricultural labourers in India over the last two centuries', therefore, one postmodernist [*Prakash*, 1992: 46] finally recognises the conservative political effect of his idealist framework: the impossibility of analysing the *material* basis of exploitation, and thus formulating political solutions based on the identity of the subject as *worker*. It is necessary to ask, therefore: to what extent has this denial by those above (intellectuals, the academy) to those below (rural workers, poor peasants) of the existence/possibility/desirability of a *class* voice, as evidenced by a general refusal of politics and more particularly by a withdrawal of commitment to socialist politics, been offset by arguments/struggles for socialism by political parties of the left operating at the grassroots?

WHAT'S LEFT OF THE PAST, WHAT'S LEFT OF THE FUTURE?

Among the more serious reasons offered for the absence of a socialist India are regional/linguistic disparities, economic backwardness, the absence of a rural proletariat, and the Sino/Soviet split of 1964, with its resultant fragmentation and disunity among political parties/groups on the Indian left.[48] While all these may indeed be important contributory factors to the absence of socialism, here it is intended to focus on different causes connected with the form and content of the agrarian class struggle itself.

The central question remains, therefore, why has the attempt of the left in India to organise/mobilise rural support for socialist objectives not met with greater success? Just under three-quarters of all labour is still employed in agriculture, and landless labour – or a 'pure' agrarian proletariat – amounts to almost half of the rural population. If one adds to this the marginal holdings owned/operated by poor peasants, sharecroppers, and tenants, whose income derives mainly from the sale of labour-power and not the product of labour, there can be little doubt about the presence, size, and importance of a potential/actual socialist constituency. In short, elements which would benefit not from the present emphasis on individual peasant smallholding but rather from a programme of common ownership of the means of production, distribution and exchange. This in turn would entail not just opposition to the state – as in the case of the farmers' movements – but rather *control* of the state, which would permit a socialist government to expropriate private property and implement a system of collective agriculture, to integrate the latter into a national plan reflecting socialist (and not capitalist) objectives, to invest in raising the level of the productive forces in agriculture, and finally to protect this programme from a hostile national/international capitalist class.

Linked to this is the failure of the numerous and extensive rural mobilisations to lead to a socialist transformation. Why, therefore, have poor peasants and agricultural labourers not moved more resolutely and successfully towards socialism? Against the characterisation by Barrington Moore of rural India as politically passive, there is actually a long history of agrarian struggle.[49] It could be argued, for example, that the 1940s was a particularly fruitful time in which to put socialist ideas on the political agenda of rural India. To begin with, it was a period marked by the imminence of Independence, when the shape of the future was itself the object of discussion, conflict and decision. More importantly, the capitalist crisis of the 1930s, the 1943 Bengal famine and wartime devaluation had all combined to undermine petty commodity production in economic terms, and with it any residual 'loyalty'/legitimacy hitherto accorded to the landlord class.[50] And finally, the period was characterised by two significant and potentially revolutionary agrarian mobilisations: the *Tebhaga* or sharecroppers movement in Bengal, and the Telengana movement in Hyderabad state (now Andhra Pradesh).[51]

CLASS STRUGGLE FROM ABOVE, OR THE WEAPONS OF THE STRONG

Much of the argument about the failure of socialism in India tends to focus on problems specifically to do with socialism itself.[52] For example, the alleged incompatability between the socialist idea on the one hand,

and on the other the hard realities of everyday economic facts, as demonstrated by the impossibility of central planning, plus the inherent individualism of human nature. Socialists themselves have not only invoked these as reasons either for advocating radical changes in theory and practice or for abandoning socialism altogether, but have also contributed to this political introspection (problem = socialism) by theorising class struggle as a process waged largely – albeit unsuccessfully – from below. Implicit in such a view is the mirror image of the-struggle-from-below, or the notion that those from whom land, property, wealth, and title have been taken will meekly accept this situation and simply go away. Against such a view of ruling class passivity, there is abundant evidence that the ruling class in India has not merely struggled to great effect in order to retain/reproduce its power, but has done this relying on two weapons in particular: physical violence and dividing the opposition.

In both the colonial and post-colonial era violence and communalisation have frequently been used by the ruling class in India in the struggle to protect their interests. What is frequently underestimated, not least by socialists themselves, is the capacity of and necessity for the ruling class not merely to demobilise but also to destroy potential/actual opposition. In the case of India, therefore, violence (both actual and threatened) plays an important role in maintaining existing property relations, the major part of this violence being directed against the non-parliamentary left and its grass-roots support.[53] Over the 1982–86 period in Bihar, for example, there were around 16,000 recorded killings of labourers and poor peasants by large landholders, their private armed gangs, and the para-military agents of the state.[54] In this connection it is as well to remember two things: first, that these are officially recognised levels of agrarian violence, the actual figure being much higher; and second, that – like the 'disappeared' of Latin America – India has with the term 'encounter' similarly contributed to the international vocabulary of political torture and violent death [*Amnesty International*, 1983: 61–8].

The second important weapon utilised by the ruling class in India has been the capacity to divide and rule potential/actual opponents by communalising the agrarian struggle.[55] For example, when the power they exercised over their Tamil coolies was marginally curtailed by legislation enacted during the 1920s, and recognising that labour was becoming more independent and assertive as a result, tea planters in Ceylon turned explicitly to caste distinctions. Paying particular attention to religious observances and social custom, therefore, was a method of continuing control over labour by means of reinforcing and encouraging caste identity among their workers. For planters, the main attraction of caste was not its element of hierarchy, but rather the primacy and innateness of intra-workforce 'cultural' division; in short, a system in which everyone knew their place as ordained (and thus rendered immutable) by 'nature'. The role of the caste system in such a context was accordingly the reproduction of an inherent (or 'natural') sense of otherness *within* the ranks of the workforce that maintained a sense of unity (and thus work discipline) while simultaneously hindering any attempts to combine effectively against the planter class.[56]

This attempt to divide and rule by communalising the agrarian struggle was not confined to the British colonial ruling class. Like its British counterpart, therefore, in the course of the Tebhaga movement in Bengal and the Telengana movement in Andhra Pradesh during the 1940s, both Hindu and Muslim components of the landlord class in India invoked and emphasised communal identities in an attempt to counter the class identity constructed/exhibited by their tenants. Within the muslim community, where religious leaders discharged an important role in the transmission/reproduction of the authority and power exercised against muslim peasants by muslim landlords, religious identity was used in order to discourage muslim sharecroppers from participating in the process of agrarian mobilisation. Muslim landowners in Andhra Pradesh and Bengal emphasised that communist-led peasant unions in both contexts were first and foremost Hindu organisations. In Bengal they also repeated the Muslim League argument that the economic demands advanced by Muslim sharecroppers would be met in an independent Pakistan, thereby subordinating the class question to the national question.[57]

CLASS STRUGGLE FROM BELOW, OR THE WEAKNESS OF THE WEAPONS

It might be objected that the success of any or all these attempts to impose a particular kind of political consciousness from above is of necessity limited by the emergence from below of countervailing and antithetical forms of political consciousness. It is necessary to ask, therefore, about the extent to which just such a countervailing political consciousness has in fact developed at the rural grassroots: specifically, one that is either actually socialist or at least prefigurative of socialism.

The dangers inherent in equating 'the popular' with the existing can be illustrated in the case of India by reference to three interrelated issues. First, by the problematic espousal on the part of left political parties of nationalist and/or populist politics. Second, by the kinds of socio-economic forces (an undifferentiated peasantry) mobilised by the left as a result of this nationalist/populist political practice. And third, by the kind of ideology (communalism) it is necessary (or expedient) to invoke in this process.

The first point, about contradictory theory and practice, may be illustrated by the ambivalent manner in which the Indian left have viewed and continue to view both nationalism and Mahatma Gandhi as embodiments and expressions of 'the popular'.[58] To begin with, in the perception of the Soviet Union, Indian socialists and communists, the political role of Gandhi changed from a reactionary one during the 1920s to a progressive one in the anti-imperialist national movement during the anti-Fascist Popular Front of the 1930s.[59] More importantly, although critical of Gandhian politics, many on the Indian left nevertheless separate this from and simultaneously acknowledge his charisma and widespread personal following. To illustrate the view that leaders do not mould followers but are moulded by them, the influential CPI theoretician S.A. Dange has argued that: 'Gandhi learnt from the masses and led them. The individual became the instrument of history, made by the masses in action, who wrote with their blood the glorious pages of our freedom movement.'[60] By endorsing in this manner the view that a political leader like Gandhi unproblematically embodies 'the popular', the left necessarily becomes doubly entrapped: not only by having to support all those he claims to represent (the socio-economically undifferentiated 'masses') but also in the specific ways designated by him (nationalist/populist discourse and practice).

Having identified 'feudalism' and not capitalism as the principal enemy and focus of struggle in the countryside, therefore, the CPI have used this as a means for postponing revolutionary action in furtherance of socialism, and advocated instead political alliance with the 'progressive' national bourgeoisie against an external monopoly capitalism (plus its internal ally, feudalism). But even in cases where revolutionary action has been undertaken by the Indian left, its connection with socialism remains problematic. Ignoring the fact that for Marxism the peasantry does not itself form a class but is internally divided along class lines, and for this reason has no independent historical role, the CPI, CPI(M) and CP(ML) have – like the neo-populist opponents of Marxism – insisted on the political unity of the peasantry. Consequently, sections of the left have not only avoided confronting the economic issues which divided peasants along class lines but – in the spurious name of national and/or peasant unity – have also on occasion actively supressed an emerging class consciousness among poor peasants and agricultural labourers.

For example, in the late 1930s the CPI refused to continue in alliance with untouchable or Dalit organisations because the latter wished to make all landlords and industrialists the object of struggle; that is, those in the Congress Party as well as the British. By contrast, the CPI maintained that as Congress had to lead the 'joint national struggle against imperialism', it could not itself be the object of struggle.[61] Similarly, in the course of the sharecroppers' movement which took place in Bengal during the late 1940s, when tensions arose between peasants who employed sharecroppers and sharecroppers themselves, CPI activists in the peasant union attempted to encourage compromise, and argued that the focus of the peasant movement should be on anti-landlord policies, or the abolition of the *zemindari* system, on which no difference existed between rich and poor peasants.

Much the same occurred in Kerala during the 1960s, where a class of agrarian capitalists emerged from among the ranks of tenants who had themselves been active in the anti-landlord struggles led by the CPI(M), and who were also the beneficiaries of the land reform carried out during the 1960s.[62] Contradictions subsequently arose within this anti-landlord front when on the wages question, agricultural labourers encountered fierce opposition from their rich and middle peasant employers, activists who had been in the vanguard of the earlier struggles against the landlord class. The same was true of Andhra Pradesh during the 1980s, where in order to maintain 'peasant unity' the CPI (M) refused to act against rich and middle peasants who employed bonded labour.[63] Significantly, evidence from both Northeastern and Southern India suggests that tribals and poor peasants *are* willing to be organised along class lines and, where the left has formed a separate union for agricultural workers, a specifically class consciousness has indeed emerged.[64]

Instead of encouraging the development of class consciousness, however, there is in India a long history of communist support for communal groups. In other words, just like parties of the right, those on the left have actively promoted and encouraged communalisation, in the form of ethnic, caste or tribal consciousness. For example, in order to gain the support of the local tribal population in Tripura during the 1930s, the CPI advocated the disenfranchisement of royal ministers and bureaucrats not on the grounds of class but because they were immigrant Bengalis.[65] In Kerala during the 1940s and 1950s the CPI not only recruited a mass base by means of caste mobilisation through caste associations but also – like other political parties – chose parliamentary candidates from among the regionally dominant religious/ethnic community (Hindu, Christian, or Muslim) in order to attract the maximum support in that area.[66] In West Bengal over the 1967–71 period Naxalites from the CPI (ML) not only mobilised tribal support on the basis of cultural particularism, claiming that no difference existed between present struggles and those of the 1855 tribal insurrection, but also organised guerrilla activity on the basis of existing tribal and kin group authority at the village level.[67] Unsurprisingly, therefore, by the late 1980s, the CPI (ML) was engaged not in class but in caste struggle, mobilising backward caste Yadavs against high-caste Rajputs. Although Rajputs have traditionally consisted of substantial proprietors, a few of the latter are now also to be found among the ranks of the Yadavs, so in this situation caste does not correspond to class.[68]

In the light of all this, it is necessary to ask a number of difficult questions: how is it possible to advocate socialism and construct a specifically socialist politics when no account is taken of the fact that tribals and peasants are not just internally differentiated along class lines, but are willing to mobilise on this basis; when it is implied that the future for which socialists are fighting is no different from an idealised tribal past; and when no attempt is made to create prefigurative socialist forms, rather merely to lock onto existing ones, and operate through these. When, in short, what is promoted or engaged in is not merely non-socialist but actually *anti*-socialist political practice. The significance of this is that it both legitimizes and creates a space for communal discourse and practice, which can then be reappropriated by the parties of the political right in order to undermine any class solidarity that has been achieved.

CONCLUSION

Any attempt to analyse the rise of the new farmers' movements in India, and more generally the new social movements worldwide, must begin by locating this process in the context of post-war capitalist development. The latter has been characterised by a shift in production from metropolitan countries to newly industrialising and less developed countries, a relocation made possible (amongst other things) by the globalisation of the industrial reserve army of labour, leading to the loss of landholdings, livlihood and employment on the part of many peasants and workers in the so-called Third World. It is only as a response to this process of internationalisation of capitalism, and the resulting proletarianisation of the petty-bourgeoisie (petty commodity producers, artisans) and the deproletarianisation of workers, therefore, that the resurgence in many parts of the globe of populist movements proclaiming resistance/empowerment on the basis of a romantic anti-capitalism, anti-modernity, nationalism, even fascism, can be understood.

In this conservative and reactionary political climate, the role of the academy in general and intellectuals in particular has been to provide not so much explanations for this shift as justifying ideologically that which happens to exist.[69] Many non-/anti-Marxist intellectuals now espouse a form of laissez-faire politics/ideology (choice-making individuals selecting an identity through which to achieve empowerment by means of resistance) to match the laissez-faire economics of neo-liberal capitalism (the exercise of subjective preference in the free market by choice-making individuals). Consequently, in much contemporary analysis of the micro-level agrarian mobilisation occurring in the so-called Third World (the grassroots response to this globalisation and market liberalisation), the prevailing orthodoxy within the academy is that political empowerment/resistance structured by a postmodern rejection of meta-narratives/universals always and everywhere constitutes an unproblematically desirable end, a view arrived at without asking by whom and for what such a process is conducted.

The political dangers inherent in unproblematically equating the 'popular' with the existing, or an unmediated (and hence 'authentic') voice-from-below, is evident both from the socio-economic forces that have (and continue to be) mobilised in rural areas by the Indian left and from the ideology it uses for this purpose. In order to maintain what is in effect a spurious peasant unity, therefore, the CPI, the CPI (M) and the CPI (ML) have not merely avoided confronting issues which divide the peasantry along class lines but on occasion actively supressed an emerging class consciousness among poor peasants and agricultural labourers. Rather than class as a mobilising ideology, the left has – like its political opponents – frequently communalised the agrarian struggle, either by promoting/encouraging or by not challenging caste and/or tribal consciousness, thereby legitimising and creating a politico-ideological space for the anti-socialist communal discourse and practice of the political right.

In the case of India (and not only India), the conjunctural importance of this lies in its impact on the political response to economic depression. Like the 1930s, therefore, the current capitalist crisis licenses a politics of right-wing reaction, and in particular a nationalist resurgence; unlike the 1930s, however, *a strong countervailing socialist politics, with its emphasis on class and internationalism, is largely absent*. In part, this absence is due to the attempt by intellectuals generally and some Indian socialists in particular to replace socialism with an idealist form of anti-capitalist theory tainted with nationalist and/or fascist links. Contrary to received wisdom, therefore, the argument advanced here is that – in the case of India – socialism has failed to prosper not because the ground has been unfertile, nor because socialist ideas are unacceptable to workers, but much rather because the proponents of socialism have not been socialist enough, and consequently a socialist agenda has not actually been offered to workers. The significance of the latter is, as Rosa Luxemburg reminds us, that political choice is and can only ever be one between socialism and barbarism.

NOTES

1. What follows expands on some of the themes presented in my earlier contribution to this volume.
2. Given this neo-liberal capitalist expansion, it is necessary for marxists to ask whether self-empowerment *as peasants* is possible or even desirable. As is clear from the many entries on the relevant subjects contained in Bernstein, Brass and Byres [1994], the debate about the persistence/disappearance of 'peasant economy' – together with the accompanying development/planning/political strategies – is global in its scope.

2a. A similar point is hinted at by Varshney [1993: 195], who notes that the demand by the Indian farmers' movements to be allowed to export foodgrains may be determined in part by their perception of the lack of domestic consuming power sufficient to absorb surpluses generated by overproduction.

3. There is now a vast literature on the new international division of labour. For more recent texts on this subject, covering a variety of production processes in different contexts, see (among others) Boyd, Cohen and Gutkind [1989], Bustamante *et al.* [1992], Castles and Miller [1993], Chapkis and Enloe [1983], Chossudovsky [1986; 1988], Cohen [1987], Deyo [1989], Henderson & Castells [1987], Hoogvelt [1987], Kaplinsky [1993], Levidow [1991], Mitter [1986], Munck [1988], Ong [1987], Portes *et al.* [1989], Sanderson [1985], Sassen [1988], Sawers and Tabb [1984], Sklair [1990], Southall [1988], Stichter and Parpart [1990], Watts [1992], and Younghong [1989]. It is important to note that, in contexts where there is a history of successful working class movements and/or organisation, the neo-liberal economic policies associated with the new international division of labour require an un-/anti-democratic goverment and repressive politics (a strong state or military regime), in order either to pre-empt or to roll back gains obtained by local/migrant workers. In the case of Chile, for example, on the advice of the neo-liberal economists belonging to the Chicago school the Pinochet dictatorship restored expropriated land to previous owners, banned political activity, cut wages, ended food price controls for the urban working class and subsidies to smallholders. With the resulting collapse of domestic purchasing power, and the reversal of the internally-oriented development strategy advocated by the Economic Commission for Latin America (ECLA), agrarian capitalists in Chile now export traditional staple foods which the locals can no longer afford to international markets [*Hojman*, 1990; 1993; *Korovkin*, 1992; *Silva*, 1990]. In the case of the Philippines, it was not the product of labour but labour-power itself which has been inserted into the global circuits of capital, policed by an equally opressive regime: accordingly, it was the Marcos dictatorship itself which promoted and profited from the world trade in Filipino migrants [*CIIR*, 1987].
4. This particular development, linking the continuation of capitalist accumulation worldwide to an expansion in the global industrial reserve army of labour, would have come as no surprise to those Marxists belonging to earlier generations (such as Maurice Dobb) who both knew their Marx and remained marxists. Writing in 1950, amidst the bout of end-of-ideology triumphalism which accompanied claims that a Keynesian solution had banished recurring capitalist crises, Dobb [1955: 215–25] warned against the illusion that capitalism was compatible with a stable condition of full employment ('a situation where the sack had lost a good deal of its sting as a

disciplinary weapon, with the virtual disappearance of the industrial reserve army'), and pointed out that sooner or later capitalist profitability would require the restoration of unemployment.

5. It is important to note that the continuing disintegration of 'peasant economy' is due as much to economic stagnation as to growth. Although Green Revolution programmes have been effected in both India and China, therefore, export processing zones draw their labour-power from those who have been expelled from the land both as a result of more efficient productive technique and because of a lack of investment in agriculture. Hence the example of India, and in particular the pattern of migration from Bihar to Calcutta, suggests that as important as the displacement of rural labour due to economic development is the displacement of rural labour due to economic stagnation. And as the example of India [*Kumar*, 1989] also confirms, export processing zones are not merely a method whereby international capital circumvents domestic legislation regarding minimum wages, welfare provisions, employment of women and legal minors, trade union membership and the right to strike. Local capital producing for export also utilises export processing zones to get around regulations protecting its own workforce. In this respect, workforce restructuring effected by international capital is in fact no different from the workforce restructuring by national (as well as international) capital effected through the informal sector economy.
6. Consequently, it could be argued that only when the actually-existing forms of socialism (perhaps more accurately described as 'state capitalism') have finally been absorbed into the capitalist system, and the latter consequently comes to be seen as the only and obvious source of all our ills, will a truly socialist transition once again be on the political agenda.
7. The resurgence of the European political right extends from the Italian 'Alliance for Freedom' (composed of the Northern League of Umberto Bossi, Forza Italia of Silvio Berlusconi, and the neo-fascist National Alliance or MSI of Gianfranco Fini), the Republicaner Party in Germany, the National Front of Le Pen in France, to attempts in Spain to rehabilitate Franco [*Cheles, Ferguson and Vaughan*, 1991; *Ford*, 1992; *Gunn* 1989]. In North America, the resurgence of the political right has taken the form of populist politics advocated by Ross Perot in the USA and Preston Manning in Canada, and in Russia the populist politics of Yeltsin have created a space now occupied by the 'ultra-nationalist'/(fascist) Zhirinovsky.
8. Among this second group are to be found Ernesto Laclau, Chantal Mouffe, André Gortz, Julia Kristeva, David Selbourne, Paul Hirst, and Marvin Harris. For recantations, together with reasons, see *inter alia*, Gortz [1982], Hall and Jacques [1989], Harris [1992], Laclau [1990: 97ff.], Selbourne [1985: 181–210; 1987]. For critiques of this kind of political shift, see (among others) the texts by Callinicos [1989], Miliband [1985], Norris [1993: 1–28], Palmer [1990] and Sivanandan [1990: 19–59]. Significantly, in the light of the connection between populism and ecology, a number of ex-socialists have changed their political colour from red to green [*Bahro* 1982; *Gortz* 1980; *Lipietz* 1992].
9. Socialism is dismissed in this way by, among others, ecofeminism, new social movements and subaltern studies theory (see the other contribution to this volume by Brass). In this regard it is perhaps salutary to recall comments made by Trotsky about a similar period of socialist disarray during the First world war, when nationalist divisions among socialists resulted in the collapse of the Second International. 'At first glance', he observed,

   > it may appear that the social revolutionary prospects of the future are wholly deceptive. The insolvency of the old Socialist parties has become catastrophically apparent. Why should we have faith in the future of the Socialist movement? Such skepticism, though natural, nevertheless leads to quite an erroneous conclusion. It leaves out of account the good will of history, just as we have often been prone to ignore its ill will ... It is not Socialism that has gone down, but its temporary historical external form. The revolutionary idea begins its life anew as it casts off its old rigid shell. This shell is made up of ... an entire generation of Socialists that has

become fossilized in self-abnegating work of agitation and organization through a period of political reaction, and has fallen in the habits and views of national opportunism or possibilism [*Trotzky*, 1918: 34–6].

10. Historically associated with the formulation of rules, the objectification of knowledge (= science), and the legitimation/exercise of power [*Chomsky*, 1982; *O'Brien and Vanech*, 1969; *Said*, 1994], intellectuals generally have been distrusted by populist movements. Such anti-intellectualism notwithstanding, as the example of not only Sharad Joshi himself but also Vandana Shiva and Gail Omvedt demonstrate, intellectuals do in fact discharge important agenda-setting roles in the farmers' movement in India. In short, the political views of intellectuals *are* important, and *do* matter.
11. General theoretical interpretations of populism include Ionescu and Gellner [1969], Laclau [1977], Kitching [1982], and Worsley [1984: 112ff., 293–95]. Other, more specific aspects to do with populism and peasant economy are covered in Byres [1979], Bernstein [1990], Brass [1991a] and de Janvry [1980].
12. For the link between populism and fascism, see the texts by among others Ferkiss [1957; 1961], Holbo [1961], Preston [1990], Sohn-Rethel [1978: 122–3] and Wiles [1969: 176–7]. For the link between populism and anti-semitism, see Eidelberg [1974], Ionescu [1969: 116–18] and Pavloff [1978: 84ff.]. The reactionary character of such kinds of anti-capitalism is evident from the utterances of those associated not only with Nazism in Germany and Fascism in Italy during the 1930s but also with the resurgent political right in the present conjuncture. Hence the reactionary/anti-Enlightenment proclamation of Italian fascists that '[w]e represent the antithesis . . . of all that world of the "immoral principles" of 1789', while the Nazis stated analogously that 'The year 1789 will be erased from history . . . [w]e wish to destroy the immoral ideology of the French Revolution' (quoted in Guerin [1974: 168]; for opposition to the French Revolution and to the Enlightenment on the part of fascism generally, see Nolte [1965]). Similarly attributing an 'alien'/'cosmopolitan' communism to an equally 'alien'/'cosmopolitan' capitalism, Zhirinovsky describes his agenda for Russia as follows:

    > Today we are in the bath-house. We are washing off this muck, this filth, plastered on us by the twentieth century. Sometimes this calls forth blood. It's bad, but apparently necessary for us and our bitter country, so that we can finally wash away the satanic dirt [= Bolshevism] which came to us at the beginning of the century, let loose on us by the West to poison this country and destroy us from within . . . via cosmopolitanism, via the influence of alien religions, alien ideas and an alien way of life. We will get rid of it all ('Bear with a Sore Head', *The Guardian*, London, 7 Jan. 1994).

13. An example of the postmodern 'refusal of politics' is Foucault [1991: 173]. There are many variants of this 'refusal of politics'. One is to announce, as many anthropologists have done [*Clifford and Marcus*, 1986; *Geertz*], 1988, that after all their form of practice is too subjective, and thus a way of knowing about the 'self' rather than the 'other'. In part, this reconstituting of participant/observation research methodology as a variety of literary practice (anthropology = fiction) is a conjuncturally symptomatic way of abolishing/denying the politically unpalatable reality (the effects of capitalist development, the non-existence of the 'noble savage') that much contemporary fieldwork discloses (for evidence of which see Geertz [1988: 99–101], although he himself does not make this point). Another variant of this 'refusal of politics', also in the realm of development discourse, is the concept of 'rent-seeking' associated with neo-classical/neo-liberal 'new political economy', a theory whereby the political right challenges what it perceives as the illegitimate operation of government monopoly in the capitalist market. As Bagchi [1993: 1729] correctly observes, 'there is nothing particularly novel about the idea of earning rent as an obstacle to progress. What is novel is a deliberate restriction and in some cases an arbitrary redefinition of the concept of rent-seeking and its application to denigrate all government intervention and virtually abolish the domain of politics in LDCs.' It scarcely needs pointing out that the postmodern 'refusal of politics' from below coincides rather too neatly with the

argument from above about the desirability of a similar 'refusal of politics'; unsurprisingly, the reason why the political right advocates that the state should not be an object of class struggle is precisely because its capture by the proletariat is the one (revolutionary) act that ruling classes everywhere fear most.

14. The redemptive myth of a 'golden age', which structures the many and recurring proclamations in the midst of capitalism by populists/populism announcing the 'end-of-history' and the 'end-of-ideology', is also present in the symbols, rites, and religious customs/ceremonies of most non-capitalist social formations [*Eliade*, 1954], where it involves the ideological attempt to replace the mortality of profane time (= history) with the immortality of sacred time (= the eternal present in the Garden of Eden). Far from disappearing, it is argued by Bausinger [1990] that such traditional beliefs expand/extend to accompany the spread of capitalism, a process structured by the commodification/reinvention of folklore. As Williams [1973: 8–12] reminds us, in the case of English culture the literary invocation of a pastoral myth is the subject of infinite historical regression, stretching back at regular intervals from the 1930s to the 1370s, at each stage of which there is said to exist an image of a (vanishing-to-be-recuperated) 'golden age' constituted by the timeless agricultural rhythms of 'Old England'. It is not necessary to endorse the conclusion presented in the text by Wiener [1981], that in England from the mid-nineteenth century onwards the pastoral myth blocked the development of industrial capitalism, therefore, to accept the validity of his argument regarding the *ideological* pervasiveness of this myth. In a sense this is unsurprising, since as Deutscher [1955: 44–5] and others have pointed out, Marxism – which challenges such myths in the name of history – has had little impact on English intellectuals.

15. Seemingly antithetical, these concepts of 'nature' are actually different sides of the same ideological coin, and constitute a Social Darwinist discourse in which humanity (instead of shaping) is shaped by 'nature'. Accordingly, the harmony which exists in the pastoral version is in fact underwritten by the violence of the 'red-in-tooth-and-claw' variant, in that a 'natural' order is not merely inscribed in 'nature' but the latter periodically exercises its physical power in order to restore/maintain this. A synthesis of these apparently antithetical views about 'nature' is contained in the work of Hardin (see below), for whom the 'natural' violence of famine, floods, drought, infanticide and so on, in so-called Third World countries is nothing other than 'nature' systematically restoring the 'natural' carrying capacity (= 'harmony') of given national populations in these contexts [*Hardin*, 1977: 63–4, 68, 93–5, 113–14; 1993: 175; *Hardin and Baden*, 1977: 113–25]. Unlike Hardin, for whom the violence of 'nature' is rational, for Foucault it represents the desirable 'otherness' of irrationality: as suggested by Miller [1993], therefore, the Dionysian rejection of reason on the part of Foucault is an attempt to recuperate a concept of 'the pre-rational/primitive', a process whereby the act of death/self-obliteration itself becomes a surrender to the ultimately unconquerable and innate power of 'nature'.

16. That an apparently progressive endorsement of diversity/difference is not merely compatible with but actually supportive of the political right is evident from the following observation [*Epstein*, 1970: 115]:

> Conservatives not only emphasize variety, they also love it. The spontaneous development of human society has led to a colorful richness which conservatives find emotionally and aesthetically satisfying. They do not bother to rationalize this preference in terms of any metaphysical system, for they consider it to be simply 'natural', that is in accordance with the 'real' needs of 'uncorrupted' human nature. Conservatives usually accuse radicals of wishing to destroy existing variety – expressing what is old and familiar – by implementing the precepts of an abstract and uniform rationalism ... The conservative view of the world affirms in theory (not always in practice) the existence of a plurality of competing values.

That diversity/difference has an important place in the conservative canon is also confirmed in the influential text by Kirk [1954: 17–18]. The reactionary programmatic application of diversity/difference is evident not just from the obvious example of 'separate development which structured the Apartheid system in South Africa, but also from the recent pronouncements of Gianfranco Miglio, an organic intellectual of the Northern League in Italy, whose secessionist proposal to re-establish 'Etruria' is based on claims of ethnic difference/diversity between the productive inhabitants of the Northern region and the unproductive/parasitical Mediterranean 'mentality' of southern Italy ('Prophet of Italy's Loss', *The Guardian*, London, 1 December 1993). Like the de-internationalised/anti-universalist ultra-nationalism/(fascism) of Zhirinovsky in Russia, it is only by a process of 'ethnic cleansing' that the nationalism of the Northern League can be recuperated and restored to a pristine authenticity within Italy as a whole, so as to be able then to co-exist and/or compete with other such (internally 'cleansed' but externally 'polluting') nationalisms (see below for the theorisation by Rorty of the 'new nationalisms').

17. Unless it is to be regarded as *innate*, immutable, and therefore part of 'nature', any concept of 'difference' has – and can only ever have – its origin in a class structure which first assembles and then ideologically consecrates it. By conferring a 'natural' fixity on 'difference, postmodernists who reify/essentialise it simultaneously naturalize the (bourgeois) socio-economic order which constructs this (historically-specific notion of) 'difference' in the first place.
18. Like new social movements, much NGO activity is frequently built around a single issue (gender, region, religion, ethnicity, or ecology), is non-class-specific, is anti-state, and seeks to improve – but not transcend – bourgeois democracy. In part, therefore, the current acceptability of voluntary organisation activity in many so-called Third World countries can – again like new social movements – be attributed to the attempt to foster development without politics in general, and without the politics of class in particular.
19. That NGOs are not merely conservative (see, for example, Sherman [1992]) but in some instances profoundly reactionary is clear from the case of what proudly claims to be 'the oldest human rights organization in the world', the Anti-Slavery Society. During the mid-1980s, one of the members of its governing body published a text (Sawyer [1986]) defending the apartheid system in South Africa, a book which carried an endorsing forword by the joint President of the Society. That complicity of this kind has a long history where this particular NGO is concerned is evident from the experiences of Sol Plaatje, the first secretary of the African National Congress, who described the Anti-Slavery Society as 'the South African government's most sturdy defender' [*Willan* 1984: 201].
20. Much of this kind of theorisation is associated with the arguments of those (e.g. Colburn [1989]; Haynes and Prakash [1991]), who adhere to the currently fashionable 'everyday forms of resistance, framework derived from the analytical approach of Scott [1976; 1985; 1990]. What such theorisations overlook is that, in a period of capitalist crisis when an authentically socialist alternative is absent (in other words, where parties of the left are reformist, on the retreat, and trade unions are under attack), empowerment/resistance arising from working class opposition to and protest about capitalism can easily be channelled into the romantic/reactionary form of anti-capitalism of the political right. This is especially true of situations where a lack of trade union and class solidarity/experience is combined with a capitalist restructuring of its workforce that results in competition for jobs among workers of different ethnic/national/gender identities. In such circumstances, the result is that anti-capitalist antagonism/conflict is projected in the (racist/nationalist/communal/sexist) idiom of ethnicity/nationality/gender.

21 It can now be argued that, because women are (obviously) neither passive nor ignorant, whatever they do is what they choose to do. In the case of gendered economic activity such as informal sector participation in so-called Third World contexts, therefore, it follows that women 'choose' and benefit from low-paid forms of self-emploment such as street vending (see, for example, Nuñez [1993]). With this kind of essentialist assertion, it is possible to not merely to justify but actually to characterise as empowerment any and all forms of economic exploitation. For a

critique of postmodern concepts of 'self-empowerment' mediated through the institutions of 'popular culture', a process whereby unfree workers symbolically 'win' battles in the ideological domain which in economic terms they either lose or do not fight, see Brass [1993b]. For examples of this process as applied to unfree labour in Peru and India, see Taussig [1984] and Prakash [1992].

22. As the case of the German *historikerstreit* suggests, historiographical revisionism of all kinds begins by relativising horror/terror/(exploitation/unfreedom) and ends up by rehabilitating it. Like the attempt to 'normalise' fascism, revisionist historiography about unfree labour during the nineteenth-century attempts to combat negative portrayals of black slaves on the cotton plantations of the antebellum American South [*Fogel and Engerman*, 1974; *Fogel*, 1990], of bonded labour in the Indian state of Bihar [*Prakash*, 1990a; 1990b], and of Pacific island labour employed on the sugar plantations of Queensland [*Shlomowitz*, 1981; 1985] by emphasising what is claimed to be the 'positive' aspects of economic and/or politico-ideological autonomy. For adherents of this viewpoint, the driving force in this tension-free economic model is not the coercion associated with class struggle and surplus extraction but rather the non-conflictive process of individual choice-making workers exercising autonomy ('subjective preference') by responding to 'pecuniary rewards' in an harmonious free market. Accordingly, slave labour on the cotton plantation of the American South, bonded labour in Bihar, and indentured Pacific islanders in Queensland are consequently depicted by this revisionist historiography as uncritical collaborators in their own exploitation by the planter, moneylender or farmer. For critiques of revisionist arguments about unfree labour in Latin America, Asia, and elsewhere, see among others Brass [1990; 1991b; 1993a; 1993b] and Brass and Bernstein [1992].

23. There is an overwhelming sense of *deja vu* regarding the current rush within the academy to distance itself from marxism. In their reviews of the history of the 'post-Marxist' retreat of intellectuals, both Callinicos [1989: 162ff.] and Petras [1990: 2145] show how exactly the same kind of arguments claiming to have superseded Marxism were deployed in the 1930s, the 1950s and the 1960s. As suggested by the case of the media publicity accorded in the mid-1970s to the 'new philosophers' [*Jenkins*, 1977: 116–24], a group of vehemently (ex-)/anti-Marxists proclaiming 'end-of-ideology'/'a political' views such as 'in the end, there is no world, only discourse', 'reason is totalitarianism', and celebrating the 'new resistants' (feminists, ecologists, minority groups), it cannot be accidental that the increasing access of intellectuals to a mass audience via the electronic media [*Debray*, 1979] is accompanied by a self-imposed or – more usually – a willingly espoused conservatism/conformity.

24. Significantly, one important political effect of the challenge by postmodernism to the notion of representation is that – in the name of 'self-empowerment' – it henceforth frees intellectuals from the need to base their arguments on the views of an 'other' (about which, see Foucault [1991: 159–60]), and in particular of a working class 'other'. They can now espouse bourgeois ideology without guilt.

25. On this point, see Lehman [1991: 73, 74–5], who refers to depoliticised deconstruction as 'yuppie radicalism', a non-threatening (pseudo-) oppositional form designed to give the impression of dissent in an increasingly conservative academic environment subject to cutbacks and declining employment/promotion opportunities. There is more than a little truth in a recent fictional account [*Adams*, 1985: 77] of just this kind of process: accused by philosophers that it would displace them, the Deep Thought computer programmed to discover the meaning of Life, the Universe and Everything, replied that

> it occurs to me that running a programme like this is bound to cause sensational public interest and so any philosophers who are quick off the mark are going to clean up in the prediction business ... Obviously you just get on the pundit circuit. You all go on the chat shows and the colour supplements and violently disagree with each other about what answer I'm eventually going to produce, and if you get yourselves clever agents you'll be on the gravy train for life.

26. For an example of an economist who reduces development theory to an epiphenomenon of mathematics, see Srinivasan [1989].

27. For attempts to apply a postmodern/(post-structuralist) framework to development theory, see the texts collected in Pieterse [1992] and Hobart [1993]. Although rightly seeking to locate labour studies in a global context, and similarly aware of the threat that postmodernism constitutes for such a project, Bergquist [1993] nevertheless insists on the value of a postmodern approach in the process of 'constructing a viable democratic politics in the world today'. It is not necessary to consider here the self-styled and self-serving 'impasse debate' (Schuurman [1993]), which is currently in the process of vanishing up its own cul-de-sac. The 'new' agenda for development theory proposed by Booth [1993] in the most recent contribution to this 'debate' turns out to be nothing more than yet another thinly-disguised postmodern endorsement of 'resistance/empowerment' inside the capitalist system, a process based on plural identities celebrating 'diversity', 'difference' and 'choice'. The suspicion remains that, as in the case of postmodernism itself, the problem for Booth lies not so much with the agenda for the 1990s as with that of the 1790s.
28. As with all fields of academic study, development theory has at the margins its share of practitioners who, not having anything of significance to say, nevertheless feel sufficiently emboldened to proclaim old/new political allegiances in keeping with these neo-liberal times. Some have now emerged from the political closet: unsurprisingly, therefore, the 'search' by one such (Hawthorn [1991; 1993a; 1993b]) for a 'new' text about Third World politics leads back to Hume and Constant (for the latter's endorsement of views about the sacredness of individual property and the market, the central emplacements of 1990s neo-liberalism, see Fontana [1988]; for Constant's position in the pantheon of conservatism, and evidence of his now-fashionable pessimism structured both by a nostalgia for 'ancient liberties' and by a distinctly postmodern aporia, see Hayek [1967: 160], O'Sullivan [1976: 44–52] and Eatwell [1989: 66–671]). Others, like Booth (see previous footnote), have held the same views all along, and can thus legitimately claim to have been consistent. Yet others have changed their minds and end up endorsing in the 1990s the very theory criticised in the 1970s. There is perhaps a different kind of consistency at work here: the views espoused in each decade were/are the mainstream academic orthodoxies of their period.
29. As Petras [1990: 2146] comments wryly: 'Under conditions of maximum capitalist power ... the cost to the intellectuals of retaining their Marxist commitments goes up and the benefits go down, increasing the incentives to rationally choose to operate within the framework of neo-liberal political economics.' That even Social Darwinist discourse has penetrated the agenda of development strategy is evident from the transformation that has taken place in the discussions of the political right concerning famine. This is best illustrated by comparing two symptomatic texts, both by important members of the (Atlantic) ruling class, but with the crucial difference that one was made in the development decade of the 1960s and the other during the less optimistic (post-modern/neo-liberal) present, when the hitherto unutterable is once again back on the political agenda of capitalism. In the opening address to the Conference on '*Subsistence and Peasant Economics*' in 1965, John D. Rockefeller announced that the main issue confronting humanity was to increase food supply to meet the rising population levels (see Wharton [1970: 3–5]). His proposed solution was to expand the output of the subsistence producer, an objective of the subsequent Green Revolution programme. Nearly a quarter of a century later, the position has been reversed. In another keynote intervention, the Duke of Edinburgh [1989], who married into a large landowning family, argued in the 1989 Richard Dimbleby Lecture that humanity was now in a situation where the 'natural' balance has been upset. According to this view, ecological disaster threatens because demographic growth nowadays is due to the fact that more efficient food production permits more people to survive. In other words, whereas for Rockerfeller in 1965 the main problem was that population increase had to be met with a corresponding increase in food production (that is, the objective is to buy off potential opponents), for the Duke of Edinburgh in 1989 the main problem had now become one where an increase in food output itself enabled more people to

survive, which in turn threatened humanity with ecological disaster. From this discourse it follows that, to maintain the existing ecological balance requires less food, the desired object of which is to enable less people to survive (that is, the policy has now become to kill off potential opponents). The subtext of this argument is nothing other than a 'green' variant of Social Darwinism which synthesises ruling class fears about population growth as a threat to its power with popular concerns about food overproduction and ecological destruction. The price humanity is being asked to pay to avoid the latter and maintain 'nature' itself in a 'natural' balance is once more to accept the inevitability (or 'naturalness') of famine as a solution to population growth in the so-called Third World. That Social Darwinism continues to flourish within the academy itself is evident, for example, from the 'lifeboat ethics' associated with the work of Garrett Hardin ([1960; 1977; 1993]; see also Hardin and Baden [1977]), a 'deep ecologist' whose views about the demographic impact on the environment of the removal of Malthusian 'checks' are perhaps the most sinister confronting development strategy. Like the Duke of Edinburgh, Hardin posits a 'natural scarcity' in which resources are finite, and is accordingly opposed to technical progress and development generally because these overload global 'carrying capacity' and threaten existing (= capitalist) property relations. Hardin's view is that global resource transfers from rich to poor nations either discourage self-sufficiency (economic aid = 'permanent parasitism', a view echoed by Kirk [1968]) or deplete common resources (= non-individual property); consequently, he maintains that inequality is functional for survival, he defends private property as a 'natural' arrangement, and to protect the latter he advocates the adoption of immigration controls by rich nations [*Hardin*, 1977: 46ff, 80–81, 92–3, 125–6; 1993: 23–5, 278ff., 300, 309; *Hardin and Baden*, 1977: 16ff., 27, 67]. For Hardin [1960: 53, 55, Figures 3–4 and 3–5], therefore, for whom the laws of 'nature' must be obeyed, the equilibrium of neo-classical economic theory represents within society exactly the same kind of 'natural' balance as the Darwinian scheme favouring the 'survival of the fittest' in nature itself. His reactionary views combine the sociobiology of Wilson, Ardrey and Dawkins with (among other things) the politics of Edmund Burke and the economics of Soddy, a 'money-reformer' with fascist connections [*Hardin*, 1977: 98, 112–13, 137, 145; 1993: 76]. (For the epistemological link between on the one hand sociobiology, and on the other racism, conservative ideology and Hume's philosophy of nature, see Barker [1981]; for the influence of Hardin's views on debates about ecology, population and the environment in so-called Third World contexts, see Basu and Mishra [1993], Bradford [1989], Bramwell [1989: 217–18], Davis and Bernstein [1991: 315ff., 323ff.], Ferkiss [1993: 176–7], Jodha [1990], McCormick [1992: 69ff.], Mellor [1989: 32–33], Merchant [1992: 66–8] and Thompson [1992: 14–15, 129–31, 162, 164–5, 172–5].)

30. This theme is explored more fully in my other contribution to this volume.
31. In seeking to understand the link between intellectuals, nationalism, peasants and populism, it is necessary to recognise just how deeply entrenched conservatism is in many of the academic institutions of metropolitan capitalist countries. Thus the emergence in North American and Australian academic circles of a revisionist historiographical approach to the issue of chattel slavery in the antebellum American South and Pacific island indentured labour in Queensland has (amongst other reasons) been due to the need to create a 'usable history', or a requirement on the part of the inheritors to present the process of plantation slavery and colonisation in a more favourable light. In the UK the process has been somewhat different, since behind the rhetoric of plurality and democracy the ancient academic institutions continue to be under the sclerotic political control of the same kind of madrigal singers and recorder players so accurately depicted 40 years ago by Kingsley Amis [1961]. Like the Welches, therefore, those who subscribe to a culturally-determined concept of 'Merrie England' nearer home unsurprisingly extend this same analytical framework into the cultural domain of the 'other' in so-called Third World contexts. Celebrating culture on their own account, they are quick to identify in the cultural *specifica diferentia* of the 'other' a similar form of empowerment within the existing socio-economic system,

contributing thereby to the now increasingly familiar refrain of 'Merrie Everywhere Else'.

32. Concerning the contradiction which derives from the privileging of the migrant-in-exile without taking into account the class origin of this subject, and the way in which this structures the political content of his/her discourse, Ahmad [1992: 12–13] observes that

    the ideological ambiguity in these rhetorics of migrancy resides in the key fact that the migrant in question comes from a *nation* which is subordinated in the imperialist system of intra-state relationships but, simultaneously, from the *class*, more often than not, which is the dominant class within that nation [which] makes it possible for that migrant to arrive in the metropolitan country to join not the working classes but the professional middle strata, hence to forge a kind of rhetoric which submerges the class question ... (original emphasis).

33. For the theorisation of the 'new' nationalism(s), see Billig [1993]. Significantly, the concept of 'new nationalism(s)' finds an exact echo in Hardin [1993: 295], for whom the 'formula for survival and progress is ... [u]nity within each sovereignty: diversity among sovereignties'. Equating nationalism with a 'natural' tendency towards 'tribalism' and 'tribal competitiveness/warfare' (tribe = nation = nature), Hardin [1977: 132] accepts that such a position amounts to a naturalisation of the existing socio-economic system (= bourgeois nationalism), and hence a justification of its inequalities. Although he notes that a system based on 'many antagonistic but co-existing tribes ... sounds very much like the world we now live in', and is thus profoundly conservative, Hardin [1977: 133] nevertheless concludes that 'it is essential that we see that it would be unwise to try to escape this condition'.

34. Hence the observation [*Billig*, 1993: 78] that:

    ... the phase 'the institutions of democracy' (which Rorty often uses) omits something crucial. In the modern age, democratic institutions developed within the nation-state, and, therefore, nationhood can be seen as one of the institutions of democracy. If so, then Rorty's argument has an unstated theme: to protect democracies and their institutions, one ('we') must protect the 'societies' in which they are situated. Unless otherwise stated, this means protecting the institutions of nationhood ('our' nationhood). To protect a nation is to protect a national identity, which, as Rorty recognizes, distinguishes that community from other communities. In the context of nations, this means preserving the nationalist myths by which nations depict themselves as unique 'imagined communities' – as 'our country'. In this way, Rorty's argument contains within itself an implicit defence of the world of nations, and thus a world of nationalisms.

35. For the fascist sympathies/complicity of Heidegger, Blanchot, de Man, and McLuhan, and more generally on the connection between postmodernism, linguistic deconstruction, decentring/deprivileging, and fascism, see Farias [1989], Ferry and Renaut [1990], Kermode [1991: 102–18], Lehman [1991], Marchand [1989: 27], Mehlman [1980: 808–29], Ott [1993], and Sluga [1993]. As worrying as the postmodernism/fascism link – or, indeed, perhaps more so – is the refusal of those such as Derrida either to accept the fact of this complicity or to acknowledge its importance (about which, see Ferry and Renaut [1990: 52–3], Lehman [1991: 234ff.]). Others are less hesitant: the Italian neo-fascist MSI describes itself as 'post-fascist' [sic].

36. Even in the case of Bataille, an (perhaps 'the') important precursor of the postmodern problematic [*Pefanis*, 1991], there exists an uneasy relationship between his anti-fascism on the one hand and his Nietzschean philosophy on the other, a contradiction unsatisfactorily explained in terms of the absence of a clearcut distinction between the politics of left and right during the 1930s. Of significance, therefore, is the fact that during the mid-1930s not only was Bataille accused by Breton of being *sur-fasciste*, and he himself admitted to a 'paradoxical fascist tendency', but the 'endorsement' Bataille extended to the Popular Front in France was on account of its force/violence rather than its politics (Bataille [1985: xi,xviii, 161–8]). Like Foucault, who identifies both Blanchot and Bataille as seminal influences [*Foucault*, 1991; *Foucault and Blanchot*,

1990] and whose own work is described in turn by Blanchot [*Foucault and Blanchot*, 1990: 95–8] as being about a 'society of blood', there is in the case of Bataille an obsession with and an emphasis on death, destruction, execution and torture, amounting at times to a Nietzschean celebration of the nihilistic/irrational. Interestingly, for Foucault [1975: 24–9] the eroticisation of power/(death) embodied in the aethetics of Nazism leads almost to 'normalisation' of fascism in the name of 'popular culture'. According to Bataille [1991: 367,399–400,457], who rather weakly disavows the existence of a link between fascism and Nietzsche, the latter recognised that the effect of an 'anything-goes' philosophy, or 'the sovereignty of a "free spirit"', would be moral relativism, or precisely the licence that postmodern theory extends to fascism (= 'horror'). The attempt to exculpate Nietzschean *volkische* beliefs is equally unconvincing: having proclaimed his own concept of 'sovereignty' innocent of a desire to recuperate an idealised agrarian past, Bataille somewhat arrogantly accuses Nietzsche of not being aware of the difference between a 'nostalgia for the feudal' (= traditional sovereignty) and Bataille's own sovereignty of the 'free spirit'. That the latter is in fact itself similarly structured by romantic/folkloric concepts of the 'primitive', however, is clear not only from his celebration of the elemental/(destructive) forces of 'nature', his explanation of capitalism largely in terms of pre-capitalist socio-economic forms (the sacred, sacrifice-as-expenditure) but also from his wish 'to stimulate a rebirth of the kind of social values [he] espoused ... the rebirth of myth and the touching off in society of an explosion of the primitive communal devices leading to sacrifice' [*Bataille*, 1985: xix–xx, 200–201; 1992]. The suspicion remains that the combination of destruction/sacrifice/nature which so fascinates Bataille and structures his 'transgression'/(otherness) is in the end no different from the ideology/(worship-of-the-sacredness) of violence/blood/soil which characterises fascism. (It is precisely this dimension, reactionary anti-capitalism, that Habermas [1987: 211ff.] overlooks in the course of identifying Bataille's heterology simply as a 'discourse-against'; at some point, therefore, the seeking out of 'otherness' merely in order to transgress cannot but posit the notion of 'fascinating fascism'.)

37. This complicity with fascism, in the name of 'popular culture' suggests the continued relevance of the observation [*Walicki*, 1969: 3] about Russian populism that '... in the [eighteen] eighties and nineties, the view that the ideas of the intelligentia should give way to the [unmediated] opinions of the people was upheld, and came close to reactionary obscurantism'.
38. It should be remembered that the defence of plantation slavery in the Antebellum American South, initially by apologists such as Fitzhugh [1960] and subsequently by the Southern Agrarians [*Twelve Southerners*, 1951: 14, 76ff.], was based on a similar objection to modernity and capitalism. Arguing that slaves were provided with a guaranteed subsistence, shared in any benefits which accrued to their master (= 'trickle down' theory), and were generally happy with the paternalistic regime on the plantation, Fitzhugh defended the Southern conservative agrarian tradition against Northern industrial capitalism on the grounds that the latter would generate a socially and economically disruptive process of class struggle leading to the eventual destruction of the 'natural' social order which its supporters believed the system of plantation slavery to be. (As is noted in the other contribution by Brass, Gandhi objected to western capitalism for exactly the same reason: that the price of industrialisation was the accompanying growth of an urban proletariat which was both politically disruptive and a bearer of 'alien' beliefs/values.) (It is precisely this dimension, reactionary anti-capitalism, that Habermas [1987: 211ff.] overlooks in the course of identifying Bataille's heterology simply as a 'discourse-against'; at some point, therefore, the seeking out of 'otherness' merely in order to transgress cannot but posit the notion of 'fascinating fascism'.)
39. For the influence on McLuhan of agrarian populism, see Marchand [1989: 27], Miller [1971: 22ff.] and Kermode [1991: 82–92]. Of particular interest in this regard is the link between on the one hand a decentred postmodernism, where all views are deprivileged, and on the other the McLuhanite concept of the 'acoustic', together with

its chain of signification. For McLuhan [1967: 111], therefore, not only is the more desirable 'acoustic' itself decentred ('the ear favors no particular "point of view"'), but discursively it is linked to other key concepts (acoustic = the South = 'the desirable' = tradition = rural = primitive = intuitive = 'the natural') in his framework (see Marchand [1989: 67, 95, 260]). By contrast, for McLuhan the visual is equated with the undesirable, which in turn is linked discursively with the North, the logical, industrialisation, urbanisation, and (unsurprisingly) technology. This framework gives rise to the following politico-ideological oppositions:

desirable	:	undesirable
acoustic	:	visual
intuition	:	logic
primitive	:	modern
South	:	North
rural	:	urban
tradition	:	industry
nature	:	technology

40. The intellectually unfashionable status of McLuhan during the recent past can be gauged from a patronising reference to him by Debray [1979: 139] as 'a curious gentleman'. Interestingly, in acknowledging the influence of Mumford and Giedion on the one hand, and on the other the New Criticism of the 1930s, McLuhan anticipates postmodernism by constructing a theory about the social based originally on ideas about architecture and literature. The latter's role in this genealogy is particularly significant, since both McLuhan and postmodernism have roots in the romantic nostalgia of the Southern Agrarians in the United States (for which see Twelve Southerners [1951], Nash [1976: 36ff., 57ff., 70, 199ff.], and – more generally – Kirk [1954: 137–39]), who not only attempted to recuperate pre-industrial values, among them slavery, but also via the work of Robert Penn Warren, John Crowe Ransom and the *Kenyon Review* influenced the revival of an a-historical, desocialised, innate aestheticism associated with the New Criticism (for which see Eagleton [1983: 47–53]).
41. For McLuhan's views on these issues, see Marchand [1989: 144, 196, 222]. In addition to his nostalgic and idealised vision of a rural 'world-we-have-lost', the anti-modern/anti-Marxist views of McLuhan were also structured by his Roman Catholicism, his views about the sanctity of the family and the importance of individual liberty, a general admiration for the traditions of a Christian Europe – which he counterposed to socialism, and the strong influence of G.K. Chesterton [*Marchand*, 1989: 23–4, 27]. (Significantly, the anti-modern/anti-socialist views of Chesterton himself can be traced to the populism of A.R. Orage, an early populariser of Nietzschean thought whose reactionary distributism embraced Catholicism and advocated a decentralised form of social organisation based on smallscale property.) In part, McLuhan's antagonism towards Marxism derived from what he regarded as its technological bias, and by implication its role in hastening the kind of future he was trying to avoid (see, for example, McLuhan [1951: 34]).
42. For a genuflection in the direction of McLuhan by the high priest of postmodernism, see Baudrillard [1981: 164ff; 1983: 35]. That the work of the latter is prefigured in that of the former is also recognised by Rose [1991: 25–8], who – unlike the position taken here – nevertheless links their views on the electronic media to the project of modernity rather than to postmodernism.
43. On these points, see McLuhan [1951], and also Marchand [1989: 107, 121, 144]. Like McLuhan, Bataille [1988, 1991] also based his theory of general economy on the primacy of consumption (expenditure of wealth) rather than production.
44. On these points, see Marchand [1989: 186, 207]. About politics, McLuhan is on record [*Marchand*, 1989: 186, 216] as observing not just that political parties were a thing of the past but also that: 'Instead of having a line or party to follow, the political candidate must become an image capable of including all the hopes and wishes of the electorate.' These utterances reveal a symptomatic political combination of populism ('above-

politics', or the absence of class) + new social movements theory ('no more parties', or non-political mobilisation) + postmodernism ('politics-as-image').

45. For his critique of modernity/media/industrialisation, see McLuhan [1951]. '[T]he process of renewal', observes McLuhan [1949: 15],

> can't come from above. It can only take the form of reawakened critical faculties. The untrancing of individuals by millions of individual acts of the will. Psychological decentralization. A merely provisional image of how it might (not how it should) occur could be formed by supposing every mechanical agency of communication in the world to be suspended for six months. No press. No radio. No movies. Just people finding out who lived near them. Forming small communities within big cities ... if something like this doesn't happen it is quite plain what will happen ... The machine is power. And practical politics mean quite simply that the machine must assume increasingly its most powerful form. The shape and rational form of man is now irrelevant.

46. For McLuhan's endorsement/advocacy of the 'preliterate', see Marchand [1989: 131]. That for McLuhan the 'global village' was a return to the 'normality' of a *tribal* village, or the *ruralisation* of decentralisation, is clear from the visual material he presents in support of his argument [*McLuhan and Fiore* 1967: 66–7]. '"Time" has ceased, "space" has vanished', he observes [*McLuhan and Fiore* 1967: 83], 'We now live in a *global* village ... we are back in acoustic space. We have begun again to structure the primordial feeling, the tribal emotions from which a few centuries of literacy divorced us.' In this regard, McLuhan himself was influenced by the views of Mumford [1934], who, in order similarly to counter the expansion of large-scale factory production and its accompanying process of urbanisation, advocated a decentralisation to and restoration of rural, community-based artisan production ('small-is-beautiful').
47. For the connections between Heideggerian philosophy, German fascism and the theory of 'deep ecology', see among others Lukacs [1980: 489–522], Bramwell [1989], Taylor [1992] and Ferkiss [1993: 164–7].
48. Banaji [1980: 233], for example, attributes the political dominance of the Indian bourgeoisie to the 'exceptional backwardness of the Indian Communist Party in its early phases of attempted formation'. Das, Rojas and Waterman [1984], by contrast, regard the Indian left as too vanguardist, and like the left generally in peripheral capitalist societies of the so-called Third World, too focused on the mobilisation of organised workers in the urban sector. Instead, Das *et al.* advocate the adoption of an Autonomist position, whereby all 'labouring people' and not just the proletariat are mobilised outside formal party structures in a common struggle for autonomy from capital and the state. The problem with this view is that – like populism – it fails to distinguish between the two different forms of anti-capitalism outlined above, and thus conflates petty-bourgeois elements, such as artisans and petty commodity producers which are opposed not to capitalism but only to specific variants of this (finance capital, large-scale industry, foreign/international capital), with urban/rural proletarians opposed to capitalism *per se*. As has been noted above, whereas the latter have an interest in socialism, the former do not, and are in some instances strongly anti-socialist in political outlook.
49. See Moore [1967: 202], and for the many instances of peasant mobilisation spanning the Moghul and the post-Independence era, see Gough [1979: 85–126].
50. For the link between on the one hand the capitalist crisis of the 1930s, the war-time devaluation, the development of what Patnaik identifies as a 'pre-famine conjuncture', and the 1943 Bengal famine, and on the other the politico-ideological delegitimisation of the landlord class in Bengal and the subsequent participation by their sharecroppers and tenants in the *Tebhaga* movement, see Patnaik [1991], Greenhough [1982], and Cooper [1988: 247–48].
51. Given the importance of both these peasant movements, the literature on them is large. For background, together with debates by participants and others (about social composition, political alliances, possible outcomes and so on), see Sen [1972], Sundarayya [1972], Rao [1972], Pavier [1981], and Cooper [1988].

52. For example, Yadav [1993] not only unproblematically blames socialism for its own political difficulties but also proposes a 'rethought' variant of the same that no longer resembles the original. Accordingly, his 'socialism' is unconnected with metanarratives (= 'European models'), requires the abandonment of the concept 'false consciousness' and a corresponding political acceptance (= 'understanding') of the 'existing moral traditions' (caste, religion, 'popular culture', 'rural society') that amounts to no more than a diluted variant of the nationalism/populism of the subaltern studies project. The latter as a way forward is similarly endorsed by Chakrabarty [1992: 83–84], who observes that: 'serious and undogmatic discussions on Gandhi (and Gandhian politics) in the pages of *Subaltern Studies* have now opened up, in India, an intellectual space for dialogue between Marxists critical of Eurocentrism and non-Marxist, liberal Indian thinkers ... who have developed criticisms of Eurocentric ideas of modernity'.
53. Recent reports suggest that military dictatorship following a violent coup is one option being considered by ruling class elements linked to the political right in India [*Roy* 1993].
54. Official statistics published in the *Indian Express*, 14 April, 1987. Gough [1979: 118] reports that some 10,000 peasants linked to the communists in India were killed during the 1967–70 period of the Naxalite movement. For the continuing incidence and impact of landowning class violence in Bihar, see Prasad [1989: 75–94].
55. It is important to note in this connection that the communalisation of struggle from above frequently triggers a corresponding communalisation as a response from below, resulting in a mutually constructed discourse that leads to the displacement of class. For example, arguing that it would have been possible for Gandhi to have advanced an anti-touchability campaign if he had been serious about it, Ambedkar [1946: 257] observes that: 'He [Gandhi] could have proposed that if a Hindu wishes to enroll himself as a member of Congress he should prove that he does not observe untouchability and that the employment of an Untouchable in his household should be advanced in support of his claim in this behalf. ...' The practicality of such a test, Ambedkar continues, lay in the fact that 'almost every Hindu, certainly every high caste Hindu, keeps more than one servant in his household'. In other words, Ambedkar was challenging untouchability while simultaneously accepting the class structure of which it was a part. That Hinduism was for Ambedkar the enemy is a point conceded by Omvedt and Patankar [1992: 386]; that is, the framing (or acceptance) of conlict in ethnic terms cannot but elicit an opposite reaction in similarly ethnic terms (on this point, see also Engineer [1992]). Unsurprisingly, therefore, not only have the 1993 Assembly elections in the states of northern India been characterised by a process of ethnic/caste/communal consolidation (from below as well as from above), but opposition to the existing structure on the part of the *Dalit Voice* speaks from the perspective of a petty-bourgeois dalit cultural nationalism against a 'Brahmanical Social Order' [*Omvedt*, 1993: 2403–4].
56. A manual by Green [1925] advising planters on the importance of caste ritual/practice makes explicit the political object of reinforcing caste distinctions among the plantation workforce.
57. Much the same kind of argument ('we appeal to peasants not to launch direct action this year ... [t]he new government of independent India ... must be given an opportunity for fulfilling its promises through legal channels') was used by the CPI similarly to defuse agrarian class struggle in Bengal during this period [*Pouchepadass*, 1980: 151].
58. Generally speaking, the potentially reactionary nature and mobilising role of non-politically-specific (= 'apolitical') concepts of 'the popular' can be illustrated by reference to the epistemological overlap between Gandhian philosophy and anarchism, and between variants of the latter and much current right-wing libertarian theory [*Barry*, 1986: 161–91; *Block and Rothwell*, 1988; *Pirie*, 1988; *Nash*, 1976: 313–19; *Nozick*, 1974; *Rothbard*, 1978: 191–207]. Hence anarchist views about the desirability of political decentralisation and individual freedom/self-empowerment coincide with the view of the libertarian right concerning the importance of the competitive 'choice-making' individual in the context of the 'minimal' state.

59. For Soviet perceptions of Gandhi, see Kautsky [1956] and Tidmarsh [1960: 86–115]. Throughout the 1920s and 1930s, Gandhi was regarded by the CPSU in a somewhat contradictory light: as a reactionary, but nevertheless necessary, component of the nationalist struggle for independence from British colonialism. Although located politically on the right wing of the Indian nationalist movement by Soviet theoreticians, therefore, his reformism was in many ways an accurate reflection of the primacy accorded to national revolution by Comintern strategy during the 1935–47 period. From 1949 onwards, the Soviet Union turned to the People's Republic of China as an ally against western imperialism, and correspondingly downgraded the importance of class struggle in India. Accordingly, Gandhi was henceforth described as a 'progressive' who fulfilled a 'major and positive role ... in the history of the struggle of the Indian people'; his non-violence was now reinterpreted in positive terms, as was his emphasis on tribal self-determination and more generally the mobilization of the masses in support of the independence movement. Most significantly, the reactionary elements of Gandhian philosophy were now recast. Not only were the negative aspects of his anti-industrial views dismissed as insignificant, but his opposition to western technology was reinterpreted as being politically acceptable: as evidence of an authentic Indian rejection of Western European colonial tradition, and thus the only way in which the peasantry could be persuaded to oppose/overthrow colonialism. This rehabilitation of Gandhi at the very moment when the Indian bourgeoisie assumed power sanctified not merely the continuation of an anti-imperialist (= nationalist) rather than an anti-capitalist (= socialist) programme but also a reactionary version of this, and thus could not but legitimise the politics of class collaboration subsequently pursued by the CPI.
60. See Dange [1969: 10]. Much the same point has been made by R. Palme Dutt and E.M.S. Namboodiripad (see Ghose [1971: 121,133], Namboodiripad [1959: 111ff.; 1966: 46]).
61. Omvedt [1990: 12–22].
62. Krishnaji [1986: 384–402].
63. Balagopal [1986: 1401–1405].
64. As the work of Alexander [1981], George [1984: 47–51], Gough [1989: 473–77, 478ff.] and Kannan [1988: 248ff.] shows, in parts of Kerala and Tamil Nadu, where the left has organised on the basis of class and excluded small farmers and tenants from unions of agricultural labourers, not only have the latter succeeded in obtaining higher wages and better working conditions but higher and backward caste workers have become members of the same union.
65. On this, see Bhattacharya [1990: 2209–14]. The similarity between the 'anti-foreigner' position adopted by the CPI with respect to Tripura in the 1930s and that of new social movements in Assam during 1979–80 is noted by Brass earlier in this volume.
66. On this point, see Hardgrave [1973: 134]. By contrast, an ethnically-specific ideology is an appropriate mobilising discourse for agrarian capitalists, as the case of the new farmers' movements demonstrates. In Uttar Pradesh, for example, the organisational success of the BKU has been attributed to caste and clan solidarity among the Jats, clan heads having acquired leadership of BKU units, and the support for the new farmers' movement in Karnataka is strongly rooted among the Lingayat and Okkaliga castes [*Dhanagare*, 1988: 30; *Nadkarni*, 1987] (see also the contributions to this volume by Dhanagare, Hasan and Gill).
67. According to Duyker [1987: 89, 103–4, 118], CPI (ML) grassroots organisation in the Midnapore and Birbhum districts of West Bengal 'owed more to indigenous cultural factors than its April 1969 resolution on political organization'. Hence one CPI (ML) leader noted that: 'When we went to the Santals we used to emphasize their [1855 Insurrectionary] heroes ... We told them that Sidhu and Kanhu were our predecessors and that "New Democracy was no different from what they had fought for".' Similarly,

> Naxalite cells and action squads had hierarchies, lines of communication and logistic support which were rooted in the local kinship system ... as whole families of Santals joined the movement, kinship organization began to parallel guerrilla organization ... the natural authority of elders, i.e. fathers, uncles and husbands,

appears to have become a political and military authority over sons, nephews and wives who also joined the movement.

In other words, guerrilla activity mobilised through the kinship system was actually structured by (and thus could not but reflect the interests of) the *existing* socio-economic order, as embodied in the authority of tribal elders. The difficulty with this is that even in a tribal context such authority can also correspond to that exercised by rich peasants over agricultural labourers and sharecroppers, all of whom happen to be tribal kinsfolk.

68. In Bihar, the Maoist Communist Centre was by 1987 engaged not in class but in caste struggle, a communalisation that culminated in the killings of landowning Rajputs by Naxalite-led Yadavs in Aurangabad district. Despite their traditionally lower caste status, Yadavs can no longer be considered as uniformly exploited: as one commentator observed, 'Over the years, the new, better-off class among the backward castes transformed itself into the kulak lobby. Today, the same people who were one in the forefront of the Kisan Sabha movement are the oppressors.' Kanchan Gupta, 'Communism Through Caste in Bihar', *The Statesman*, 16 June 1987.

69. As noted by one observer [*Williamson*, 1989: 33–34], in the UK this amounts to an attempt 'to align political perspectives with the way things *already* are – to take over, rather than to transform, the agenda of the [political] right' (original emphasis).

REFERENCES

Adams, D., 1985, *The Hitch-Hiker's Guide to the Galaxy – the Original Radio Scripts*, London: Pan Books.

Ahmad, A., 1992, *In Theory: Classes, Nations, Literatures*, London: Verso.

Alexander, K.C., 1981, *Peasant Organizations in South India*, New Delhi: Indian Social Institute.

Ambedkar, B.R., 1946, *What Congress and Gandhi have done to the Untouchables*, Bombay: Thacker & Co. Ltd.

Amis, K., 1961, *Lucky Jim*, Harmondsworth: Penguin Books.

Amnesty International, 1983, *Political Killings by Governments*, London: Amnesty International Publications.

Bagchi, A.K., 1993, '"Rent-Seeking", New Political Economy and Negation of Politics', *Economic and Political Weekly*, Vol. 28, No. 34.

Bahro, R., 1982, *Socialism and Survival*, London: Heretic Books.

Balagopal, K., 1986, 'Agrarian Struggles', *Economic and Political Weekly*, Vol. 21, No. 32.

Banaji, J., 1980, 'The Comintern and Indian Nationalism', in K.N. Panikkar (ed.), *National and Left Movements in India*, New Delhi: Vikas Publishing House.

Barker, M., 1981, *The New Racism: Conservatives and the Ideology of the Tribe*, London: Junction Books.

Barry, N.P., 1986, *On Classical Liberalism and Libertarianism*, London: Macmillan.

Basu, K. and A. Mishra, 1993, 'Sustainable Development and the Commons Problem: A Simple Approach', in P. Bardhan, M. Datta-Chaudhuri and T.N. Krishnan (eds.), *Development and Change: Essays in Honour of K.N. Raj*, Bombay: Oxford University Press.

Bataille, G., 1985, *Visions of Excess: Selected Writings, 1927–1939*, Manchester: Manchester University Press.

Bataille, G., 1988, *The Accursed Share – Volume I*, New York: Zone Books.

Bataille, G., 1991, *The Accursed Share – Volumes II and III*, New York: Zone Books.

Bataille, G., 1992, *Theory of Religion*, New York: Zone Books.

Baudrillard, J., 1981, *For a Critique of the Political Economy of the Sign*, St Louis, MO: Telos Press.

Baudrillard, J., 1983, *In the Shadow of the Silent Majorities, or The End of the Social*, New York: Semiotext(e).

Bausinger, H., 1990, *Folk Culture in a World of Technology*, Bloomington, IN: Indiana University Press.

Bergquist, C., 1993, 'Labor History and Its Challenges: Confessions of a Latin Americanist', *The American Historical Review*, Vol. 98, No. 3.

Bernstein, H., 1990, 'Taking the Part of Peasants?', in H. Bernstein *et al.* (eds.), *The Food Question: Profits versus People*?, London: Earthscan.

Bernstein, H., Brass, T. and T.J. Byres, 1994, *The Journal of Peasant Studies: A Twenty Year Index, 1973–93*, London: Frank Cass.

Bhattacharya, H., 1990, 'Communism, Nationalism and the Tribal Question in Tripura', *Economic and Political Weekly*, Vol. 25, No. 39.

Billig, M., 1993, 'Nationalism and Richard Rorty: The Text as a Flag for *Pax Americana*,' *New Left Review*, 202.

Block, W. and L.H.J. Rockwell (eds.), 1988, *Man, Economy and Liberty: Essays in Honor of Murray Rothbard*, Auburn,AL: Ludwig von Mises Institute.

Booth, D., 1993, 'Development Research: From Impasse to a New Agenda', in Schuurman (ed.) [1993].

Boyd, R., Cohen R. and P. Gutkind (eds.), 1989, *International Labour and the Third World: The Making of a New Working Class*, Aldershot: Avebury.

Bradford, G., 1989, *How Deep is Deep Ecology*?, Hadley, MA: Times Change Press.

Bramwell, A., 1989, *Ecology in the Twentieth Century*, New Haven, CT: Yale University Press.

Brass, T., 1990, 'The Latin American *Enganche* System: Some Revisionist Reinterpretations Revisited', *Slavery and Abolition*, Vol. 11, No.1.

Brass, T., 1991a, 'Moral Economists, Subalterns, New Social Movements, and the (Re-) Emergence of a (Post-) Modernised (Middle) Peasant', *Journal of Peasant Studies*, Vol. 18, No.2.

Brass, T., 1991b 'Market Essentialism and the Impermissibility of Unfree Labour', *Slavery and Abolition*, Vol. 12, No. 3.

Brass, T., 1993a, 'Some Observations on Unfree Labour, Capitalist Restructuring, and Deproletarianization,' in T. Brass, M. van der Linden and J. Lucassen (eds.), *Free and Unfree Labour*, Amsterdam: International Institute for Social History.

Brass, T., 1993b, 'A-Way with Their Wor(l)d: Rural Labourers through the Postmodern Prism', *Economic and Political Weekly*, Vol. 28, No.23.

Brass, T. and H. Bernstein, 1992, 'Proletarianization and Deproletarianization on the Colonial Plantation', in E.V. Daniel, H. Bernstein and T. Brass (eds.), *Plantations, Proletarians and Peasants in Colonial Asia*, London: Frank Cass.

Bustamante, J.A. *et al.* (eds), 1992, *US–Mexico Relations: Labor Market Interdependence*, Stanford, CA: Stanford University Press.

Byres, T.J., 1979, 'Of Neo-populist Pipe-dreams: Daedalus in the Third World and the Myth of Urban Bias', *Journal of Peasant Studies*, Vol. 6, No.2.

Callinicos, A., 1989, *Against Postmodernism*, Cambridge: Polity Press.

Castles, S. and M.J. Miller, 1993, *The Age of Migration: International Population Movements in the Modern World*, London: Macmillan.

Catholic Institute for International Relations (CIIR), 1987, *The Labour Trade: Filipino Migrant Workers Around the World*, London: CIIR.

Chakrabarty, D., 1992, 'Marxism and Modern India', in A. Ryan (ed.), *After the End of History*, London: Collins & Brown.

Chapkis, W. and C. Enloe (eds.), 1983, *Of Common Cloth: Women in the Global Textile Industry*, Washington: Transnational Institute.

Cheles, L., Ferguson, R. and M. Vaughan (eds.), 1991, *Neo-Fascism in Europe*, London: Longman.

Chomsky, N., 1982, *Towards a New Cold War: Essays on the Current Crisis and How We Got There*, London: Sinclair Browne.

Chossudovsky, M., 1986, *Towards Capitalist Restoration? Chinese Socialism after Mao*, London: Macmillan.

Chossudovsky, M., 1988, 'World Unemployment and China's Labour Reserves', in R. Southall (ed.) [1988].

Clifford, J., and G. Marcus (eds.), 1986, *Writing Culture: The Poetics and Politics of Ethnography*, Berkeley, CA: University of California Press.

Cohen, R., 1987, *The New Helots: Migrants in the International Division of Labour*, Aldershot: Gower Publishing Co.

Colburn, F.D. (ed.), 1989, *Everyday Forms of Peasant Resistance*, New York: M.E. Sharpe, Inc.

Cooper, A., 1988, *Sharecropping and Sharecroppers' Struggles in Bengal 1930–1950*, Calcutta: K.P. Bagchi & Co.

Dange, S.A., 1969, *Driving Forces of History: Heroes and Masses*, New Delhi: People's Publishing House.

Das, A.N., Rojas, F. and P. Waterman, 1984, 'The Labour Movement and Labouring People in India', in Das, Nilkant and Dubey (eds.) [1984].

Das, A.N., Nilkant, V. and P.S. Dubey (eds.), 1984, *The Worker and the Working Class: A Labour Studies Anthology*, New Delhi: Public Enterprises Centre for Continuing Education.

Davis, K. and M.S. Bernstein (eds.), 1991, *Resources, Environment, and Population: Present Knowledge, Future Options*, New York: Oxford University Press.

Debray, R., 1979, *Teachers, Writers, Celebrities*, London: Verso.

Deutscher, I., 1955, *Heretics and Renegades*, London: Hamish Hamilton.

DeWind, J. *et al.*, 1979, 'Contract Labor in US Agriculture: The West Indian Cane Cutters in Florida', in R. Cohen, *et al.* (eds.), *Peasants and Proletarians*, London: Hutchinson University Library.

Deyo, F.C., 1989, *Beneath the Miracle: Labor Subordination in the New Asian Industrialism*, Berkeley, CA: University of California Press.

Dhanagare, D.N., 1988, 'An Apoliticist Populism', in A.N. Das (ed.), *Farmer Power*, a special issue of *Seminar*, No.352.

Dobb, M., 1955, 'Full Employment and Capitalism [1950]', in *On Economic Theory and Socialism: Collected Papers*, London: Routledge & Kegan Paul.

Duyker, E., 1987, *Tribal Guerrillas: The Santals of West Bengal and the Naxalite Movement*, New Delhi: Oxford University Press.

Eagleton, T., 1983, *Literary Theory*, Oxford: Basil Blackwell.

Eatwell, R., 1989, 'The Nature of the Right, 2: The Right as a Variety of "Styles of Thought"', in R. Eatwell and N. O'Sullivan (eds.), *The Nature of the Right*, London: Pinter Publishers.

Edinburgh, Duke of, 1989, *Living Off the Land*, London: BBC Books.

Eidelberg, P.G., 1974, *The Great Rumanian Peasant Revolt of 1907*, Leiden: E.J. Brill.

Eliade, M., 1954, *The Myth of the Eternal Return*, New York: Pantheon Books Inc.

Engineer, A.A., 1992, 'Communal Conflict after 1950: A Perspective', *Economic and Political Weekly*, Vol.27, No.34.

Farias, V., 1989, *Heidegger and Nazism*, Philadelphia, PA: Temple University Press.

Epstein, K., 1970, 'Three Types of Conservatism', in M. Richter (ed.), *Essays in Theory and History*, Cambridge, MA: Harvard University Press.

Ferkiss, V.C., 1957, 'Populist Influences on American Fascism', *Western Political Quarterly*, Vol.10, No.2.

Ferkiss, V.C., 1961, 'Populism: Myth, Reality, Current Danger', *Western Political Quarterly*, Vol.14, No.3.

Ferkiss, V., 1993, *Nature, Technology, and Society: Cultural Roots of the Current Environmental Crisis*, London: Adamantine Press.

Ferry, L. and A. Renaut, 1990, *Heidegger and Modernity*, Chicago, IL: University of Chicago Press.

Fitzhugh, G., 1960, 'Sociology for the South [1854]', and 'Cannibals All! [1857]', in H. Wish (ed.), *Antebellum: The Writings of George Fitzhugh and Hinton Rowan Helper on Slavery*, New York: Capricorn Books.

Fogel, R.W., 1990, *Without Consent of Contract: The Rise and Fall of American Slavery*, London: Norton.

Fogel, R.W. and S.L. Engerman, 1974, *Time on the Cross: The Economics of American Negro Slavery*, London: Wildwood House.

Fontana, B., 1988, *Benjamin Constant: Political Writings*, Cambridge: Cambridge University Press.
Ford, G., 1992, *Fascist Europe: The Rise of Racism and Xenophobia*, London: Pluto Press.
Foucault, M., 1975, 'Film and Popular Memory: An Interview with Michel Foucault', *Radical Philosophy*, No.11.
Foucault, M., 1991, *Remarks on Marx*, New York: Semiotext(e).
Foucault, M. and M. Blanchot, 1990, *Foucault/Blanchot*, New York: Zone Books.
Friedland, W.H. *et al.*, 1981, *Manufacturing Green Gold*, Cambridge: Cambridge University Press.
Friedland, W.H., 1991, 'Shaping the New Political Economy of Advanced Capitalist Agriculture', in W.H. Friedland *et al.* (eds.), *Towards a New Political Economy of Agriculture*, Boulder, CO: Westview Press.
George, J., 1984, *Politicization of Agricultural Workers in Kerala – A Study of Kuttanad*, Calcutta: K.P. Bagchi & Co.
Geertz, C., 1988, *Works and Lives: The Anthropologist as Author*, Stanford, CA: Stanford University Press.
Ghose, S., 1971, *Socialism and Communism in India*, Bombay: Allied Publishers.
Gortz, A., 1980, *Ecology as Politics*, Boston, MA: South End Press.
Gortz, A., 1982, *Farewell to the Working Class*, London: Pluto Press.
Gough, K., 1979, 'Indian Peasant Uprisings', in A.R. Desai (ed.), *Peasant Struggles in India*, Bombay: Oxford University Press.
Gough, K., 1989, *Rural Change in Southeast India 1950s to 1980s*, Delhi: Oxford University Press.
Green, L.B., 1925, *The Planter's Book of Caste and Custom*, Colombo: The Times of Ceylon Co., Ltd.
Greenhough, P.R., 1982, *Prosperity and Misery in Modern Bengal: The Famine of 1943–44*, New York: Oxford University Press.
Guerin, D., 1974, *Fascism and Big Business*, New York: Pathfinder Press.
Gunn, S., 1989, *Revolution of the Right: Europe's New Conservatives*, London: Pluto Press.
Habermas, J., 1987, *The Philosophical Discourse of Modernity*, Cambridge, MA: The MIT Press
Hall, S. and M. Jacques (eds.), 1989, *New Times: The Changing Face of Politics in the 1990s*, London: Lawrence & Wishart.
Hardgrave, R.L., 1973, 'The Kerala Communists: Contradictions of Power', in P.R. Brass and M. Franda (eds.), *Radical Politics in South Asia*, Cambridge, MA: MIT Press.
Hardin, G., 1960, *Nature and Man's Fate*, London: Jonathan Cape.
Hardin, G., 1977, *The Limits of Altruism: An Ecologist's View of Survival*, Bloomington, IN: Indiana University Press.
Hardin, G., 1993, *Living Within Limits: Ecology, Economics, and Population Taboos*, New York: Oxford University Press.
Hardin, G. and J. Baden (eds.), 1977, *Managing the Commons*, San Francisco, CA: W.H. Freeman and Company.
Harris, M., 1992, 'Anthropology and the Theoretical and Paradigmatic Significance of the Collapse of Soviet and East European Communism', *American Anthropologist*, Vol.94, No.2.
Harvey, D., 1989, *The Condition of Postmodernity*, Oxford: Blackwell.
Hawthorn, G., 1991, '"Waiting for a Text?": Comparing Third World Politics', in J. Manor (ed.), *Rethinking Third World Politics*, London: Longman.
Hawthorn, G., 1993a, 'Liberalization and "Modern Liberty": Four Southern States', *World Development*, Vol.21, No.8.
Hawthorn, G., 1993b, 'Listen to the Women', *London Review of Books*, Vol.15, No.20.
Hayek, F.A., 1967, 'The Principles of a Liberal Social Order', in *Studies in Philosophy, Politics and Economics*, London: Routledge & Kegan Paul.
Haynes, D. and G. Prakash (eds.), 1991, *Contesting Power: Resistance and Everyday Social Relations in South Asia*, Delhi: Oxford University Press.
Heidegger, M., 1969, *Discourse on Thinking*, New York: Harper & Row.

Henderson, J. and M. Castells (eds.), 1987, *Global Restructuring and Territorial Development*, London: Sage.
Hobart, M. (ed.), 1993, *An Anthropological Critique of Development*, London: Routledge.
Hojman, D.E. (ed.), 1990, *Neo-liberal Agriculture in Rural Chile*, London: Macmillan.
Hojman, D.E. (ed.), 1993, *Change in the Chilean Countryside*, London: Macmillan.
Holbo, P.S., 1961, 'Wheat or What? Populism and American Fascism', *Western Political Quarterly*, Vol.14, No.3.
Hoogvelt, A., 1987, 'The New International Division of Labour', in R. Bush, G. Johnston and D. Coates (eds.), *The World Order: Socialist Perspectives*, Oxford: Polity Press.
Ionescu, G., 1969, 'Eastern Europe', in Ionescu and Gellner (eds.) [1969].
Ionescu, G. and E. Gellner (eds.), 1969, *Populism*, London: Weidenfeld & Nicolson.
de Janvry, A., 1980, 'Social Differentiation in Agriculture and the Ideology of Neopopulism', in F.H. Buttel and H. Newby (eds.), *The Rural Sociology of the Advanced Societies: Critical Perspectives*, London: Croom Helm.
Jenkins, T., 1977, 'The Death of Marx: A Media Event', *Journal of the Anthropological Society of Oxford*, Vol.VIII, No.3.
Jodha, N.S., 1990, 'Depletion of Common Property Resources in India: Micro-Level Evidence', in G. McNicoll and M. Cain (eds.), *Rural Development and Populations: Institutions and Policy*, New York: Oxford University Press.
Kannan, K.P., 1988, *Of Rural Proletarian Struggles: Mobilization and Organization of Rural Workers in South-West India*, Delhi: Oxford University Press.
Kaplinsky, R., 1993, 'Export Processing Zones in the Dominican Republic: Transforming Manufactures into Commodities', *World Development*, Vol.21, No.11.
Kautsky, J.H., 1956, *Moscow and the Communist Party of India*, New York: MIT Press.
Kermode, F., 1991, *The Uses of Error*, Cambridge, MA: Harvard University Press.
Kirk, R., 1954, *The Conservative Mind*, London: Faber & Faber.
Kirk, R., 1968, 'The African Example: American Ritualistic Liberalism in Action', in J.G. Kirk (ed.), *America Now*, New York: Antheneum.
Kitching, G., 1982, *Development and Underdevelopment in Historical Perspective*, London: Methuen.
Korovkin, T., 1992, 'Peasants, Grapes and Corporations: The Growth of Contract Farming in a Chilean Community', *Journal of Peasant Studies*, Vol.19, No.2.
Krishnaji, N., 1986, 'Agrarian Relations and the Left Movement in Kerala: A Note on Recent Trends', in A.R. Desai (ed.), *Agrarian Struggles in India after Independence*, Delhi: Oxford University Press.
Kumar, R., 1989, *India's Export Processing Zones*, Delhi: Oxford University Press.
Laclau, E., 1977, *Politics and Ideology in Marxist Theory*, London: New Left Books.
Laclau, E., 1990, *New Reflections on the Revolution of Our Time*, London: Verso.
Lehman, D., 1991, *Signs of the Times: Deconstruction and the Fall of Paul de Man*, New York: Poseidon Press.
Lipietz, A., 1992, *Towards a New Economic Order: Postfordism, Ecology and Democracy*, Cambridge: Polity Press.
Levidow, L., 1991, 'Women Who Make the Chips', *Science as Culture*, 10.
Lukacs, G., 1980, *The Destruction of Reason*, London: The Merlin Press.
Luxemburg, R., 1950, *The Accumulation of Capital*, New York: Monthly Review Press.
McCormick, J., 1992, *The Global Environmental Movement: Reclaiming Paradise*, London: Bellhaven Press.
McLuhan, M., 1949, 'The Psychopathology of Time & Life', *Neurotica*, 5.
McLuhan, M., 1951, *The Mechanical Bride: Folklore of Industrial Man*, New York: The Vanguard Press, Inc.
McLuhan, M. and Q. Fiore, 1967, *The Medium is the Massage*, New York: Bantam Books.
Marchand, P., 1989, *Marshall McLuhan: The Medium and the Messenger*, New York: Ticknor & Fields.
Mehlman, J., 1980, 'Blanchot at *Combat*: Of Literature and Terror', *MLN*, Vol.95, No.4.
Mellor, M., 1989, 'Turning Green: Whose Ecology?', *Science as Culture*, No.6.

Merchant, C., 1992, *Radical Ecology: The Search for a Livable World*, London: Routledge.
Miliband, R., 1985, 'The New Revisionism in Britain', *New Left Review*, No.150.
Miller, Jonathan, 1971, *McLuhan*, London: Fontana.
Miller, James, 1993, *The Passion of Michel Foucault*, London: Harper Collins.
Mitter, S., 1986, *Common Fate, Common Bond: Women in the Global Economy*, London: Pluto Press.
Moore, B., 1967, *Social Origins of Dictatorship and Democracy: Lord and Peasant in the Making of the Modern World*, London: Allen Lane.
Muford, L., 1934, *Technics and Civilization*, London: Routledge.
Munck, R., 1988, *The New International Labour Studies*, London: Zed Press.
Nadkarni, M.V., 1987, *Farmers' Movements in India*, New Delhi: Allied Publishers.
Namboodiripad, E.M.S., 1959, *The Mahatma and the Ism*, New Delhi: People's Publishing House.
Namboodiripad, E.M.S., 1966, *Economics and Politics of India's Socialist Pattern*, New Delhi: People's Publishing House.
Nash, G.T., 1976, *The Conservative Intellectual Movement in America*, New York: Basic Books.
Nolte, E., 1966, *The Three Faces of Fascism*, New York: Holt, Reinhart & Winston.
Norris, C., 1993, *The Truth about Postmodernism*, Oxford: Blackwell.
Nozick, R., 1974, *Anarchy, State and Utopia*, Oxford: Basil Blackwell.
Nuñez, L., 1993, 'Women on the Streets: Vending and Public Space in Chile', *Economic and Political Weekly*, Vol.28, No.44.
O'Brien, C.C. and W.D. Vanech (eds.), 1969, *Power and Consciousness*, New York: New York University Press.
Omvedt, G., 1990, 'Ambedkar and Dalit Labor Radicalism: Maharashtra, 1936–1942', *South Asia Bulletin*, Vol.10, No.1.
Omvedt, G., 1993, 'Of Brahmins, Sacred and Socialist', *Economic and Political Weekly*, Vol.28, No.44.
Omvedt, G. and B. Patankar, 1992, 'The Non-Brahman Movement and the Class–Caste Debate', in G. Shah (ed.), *Capitalist Development: Critical Essays*, London: Sangam Books.
Ong, A., 1987, *Spirits of Resistance and Capitalist Discipline: Factory Women in Malaysia*, Albany, NY: State University of New York Press.
O'Sullivan, N., 1976, *Conservatism*, London: J.M. Dent & Sons Ltd.
Ott, H., 1993, *Martin Heidegger: A Political Life*, London: Harper Collins.
Palmer, B.D., 1990, *Descent into Discourse: The Reification of Language and the Writing of Social History*, Philadelphia, PA: Temple University Press.
Patnaik, U., 1991, 'Food Availability and Famine: A Longer View', *Journal of Peasant Studies*, Vol.19, No.1.
Pavier, B., 1981, *The Telengana Movement 1944–51*, New Delhi: Vikas Publishing House.
Pavloff, V.N., 1978, 'Revolutionary Populism in Imperial Russia and the National Question in the 1870s and 1880s', in E. Cahm and V.C. Fisera (eds.), *Socialism and Nationalism*, Volume 1, Nottingham: Spokesman.
Pefanis, J., 1991, *Heterology and the Postmodern: Bataille, Baudrillard and Lyotard*, Durham NC: Duke University Press.
Petras, J., 1990, 'Retreat of the Intellectuals', *Economic and Political Weekly*, Vol.25, No.38.
Pieterse, J.N. (ed.), 1992, *Emancipations, Modern and Postmodern*, a special issue of *Development and Change*, Vol.23, No.3.
Pirie, M., 1988, *Micropolitics: The Creation of Successful Policy*, Aldershot: Wildwood House.
Portes, A. *et al.*, 1989, *The Informal Economy: Studies in Advanced and Less Developed Countries*, London: The Johns Hopkins Press.
Pouchepadass, J., 1980, 'Peasant Classes in Twentieth Century Agrarian Movements in India', in E.J. Hobsbawn, W. Kula, Ashok Mitra, K.N. Raj and Ignacy Sachs (eds.),

Peasants in History: Essays in Honour of Daniel Thorner, Calcutta: Oxford University Press.

Prakash, G., 1990a, *Bonded Histories: Genealogies of Labour Servitude in Colonial India*, Cambridge: Cambridge University Press.

Prakash, G., 1990b, 'Bonded Labour in South Bihar: A Contestatory History', in S. Bose (ed.), *South Asia and World Capitalism*, Delhi: Oxford University Press.

Prakash, G., 1992, 'The History and Historiography of Rural Labourers in Colonial India', in G. Prakash (ed.), *The World of the Rural Labourer in Colonial India*, Delhi: Oxford University Press.

Prasad, P.H., 1989, *Lopsided Growth: Political Economy of Indian Development*, Bombay: Oxford University Press.

Preston, P., 1990, 'Populism and Parasitism: the Falange and the Spanish Establishment 1939–75', in M. Blinkhorn (ed.), *Fascists and Conservatives: The Radical Right and the Establishment in Twentieth Century Europe*, London: Unwin Hyman.

Rao, C. Rajeswara, 1972, *The Historic Telengana Struggle: Some Useful Lessons from its Rich Experience*, New Delhi: Communist Party of India.

Rose, M.A., 1991, *The Post-Modern and the Post-Industrial: A Critical Analysis*, Cambridge: Cambridge University Press.

Rothbard, M.N., 1978, 'Society without a State', in J.R. Pennock and J.W. Chapman (eds.), *Anarchism*, New York: New York University Press.

Roy, A., 1993, 'Pressure to Curb People's Movements', *Economic and Political Weekly*, Vol.28, No.52.

Said, E., 1994, *Representations of the Intellectual*, London; Random House.

Sanderson, S.E. (ed.), 1985, *The Americas in the New International Division of Labor*, New York: Holmes & Meier Publishers, Inc.

Sassen, S., 1988, *The Mobility of Labor and Capital: A Study in International Investment and Capital Flow*, Cambridge: Cambridge University Press.

Sawers, L. and W.K. Tabb (eds.), 1984, *Sunbelt/Snowbelt: Urban Development and Regional Restructuring*, New York: Oxford University Press.

Sawyer, R., 1986, *Slavery in the Twentieth Century*, London: Routledge & Kegan Paul.

Schuurman, F.J. (ed.), 1993, *Beyond the Impasse: New Directions in Development Theory*, London: Zed Press.

Scott, J.C., 1976, *The Moral Economy of the Peasant: Rebellion and Subsistence in Southeast Asia*, New Haven, CT: Yale University Press.

Scott, J.C., 1985, *Weapons of the Weak: Everyday Forms of Peasant Resistance*, New Haven, CT: Yale University Press.

Scott, J.C., 1990, *Domination and the Arts of Resistance: Hidden Transcripts*, New Haven, CT: Yale University Press.

Selbourne, D., 1985, 'A Political Morality Re-examined', in D. Selbourne (ed.), *In Theory and in Practice: Essays on the Politics of Jayaprakash Narayan*, Delhi: Oxford University Press.

Selbourne, D., 1987, *Left Behind: A Journey Through British Politics*, London: Jonathan Cape.

Sen, S., 1972, *Agrarian Struggle in Bengal 1946–47*, New Delhi: People's Publishing House.

Sherman, A.L., 1992, *Preferential Option: A Christian and Neoliberal Strategy for Latin America's Poor*, Washington, DC: The Institute on Religion and Democracy.

Shlomowitz, R., 1981, 'Markets for Indentured and Time-expired Melanesian Labour in Queensland, 1863–1906', *Journal of Pacific History*, Vol.16, No.2.

Shlomowitz, R., 1985, 'Time-expired Melanesian Labor in Queensland: An Investigation of Job Turnover, 1884–1906', *Pacific Studies*, Vol.8, No.2.

Silva, P., 1990, 'Agrarian Change Under the Chilean Military Government', *Latin American Research Review*, Vol.25, No.1.

Sivanandan, A., 1990, *Communities of Resistance: Writings on Black Struggles for Socialism*, London: Verso.

Sklair, L., 1990, 'Regional Consequences of Open-door Development Strategies: Export Zones in Mexico and China', in D. Simon (ed.), *Third World Regional Development: A*

Reappraisal, London: Paul Chapman Publishing Ltd.
Sluga, H., 1993, *Heidegger's Crisis: Philosophy and Politics in Nazi Germany*, Cambridge, MA: Harvard University Press.
Sohn-Rethel, A., 1978, *Economy and Class Structure of German Fascism*, London: CSE Books.
Southall, R., 1988, *Labour and Unions in Asia and Africa*, London: Macmillan Press.
Srinivasan, T.N., 1989, 'On Choice among Creditors and Bonded Labour Contracts', in P. Bardhan (ed.), *The Economic Theory of Agrarian Institutions*, Oxford: Clarendon Press.
Stichter, S. and J.L. Parpart (eds.), 1990, *Women, Employment and the Family in the International Division of Labour*, London: Macmillan.
Sundarayya, P., 1972, *Telengana People's Struggle and its Lessons*, Calcutta: Communist Party of India (Marxist).
Taussig, M., 1984, 'Culture of Terror – Space of Death: Roger Casement's Putumayo Report and the Explanation of Torture', *Comparative Studies in Society and History*, Vol.26, No.3.
Taylor, C., 1992, 'Heidegger, Language and Ecology', in H.L. Dreyfus and H. Hall (eds.), *Heidegger: A Critical Reader*, Oxford: Blackwell.
Thompson, P.B., 1992, *The Ethics of Aid and Trade*, Cambridge: Cambridge University Press.
Tidmarsh, K., 1960, 'The Soviet Reassessment of Mahatma Gandhi', in R. Iyer (ed.), *South Asian Affairs*, Illinois: Southern Illinois University Press.
Trotzky, L., 1918, *The Bolsheviki and World Peace*, New York: Boni and Liveright.
Twelve Southerners, 1951/[1930], *I'll Take My Stand: The South and the Agrarian Tradition*, New York: Peter Smith.
Varshney, A., 1993, 'Self-Limited Empowerment: Democracy, Economic Development and Rural India', *Journal of Development Studies*, Vol.29, No.4.
Walicki, A., 1969, *The Controversy over Capitalism*, Oxford: The Clarendon Press.
Watts, M., 1992, 'Peasants and Flexible Accumulation in the Third World: Producing under Contract', *Economic and Political Weekly*, Vol.27, No.30.
Wharton, C.R. (ed.), 1970, *Subsistence Agriculture and Economic Development*, London: Frank Cass & Co.
Wiener, M.J., 1981, *English Culture and the Decline of the Industrial Spirit 1850–1980*, Cambridge: Cambridge University Press.
Wiles, P., 1969, 'A Syndrome, Not a Doctrine', in Ionescu and Gellner (eds.) [1969].
Willan, B., 1984, *Sol Plaatje: South African Nationalist 1876–1932*, London: Heinemann.
Williams, R., 1973, *The Country and the City*, London: Chatto & Windus.
Williamson, J., 1989, 'Even New Times change', *New Statesman*, 7 July.
Worsley, P., 1984, *The Three Worlds: Culture and World Development*, London: Weidenfeld & Nicolson.
Yadav, Y., 1993, 'Towards an Indian Agenda for the Indian Left', *Economic and Political Weekly*, Vol.28, No.41.
Yonghong, S., 1989, 'Export Processing Zones in China', *Economic and Political Weekly*, Vol.24, No.7.

Abstracts

Introduction: The New Farmers' Movements in India
TOM BRASS

Contextualising the new farmers' movements which emerged in India during the 1980s in terms of economic developments both at the national and the international level, the contributions to this volume are grouped round four themes. First, the extent to which the farmers' mobilisations in India are part of a general global trend towards new social movements. Second, the historical background and future direction of the new farmers' movements in India. Third, their class composition and regional specificity. And fourth, the kind of mobilising ideology (anti-state, anti-urban, anti-capitalist) they use and the degree to which this discourse reinforces or negates other politico-ideological issues currently topical in India, in particular those associated with the BJP.

The Politics of Gender, Nature and Nation in the Discourse of the New Farmers' Movements
TOM BRASS

Together with the environmental and women's movements which emerged in India during the 1980s, the farmers' movement is viewed as part of a new and authentically grassroots form of apolitical/anti-state mobilisation. However, it is argued here that the peasant/gender essentialisms invoked in the discourse shared by the new farmers' movement, ecofeminists and some sections of the left, have been those associated historically with the politics of populism/nationalism. In the the Indian context, such idioms are particularly supportive of the neo-populist/communal/nationalist discourse of the political right. One consequence of this discursive fusion has been the reproduction of a politico-ideological space that has now been (re-) occupied by the BJP/VHP/RSS.

The Class Character and Politics of the Farmers' Movement in Maharashtra during the 1980s
D.N. DHANAGARE

This analysis seeks to bring out the dominant class character of the new farmers' movement in Maharashtra. Providing the background of its specific agitations launched from the late 1970s through the 1980s, it analyses the Shetkari Sanghatana's ideological pronouncements as well as demands. It argues that the movement heralds the emergence of a class of rich farmers whose interests it serves the best. The study further suggests that the strong flavour of economistic populism in the ideology of the farmers' movement is neither accidental nor without purpose. On the contrary, populism is that form in which the hegemony of the dominant class – in sum and substance – manifests itself. None the less the

Sanghatana's politics of populism breeds political ambivalence, and its pragmatism in the pursuit of power severely limits the potential of populist discourse.

New Farmers' Movements in India as Structural Response and Collective Identity Formation: The Cases of the Shetkari Sanghatana and the BKU
STAFFAN LINDBERG

A closer look at the new farmers' movements in India shows that during the last 20 years there seems to have been an important shift in the character of peasant political activities. Today the scene is dominated by the so-called 'Farmers' agitation' representing the upper and middle strata of the peasantry, standing in sharp contrast to the main strand of the traditional peasant movements, which represent the lower and proletarian strata of the peasantry. The article tries to discern the main causes of this shift in the character of peasant politics in India, and to analyse the social construction and potential development of these new farmers' movements. To analyse the movements two perspectives are applied, one emphasising the structural features of the agrarian economy and its recent transformation, and the other looking at social processes of interaction, identity formation and collective action. It is found that both perspectives are needed if we are to understand the new farmers' movements.

'We Want the Return for Our Sweat': The New Peasant Movement in India and the Formation of a National Agricultural Policy
GAIL OMVEDT

Debates and struggles over national agricultural policy in India reveal a clear distinction between the leaders of the farmers' movement in Uttar Pradesh, whose programme is producer oriented, and Sharad Joshi, whose demands include not just higher crop prices for producers but also higher wages for rural workers. Criticising the Nehruvian development path, which involves extracting surpluses from agriculture by the price mechanism, a consequence of which is faltering growth and the immiseration of rural workers, Joshi maintains that rural labour will benefit from higher crop prices. Arguing that economic growth in the agrarian sector is generated not just by wage labour but also by the unpaid labour of petty commodity producers and women, Joshi's view is that the retention of surpluses in the agrarian sector will lead to increased capital accumulation in agriculture and labour-intensive rural industries.

Shifting Ground: Hindutva Politics and the Farmers' Movement in Uttar Pradesh
ZOYA HASAN

Politics in the rural areas of Uttar Pradesh has been transformed by the emergence of a powerful farmers' movement with strong support among the prosperous peasantry. Studies of farmers' movement have placed a different emphasis on the importance of class and caste factors, as well as drawn attention to the important role of the middle peasants in agrarian mobilisation. This study attempts to situate the nature of and shifts in the farmers' movement in the context of agrarian transition and political change in UP. A central paradox is that although the movement was dominated by and reflected the economic interests of surplus producing farmers, its principal mobilising ideology and strategy during the campaigns was non-economic. It was embedded in existing caste and religious cleavages. For this reason, the movement was soon overtaken by the sway of Hindutva politics in western UP. Two particular factors, the intensification of caste and communal politics, are considered in explaining the rise and decline of the movement. It is argued hat the fortunes of the farmers' movement are crucially influenced by larger social forces which are reshaping political processes in north India. This aspect has been neglected in most of the analyses of the farmers' movements.

The Farmers' Movement and Agrarian Change in the Green Revolution Belt of North-west India
SUCHA SINGH GILL

Part of a long history of peasant struggle in this region, the recent upsurge of the farmers' movement in the Green Revolution belt of Northwestern India is due to a combination of factors. In economic terms, these include the expansion of the market nexus coupled with declining agricultural profitability, and the lack of non-farm employment. Its populism notwithstanding, in class terms the beneficiaries of the BKU economic programme and organizational activities in Punjab, Haryana and western Uttar Pradesh have been the better-off rural elements. The politico-ideological conditions favouring such mobilisation include the capacity to sustain both a non-party political image and peasant solidarity against hired labour. However, the divisive effect of ethnic idioms/symbols used in the mobilisation process itself and spilts within the farmers' leadership, constitute limits to the effectiveness of the movement.

'Khadi Curtain', 'Weak Capitalism' and 'Operation Ryot': Some Ambiguities in Farmers' Discourse, Karnataka and Maharashtra 1980–93
MUZAFFAR ASSADI

This article examines programmatic, strategic and ideological ambiguities in the discourse of the farmers' movement in Karnataka and Maharashtra. It focuses specifically on the way in which both the KRRS and Shetkari Sanghatana claim to be 'new' agrarian mobilisations, how they identify potential/actual membership and alliances, the manner in which they confront and/or collaborate with the state, and in particular how they conceptualize externally-derived exploitation. The latter is linked to the continued existence in India of a subordinated 'weak' capitalism which perpetuates not only colonial dependency on foreign capital but also endemic rural poverty and urban bias, and the eradication of which requires either a 'Khadi Curtain' or an 'Operation Ryot'. That is, inter-national egalitarianism based on non-exploitative relations (favourable terms of trade and remunerative prices).

The Farmers' Movements: A Critique of Conservative Rural Coalitions
JAIRUS BANAJI

Reflecting the loss of Congress hegemony in rural areas during the 1980s, farmers' movements in India are mass organisations led by sections of the rural elite. Politically, such movements are conservative mobilisations that seek to reinforce existing property rights and consolidate a broad-based and diversified rural capitalism. In Gujarat as well as Maharashtra and Uttar Pradesh, these movements represent the economic power of emerging rural capitalists whose business activities straddle the rural/urban divide. In both economic and political terms, therefore, the new farmers' movements can be said to represent an extension of 'Bharat' into 'India'.

Post-Script: Populism, Peasants and Intellectuals, or What's Left of the Future?
TOM BRASS

The current global expansion of neo-liberal capitalism, which is attempting to incorporate large sections of not just the farmers' movements in India but also the peasantry in Third World and ex-/actually-existing socialist countries into an international industrial reserve army of labour, is being accompanied by a worldwide resurgence of nationalism and a corresponding displacement of socialist ideas by populist ones. It is argued here that, because of a failure to distinguish between a progressive/modern anti-capitalism which seeks to transcend bourgeois society, and a romantic anti- (or post-) modern form the roots of which are located in agrarian nostalgia and reactionary visions of an innate 'nature', the response by many academics/intellectuals/activists to this process of economic globalisation has been (and continues to be) supportive of conservative/nationalist/(fascist) ideology.

For Product Safety Concerns and Information please contact our EU representative GPSR@taylorandfrancis.com
Taylor & Francis Verlag GmbH, Kaufingerstraße 24, 80331 München, Germany

www.ingramcontent.com/pod-product-compliance
Ingram Content Group UK Ltd.
Pitfield, Milton Keynes, MK11 3LW, UK
UKHW042200240425
457818UK00011B/319

* 9 7 8 0 7 1 4 6 4 1 3 4 8 *